Crisis and Innovation in Asian Technology

In mid-May 1997 a financial crisis erupted in Asia after an attack by private investors on the baht, the Thai currency. The crisis spread quickly across the region, where investor confidence plummeted, resulting in massive capital outflows, stock market collapses, high unemployment, and even insurrection. The crisis was unprecedented in its scale, scope, and duration. The Asian "economic miracle"that had stimulated so much awe and even dread now invoked empathy and apprehension in greater measure.

The contributors to this volume investigated change in the innovation and production systems of Asian states in response to economic and political upheaval. They conducted empirical studies of several regional industries – autos, semiconductors, and hard disk drives – and seven different national economies: China, Malaysia, Japan, Singapore, South Korea, Thailand, and Taiwan. In the face of crisis and global competition, the Asian states did not converge on more open or "liberal" economic norms. Instead, they superimposed change at the margins, seeking unique technohybrid solutions to build capabilities to compete in local, regional, and even global markets.

William W. Keller is Wesley W. Posvar Professor of International Studies at the University of Pittsburgh, where he is the Director of the Ridgway Center for International Security Studies. His books include *The Myth of the Global Corporation* (1998) and *Arm in Arm: The Political Economy of the Global Arms Trade* (1995). He is a past Executive Director of the Center for International Studies at the Massachusetts Institute of Technology.

Richard J. Samuels is Ford International Professor of Political Science at the Massachusetts Institute of Technology, where he is Director of the Center for International Studies. He is a member of the Council on Foreign Relations and has written or edited seven books, including the prize-winning *"Rich Nation, Strong Army"*: *National Security and the Technological Transformation of Japan* (1994).

Crisis and Innovation in Asian Technology

Edited by

WILLIAM W. KELLER
University of Pittsburgh

RICHARD J. SAMUELS
Massachusetts Institute of Technology

CAMBRIDGE
UNIVERSITY PRESS

PUBLISHED BY THE PRESS SYNDICATE OF THE UNIVERSITY OF CAMBRIDGE
The Pitt Building, Trumpington Street, Cambridge, United Kingdom

CAMBRIDGE UNIVERSITY PRESS
The Edinburgh Building, Cambridge CB2 2RU, UK
40 West 20th Street, New York, NY 10011-4211, USA
477 Williamstown Road, Port Melbourne, VIC 3207, Australia
Ruiz de Alarcón 13, 28014 Madrid, Spain
Dock House, The Waterfront, Cape Town 8001, South Africa

http://www.cambridge.org

First published 2003

Printed in the United Kingdom at the University Press, Cambridge

Typeface Sabon 10/12 pt.   *System* QuarkXPress   [TB]

A catalog record for this book is available from the British Library.

Library of Congress Cataloging in Publication data

Crisis and innovation in Asian technology / edited by William W. Keller, Richard J. Samuels.
    p.   cm.
    Includes bibliographical references and index.
    ISBN 0-521-81871-0 – ISBN 0-521-52409-1 (pb.)
        1. Technological innovations – Economic aspects – East Asia.   2. Technological
    innovations – Economic aspects – Asia, Southeastern.   3. Financial crises – Asia,
    Southeastern.   4. Competition, International.   5. Microelectronics industry – East Asia.
    6. Microelectronics industry – Asia, Southeastern. I. Keller, William W. (William Walton),
    1950– II. Samuels, Richard J.

HC460.5Z9 T423   2002
338'.064'095–dc21   2002023345

ISBN 0 521 81871 0 hardback
ISBN 0 521 52409 1 paperback

Printed in the United States of America

To Pat Gercik
in friendship and in recognition
of her many contributions to the MIT Japan Program

Contents

Figures and Tables   *page* viii
Contributors   ix
Acknowledgments   xi

1   Innovation and the Asian Economies
    William W. Keller and Richard J. Samuels   1
2   Japanese Production Networks in Asia:
    Extending the Status Quo
    Walter Hatch   23
3   Crisis and Innovation in Japan: A New Future through
    Technoentrepreneurship?
    D. H. Whittaker   57
4   Crisis, Reform, and National Innovation in South Korea
    Linsu Kim   86
5   From National Champions to Global Partners: Crisis,
    Globalization, and the Korean Auto Industry
    John Ravenhill   108
6   Crisis and Adaptation in Taiwan and South Korea:
    The Political Economy of Semiconductors
    William W. Keller and Louis W. Pauly   137
7   China in Search of a Workable Model: Technology
    Development in the New Millennium
    Barry Naughton and Adam Segal   160
8   Economic Crisis and Technological Trajectories:
    Hard Disk Drive Production in Southeast Asia
    Richard F. Doner and Bryan Ritchie   187
9   Continuity and Change in Asian Innovation
    William W. Keller and Richard J. Samuels   226

Index   243

Figures and Tables

Figures

1.1 Percent Change in Real GDP of Selected Asian Countries   *page* 4
2.1 Japanese Manufacturing FDI to Asia   29
2.2 Business Start-up and Closure Rates   55
2.3 Character of Start-up in Different Periods   56
3.1 Start-ups and Closures in Japan, 1966–96   72
5.1 Korean Motor Vehicle Production and Exports   110
7.1 Main Modes of Technology Imports   171

Tables

2.1 Flow of JICA Experts to Asia   28
2.2 Japan's Technology Exports to Asia   30
2.3 Export-Import Bank Loans for JFDI to Asia   36
2.4 Japanese Subcontractors Moving into Asia   38
2.5 Japanese Expatriates in Private Firms in Asia   41
3.1 Small-Firm Employment Share in High-Tech Manufacturing
    Industries in Japan, the United States, and the United Kingdom   71
4.1 Research and Development Expenditures, 1965–98   99
5.1 Partners in the Korean Auto Industry Pre- and Postcrisis   126
8.1 New Government Initiatives since 1997   218
8.2 HRDF and SDF Comparison   222

Contributors

Richard F. Doner is Associate Professor of Political Science at Emory University, Atlanta, Georgia.

Walter Hatch is Lecturer and Tamaki Fellow at the Jackson School of International Studies, University of Washington, Seattle, Washington.

William W. Keller is Wesley W. Posvar Professor of International Studies and Director of the Ridgway Center for International Security Studies at the University of Pittsburgh, Pittsburgh, Pennsylvania.

Linsu Kim is Professor of Management at Korea University, Seoul, Korea. He also serves as Chairman of the Korean Council of Humanities and Social Research Institutes.

Barry Naughton is Professor of Political Science at the University of California, San Diego, California.

Louis W. Pauly is Professor of Political Science and Director for the Center for International Studies at the University of Toronto, Toronto, Canada.

John Ravenhill is Professor at the University of Edinburgh, Edinburgh, Scotland.

Bryan Ritchie is Assistant Professor at James Madison College at Michigan State University, East Lansing, Michigan.

Richard J. Samuels is Ford International Professor of Political Science and Director of the Center for International Studies at the Massachusetts Institute of Technology, Cambridge, Massachusetts.

Adam Segal is Next Generation Fellow, Asia Studies, at the Council on Foreign Relations, New York, New York.

D. H. Whittaker is Reader at the University of Cambridge, Cambridge, United Kingdom, and Visiting Professor at Doshisha University, Japan.

Acknowledgments

This book arose out of two workshops held at the Center for International Studies at the Massachusetts Institute of Technology in the summer of 1999 and the fall of 2000. We wish to thank each of the authors for his intellectual generosity and commitment to the overall success of the project. We also benefited from the thoughtful contributions of Martin Beversdorf, Douglas Fuller, Gerald Hane, Andrew Procassini, Rahardi Ramelon, and John Zysman. Peter Katzenstein deserves special thanks for serving as discussant and mentor throughout the project. We also wish to acknowledge the able research assistance of Wenkai He. Finally, our job as the project organizers was made immeasurably easier by the organizational and editorial skills of Amy Briemer, Andrea Gabbitas, Tisha Gomes, and Laurie Scheffler.

Innovation and the Asian Economies

William W. Keller and Richard J. Samuels

This book is about crisis and choice, an enduring relationship in world politics and, especially, in economic change. Modern social science is filled with "shock adjustment" metaphors invoked to characterize the ways in which change occurs.[1] Much like our understanding of evolutionary biology, notions of "punctuated equilibrium" or "paradigm shifts" presume that significant institutional and normative adjustments follow sudden major challenges to a previously stable system. War is the most common "punctuation." We speak confidently of a post–World War II world that operated under different rules (as set by the superpower confrontation) and with different institutions (e.g., those of Bretton Woods) than the prewar one. New ideas, such as Keynesianism or communism, can have the same effect.[2]

[1] Peter J. Katzenstein, *Small States in World Markets: Industrial Policy in Europe* (Ithaca: Cornell University Press, 1985); and Peter Gourevitch, *Politics in Hard Times* (Ithaca: Cornell University Press, 1986), are particularly important studies in this genre. Both look at war and depression as institution-shifting events in Western Europe. Alexander Gershenkron, *Economic Backwardness in Historical Perspective: A Book of Essays* (Cambridge, Mass.: Harvard University Press, 1966), posits the industrial revolution as the shock that transformed the developmental strategies of late-developing states. See Wade Jacoby, *Imitation and Politics: Redesigning Modern Germany* (Ithaca: Cornell University Press, 2000), for a more recent example. Earlier work includes the essays in Gabriel Almond et al., eds., *Crisis, Choice, and Change* (Boston: Little, Brown, 1973). Robert Putnam, *Making Democracy Work* (Princeton: Princeton University Press, 1993), is weighted in the other direction. It privileges stability and discounts disequilibrating shocks. For recent theoretical treatment, see Ellen M. Immergut, "The Theoretical Core of the New Institutionalism," *Politics and Society* 26, no. 1 (March 1998): 5–34; and Ira Katznelson, "Structure and Configuration in Comparative Politics," in Mark Irving Lichbach and Alan S. Zuckerman, eds., *Comparative Politics: Rationality, Culture, and Structure* (Cambridge: Cambridge University Press, 1997). Brett Kubicek, "Social Mechanisms and Political Creativity" (Ph.D. dissertation, Massachusetts Institute of Technology, forthcoming) is an important critique of this model.

[2] The standard theoretical treatment of this is the notion of scientific revolution introduced in Thomas Kuhn, *The Structure of Scientific Revolutions,* 3rd ed. (Chicago: University of Chicago Press, 1996). For the example of Keynesianism, see Peter Hall, ed., *The Political Power of Economic Ideas: Keynesianism across Nations* (Princeton: Princeton University Press, 1989).

Similarly, technological innovations – in transportation, communication, or other elements of infrastructure – can also provide dramatic "punctuation" of a stable order.[3] Entrepreneurs had different expectations of markets before the Industrial Revolution than later, before the diffusion of railways or of telephones than afterward, or prior to the introduction of just-in-time production than they do today. Similarly, microelectronics and then the Internet each transformed the business models deployed for generating wealth and profit. In each case, new technology led to the redistribution of economic and political power. New products, like new world orders, can transform what we believe to be the "normal" social, political, and economic conditions within which we make choices.

Stephen Krasner captures the way in which social science focuses on the effects of the adjustment, effects that canalize choice and set in place new institutions that channel and constrain action in a new "normal" political economy. The resulting institutions in turn are dislodged only by shocks of equal or greater magnitude: "New structures originate during periods of crisis. They may be imposed through conquest or be implanted by a particular fragment of the existing social structure. But once institutions are in place they can assume a life of their own, extracting societal resources, socializing individuals, and even altering the basic nature of civil society itself."[4]

The contributors to this volume test these ideas against the Asian financial crisis of 1997–98, the most significant challenge to the ways in which innovation and production had been organized in the most dynamic corner of the global economy at the turn of the past century. While the crisis was financial, at least initially, the choices and outcomes on which our authors focus are technological ones. Their chapters seek to understand and explain whether and to what extent the Asian financial crisis shifted the institutions of science, technology, and innovation in Asia and across the globe.

In mid-May 1997 a financial crisis expanded outward from Southeast Asia after a broad and deep attack by private investors on the baht, the Thai currency. The crisis spread rapidly across the region. The five "crisis countries" – Thailand, Malaysia, Indonesia, the Philippines, and South Korea – all experienced similar symptoms, including massive capital outflows, collapse of the stock market, exhaustion of foreign reserves, and successive currency depreciations. The central banks at first responded by intervening to defend currency values. They raised interest rates and, as one contemporary institutional

---

[3] See Christopher Freeman, *Technology Policy and Economic Performance* (London: Pinter, 1987).

[4] Stephen D. Krasner, "Approaches to the State: Alternative Conceptions and Historical Dynamics," *Comparative Politics* 16, no. 2 (January 1984): 240. For recent theoretical treatments of these relationships, see Paul Pierson, "Increasing Returns, Path Dependence, and the Study of Politics," *American Political Science Review* 94, no. 2 (June 2000): 251–68; and James Mahoney, "Path Dependence in Historical Sociology," *Theory and Society* 29 (2000): 507–48.

account put it, "tightened capital and exchange controls, particularly on forward or derivative transactions and their financing. However, these responses failed to restore investor confidence, and further capital outflows, sharp depreciations of the exchange rate, and falls in the stock market took place."[5]

The scale of this crisis was unprecedented.[6] The five "crisis countries" sustained a net reversal of more than $100 billion in private capital flows, approximately 11 percent of GDP, during the last half of 1997. Concurrently, the value of the currencies in these countries continued to fall sharply.[7] The Asian nations listed in Figure 1.1 experienced declines in GDP from 1.1 to 13.1 percent in 1998. Within a year, the crisis had taken on global dimensions.

The timing and depth of the crisis varied widely from country to country across the region. Thailand's economy contracted almost immediately following the onset of the financial crisis, even for the year 1997. Japan, Korea, Indonesia, Malaysia, and Thailand all lost ground the following year. Of the countries displayed in Figure 1.1, only China and Taiwan were relatively unaffected in terms of overall economic growth. Over the next two years, all of these countries, except Japan, experienced a significant rebound in part due to a powerful upsurge in the silicon cycle, driven by consumer demand for electronic equipment and corporate demand for telecommunications infrastructure.

The slowing of the U.S. and European economies that began in 2001, however, hampered the Asian recovery. Sales in the semiconductor industry – which is often considered a bellwether for the electronics-oriented economies of East Asia – were forecast to fall 26 percent to $35 billion for the Japanese market, and 23 percent to $39 billion for the Asia Pacific market in 2001.[8] A generalized slump in the information technology industries, especially telecommunications, extended and broadened the nature of the Asian economic downturn. By mid-2001 Japan's trade surplus was half the level of its 1998 peak. The Asian "economic miracle" that had stimulated so much awe, admiration, and even dread, now invoked empathy and apprehension in greater measure.

Of course, these concerns may well be premature or misplaced. It remains to be seen if the economies of East and Southeast Asia will heal and, if in doing so, they might once again provide alternative models for the organization of innovation and economic development. During the final decades of the past century, there was an intense debate about forms of capitalism in general and about the organization of national scientific and technological

[5] International Monetary Fund, "The East Asian Crisis: Macroeconomic Development and Policy Lessons," Working Paper, Washington, D.C., August 1998, p. 20.

[6] Stephan Haggard, *The Political Economy of the Asian Financial Crisis* (Washington, D.C.: IIE, 2000), p. 1.

[7] OECD, *Asia and the Global Crisis: The Industrial Dimension* (Paris, 1999), p. 9.

[8] SIA Press Release, "Semiconductor Industry Association Forecasts Semiconductor Recovery for 2002–2004," November 8, 2001.

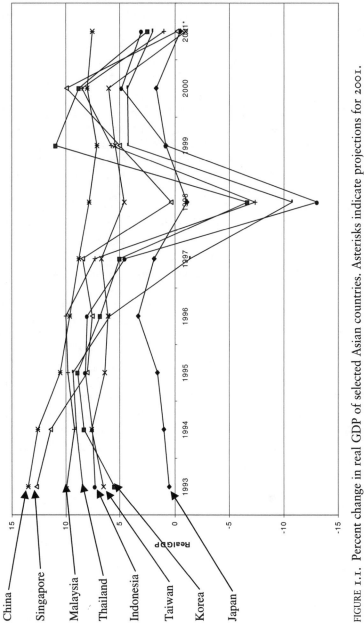

FIGURE 1.1. Percent change in real GDP of selected Asian countries. Asterisks indicate projections for 2001.
Source: IMF, *World Economic Outlook May 2001,* Statistical Appendix, table 1.7, p. 32. IMF, *World Economic Outlook,* Statistical Appendix, tables 2 and 6, p. 166, p. 173.
<http://www.imf.org/external/pubs/ft/weo/2001/01/pdf/append.pdf>.

infrastructures in particular.[9] National governments, with their governing ideologies and industrial policies, were seen by many as exerting a profound influence on the development of science and technology within their borders. Domestic scientific and technological capabilities, in turn, were seen as key to national economic success – and to national security – at the dawn of the new millennium.

This debate was only the latest version of one that has framed the choices of states and firms for centuries. Following Adam Smith in the late eighteenth century, liberals have emphasized the self-regulating virtues of politics and markets. Governments would always distort the essentially benign workings of markets, and states should do no more than provide rules that safeguard private property. The government could properly protect private property and provide collective goods such as education or defense but should otherwise stand clear of the more efficient marketplace. Where markets were most open and where trade was most unfettered by tariffs or by regulation, innovation would flourish and wealth would be generated.

Friedrich List was the most prominent among several influential nineteenth-century "national economists," who expressed doubt about the self-regulating virtues of markets. List disagreed fundamentally with free-trade liberals, whose views derived from Adam Smith and David Ricardo, over how to ensure the generation of national wealth. On his account, the productive power of manufactures was central to national security, and the provision of national security could not be left to competition among narrowly constituted private interests. Some sectors needed protection before they could succeed. They could not be expected to produce the collective goods upon which national wealth and security depend unless they were nurtured to maturity. Free trade was fine, indeed desirable, but only after critical national industrial capabilities were assured. List argued that national advantage was not only bequeathed by history and by naturally occurring factor endowments; it could (indeed, it should) be created through temporary insulation from world markets if need be. List's view has resonated ever since in the industrial policies of late-developing states.

Indeed, despite the dramatic increases in trade and cross-border investment associated with "globalization" in the 1980s and 1990s, some economies

---

[9] Although the success of Japan in the 1980s stimulated considerable debate about the varieties of capitalism (see, e.g., Chalmers Johnson's landmark study of Japan as a "developmental state": *MITI and the Japanese Miracle* [Stanford: Stanford University Press, 1982]), research on the varieties of capitalism has long been a staple of comparative political economy. See Gershenkron, *Economic Backwardness in Historical Perspective*; Andrew Shonfield, *Modern Capitalism: The Changing Balance of Public and Private Power* (New York: Oxford University Press, 1965); Michel Albert, *Capitalism vs. Capitalism* (New York: Four Walls Eight Windows, 1993); and Peter A. Hall and David W. Soskice, eds., *Varieties of Capitalism: The Institutional Foundations of Comparative Advantage* (New York: Oxford University Press, 2001).

seemed to nurture more insular systems of innovation. They were more likely than others to apply science and technology policy to explicit national goals. The success of "developmental" programs, involving both direct and subtler state intervention, suggested that there were ways to deploy public policy to accelerate and deepen economic advancement for the benefit of a nation's citizenry. On the other hand, more "liberal" economies seemed headed inexorably toward the same sorts of relatively more open scientific and technological institutions associated with the industrial states of Western Europe and North America.[10] This was a high stakes debate. Getting capitalism and the institutions of investment and innovation "right" could mean millions of jobs, billions of dollars of profits, and realignment in the global balance of power.[11]

But, as the contributors to this volume reveal, "getting it right" has meant different things to different actors. The industrial and industrializing economies of Asia that have received so much attention have never been monolithic. Nor do they seem likely to become so, theories of convergence to neoliberal institutions and ideologies notwithstanding. China (since 1979) and several of the ASEAN states were relatively open to direct foreign investment and to dependence on the foreign technology that often accompanies such investment.[12] While not "liberal" in a neoclassical sense, they appeared willing to pay some of the costs in reduced autonomy that can result from foreign control over domestic assets.

Other states in the region, such as Japan and the Republic of Korea, made a different calculation. While they, too, were eager to acquire foreign technology, they chose to do so at a more distant arm's length, eschewing the foreign influence that comes with direct foreign investment. Their rather more mercantile orientation invited intense pressures from foreign firms and governments for liberalization. Not opening their markets indiscriminately required that they bear a greater share of the costs of nurturing their more autonomous technology systems.

Whether relatively open or closed, each of the economies in East and Southeast Asia had grown enormously in the last quarter of the twentieth century. And each faced a crisis that might force it to change.

[10] See the essays in Suzanne Berger and Ronald Dore, eds., *National Diversity and Global Capitalism* (Ithaca: Cornell University Press, 1996). Accounts of the "developmental state" are Johnson, *MITI and the Japanese Miracle*; Meredith Woo-Cummings, ed., *The Developmental State* (Ithaca: Cornell University Press, 1999).

[11] See Wayne Sandholtz et al., eds., *The Highest Stakes* (New York: Oxford University Press, 1992), for a snapshot of these concerns during the precrisis years when the United States seemed in secular decline.

[12] ASEAN is the acronym for Association of South East Asian Nations. The member states are Brunei Darussalam, Cambodia, Indonesia, Laos, Malaysia, Miramar, Philippines, Singapore, Thailand, and Vietnam.

Modeling Crisis and Choice

In general, there are four classes of factors that constrain and channel choice in the face of crisis: the institutional configuration of states, the ideological preferences of political actors, the material capabilities of economic actors, and the creativity of political and economic leaders. Here we introduce each set of factors in turn and match them briefly to the technology and manufacturing base of the national economies examined in this volume.

Institutions

The elements of institutional configuration of a political economy – its regulatory structure, the organization of private interests, their relationship to the state, and the location of local firms in the value-added supply chain – may each be critical in determining its capacity to resist external shocks. For the purposes of this volume, however, the "innovation system" is the institutional configuration of greatest significance. The concept of national innovation systems was introduced in the mid-1980s by scholars who were dissatisfied with the neoclassical treatment of innovation as an exogenous variable. It has drawn largely from the field of evolutionary economics, stressing the endogenous nature of innovation in its own development. An innovation system is "the network of institutions in the public and private sectors whose activities and interactions initiate, import, modify and diffuse new technologies."[13]

A *national* innovation system comprises firms, universities, nonprofit entities, and public agencies that produce or support the production of science and technology within national borders. There seem to have been enduring differences in the national innovation systems of the leading industrial states in North America, Europe, and Asia – differences in the style and focus of supporting policies, in the ways in which research and development (R&D) is funded, where it is conducted, and in the technical orientation of industrial research.[14] On this view, innovation systems that span sectors in the same country have more in common with each other than they do with the same industrial sector in other countries. It follows that one wonders if firms ever really leave their nationality at the shores of their home economy. Are they really amoral utility maximizers, shorn of their nationality when they cross borders? Or are Japanese firms still Japanese, and U.S. firms still American, and German firms still European when they invest and operate in Singapore, Taiwan, or Guangdong? Would Chinese and South Korean business executives hold different views on this subject?

The host economies are also important in the *national* innovation system model. The national economies, in which multinationals invest, shape

[13] Freeman, *Technology Policy and Economic Performance.*
[14] Paul N. Doremus, William W. Keller, Louis W. Pauly, and Simon Reich, *The Myth of the Global Corporation* (Princeton: Princeton University Press, 1998), p. 60.

innovation within their borders through public policies and political ideology. On this view, their policies and interventions are likely to be consistent and have similar effects across sectors. Whether these policies conflict with, or respond to, the preferences of indigenous firms, political battles involving R&D tax incentives, subsidies, technology transfer requirements, capital controls, or even educational reforms will determine much of the character of innovation within national borders.

The alternative institutional perspective is *sectoral*. A sectoral innovation system comprises similar relationships and institutions, but they interact within a functionally delimited domain, which may be nationally, regionally, or globally distributed. On this view, firms in the same business, even if in different countries, have more in common with one another (and organize their R&D in the same ways) than do firms in different sectors in the same country. Companies, and the states that hope to nurture them, have to respond to similar sets of technological imperatives. Here there is more coherence within types of production or processes than within types of states. Aerospace industries in Russia, Japan, and Indonesia – like computer industries in Korea, Taiwan, and India – have more in common with one another than do aerospace firms and computer firms in any one of these states.

Clearly there is a division of labor in the same industrial sector across states, sometimes referred to as the "regional" R&D and production systems model. Richard Doner and Bryan Ritchie argue in this volume, for example, that Singapore, Malaysia, and Thailand occupy quite different rungs in a regional hierarchy of countries that produce hard disk drives. Walter Hatch suggests that the Japanese dominate sectoral production systems by integrating them vertically across the region from headquarters in Tokyo or Osaka. As these contributors and others demonstrate, institutional arrangements vary considerably across the region, and by sector. Each is interested in delineating these differences and in determining for our readers how they vary systematically.

Whether an innovation system is bounded by a national economy or by an industrial sector, it can be understood to comprise (or be animated by) distinctive political norms. But politics has rarely been incorporated into models of innovation systems. Economists who focus on national characteristics to explain innovation argue that certain country-specific institutional variables, such as market structure or legal systems, shape innovative processes across sectors within national borders. Those who focus on sectors see a functional logic specific to particular business segments or supply chain characteristics. Although some political scientists have addressed the politics of innovation systems, the strategic, normative, and material bases for R&D are usually left unexplored.[15] All agree that technological innovation

---

[15] Herbert Kitschelt, "Industrial Governance Structures, Innovation Strategies, and the Case of Japan: Sectoral or Cross-National Comparative Analyses?" *International Organization* 45, no. 4 (1991): 453–93, is an exception. He has gone furthest in endeavoring to combine

is one of the most important engines of economic growth. All agree that investment in learning and innovation repays firms and nations. But few examine the extent to which the dynamics of innovation are politicized – that is, determined by power relations among and within states, and between states and firms, both domestic and foreign. We turn, therefore, to ideology as an alternative to institutions.

Ideology

Different institutions and different capabilities may be informed by different ideas, and the strength and resilience of these ideas may be tested in times of crisis. The ideological preferences of actors in the world of innovation and production systems and their fundamental assumptions about the value of indigenous research and development can be characterized ideal-typically as the difference between technonationalism and technoglobalism.[16]

States that embrace "technonational" norms are less willing to open their markets to direct foreign investment out of a concern that more mature foreign-based firms and technologies would snuff out nascent domestic ones. Technonationalists are convinced that their domestic economies need protection not only from predatory foreign investors, but also from the foreign technology and competition that they would introduce. They believe that a domestic economy can be mature, and the nation secure, only if it exerts substantial control over the generation of knowledge and the standards by which design and manufacture are undertaken. Importantly, this perspective informs choices independent of public policy. That is, conational firms that operate under technonational assumptions may be more comfortable with one another and more willing to cooperate than are firms that are – as in the neoclassical paradigm – rational utility maximizers, always poised to change production locations or suppliers to achieve further advantage. Firms that adhere to a technonational ideology are more likely to maintain supply chain relationships with conationals without regard to geographic location, striving to keep the higher value-added activities in their domestic economies.

---

the sectoral and national approaches. For a variety of national and sectoral analyses by economists, see Bengt-Ake Lundvall, ed., *National Systems of Innovation* (London: Pinter Publishers, 1992); David C. Mowery, *Science and Technology Policy in Interdependent Economies* (Boston: Kluwer Academic Publishers, 1994); Sylvia Ostry and Richard R. Nelson, *Techno-Nationalism and Techno-Globalism* (Washington, D.C.: Brookings Institution, 1995); Richard R. Nelson, ed., *National Innovation Systems: A Comparative Analysis* (Oxford: Oxford University Press, 1993); and U.S. Congress, Office of Technology Assessment, *Multinationals and the U.S. Technology Base*, OTA-ITE-612 (Washington, D.C.: U.S. Government Printing Office, September 1994).

[16] Robert Reich, "The Rise of Techno-Nationalism," *Atlantic* 259, no. 5 (May 1987): 62–69. See Richard J. Samuels, *"Rich Nation, Strong Army": National Security and the Technological Transformation of Japan* (Ithaca: Cornell University Press, 1994); chapter 1 provides a short intellectual and economic history of "technonationalism."

Technonationalists discern a difference between proprietary and generic technical information that has national, rather than corporate, borders. Under technonational assumptions, when conational firms share information in the development of new technology, they are collaborating. Such collaboration, which may involve joint research and technology sharing, is viewed as a public good that would not otherwise be provided. And as a public good, it transcends antitrust or competition policy considerations. In a technonational setting, firms may also enter into intense competition, which may be muted by the state in infant industries or used as a device to winnow out the weaker players to promote a limited number of world-class contenders. Thus, the technonationalist perspective emphasizes autonomy over dependence on foreign technology, the diffusion of knowledge among national users, and the nurturance of domestic scientific and technological capabilities. A "developmental state" may be the spider in the national web of technology development, but the connections and mutual trust among conationals do not require state sanction.[17]

Japan is the paradigmatic case of technonationalism.[18] For more than 150 years, Japanese firms and the Japanese governments embraced technology and the economy as matters of national security. State planners and technonationalists in the private sector fused industrial, technological, and security priorities. These were driven by military ambition in the first half of Japan's industrialization and by commercial needs in the second. Japanese planners carefully and consciously navigated between the Scylla of technological backwardness and the Charybdis of foreign dependence. As a result, each subsequent generation of Japanese products – whether aircraft, machine tools, eyeglasses, or chemicals – depended less than its predecessor on foreign technology. As one MITI official put it: "ichigo yūnyū, nigo kokusanka" (the first time, we import, the second time, we do it ourselves). This helps explain why as late as the early 1990s as much as half of Japanese manufactured imports came from Japanese firms abroad, and why as much as 70 percent of the growth in Japanese imports between 1990 and 1997 came from "captive" (Japanese owned) firms.[19] In Japanese practice, technology was often a quasi-public good developed and distributed through elaborate networks of producers and bureaucracies. As a consequence, Japan built an extensive network of "technology highways" – an infrastructure comprising at least as many lanes, but perhaps fewer roadblocks than in counterpart systems where antitrust and collusion were of greater concern.

In Japanese thinking, institutions such as research consortia and manufacturing alliances enable competitors to achieve common technical goals before

---

[17] Johnson, *MITI and the Japanese Miracle*, introduces the concept of the "developmental state."
[18] Samuels, "*Rich Nation, Strong Army.*"
[19] Richard D. Katz, "Foreign Direct Investment, Shareholder Power, and Competition: Promoting a Virtuous Cycle," Research Institute on Economy, Trade and Industry (RIETI), May 21, 2001, Tokyo.

they compete with each other in the market. Japanese firms therefore have cooperated in consortia at every level of the development cycle, including basic research, systems development, and even in device manufacturing. Although the form and function of these consortia has varied – and competition among the participating firms never disappears and is often extremely vigorous – collaboration persists as a highly valued norm in Japan. Elsewhere it is denigrated as "collusive" or "anticompetitive." Firms and the government vigilantly monitor the economy to mitigate the worst effects of market shifts and technological revolutions. To *nurture* Japanese firms, they deploy a wide range of "TIPS" (technology and industrial policies), including generous subsidies, tax breaks, loans, depreciation allowances, and R&D grants.[20] Taken together, Japan provided a model of successful technonationalism, at least until the Japanese economic bubble burst in the early 1990s.

Technoglobalists, on the other hand, base their arguments on a more liberal and individualistic set of assumptions. They tend to reject collaboration as suboptimal, and state regulators interpret collaboration as collusion. Such collaboration may distort economic growth rather than enhance it. From a technoglobal standpoint, although states should provide infrastructure to set the conditions for progress in basic science, by and large individual firms are responsible for technical advance and product innovation. States may intervene when public goods such as R&D and technical education are insufficient, but they normally do so at the level of "basic" or "fundamental" scientific research, not at the level of "applied" product or process technology development. Because, on this account, firms make the greatest contributions when global barriers to the transfer and diffusion of technology are lowest, technoglobalists press policy makers to reduce the barriers to the diffusion of innovation worldwide.

Singapore and Hong Kong may be the classic technoglobalist states of Asia. Both economies embrace open, free-trade principles that encourage unfettered capital mobility, accompanied by low tariffs, within a relatively laissez-faire regulatory system. Historically, each has attracted significant direct foreign investment, and both have functioned as the regional headquarters for a number of the world's leading multinational corporations. Perhaps as important, Singapore in particular, but also Hong Kong, has worked to create an environment conducive to high-technology manufacturing. These two "city-states" have overtly courted foreign-based companies as a means of acquiring and diffusing technology and technical learning as broadly as possible within their respective populations. Singapore has been singularly successful, for example, in capturing the high end of global disk drive production, although there are increasing signs that Singapore's technoglobal orientation may be more circumspect in the future.

[20] Saadia Pekkanen, "The Logic of Industrial Selection: Theory, Perceptions, and Policy in Postwar Japan" (Ph.D. dissertation, Harvard University, 1996), is a full account of these TIPs.

Between these two ideal types, our empirical research indicates, lies an intermediate third option or range – what we call technohybrids. Some countries have embraced a limited form of technoglobalism in order to become vital players in multinational production networks. These hybrids self-consciously invite high-technology foreign direct investment as a means of technical learning in order to achieve explicit national goals and a higher standard of living for their citizens. In so doing they adopt strategic technology and industrial policies that both attract foreign-based multinationals and position domestic firms to capture some portion of added value in the production process. They invest substantial funds in national laboratories and infrastructure for technical education. In time, such states may spawn and privatize companies that reach state-of-the-art production in technically sophisticated industries.

Unlike technonational regimes that restrict or channel foreign technology investment, and unlike technoglobal ones that are largely indifferent to it, technohybrids may permit or even initially encourage a substantial degree of foreign control over domestic technological assets. As a developmental strategy, they may seek foreign assistance in the creation of a domestic technology infrastructure. Like technonational regimes, such states make determined efforts to attract and train scientists and engineers, often initially sending their best and brightest abroad, while upgrading indigenous universities to increase the supply of technical talent to local industry. In time their firms may acquire foreign subsidiaries to gain direct access to intellectual property and cutting-edge technologies. Unlike technonational systems, however, technohybrids open their markets to foreign direct investment in ways that generate mutual dependence between foreign-based multinationals and domestic producers.

Taiwan offers the paradigmatic example of the technohybrid regime – especially in the semiconductor industry, where local foundries mass-produce hundreds of different kinds of integrated circuits for foreign firms, using designs supplied by their customers. Increasingly, these customers are U.S. or European firms that do not have chip production facilities of their own. When demand is strong, foreign firms may have to wait on line, even as the Taiwanese foundries aggressively add capacity. When demand is weak, the foundries quietly supply local industries with excess production at reduced costs or, more recently, suffer the consequences of lower capacity utilization rates. China, too, has embraced elements of this approach. For more than two decades, portions of the economy as a whole, and the technology system in particular, have been decentralized and exposed to direct foreign associations. Centralized research and development and state-owned enterprises are gradually being displaced by links to foreign research laboratories and private entrepreneurs. The "not quite liberal" yet "not quite mercantile" technology systems of Taiwan and parts of China suggest alternatives to the dominant extant models.

Capabilities

Different ideas and different institutions do not map perfectly across different economic or political capabilities. Nor do they necessarily predict if states and firms will respond effectively in a crisis. By capabilities we refer to several structural features, including the size of the economy or in the case of China, for example, the projected size of its economy and markets. China's vast population and its dramatically expanding economy bestow capabilities that are unavailable to smaller states without regard to their institutional or ideological preferences. Unlike the ASEAN states, China can pursue a range of technology acquisition strategies and industrial policies, which are independent and may even appear contradictory or internally inconsistent.

In another example, the world's second largest economy, Japan, has been able to maintain a higher standard of living and continue to restrict foreign direct investment into its manufacturing sector to levels far lower than those of other advanced industrial states. And it has done so even in the face of regional financial contagion that fell in the middle of a decade of Japanese economic stagnation. Such options are simply unavailable to the smaller economies in Asia, which must find means of inserting their capabilities into regional production networks that are usually dominated by foreign-based multinational corporations.

The foreign reserves available to central bankers also constitute a distinct capability and affect the range of available choices in the face of economic crisis. In 1998, when the full effect of the Asian financial contagion was felt, countries with more than $30 billion in foreign exchange were – with the exception of Japan – all able to avoid recession. These included China, Taiwan, and Singapore with foreign reserves of $142.8, $84.0, and $74.5 billion respectively in the spring of 1998. On the other side of the ledger, the economies of South Korea, Indonesia, Malaysia, and Thailand all contracted between 6.7 and 10.8 percent in 1998, and all had foreign reserves of between $15.5 and $30.3 billion. Countries with large foreign reserves were better able to defend their currencies from speculators and to stave off significant recession in the immediate aftermath of the 1997–98 financial crisis.[21]

Finally, more differentiated economies – those hosting a wider range of economic activities or less dependent on particular export markets or products – are typically in a better position to weather crises that weaken or bring down more narrowly constituted ones. Small countries that have attracted major foreign direct investment may also be better positioned. The onset of the Asian economic crisis coincided with a decrease in demand for goods produced by the information technology industries, sometimes referred to as a downturn in the "silicon cycle." Economies like China's and

---

[21] As of May 1998, the foreign reserves of selected East Asian states were as follows (in $billions): Japan, 205.7; South Korea, 30.3; Singapore, 74.5; Taiwan, 84.0; China, 142.8; Indonesia, 15.5; Malaysia, 20.4; and Thailand, 28.6. *Asian Banker Journal* <www.theasianbanker.com>.

Japan's that have significant levels of activity in a wide variety of industries tended to be better insulated than economies like South Korea's and Malaysia's, whose manufactures are more concentrated in electronics.

Leadership

Leadership is a final, additional factor that intervenes between crisis and change. Unlike institutions, ideologies, and capabilities, leadership is a matter of agency. Being neither structural nor normative, it is accordingly more difficult to model. Leadership matters.[22] How George W. Bush and Tony Blair responded to the terrorist attacks of September 2001 clearly will determine the destiny of a great many persons. Few will disagree that Martin Luther King transformed apartheid in America or that Mao and Gandhi inspired epochal change in China and India. Given how obvious this is, it is puzzling that so many intellectuals routinely subordinate the strategies and choices of individuals to forces that exist beyond their control. When asked directly, few embrace the idea that there is no choice in history; similarly, no one admits to holding the view that leaders do only what "great forces" dictate. Yet, in our collective retelling, choices are routinely limited by a mixed configuration of inherited resources, institutions, or ideas. The choices actors make are largely self-evident, if they are not always singular. Social science privileges constraint over choice.

To be sure, it is no less obvious that constraints matter. Not everything under the sun is possible. A great deal is beyond the control of even the most able strategist. Moreover, we can be certain that far more opportunities are lost than are seized in history. But if determined individuals can deliberately and systematically make their political space more capacious – if they can "stretch their constraints" – then analysts who privilege constraint risk missing how political actors mobilize creativity, prejudice, spite, passion, history, religion, and philosophy to thwart adversaries and expectations. In the real world, some leaders do little more than bob like corks on a restless sea. But others, many others, do much more. Some revolutionaries invent futures using wholly new materials of their own design. Others tinker with materials at hand, first making a new past before constructing a future. And even those who do not construct elaborate strategies may select among equally plausible alternatives in the normal course of events. In short, constraints may be greater in the telling than in the acting, not least because the weight of great inertial forces in society and economy can be tipped into the balance for the leader's scheme.

Leaders are political and economic actors with a greater range of potential assets at their disposal. They can "stretch" the constraints that geography, natural resources, old legacies, and international location provide. In the world of economy and technology, it can make an enormous difference

---

[22] This discussion is derived from Richard J. Samuels, *Machiavelli's Children: Leaders and Their Legacies in Italy and Japan* (Ithaca: Cornell University Press, forthcoming).

that some individuals deploy these assets more adroitly and more purpose-
fully than do others.

During the Asian financial crisis of 1997–98, there was no more creative
leader than Mahathir Mohamad of Malaysia. Although the initial manifestations of the crisis in Malaysia were similar to those elsewhere,[23] Malaysia
met the crisis without succumbing to intervention by the International
Monetary Fund (IMF). Instead, Prime Minister Mahathir took the reigns,
pointing to currency speculators as the true scoundrels in the unfolding
drama. Wasting little time, Malaysia instituted capital controls in September
1998 to stem short-term portfolio flows and to quell the offshore ringgit
market in Singapore. High-tech infrastructure projects were put on hold,
reducing government obligations by about $10 billion; selective import
duties were imposed; and a "buy Malaysia" campaign was set in motion.[24]

A contemporary account in the *ASEAN Economic Bulletin* summarizes
the flurry of unconventional activity nicely: "On December 5, the Deputy
Prime Minister and Finance Minister, Anwar Ibrahim, unveiled a reform
package. The key elements of the package included cutting government
spending by 18 percent, postponing indefinitely all public sector investment
projects which were still in the pipeline, stopping new overseas investments
by Malaysian firms, freezing new share issues and company restructuring,
and cutting salaries of government ministers by 10 percent. With these
measures, the previous budget forecast of economic growth (7 percent) was
lowered to 4–5 percent."[25] There was, however, a great deal of political
turmoil when Mahathir, fearing Anwar's enhanced influence at home and
abroad, arrested his finance minister and consolidated his power. The central point of the Malaysian case is that no combination of institutions, ideologies, or capabilities is so strong as to force each state or economy into
the same set of choices when faced by crisis.

China emerged from the crisis relatively unscathed; little evidence suggests that its relative immunity from the Asian financial crisis was the result
of any particular policy choice or leader. China benefited more from the
backwardness of its own financial institutions than from the deft manipu-
lation of policy by sagacious leaders. Four major state-owned banks dominated the Chinese financial system circa 1997. The main liabilities in the
system were to Chinese depositors, and the main assets were loans to state-
owned firms. Thus, while the Chinese banking system was insolvent, the
enormous debt burden was denominated entirely in the yuan.

---

[23] In the manufacturing sector, for example, literally hundreds of companies failed, with many
more struggling to keep their doors open. Economist Intelligence Unit, EIU Country Profile 1999–2000, Malaysia: Manufacturing, p. 29. <http://store.eiu.com/index.asp?layout =
country_home_page&country_id=MY>.

[24] Prema-chandra Athukorala, "Swimming against the Tide: Crisis Management in
Malaysia," *ASEAN Economic Bulletin* 15, no. 3 (December 1998): 285.

[25] Ibid., p. 285.

That said, however, leadership did matter critically after the Asian financial crisis, as Chinese policy makers came to understand the challenges and nature of economic reform, using the crisis as a spur to action.[26] Prior to 1997 very few Chinese leaders were willing to acknowledge that a large portfolio of nonperforming loans actually constituted a problem. Although it was well known that state banks were dumping household deposits into negative-return investments, there was no discussion of how destructive that could be to long-term growth. That changed after 1997. Confronted with China's financial problems, Chinese leaders undertook initiatives in bank commercialization and in the elimination of state-owned enterprises. Most radically, they changed course on their strategy for accession into the World Trade Organization (WTO).

For thirteen years prior to 1999, the Chinese argued for accession to the General Agreement on Tariffs and Trade (GATT) on concessionary terms, terms that would essentially have permitted China to freeze in place a deeply distorted domestic market, including in the financial sector. Now, however, the Chinese leadership reversed itself and acceded to virtually all demands of the United States and other developed nations to transform the state bank–state monopoly situation of precrisis days. Implementing these changes has not been smooth or easy, but the leaders' decision for institutional and ideological change since 1997 was breathtaking. Private entrepreneurs were welcomed into the Communist Party. The Chinese constitution was amended to recognize the role of private firms. The insolvency of the banking system was openly acknowledged, and steps were taken to shut down state-owned firms, despite a concomitant rise in unemployment.

Previewing Our Findings

As the diverse cases of Malaysia and China suggest, the 1997–98 Asian financial crisis had many manifestations and evoked a great many national responses. It was not one crisis, but many. Japan's was the earliest – beginning in 1990 with the bursting of its financial and real-estate bubbles – and the longest-sustained. Over the course of the next decade, the economy grew by less than half the rate it did during the previous decade. Dramatically slower growth was joined by a collapse in asset values. Over the course of the 1990s the Nikkei average fell from close to 40,000 points to just over 13,000 and land prices fell by more than 50 percent from their bubble-era high. Japan struggled through a series of political crises (seven different combinations of party coalitions produced eight prime ministers in the decade after the bubble burst) and economic transformations (the *keiretsu* recombined amid plans for "Big Bang" deregulation and record

---

[26] This discussion is based on Edward S. Steinfeld, "Beyond the Transition: China's Economy at Century's End," *Current History,* no. 271 (September 1999): 271–75, and on conversations with the author.

unemployment).[27] More than a decade after it all began, public debt and unemployment were both at record levels with no end in sight.

Indonesia sustained perhaps the greatest economic and political disruption. The Indonesian currency, the rupiah, lost nearly one-third of its value within three months following the onset of the crisis. The International Monetary Fund, the World Bank, and the Asian Development Bank intervened to provide $18 billion collectively in financing commitments aimed at restoring investor confidence and bringing about an orderly economic adjustment.[28] But such assistance did not come without a political price tag. As one contemporary observer put it: "IMF supervision of Indonesian monetary and fiscal policy, and of general compliance with the IMF agreement is very, very strict. . . . So short is the leash that national sovereignty can be said to have been impaired. . . . The spectre of the national economy becoming an extension of markets of foreign multinational companies haunts sections of the domestic political community."[29] Within a year, with the country enmeshed in a cycle of hyperinflation and currency depreciation, severe civil unrest led to the resignation of President Suharto of Indonesia. Fires burned in the capital, and marshal law was imposed to restore order.

The crisis brought the Indonesian innovation system to its knees. For nearly one-quarter century, the government of Indonesia had, for example, supported the aircraft industry as an area of strategic investment in high technology. The government established a scholarship program to send its best students abroad for technical training. It created national laboratories to assist in the effort, and in the middle 1970s Indonesia entered into licensed production agreements with DASA of Germany (then MBB) and CASA of Spain to produce both helicopters and fixed-wing aircraft.

During the next two decades, Indonesia made remarkable progress in the research, design, and production of aircraft – consolidating nearly all activity in a single state-owned enterprise, the Indonesian Aerospace Company (IAe), then the Indonesian Aircraft Industry. But as a dramatic consequence of the Asian financial crisis, which for Indonesia was a full-blown economic and political disaster, all funding for aerospace technology development was terminated, and the country's innovation system stagnated for the balance of the decade and beyond.[30]

[27] Edward J. Lincoln, *Arthritic Japan: The Slow Pace of Economic Reform* (Washington, D.C.: Brookings Institution Press, 2001), is an excellent review of what did and did not change in the Japanese economy during the "lost decade" of the 1990s.

[28] Timothy Lane et al., "IMF-Supported Programs in Indonesia, Korea, and Thailand: A Preliminary Assessment," IMF Occasional Paper 178, Washington, D.C., p. 4.

[29] Mohammad Sadli, "The Indonesian Crisis," *ASEAN Economic Bulletin* 15, no. 3 (December 1998): 275, 276.

[30] This paragraph and the preceding one are based on Rahardi Ramelan, "Aircraft Technology in Indonesia: After the Crisis in the Global Market," paper prepared for the MIT Workshop on Innovation and Crisis – Asian Innovation after the Millennium, September 15–16, 2000, Cambridge, Mass.

In the Republic of Korea, the won and foreign exchange reserves both also fell precipitously. But even though monetary policy was tightened briefly, it was relaxed due to fears that higher interest rates would adversely affect the highly leveraged Korean *chaebol*. By the end of 1997 the won had slid by more than 20 percent against the dollar and foreign reserves had fallen to $6 billion from $22.5 billion. The positive impact of interventions by the IMF and other international financial institutions appeared to be temporary and superficial at best. Leading candidates for the 1997 presidential election did not support the IMF program fully, and investor confidence was once again undermined.[31]

The Bank of Thailand abandoned efforts to prop up the baht within just two months, and much of the economy came under IMF supervision. As elsewhere, however, market confidence eroded further, due in part to delays in "reforming" the financial sector. By May 1998 fiscal policy shifted to a more "accommodating" stance. Measures were adopted to shore up the banks and facilitate corporate restructuring.[32]

As Doner and Ritchie describe in Chapter 8 of this volume, the technology and industrial base of Thailand has remained bifurcated, with most high-technology products imported for assembly. Local industry is still highly protected, working at the low-tech end, and is largely oriented toward the domestic economy. Because of the country's weak engineering base, indigenous firms have been unable to absorb many technologies from abroad, and the country has been unable to develop a large pool of technical talent.

Of the seven countries analyzed in this study, China's growth trajectory appears to have been least affected by the Asian crises. The Chinese GDP maintained a steady growth of 8.8, 7.8, 7.1, and 8.0 percent for the years 1997 through 2000 respectively. In this volume, Barry Naughton and Adam Segal argue that while the crisis did cause some dislocation within China, it was not as great an economic factor as successive waves of domestic economic and political reform. Chinese leaders act on the assumption that China will once again attain great-power status. This perception influences their choices of economic and technology acquisition policies in ways that set China apart from other Asian states.

The Asian economic crises offered an extraordinary opportunity to understand the relationship between technology and finance on the one hand, and between government policy and the global marketplace on the other. It raises the possibility that our models of technoglobalism and technonationalism are inaccurate and provides a chance to investigate and modify each. After all, if the Japanese were such technonationalists, why did they allow so many jobs to migrate offshore in the 1990s? Why do they now export more technology to the United States than they import?[33] And

---

[31] Lane et al., "IMF-Supported Programs," p. 6.

[32] Ibid., pp. 2–3.

[33] Data from the Statistics Bureau of the Japanese government's Management and Coordination agency show that Japan's technology transfer balance shifted from a deficit

why did they move so vigorously to deregulate their financial system? We wonder if the financial crisis of 1997–98 generated new imperatives driven by political and economic instability. Did it clarify the ways in which Asian governments and companies think and behave regarding critical technology assets? It may be that if the Asian crises deepen, a liberal logic of "technoglobalism" – as predicted by many economists and analysts in the Washington foreign economic policy community – will prove irresistible. We wonder whether Japanese and Korean technological assets, for example, are more readily available for foreign acquisition than in the past.

On the other hand, in the face of widespread financial disintegration and new political uncertainties, technonational structures and norms may have been reinforced, reshaped, or in some cases, introduced. The costs of openness and the loss of control may drive some states to harden a mercantilist logic of retaining and building core national technical competencies. This may persist until the crisis in confidence ends and the next round of international competition comes into focus. This book was designed to sort out what we know about the behavior of Asian states and firms when financial and economic crises force reconsideration of national technoeconomic strategies.

Whether the Asian financial and economic crises of the late 1990s should be seen as agents of profound change or forces that bolstered extant state propensities, the response of Asian innovation systems to the crisis did affect macroeconomic and industrial policies. It has also affected the ways in which business is transacted throughout the region. United States and European companies have gained greater access to some formerly resistant Asian economies, through direct investment, possibly even through technology acquisitions. This observation is elaborated by several of the contributors to this book, particularly with reference to apparent change in the Republic of Korea.

In this volume, Linsu Kim argues that while the crisis created hardship for many Koreans in the short term, it also introduced an opportunity for Korea to make fundamental changes in its technonationalist orientation. Changes in industry and at the highest levels of government, he writes, will force Korea to accommodate to globalization but, he adds, it will be carried out in the Korean national interest. In a separate chapter, John Ravenhill agrees that the crisis in Korea catalyzed fundamental policy change. He argues that while the crisis paved the way for greater foreign investment in the automobile sector, it was more than a financial crisis because it was systemic in nature. For Ravenhill, the origins of the crisis that struck the Korean automobile industry are a direct consequence of a technonationalist developmental strategy gone wrong. In his view, Korean automakers took

to a surplus between 1995 and 1998. See Kagaku Gijutsu Seisaku Kenkyûjo, ed., *Nihon no Gijutsu Yûshutsu no Jittai: Nihon no Gijutsu, Shihon to tomo ni Ajia E* (The state of Japanese technology exports: Japanese technology and capital to Asia) (Tokyo: Kagaku Gijutsuchô, September 2, 1997).

on excessive debt, diversified beyond their core competencies, and sought market share in lieu of profits.

Two contributors to this volume address the extent to which Japanese technonationalism may have unraveled in the long decade of the Japanese crisis, which began in the early 1990s with the "bursting of the bubble," deepened with the onset of the more generalized Asian financial crisis in 1997–98, and continued into the next millennium. D. H. Whittaker emphasizes the changes in Japan: a restructuring of the financial sector, greater foreign participation in Japanese financial markets, and a weakening (if not the demise) of the corporate cross-shareholding system. He argues that the ongoing Japanese crisis differs from the broader Asian one. In his view, Japanese banks contributed to the more general financial crisis by making too many imprudent loans to firms in the affected countries.

Walter Hatch offers an alternative view that Japan's technonational regime is alive, if unhealthy, but only because it has been regionalized into Asia. Japanese corporations have consciously availed technological assets to different Asian countries, depending on their level of technological development. Even though it has been squeezed by advocates of global trade and investment, and there are pressures toward convergence, Japan's technonational regime has remained remarkably resilient – and has done so to the likely detriment of Japan. The Japanese system of "relationalism," he argues, has been extended in much of the rest of East Asia, prolonging the day of reckoning for Japanese companies. To a great extent, Japan's technonational regime continues to be guided by "norms and institutions of cooperation." The Asian financial crisis of 1997–98 provided a means for Japan to extend its production and financial networks more deeply into Asia, supporting Japanese transplants throughout the region. This technoeconomic system is very unlike the neoliberal regimes of Great Britain or the United States.

Asian states that have heretofore paid the costs of indigenous technology development may have become more open to foreign direct investment and licensing in areas beyond nonfinancial services. Those previously willing to license technology only in the short term for political reasons may find new advantages in the sale of knowledge. Others may be forced to maintain their technological dependence for economic and political reasons. In some sectors national and regional investment in science and technology will be curtailed severely. In others, it may be expanded.

The changes occurring today, which many observers thought unlikely a few years back, could alter fundamentally the industrial policies of Asian governments and the technology strategies of Asian, U.S., and European multinationals. The various Asian nations and firms struggling with deflated equity markets, volatile exchange rates, foreign debt, high unemployment, and political uncertainty responded to the financial crisis in different ways. Accordingly, questions regarding the nature, extent, and durability of the various innovation systems throughout Asia are empirical. They require careful mapping.

The Organization of the Volume

The editors and authors of this book refined and examined the relationship of crisis and innovation in Asia in workshops and conferences held at MIT in 1999 and 2000. As we learned on those occasions, discussions of innovation in Asia tended to move from one perspective to another, depending on the particular mix of countries and industries in question: we focused first on the politics of national innovation systems of particular countries; at other times, on specific industries, such as automobiles in Korea or semiconductors in Taiwan; and finally on technology hierarchies in cross-national production systems, such as hard disk drives in Singapore, Malaysia, and Thailand. These varying perspectives are reflected in the chapters that follow. Chapters 2 and 3 speak to the issues of continuity and change in Japanese innovation. Although the authors present very different understandings of the economic and political crises in Japan, they are in agreement that the jury is still out regarding fundamental change in the technonationalist culture of that country.

Taken together, Chapters 4 though 6 present different aspects of changes in the Korean state and economy, some of which began long before the Asian financial crisis and some that were generated by it. Of the seven Asian countries treated in this volume – China, Japan, Malaysia, Singapore, South Korea, Taiwan, and Thailand – South Korea stands out as the country that has experienced the most dramatic institutional change, both in terms of economic structure and government administration. Much of that change can be attributed to the economic and political crises that swept the region in 1997 and beyond, but as one chapter argues, the structural conditions underlying that change were put in place as fundamental building blocks in the early years of Korean industrialization. All agree that Korea has outgrown the technonational orientation that initially enabled it to achieve world-class technology and innovation in a number of global industries.

Chapter 6 also focuses on Taiwan. William Keller and Louis Pauly note that, of all the countries buffeted by the Asian crises, Taiwan was initially the least affected; however, by mid-2001 that country also slipped into recession. Indeed, there appear to have been no severe political or economic perturbations, from the onset of the financial crisis through the earthquake of September 1999, that literally bumped the island's major industries off line. In this and other ways, Taiwan presents a bit of a conundrum. Government and industry continue to impart a complementary blend of globalist and nationalist innovation strategies for nation building, even though in recent years industry appears to be playing a more dominant role in this common project to build an electronics industry powerhouse. China would also appear to fit into the "technohybrid" category. But as the authors of Chapter 7 explain, due to its sheer size and history as a great power, China has the option to deploy a variety of strategies to build its economic and technological infrastructure, and several innovation experiments may coexist side by side.

The final case study, Chapter 8, analyzes the high-technology disk drive industry that spans Southeast Asia – specifically Singapore, Malaysia, and Thailand. Here, the authors argue that a downturn in the industry, already in progress, was exacerbated by the financial contagion, beginning in the spring of 1997. All three nations participated differently in a hierarchical regional production system with Singapore at the top; and all three responded to the crisis differently, as suggested earlier. But perhaps most interesting, the authors conclude that Singapore, which had previously been seen as a quintessential technoglobal state, the "regional headquarters" for many multinational corporations, responded to the crisis by introducing technonationalist steps to create new indigenous small and medium-sized companies.

As we "interview" the industry and country case studies in this volume, we are struck by the extent to which Asian technology after the millennium is characterized both by change, as in the cases of South Korea and Singapore, and by overall continuity (with change at the margins), as typified by the cases of Japan and Taiwan. At the beginning of this chapter we suggested several ways to characterize innovation and Asian states. In the context of an increasingly global Asia, however, we think that small states will continue to mix in degrees of technonationalism with the catechism of globalization, eventually creating as many hybrid combinations as there are industrializing and industrialized states. This project, then, marks not so much the continuation of an old debate, as we first suggested, but more an Asia coming to terms with the increasingly global economy of the twenty-first century. We envisage an Asian economic landscape in which small states will have to revise their technology and industrial policies continuously, creating political space and niche markets in which their companies can maneuver for advantage. Far from the demise of the state, such policies will be necessary to offset the scale and scope of foreign-based multinationals now in the process of consolidating dominant positions in global markets.

2

Japanese Production Networks in Asia

Extending the Status Quo

Walter Hatch

Japan's technoindustrial regime, which I call "relationalism," has proved remarkably resilient in the face of powerful market and political forces for change. Despite a decade of economic setbacks capped off by the Asian financial crisis, Japan continues to be held together by a dense web of long-standing and mutually reinforcing relationships between government and business, between nominally independent firms, and between labor and management. This is not to say that Japan is immutable. It clearly is under-going change in the distribution of economic gains and losses, as evidenced by growing income inequality. The "big tent" of relationalism today protects fewer Japanese citizens than it has at any other time in the postwar period. But the tent itself is still standing tall.

This chapter confirms a key assertion pointed out by several of the authors of this volume: globalization – or, more specifically, global financial integration – does not necessarily compel heterogeneous technoindustrial regimes to converge toward a single model. Variation survives because existing institutions, norms, and capabilities (both objective and creative) stand in the middle of the transmission belt leading from exogenous pressure to political-economic response, mediating the impact. Japan's experience reveals that a very large economy held together by intraelite cooperation can absorb such exogenous pressure better than a small economy driven by intraelite rivalry – at least for a while.

Consider some of the following claims made by those who say Japan is undergoing significant structural change, as well as evidence suggesting the contrary. The government has implemented regulatory and administrative reforms that appear to diminish its once significant role in private market matters. However, the number of regulations imposed by the Japanese state between 1996 and 1998 was 8.6 percent *higher* than the number imposed between 1986 and 1988, the beginning of a decade of supposed *kisei kanwa*

I am indebted to Richard Samuels for helpful comments on an earlier draft of this chapter.

(easing of regulations). And the number of retiring bureaucrats who used the practice of *amakudari* ("descent from heaven") to take up positions in the private sector (often in firms they used to regulate) actually *increased* by 14.4 percent between 1986–88 and 1996–98.[1]

Horizontal *keiretsu* ties between firms seem to be unraveling as main banks from different corporate groups merge. At a deeper level, however, one can see that these ties are *re*raveling as four consolidated *keiretsu* take the place of the old six. Industry tie-ups, such as the ones between Sumitomo Chemicals and Mitsui Chemicals and between NKK (part of the old Fuyo Group) and Kawasaki Steel (part of the old Dai-ichi Kangyo Group) are following the pattern of bank mergers, such as the ones between Sumitomo Bank and what used to be called Mitsui Bank and between Fuji Bank and Dai-ichi Kangyo Bank.[2]

In the automobile industry, vertical *keiretsu* linkages between manufacturing assemblers and their longtime subcontractors appear to be dissolving as foreign firms such as Renault and Daimler Chrysler acquire dominant positions in heavily indebted domestic firms such as Nissan (with an estimated $21 billion in debt in 1999) and Mitsubishi Motors ($15 billion in debt in 2000). Cost-cutting managers at these troubled automakers have sought to streamline the system of parts procurement. On the other hand, competitive automakers such as Toyota and Honda have maintained or even strengthened ties with *keiretsu* suppliers. For example, in the late 1990s, Toyota increased its equity stake in its three largest suppliers (Denso, Toyota Gosei, and Aishin).

Japan suddenly seems open to foreign direct investment (FDI). Thanks to hefty investments in the automobile industry and financial services sector, foreign capital has indeed increased its position in Japan – but remains relatively minuscule. In the 1990s, the total flow of FDI into Japan was $26 billion – smaller than for any other major industrialized country and less than 3 percent the amount of FDI that found its way into the United States during that decade.

Firms appear to be restructuring by trimming payrolls. However, they are in fact achieving such reductions through natural attrition and the transfer of surplus workers to affiliated firms or dedicated subcontractors. For core employees (who are, for the most part, male, middle-aged, and

[1] These statistics, which come from the Management and Coordination Agency and Tôyô Keizai Shimpôsha, respectively, are presented in more detail in Walter Hatch, "Rearguard Regionalization: Protecting Core Networks in Japan's Political Economy" (Ph.D. dissertation, University of Washington, 2000).

[2] See Odagiri Naoto, "Kin'yû Fuan no Naka de no Senshutsu Mitsui Sumitomo ga Ippô Reedo" (In the midst of financial crisis, Mitsui and Sumitomo are moving together to lead the pack), *Ekonomisuto*, April 17, 2001, pp. 26–35. Also, see "Japan's Keiretsu: Regrouping," *Economist*, November 25, 2000, p. 74.

skilled), the job turnover rate remains about 4 percent a year – not significantly higher than it was in the mid-1980s.[3]

What, then, explains the remarkable durability of Japan's embattled technoindustrial regime? This chapter argues that Japanese government and business elites have rescued – temporarily – the system of relationalism by regionalizing it, by extending its web of relational ties into industrializing Asia,[4] where such ties still serve a useful economic function. In doing so, however, they have preserved the status quo at home, thereby delaying needed reforms.

The chapter proceeds in five steps. First, it defines "relationalism" more carefully. Second, it demonstrates how Japanese elites sought to extend the shelf life of this regime by regionalizing it. Third, it suggests that the Asian fiscal crisis of 1997–98 slowed but did not stop this process. Fourth, it asserts that the regionalization of relational networks reflects Japanese technonationalism, the quest for power or autonomy through control of strategic economic resources. Finally, the chapter shows how regionalization, by rescuing relationalism, has served to restrict the growth potential of the Japanese economy.

Relationalism Defined

A technoindustrial regime is the set of actors (bureaucrats, corporate managers, and labor elites) who generate and employ knowledge for industrial production in a specific social and spatial context; the set of norms that unite and motivate these actors; and the set of institutions through which these actors exchange information.[5] When it operates on the level of the nation-state, such a regime is much like what many scholars have referred to as a "national system of innovation."

Although squeezed by globalization and subjected to pressures for convergence, Japan remains quite unlike the relatively neoliberal and atomistic regimes of the United States and the United Kingdom. Relationships matter far more. Japanese government officials still collaborate closely with business executives on industrial policies. In 1998, for example, the Ministry of Economy, Trade, and Industry (METI, better known in the past as the Ministry of International Trade and Industry, or MITI) crafted a seven-year plan to aid the satellite industry through a series of joint research projects. In 1999 METI joined other ministries in developing a "national strategy" of catching up with the United States

---

[3] Ministry of Labor, *Rôdô Hakusho* (White paper on labor) (Tokyo, 1998), p. 123.

[4] Unless otherwise noted, "Asia" here means China, the four Asian NIEs (the newly industrializing economies of South Korea, Taiwan, Singapore, and Hong Kong), and the ASEAN-4 (the four core members of the Association of Southeast Asian Nations: Thailand, Indonesia, Malaysia, and the Philippines).

[5] I am influenced here by Pempel's use of the concept of "regime." See T. J. Pempel, *Regime Shift: Comparative Dynamics of the Japanese Political Economy* (Ithaca: Cornell University Press, 1998).

and Europe in biotechnology. And in 2000 METI set up a strategic council to promote the fledgling information technology industry.[6]

Moreover, Japanese corporations continue to maintain long-standing, mutually reinforcing ties with one another via cross-shareholding relationships. In a survey conducted in the year 2000, 719 of 731 major firms reported that they are owned, at least in part, by stable shareholders who do not trade such stock. Of those 719 firms, two-thirds indicated that more than 50 percent of their outstanding shares are held in this way. Finally, three-quarters of the firms reported that longtime employees, promoted through the ranks, occupy at least half of the seats on their boards of directors.[7]

To an unusual degree, then, Japan's technoindustrial regime has been and continues to be guided by norms and institutions of cooperation – a system of relationalism. Thus, the Economic Planning Agency of Japan concludes that this system "emphasizes the merits of cooperation based on long-term relationships between economic actors and within economic institutions. In this way, each economic actor has been able to avoid the risks associated with fierce competition, maximizing its self-interest by forging alliances within the market."[8]

Relationalism in Japan is manifested in three strands of strong, cooperative ties between conationals. The first is government-business ties. It is often difficult to distinguish the public from the private sector in Japan, where bureaucrats and business executives routinely confer over policy. Such cooperation often takes the form of "administrative guidance" (*gyôsei shidô*), an informal policy-negotiating process that is sometimes initiated by the state and sometimes by industry.

The second is business-business ties. In Japan, as in all market-oriented regimes that recognize private property rights, competition among firms is encouraged – but only up to a point. "Excess competition," manifested in bankruptcies and layoffs, is unwelcome. As a result, firms routinely cooperate through a variety of nonmarket institutions such as trade associations and *keiretsu* designed to stabilize the market. *Keiretsu* are organized both horizontally and vertically. Horizontally organized groups, such as Mitsui and Mitsubishi, typically include a main bank, a trading company, and member firms in a variety of different industries. Vertically organized groups tend to link the manufacturers of finished goods with parts suppliers and distributors.

---

[6] See Matsubara Satoru, "Yôyaku IT ni Torikumi Hajimeta Nihon Seifu" (The Japanese government is finally beginning to grapple with information technology), *Ekonomisuto*, September 25, 2000, pp. 90–91. This special issue is devoted to the "Nihon-gata IT Kakumei" (Japanese-style IT revolution), and includes a twenty-four-page section on each ministry's industrial policies to promote IT.

[7] The survey was conducted by the Research Institute for the Advancement of Living Standards. Results have been published in Inagami Takeshi, ed., *Gendai Nihon no Kôporeito Gabanansu* (Corporate governance in contemporary Japan) (Tokyo: Tôyô Keizai Shimpôsha, 2000).

[8] Economic Planning Agency of Japan, *Kôzô Kaikaku ni Chôsen: Keizai Shakai ni Dainamizumu o* (The challenge of structural reform: Bringing dynamism to the economy), a report from the Keizai Shingikai (Deliberation Council on the Economy), Tokyo, June 1998, p. 23.

The third strand of cooperation involves labor-management ties. Because they invest so heavily in on-the-job training, large companies in Japan rarely resort to layoffs. Instead, they encourage employees to stay on the job by offering seniority-based wages, as well as private pension funds and other company-specific benefits. Longtime (if not "lifetime") employees organize themselves into enterprise unions that serve to align the interests of workers and the interests of the company.

To be sure, cooperative ties provide the internal "wiring" for virtually all social systems, including a technoindustrial regime. These ties, however, are far stronger, far more durable in Japan, which is why Sakakibara refers to Japan as a "non-capitalist market economy."[9] Indeed, strong ties of cooperation have been routinized, and thus institutionalized, in many other aspects of the Japanese political economy, including some areas that are critical for technological development. For example, manufacturers in Japan do not usually recruit and hire young engineers directly from the nation's leading technical schools. Instead, they negotiate with the students' faculty advisors, who have insisted on adherence to an informally administered allocation scheme for each industry. This linkage between industry and academia has helped maintain a rough parity in skill levels between otherwise competing manufacturers and has thus reinforced business-business cooperation.

Relationalism carries both costs and benefits. The costs are, for the most part, opportunity costs associated with relatively dense and inward-looking networks that are thus closed to new sources of information from the outside. The benefits flow from reduced transaction costs associated with long-term, implicit contracting. In the 1950s, 1960s, and early 1970s, the benefits of relationalism clearly outweighed the costs as Japan struggled to catch up with more advanced industrial economies by adopting and commercializing Western technology. This cost-benefit ratio flipped, however, once Japan caught up with the West. For a surprisingly long time, Japanese firms managed to disguise their structural weakness by going on a binge of capital investment that reached as much as 40 percent of GDP. The Ministry of Finance (MOF), of course, acted as the excessively generous bartender, pouring more and more liquidity into the financial system, pushing interest rates down, and eventually fueling a speculative "bubble" characterized by massive asset inflation. Japan today is still suffering from a nasty hangover.

The Japanese Crisis

As several of the contributors of this volume have noted, the Asian crisis was many crises; that is, it was experienced differently by different economies in Asia and at different times. For Japan, the region's one and only economic giant, the crisis was a major setback in a long string of setbacks dating back

---

[9] Sakakibara Eisuke, *Beyond Capitalism: The Japanese Model of Market Economics* (Lanham, Md.: University Press of America, 1993).

TABLE 2.1. *Flow of JICA Experts to Asia*

	Number of Experts Dispatched to Asia	Share of Total Number of Experts
1991	1,292	50.3
1992	1,354	49.7
1993	1,513	51.9
1994	1,583	52.9
1995	1,565	51.4
1996	1,804	59.0

Source: MOFA, *Wagakuni no Seifu Kaihatsu Enjo no Jisshi Joukyou* (Japanese ODA), various years.

to 1991, when the bubble popped and stock prices tumbled. Indeed, one could argue that Japan's economic stagnation in the mid-1990s helped create the conditions that led to the collapse of the Thai baht in July 1997. But that is another story.

To understand how Japan responded to the regional crisis, we first must appreciate how Japanese elites responded to the domestic crisis that preceded it. In the early 1990s, as Japan sank deeper and deeper into the Heisei recession, the nation's interest in Asia seemed to rise higher and higher. Political and business elites brimmed with enthusiasm about the region. In 1992 Hosoya Yuji, then deputy director of MITI's industrial policy bureau, declared that "Japan's main target [for trade and investment] must be Asia."[10] A year later, Keidanren, Japan's big business federation, noted that Asia had become "an indispensable part of the business and procurement activities of Japanese companies." Economic ties between Japan and other countries in Asia benefit both sides and thus should be strengthened, according to the federation. "Japanese companies will have to form a closer cooperative relationship in an effort to secure their international competitiveness."[11]

This heightened rhetoric was matched by new initiatives in the region. For example, the Japanese state stepped up its Official Development Assistance (ODA), providing $4.2 billion to Asia in 1995 – a sharp increase over 1990, when it gave $3.1 billion. Although most of this money came in the form of yen loans for dams, sewers, electrical transmission lines, and other infrastructure projects, an increasing amount came in the form of technical assistance. The Japan International Cooperation Agency (JICA) dispatched more and more Japanese "experts" to Asia, where they advised host governments and local industry on everything from industrial policy to manufacturing quality standards. Table 2.1 documents the increasing presence of JICA advisers in Asia.

[10] Quoted in *Financial Times*, December 21, 1992, p. 23.
[11] *Keidanren Review*, special issue, 1993, p. 8.

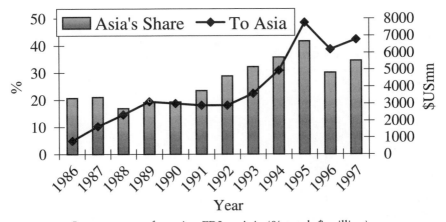

FIGURE 2.1. Japanese manufacturing FDI to Asia (% total, $ million).
Source: Calculated by the author from Ministry of Finance, *Kokusai Kinyûkyoku Nenpô*, various years.

But the more dramatic action occurred on the private side as Japanese industry began to move aggressively into Asia. As Figure 2.1 shows, manufacturing investment in the region climbed sharply in the first half of the 1990s, reaching $7.8 billion in 1995, or almost 42 percent of all foreign direct investment by Japanese producers. Represented in terms of projects rather than value of investment, the movement into Asia is even more impressive: two-thirds of all the factories set up overseas by Japanese firms are located in Asia.[12]

In addition to traditional forms of FDI, Japanese manufacturers engaged heavily in what are often called "intermediate" forms of overseas investment, particularly franchise contracts and technology licensing agreements with Asian partners.[13] As Table 2.2 indicates, Japanese technology exports to Asia doubled between 1991 and 1996, when they reached $2.75 billion. Since the mid-1990s, the region has received roughly half of all technology exports from Japan.

More than anything else, this export of Japanese capital and technology helped weave together the economies of Asia, where intraregional trade had – until the regional crisis of 1997–98 – grown faster than anywhere else in the world. Indeed, regional integration has been driven largely by the business strategies of Japanese firms, or networks of firms, which have sought to

[12] See JETRO, *Gyaku Yunyû no Jittai ni kansuru Ankeito Chôsa* (Survey report on reverse imports) (Tokyo: Kaigai Keizai Jôhô Sentaa, August 1998), p. 4.
[13] Even though MNCs engaging in such "intermediate forms" of FDI do not acquire a majority equity stake in an offshore business, they often gain de facto control over the business. This is why many economists treat them as variants of foreign direct investment.

TABLE 2.2. *Japan's Technology Exports to Asia*

	Volume (US $ billion)	Share of Japan's Total Tech Exports (%)
1986	0.69	39
1987	0.69	40
1988	0.81	41
1989	1.03	39
1990	1.23	45
1991	1.36	46
1992	1.33	44
1993	1.49	47
1994	1.71	46
1995	2.25	50
1996	2.75	49

Note: Dollar amounts are based on a constant exchange rate of ¥125 = $1.
Source: Kagaku Gijutsuchô, *Kagaku Gijutsu no Shinkô ni kansuru Nenpô Hôkoku* (Annual report on the promotion of science and technology), various years.

construct a hierarchical division of labor based on the different but complementary factor endowments and industrial structures, and thus the different but complementary comparative advantages, of Asian economies. Put simply, Japanese multinational corporations (MNCs) have tried to distribute production activities among various locations in the region according to the technological level of the host economy.

Japanese electronics firms have pursued such strategies most aggressively, creating vertically layered intrafirm or intranetwork supply chains that use technology-intensive production from Japan, capital-intensive production from the Asian newly industrialized economies (NIEs), and labor-intensive production from China and the Association of South East Asian Nations (ASEAN-4). More specifically, the Asian affiliates of these Japanese MNCs assemble finished products with high-tech components imported from Japan, slightly less complex parts imported from the Asian NIEs, and the simplest, standardized parts from China and the ASEAN-4. For example, to manufacture VCRs at its assembly plant in Bangi, Malaysia, Sony imports integrated circuits and other high-tech components from Japan and printed circuit boards from Singapore. It also purchases tape decks, as well as many other standard parts, from local suppliers in Malaysia, many of them Japanese.[14]

---

[14] This comes from interviews with Sony officials in Tokyo (July 1992) and Penang (April 1993). See Walter Hatch and Kozo Yamamura, *Asia in Japan's Embrace: Building a Regional Production Alliance* (Cambridge: Cambridge University Press, 1996), p. 25.

Automobile manufacturers, taking advantage of ASEAN programs, such as the ASEAN Industrial Cooperation scheme, to reduce tariffs on certain kinds of intraregional, intraindustry trade, have built their own supply networks in Southeast Asia. In general, these involve swapping parts that are produced in larger volumes at specified factories across the region and then assembling them in finished vehicles. Toyota, for example, used its affiliate in the Philippines as a base for specialized production of transmissions, its affiliate in Indonesia for gasoline engines, its affiliate in Malaysia for steering gears and electronic components, and its affiliate in Thailand for diesel engines and pressed parts. In 1996, only four years after it set up its regional production network, Toyota moved nearly $200 million in parts between its plants in Southeast Asia.[15]

Tamura writes that Japanese MNCs are building a regional division of labor that emphasizes technology-intensive "prototype" production in Japan and mass production of standardized products in Asia. These manufacturers, he concludes, "view Japan and Asia as one interconnected zone of activity."[16] Indeed, it has become increasingly clear that Japanese manufacturers are trying to regionalize the technoindustrial regime they helped establish over a number of years in Japan. That is, they are seeking to extend into Asia their own embattled web of strong relational ties. This should not surprise us. As Doremus, Keller, Pauly, and Reich have demonstrated, MNCs are rarely "global."[17] In most cases, they possess a national identity that is shaped by the distinctive norms and institutions embedded in their home country. Japanese MNCs are thus guided by the norms and institutions of cooperation that make up relationalism, and they have found it easier to replicate these norms and institutions in Asia, where they have some salience, than they have in Europe or the Americas.

Government-Business Ties

The Japanese state, under pressure to quit meddling in the domestic market, has found a new mission for itself in Asia. It serves as a midwife to Japanese manufacturers in the region, working to help them realize their business strategies.[18] In speeches and policy reports, government officials have argued that a regional division of labor will contribute to a dynamic process of "industrial sequencing" as more advanced economies in the region "pass down" industries in which they no longer enjoy a comparative advantage – much as an older sibling passes down outgrown clothes to a

[15] *Nikkei Weekly*, April 7, 1997, p. 22.
[16] Tamura Ei, "Wagakuni Seizô Kigyô no Kaigai Tôshi no Genjô to Kongo no Hôkô ni tsuite" (The current state and future direction of foreign investment by Japanese manufacturing firms), *Chûshô Kôkô Geppô*, November 1996, p. 22.
[17] Paul N. Doremus, William W. Keller, Louis W. Pauly, and Simon Reich, *The Myth of the Global Corporation* (Princeton: Princeton University Press, 1999).
[18] The state's ability to act as a "midwife" for industry is discussed in Peter Evans, *Embedded Autonomy: States and Industrial Transformation* (Princeton: Princeton University Press, 1995).

younger sibling. They have called this the "flying geese" pattern of regional economic development, a V-shaped pattern with Japan as the "lead goose," followed by the Asian NIEs, followed further by ASEAN and China.[19]

In the early 1990s, this concept became enshrined as official policy toward the region. Thus, Prime Minister Kaifu Toshiki told a Southeast Asian audience that "Japan will . . . continue to seek to expand imports from the countries of the region and promote greater investment in and technology transfer to these countries, in line with the maturity of their trade structure and their stage of development. And as the necessary complement to this effort, I hope that the host countries will make an even greater effort to create a climate receptive to Japanese investment and technology transfer."[20]

MITI/METI has, from time to time, tried to coordinate this effort to construct a regional division of labor, or what it officially called "complex international work sharing" based on "agreed specialization."[21] In the early 1990s it pushed the New Asian Industries Development (New AID) plan, an ambitious scheme to coordinate Japan's aid, investment, and trade policies toward the region. The plan was designed to stimulate export-oriented manufacturing throughout Asia and to help Japanese firms upgrade their domestic operations by transferring labor-intensive production to new offshore facilities. MITI vowed to implement the program in three phases: collaboration with counterparts in host countries to identify specific industries that, with some nurturing, might become internationally competitive; the drafting of proposals to promote those targeted industries, usually relying on a mixture of "hard infrastructure" (such as roads and electrical transmission lines) and "soft infrastructure" (such as new Japanese-style organizations reflecting cooperation between government and business); and issuing yen loans and dispatching experts to implement these programs.

MITI's New AID plan was heavily criticized by other ministries in the Japanese government, particularly the Ministry of Foreign Affairs, which viewed it as an effort to take over Japan's foreign aid program. So MITI dropped the plan but not the vision behind it. That vision, spelled out in its annual statement of policy priorities, continued to be "the creation of open

---

[19] The "flying geese" concept was first used by Kaname Akamatsu, "A Historical Pattern of Economic Growth in Developing Countries," *Developing Economies* 1 (1962): 3–25, to describe the process of technological assimilation that allowed a single industry in a developing economy to "graduate" from dependence on imports and eventually become a producer of internationally competitive exports. It was later appropriated by Japanese government officials, who used it to promote Japanese trade and investment in the region.

[20] The speech is reproduced in the *ASEAN Economic Bulletin* 8 (1991): 87–94.

[21] MITI, *White Paper on International Trade* (English version) (Tokyo: JETRO, 1992), pp. 101–18. For more on the role of the Japanese state in this process, see Hatch and Yamamura, *Asia in Japan's Embrace*, pp. 117–22 and 138–41; and Kit G. Machado, "Transnational Production, Regionalism, and National Development: The Case of the Japanese Motor Vehicle Industry in East Asia," *Waseda Journal of Asian Studies* 17 (1995): 35–36.

industrial networks" and "the support of Japanese business activities in Asia."[22] In the mid-1990s, MITI rolled out a new initiative to export industrial policies to Asia – the Cambodia-Laos-Myanmar Working Group (CLM-WG), which sought to promote the industrialization of those transitional economies. MITI pointed out that this new policy group was based in Bangkok, not Tokyo, and insisted that it reflected an equal partnership between ASEAN (represented by the ASEAN Economic Ministers, or AEM) and Japan (represented by MITI). In fact, however, CLM-WG was financed and staffed exclusively by MITI. The organization soon evolved into the AEM-MITI Economic and Industrial Cooperation Committee (AMEICC), and broadened its coverage to include all of Southeast Asia. It also expanded its mission by, for example, pushing for stronger industrial linkages and more liberal investment policies throughout the region.

Other Japanese government-affiliated groups, such as JICA, also use industrial policies to try to guide host states and local firms in Asia. In the mid-1990s, as Japanese assemblers sought to replicate their domestic *keiretsu* networks in Asia, this guidance often centered on how to develop supporting industries – particularly in the consumer electronics and automobile industries. For example, a JICA team in Thailand produced a detailed study that led, in 1995, to the Thai Ministry of Industry's "Master Plan for Supporting Industries." In addition, a JICA representative (the former director-general of MITI's Consumer Goods Bureau) began advising the Thai government in 1998 on how to set up a public finance corporation for small and medium-sized enterprises (SMEs).[23] MITI/METI, however, remains the most active agent in establishing and implementing this agenda. It has, for example, created a regional council, including government and industry officials from ASEAN countries, as well as government and industry officials from Japan, to propose policies designed to foster the growth of SMEs in Southeast Asia.[24]

Under MITI/METI's guidance, Japanese business groups have encouraged their Asian counterparts to build up not only nationally based trade associations but also, for the first time, regionwide industrial associations that directly reflect Japanese business interests. Thus, the Japan Automobile Manufacturers Association (JAMA) encouraged automakers in Southeast Asia to reorganize and revitalize their flagging ASEAN Automobile Federation (AAF); the Japan Electrical Manufacturers Association (JEMA) and Electric Industries Association of Japan (EIAJ) joined forces with Asian manufacturers to establish a new regional grouping, Business Dialogue; and the Communications Industry Association of Japan (CIAJ) launched the Asian Telecommunications

---

[22] See MITI, *Tsûshô Sangyô Seisaku no Jûten: Heisei 8 Nendo* (Commercial and industrial policy priorities for 1996) (Tokyo, 1995), p. 25.
[23] *Nihon Keizai Shinbun*, November 11, 1998.
[24] *Yomiuri Shinbun*, March 2, 1997.

Industry Exchange.[25] A major purpose of the new regional organizations is to harmonize product and safety standards as well as certification procedures among members. MITI noted that, although U.S. standards often become de facto global standards, the European Union has moved to establish its own regional standards in some fields. It stressed, "There is an urgent need to create standards based on the particular requirements of the Asia-Pacific region."[26]

Japanese bureaucrats advise not only host states and industries in Asia, but also Japanese firms seeking to invest in Asia, as well as Japanese firms that already have invested in Asia. When conducted in Japan, this guidance often takes the form of business counseling and is directed at SMEs looking for tips on suitable industrial sites and possible joint venture partners. Indeed, the government now publishes a manual describing all the programs available to smaller firms contemplating a move overseas. The manual (*Chûshôkigyô Kokusaika Shien Manyuaru*) was only 63 pages in 1996, when it was first published by MITI's SME Agency. Two years later, it was 116 pages.

In some cases, however, administrative guidance is aimed at large firms, and may be used to encourage cooperative or even collusive behavior. That was the case in 1992, when MITI called together representatives of the consumer electronics industry and tried to reach a loose agreement on which companies would invest how much money to manufacture what products in which countries.[27]

Outside Japan, MITI/METI uses another one of its arms, JETRO (Japan External Trade Organization), which operates 10 support centers throughout Asia, to guide Japanese firms that have already built factories.[28] In 1990 it announced a plan to create public-private councils in major cities throughout the region to provide what it called "local guidance" to those affiliates.[29] More recently, in 1996, it set up the Asian Industrial Network Program to pool information on suppliers and joint venture partners.[30] JETRO has provided an important coordinating function for Japanese affiliates in Asia; for example, in 1991 it helped broker an informal agreement

---

[25] Interviews with MITI officials, Tokyo, 1997–99.

[26] *Nikkan Kôgyô,* September 20, 1996.

[27] "MITI Urges Electronics Firms to Produce Abroad," *Nikkei Weekly,* June 13, 1992, p. 1.

[28] In 1995, for the sake of comparison, I visited the service centers operated by the U.S. Department of Commerce in places like Bangkok, Taipei, Kuala Lumpur, and Jakarta. U.S. officials stationed there described themselves as "firemen" who move into action on behalf of American firms only after those firms run into trouble with host government officials and call for help. This retroactive role was confirmed when I asked for statistics on U.S. business activities in the region. Unlike Japanese officials, U.S. officials had collected only the most general data.

[29] "Ajia Shokoku ni Sangyô Ritchi Shidô" (Industrial siting guidance in different countries across Asia), *Nihon Keizai Shinbun,* September 20, 1990, p. 5.

[30] *Nikkan Kôgyô,* October 12, 1996.

among Japanese electronic manufacturers in Malaysia that led to a wage cartel curbing competition for the scarce supply of electrical engineers in that country.[31] The Japanese government defends its role in brokering such overseas agreements by citing the threat presented by "excess competition" between Japanese MNCs in host economies.[32]

Guidance may also be packaged in the form of financial incentives. In a sharp contrast with its Western counterparts, the Japanese state actively subsidizes private overseas investment, particularly FDI to Asia. This is a source of pride for the Japan Export-Import Bank, which notes that "the use of public funds to finance private overseas investment is relatively unique to Japan, with almost no parallel in other countries."[33] Although the government's share of FDI financing has diminished in recent years as firms have drawn more heavily on their own resources and on commercial banks (particularly Japanese banks that have set up branches in Asia), its absolute contributions have actually grown quite substantially. The relative weight of FDI financing in total government lending activity has also increased. Beginning in the mid-1980s, the Export-Import Bank began to shift its focus from export credits to overseas investment loans – especially to Japanese firms setting up shop in Asia. By 1996 it was lending $331 billion to support private investment in the region – double what it lent in 1993 and twenty-eight times what it lent in 1986. As Table 2.3 shows, such financing for regionalization became nearly a quarter of the bank's total business by that time.

Besides the Export-Import Bank, which deals mainly with large firms, three government-affiliated financial institutions have used public funds (postal savings) from the Fiscal Investment and Loan Program (FILP), a key vehicle of industrial policy during the 1950s and 1960s, to guide small and medium-sized enterprises into Asia.[34] Those banks (Shôkô Chûkin; the Japan Finance Corporation for Small Business; and the People's Finance Corporation) have been given new or expanded responsibilities – in large part due to the credit squeeze facing SMEs during the long economic recession in Japan, but also in part due to the new emphasis on encouraging regionalization.

[31] JETRO intervened on behalf of Japanese producers in Malaysia who complained when Sony lured skilled technicians to its new factory there by offering wages 30 percent higher than its competitors. See "Gathering of the Clan," *Far Eastern Economic Review*, March 28, 1991, p. 52. Japanese manufacturers have established similar wage cartels in industrial parks across Asia.

[32] For example, JETRO frets openly that competition between Japanese producers in Thailand is becoming "an extremely serious problem." See JETRO, "Zai Tai Nikkei Seizôgyô Jittai Chôsa" (A survey of Japanese manufacturing affiliates in Thailand), *Tsûshô Geppô*, June 9, 1997.

[33] Japan Export-Import Bank, *Sanjûnen no Ayumi* (The past thirty years) (Tokyo 1983), p. 40.

[34] FILP is still well endowed – a function of the public's growing concern over the solvency of private banks. In 1998 it was funded to the tune of 50 trillion yen. And the program remains firmly under the control of the Ministry of Finance (MOF), which merely reports income and expenses to the Diet.

TABLE 2.3. *Export-Import Bank Loans for JFDI to Asia*

Year of Commitment	Overseas Investment Loans to Asia (billion ¥)	Share of Total Commitments (%)
1996	330.6	22.3
1995	251.2	15.3
1994	188.5	10.9
1993	163.7	13.1
1992	319.3	16.7
1991	188.7	12.7
1990	199.7	12.6
1989	135.7	8.0
1988	42.0	2.9
1987	198.7	14.1
1986	11.9	1.1
1985	41.3	4.7
1984	52.4	6.7
1983	77.0	8.0
1982	n/a	n/a
1981	90.2	5.6
1980	79.1	8.5

Source: Export-Imports Bank of Japan, *Annual Report,* various years.

For example, under a law passed in 1987 and revised in 1995, these government banks are now specifically authorized to subsidize efforts by small firms to enter new fields – including, literally, foreign fields. This program was intended to help SMEs cope with the ongoing process of "hollowing out," a process that, for them, means the loss of domestic markets as their Japanese customers (often assemblers of automobiles or electronic goods) move overseas. Ironically, though, it includes a remedy that contributes to the larger problem of "hollowing out." The Japan Finance Corporation for Small Business (JFS) has been the most aggressive lender, using nearly 70 billion yen to finance 844 overseas investment projects between 1987 and 1996. And 90 percent of those projects have been in Asia.

Business-Business Ties
In the 1990s Asia emerged as the overseas base for Japanese subcontractors in a variety of machine manufacturing industries. For example, between 1992 and 1994 Japanese affiliates manufacturing electronic components in places such as Bangkok and Penang saw their sales go up by 41 percent while their parent companies in Japan saw sales fall by 8 percent.[35] This

---

[35] Japan Machinery Exporters Association, "Wagakuni Kikai Sangyô no Ajia ni okeru Seisan Bungyô Jittai ni tsuite" (The actual state of production and division of labor by Japanese machine industries operating in Asia), an unpublished report, Tokyo, June 1994. This was

disparity in sales was especially marked in such high-tech fields as computer parts (a 101 percent increase for Japanese affiliates in Asia; a 14 percent drop for Japanese parents at home).

Equally explosive was the expansion of Japanese automobile parts suppliers into Asia. In the thirty-five years from 1962 through 1997, Japanese auto parts producers made 405 investments in the ASEAN-4 countries of Southeast Asia (Thailand, Indonesia, Malaysia, and the Philippines); but they made 223 of those investments (or 55 percent) in the final six-year period from 1991 through 1997. The peak year was 1996. Of new overseas production bases established by Japanese auto parts manufacturers that year, 76 percent were in Asia.[36] Indeed, the region has attracted the lion's share of overseas manufacturing investment by small and medium-sized firms from Japan. In 1994, 81 percent of FDI projects undertaken by Japanese SMEs ended up in Asia; even in 1997, 55.3 percent chose this region in spite of its economic woes.[37]

This concentration of investment did not occur by accident. In the 1990s Japanese machinery assemblers sought to consolidate their regional production networks by purchasing parts from Japanese-affiliated suppliers in host economies. Purely local suppliers apparently could not meet exacting standards for quality and punctuality, and a highly valued yen raised the cost of importing parts from Japan. So parent firms (machinery assemblers) leaned on their subcontractors to follow them into Asia.

One that felt the pressure was Nippon Electronics, a relatively large producer of printed circuit boards for Japanese electronics manufacturers such as Sony, Matsushita, and Sanyo. Although it fully expected to end up losing money in the short run if it built a factory in Malaysia, it decided to make the move anyway. The company felt it had a "responsibility" (*sekinin*) to its longtime customers, according to the managing director of the subsidiary outside Kuala Lumpur, "For several years, our [Japanese] customers in Southeast Asia asked us to come and support them. They asked and asked, and finally we came. We had no choice really."[38]

Regionalization has helped cement relations between assemblers and their key suppliers in Japan, relations that had threatened to unravel during the 1990s and the protracted slowdown in the domestic economy. This is in fact a stated goal of the MITI/METI agency that oversees relations between

a survey of 144 Japanese machinery manufacturers with factories in China, the Asian NIEs, the ASEAN-4, and Vietnam.

[36] Japan Finance Corporation for Small Business, "Jidôsha, Kadenkigyô ni miru Shitauke Bungyô Kôzô no Henka: Kôzô Hendô ni Tsuyoi Shitauke Kigyô no Shutsugen" (The structural transformation of supporting industries as seen in automobiles and consumer electronics: The emergence of strong subcontractors), *Chûshôkôko Repôto*, 97, no. 2 (May 1997): 35.

[37] Small and Medium Enterprise (SME) Agency, *Chûshô Kigyô Hakusho, Heisei 10-nenban* (Small business in Japan) (Tokyo: MOF Printing Bureau, 1998), p. 73.

[38] Interview, Shah Alam, Malaysia, April 24, 1993.

TABLE 2.4. *Japanese Subcontractors Moving into Asia*

	1991	1992	1993	1994	1995	1996
NIEs	2.3	0.0	3.8	10.7	23.5	13.8
ASEAN-4	6.1	8.2	17.1	17.4	32.5	24.1
China	0.0	3.4	12.2	10.2	21.3	12.8

Note: The institute asked respondents each year to identify the motivation behind their decision to invest in a particular foreign location. Multiple responses were allowed. Values represent percentage indicating they invested to "supply parts to an assembly manufacturer."
Source: Annual surveys, Research Institute on Overseas Investment (Export-Import Bank of Japan), Tokyo.

manufacturing assemblers and subcontractors in Japan. In one report, the agency encourages suppliers to "become part of the supply architecture of globally based parent companies" and thereby maintain or perhaps even strengthen ties with their customers or "parents."[39]

These linkages inspired Adachi to refer to Japanese manufacturing investment in Asia as "convoy-style" (*sendan-gata*) FDI because it typically is carried out by an assembler followed closely by his most trusted (first- and perhaps second-tier) suppliers.[40] This became especially apparent in the 1990s. Table 2.4 presents the findings of a survey showing that, by 1995, as many as 32.5 percent of all Japanese firms investing in the ASEAN-4 and as many as 21.3 percent of those investing in China indicated they had decided to make the move to "supply parts to an assembly manufacturer," meaning – in nearly all cases – a Japanese transplant. This marked a dramatic increase over previous years.

Far from abandoning their homegrown vertical *keiretsu*, then, Japanese manufacturers have tried to replicate them – and deploy them strategically – as they expand into Asia. In one statistical study, Belderbos, Capannelli, and Fukao use a probability test to explain the variation in local content ratios (measured both by local value added and the procurement of inputs from local suppliers) of 157 Japanese electronics manufacturers operating in Asia in 1992. They find that membership in a vertical *keiretsu*, especially one with strong intragroup ties, leads to increased local content, particularly for Japanese affiliates operating in places such as Southeast Asia and China, where the indigenous supply base remains weak. This result, they conclude, reflects the fact that Japanese MNCs have recreated their supply networks

---

[39] Zenkoku Shitauke Kigyô Shinkô Kyôkai, *Shitauke Kigyô ni kansuru Q&A* (Questions and answers about being a subcontractor), agency brochure, Tokyo, March 1997, p. 58.

[40] Adachi Fumihiko, "Kyûseichô suru Ajia to Nihon Chûshô Kigyô" (A rapidly growing Asia and Japanese small and medium-sized firms), in Tatsumi Nobuharu and Sato Yoshio, eds., *Shin-chûshô kigyô-ron o Manabu* (Toward a new analysis of small and medium-sized firms) (Tokyo: Yuhikaku, 1996), p. 182.

"mostly through the establishment of overseas manufacturing plants by existing Japanese manufacturers of parts and components, in which the latter were often assisted by the 'core' firm of the keiretsu."[41]

The strongest Japanese automakers have made the most significant progress in replicating their domestic *keiretsu* in Asia. At its manufacturing affiliate in Samutprakarn, just outside Bangkok, Toyota assembles vehicles with the help of thirty-two Japanese parts suppliers operating in Thailand. All but four of these suppliers are members of the Toyota supply *keiretsu* in Japan. Likewise, the giant automaker has moved into the Chinese port city of Tianjin with fourteen of its most important Japanese suppliers to manufacture passenger vehicles. Toyota, according to one news report, is "rebuilding its *keiretsu* supply system" in Tianjin.[42]

Others have unearthed equally compelling evidence that Japanese automakers are attempting to bring core members of their domestic supply networks with them as they expand into Asia. Nishioka, focusing on ASEAN, concluded that, "with the exception of those cases in which an established supplier has stayed home, we find very few examples of Japanese automakers [in Southeast Asia] engaging in transactions outside their established *keiretsu* groups."[43] Likewise, Kasahara argues that Japanese automakers in Thailand are seeking to capture "relational quasi-rents" by conducting almost all of their business with Japanese subcontractors who belong to their parent firm's *keiretsu* network.[44]

As they have done at home, Japanese automakers have established cohesive supply groups in each Asian country in which they operate. These groups, which meet regularly under the auspices of the assembler, even carry the same name as the vertical *keiretsu* in Japan after which they are patterned. Some observers, however, have suggested that Japanese automobile supply networks in Thailand, Indonesia, and Malaysia are more "open" and less exclusionary than supply networks in Japan.[45] This observation ignores the fact that automobile markets in Asia are still tiny

---

[41] Rene Belderbos, Giovanni Capannelli, and Kyoji Fukao, "Local Procurement by Japanese Electronics Firms in Asia," paper presented at a National Bureau of Economic Research seminar, June 1998, Osaka Japan, p. 12.

[42] "Chûgoku de Toyota Seisan Byôyomi" (The countdown for Toyota in China), *Asahi Shinbun*, January 28, 2000, p. 13. We should note here that the Chinese government, eager to receive investment in parts manufacturing, encouraged Toyota to replicate its *keiretsu* network in Tianjin.

[43] Nishioka Tadashi, "ASEAN ni okeru Jidôsha Sangyô no Dôkô to Wagakuni Chûshô Buhin Meikaa e no Eikyô ni tsuite" (The state of the automobile industry in ASEAN, and its influence on Japanese SME parts producers), *Chûshô Kôko Repôto*, 98, no. 1 (April 1998): 66.

[44] Hiroyuki Kasahara, "Transfer and Adaptation of Manufacturer-Supplier Relationships from Japan to Thailand: A Case of the Automobile Industry," unpublished manuscript, Tsukuba University, July 28, 1997, pp. 22–24.

[45] Among many possible examples, see Wendy Dobson, "Crossing Borders: Multinationals in East Asia," in Wendy Dobson and Chia Siow Yue, eds., *Multinationals and East Asian Integration* (Ottawa: International Development Research Centre, 1997), p. 246.

compared with the Japanese market and that parts suppliers, as a result, are unable to achieve economies of scale – and thus unable to operate at maximum efficiency – without selling to a longer list of customers. Indeed, representatives of Japanese automakers in Asia confided that, when their *keiretsu* suppliers first followed them into the region, they encouraged those suppliers to sell parts to other automakers as well. In the words of one such representative: "We wanted them to get to the point where they could be really efficient and produce parts cheaply. They couldn't get there by relying solely on us."[46]

In the long run, as automobile markets in the region expand, we should find that the membership of these Asian supply groups begins to resemble the membership of corresponding networks in Japan. That is, the need to engage in extra-*keiretsu* transactions will lessen as suppliers begin to achieve economies of scale by selling only – or chiefly – to their primary customers. Higashi states this most simply: "As the market grows, the emphasis on *group-ka* [tighter ties inside the group] also grows."[47]

Management and Labor

Japanese manufacturers have incorporated their Asian operations into regionwide personnel systems that allow them to protect better the job security of core or lifetime workers. In this way, the regionalization of Japanese manufacturing has helped block or inhibit structural change in the Japanese employment system. More specifically, it has helped maintain the strong relational ties that have bound longtime employees to their employers.

During the protracted economic slump of the 1990s, the managers of those manufacturing firms scrambled to cut production costs, especially labor costs. Due to long-standing norms and institutions in the domestic political economy of Japan, however, they were not inclined to lay off core or lifetime workers. Instead, they relied on less drastic means such as *shukkô* ("seconding," or the temporary transfer of employees) – including what could be called "cross-border *shukkô*" – to trim their payrolls. Asia, home to an expanding list of Japanese manufacturing affiliates, has thus served as a holding pen, a place to store surplus white-collar workers from Japan.

In the mid-1990s, when Asia was still booming, Honda transferred a large number of supervisors from Japan to its affiliates in the region, especially Thailand. This eased some of the growing pressure at home, according to a Honda spokesman. "Our network of operations [in Asia] provides us with more flexibility in personnel management."[48] Nissan used its Asian

[46] Interview, Bangkok, Thailand, September 2, 1997.
[47] Higashi Shigeki, "Thai no Jidôsha Sangyô: Hogo Ikusei kara Jiyûka e" (The Thai automobile industry: From protection to liberalization), *Ajiken Waarudo Torendo*, no. 4 (July 1995): 46–47.
[48] Interview, Tokyo, October 13, 1998.

TABLE 2.5. *Japanese Expatriates in Private Firms in Asia*

	Japanese Employees in Asia (total number)	Percentage of All Japanese Employees Overseas	Percent Change (year on year)
1996	103,688	35.7	+ 9.6
1995	94,589	34.4	+ 13.3
1994	83,474	31.7	+ 7.4
1993	77,708	28.5	+ 8.5
1992	71,608	26.4	+ 10.2
1991	64,990	24.5	+ 16.9
1990	55,590	23.1	+ 10.8
1989	50,177	22.9	+ 9.7
1988	45,750	23.5	+ 8.1
1987	42,305	24.1	

Source: Ministry of Foreign Affairs, *Kaigai Zairyû Hôjinsû Chôsa Tôkei*, various years.

affiliates in much the same way. "We have too many managers at Nissan Motors in Japan," confides an executive for the automaker. "Our overseas operations give us a convenient way to relieve this excess supply of management staff."[49]

In the 1990s, when it struggled to reduce its domestic employment by 10,000 workers, Hitachi relied heavily on natural attrition, an early-retirement program, and temporary transfers, including cross-border *shukkô*.[50] In 1991 the electronics giant had 450 Japanese managers stationed overseas, including Asia; by 1996 that number had nearly doubled to 830. Hitachi's experience is not extraordinary. As Table 2.5 shows, the total number of Japanese employees at private firms in Asia increased almost twofold over that period, reaching 103,688 by 1996.

Cross-border *shukkô* can, of course, move in either direction. Parent companies in Japan, using what they call "on-the-job training programs," routinely import less-skilled Asian workers from their regional affiliates and put them to work on home-based assembly lines, and particularly in the "dangerous, difficult, and dirty" jobs. This can happen either when the supply of Japanese workers willing to perform such labor in Japan is low, or when the supply of Asian workers at overseas affiliates becomes excessive. For example, in 1992 Toyota sent about 200 workers from its assembly plant in Indonesia to its plants in Japan to receive on-the-job training. This was double the number of "trainees" sent in an average year. Why? Nakamura and Padang provide a succinct explanation: the parent company in Japan "was experiencing a boom and faced a shortage of manpower . . .

[49] Interview, Tokyo, July 24, 1992.
[50] Interview, Hitachi-city, July 29–30, 1998.

[while its affiliate in Indonesia] did not have favorable market conditions and suffered from excessive manpower."[51] In addition, parent companies in Japan may move export-oriented assembly lines – and thus jobs – back to Japan when relative costs shift in response to exchange rate adjustments. For example, in 1997, when the yen weakened against the dollar, Matsushita moved its production of sixteen-inch and twenty-five-inch color television sets back to Japan from Malaysia – even though it anticipated having to run its Japanese plants at a loss for at least a short time. It did so because it wanted to protect domestic jobs, according to Shirafuji Hiroyuki, managing director of Matsushita TV.[52]

Thanks to this ongoing concern about domestic employment, leading Japanese labor organizations have been able to express qualified support for business plans to "rationalize" production activities through regionalization. In one report, Denki Rengô – the Electrical Workers Union, a subset of the conservative Rengô (Japan Trade Union Confederation) – argues that Japanese manufacturing investment in Asia, carried out as part of a regional division of labor, can actually protect the jobs of skilled core employees in Japan.[53] This position is quite different from the one taken by Rengô's U.S. counterpart, the AFL-CIO, in the debate over the North American Free Trade Agreement.

From Japanese to Asian Crisis

In 1997, six years after Japan's domestic crisis began, a debt crisis erupted in Thailand and then spread quickly, like a virus, through much of Asia, enfeebling what until then had looked like healthy, even vibrant economies. Surprisingly, though, the crisis did not undermine ongoing efforts to extend the Japanese system of relationalism into Asia. Domestic business and political elites coped with the dramatic contraction of those markets by resorting to extraordinary measures. This simply reinforces a point made in Chapter 1 of this volume: actors have varying capabilities, and thus do not experience a crisis in the same way or to the same degree. Occupying central positions within the region's web of exchange networks, Japanese elites

---

[51] Keisuke Nakamura and Padang Wicaksono, *Toyota in Indonesia: A Case Study on the Transfer of the TPS* (Jakarta: Center for Japanese Studies, University of Indonesia, 1999), p. 93. In interviews, host government officials often complained that training programs set up by Japanese manufacturers are nothing more than a way to supply their domestic factories with cheap labor from their other Asian factories.

[52] "Manufacturers Shift Strategies in Asia," *Nikkei Weekly*, July 15, 1997, p. 19. This motive also helps explain Japan's relatively low level of "reverse imports" from manufacturing affiliates in Asia.

[53] Denki Rengo, *Nikkei Denki Kigyô no Kaigai Shinshutsu to Kokunai Sangyô/Koyô e no Eikyô* (Foreign direct investment by Japanese electronics firms and the impact on domestic production and employment) (Tokyo: Denki Sogo, June 1998), p. 169.

were able to ride out the roughest part of the storm. Indeed, they actually may have consolidated some of their positions in Asia.

For example, between November 1997 and January 1999, 244 joint ventures in Thailand received life-saving transfusions of capital from their foreign parents – and nearly two-thirds of that money came from Japan.[54] In other words, while many American, European, and Korean manufacturers reduced their presence in the market, Japanese MNCs held on for dear life.[55]

By late 1999, when the crisis showed signs of easing, this "hang tough" strategy appeared to be paying off. In Thailand, Mitsubishi Motors was preparing to quadruple its annual production of automobiles and was moving ahead with plans to use some of its increased capacity to build an "Asian car."[56] In Indonesia, Toshiba was able to begin expanding production of cathode ray tubes for color televisions after Korean producers closed their assembly lines. "In some areas, we are facing less competition," said Tsubota Yutaka, manager of the conglomerate's Asian operations. "We are already as profitable [in the region] as we were before the crisis." Toshiba apparently was not alone. JETRO reported that 75 percent of Japanese manufacturers in Southeast Asia expected to break even or turn a profit in 1999.[57]

In the face of this crisis, Japanese manufacturers managed to hold onto their all-important supply networks in Asia. For example, in Thailand, where scores of local suppliers went bankrupt and an equivalent number of foreign suppliers shut down their factories, not a single Japanese parts producer gave up – despite having to operate at sometimes as little as 20 percent of production capacity.[58] How did they do it? The answer reveals an interesting twist: in this instance, relationalism actually bailed out regionalization.

Consider what happened in the automobile industry. Parent companies in Japan pursued a three-pronged strategy to help Japanese subcontractors in Asia. First, they provided emergency financial assistance to members of their regional supply groups. Toyota, for example, agreed to make advance payments to its parts producers throughout Asia and financed critical but

---

[54] "Japanese Companies Gave Most Aid to Thai Joint Ventures in Crisis," *Nikkei Weekly*, June 14, 1999, p. 20. The *Far Eastern Economic Review*, July 29, 1999, p. 52, reported that the Japanese government – through the Export-Import Bank – helped finance a number of these capital injections.

[55] In Thailand, for example, the number of Japanese FDI projects increased from 158 in 1998 to 188 in 1999, according to the Thai Board of Investment. The number of U.S. and European projects, meanwhile, fell from 62 to 53, and from 123 to 83, respectively.

[56] *Asahi Shinbun*, April 14, 2000, p. 10.

[57] Emily Thornton, "Japan's Asian Comeback," *Business Week*, November 1, 1999, pp. 18–19.

[58] See JETRO, *Tsûshô kôhô*, May 31, 1999, p. 10. Indeed, a large percentage of the Japanese manufacturing affiliates that injected capital into established operations in Asia, and thereby increased their equity position in those joint ventures, were parts producers. These included Showa and Keihin, Honda suppliers in Thailand, and Unisia Jecs, a Nissan supplier in South Korea. See *Nikkei Weekly*, June 15, 1998, p. 18.

short-run expenses, such as the lease of equipment.[59] Nissan also came to the defense of its beleaguered parts suppliers in Thailand, subsidizing up to $26 million in production there.[60]

Second, to breathe some life into an otherwise flat market, the parent companies temporarily assigned to their affiliates in Asia some of the production chores that had, until then, been done entirely in Japan. Toyota, for example, gave its Thai affiliate the responsibility of manufacturing – and then exporting – a line of pickup trucks. Stanley Electric transferred a share of the production of headlights to its affiliate in Thailand.[61] Mitsuba, meanwhile, turned over all production of IC flasher relays to its Thai affiliate, which then exported the goods back to Japan.[62]

Third, parent firms dramatically boosted the import of parts from struggling parts suppliers in Asia. Toyota was buying only 2.5 billion yen worth of auto parts from Japanese subcontractors in Asia in 1997, when the region's economic crisis began; by 2000, however, it was planning to import auto parts valued at 14 billion yen – a nearly sixfold increase.[63] In just one year (1998), Honda increased its import of auto parts manufactured in Thailand by 150 percent.[64] Mitsubishi Motors, likewise, began importing parts from Japanese suppliers in Thailand and using them in its Galant, produced in the United States, and its Lancer, produced in Japan.[65]

To ride out the economic storm in Asia, Japanese automakers had to do more than just shore up their supply base; they also had to hang onto their labor force. Here, too, regionalized relationalism came in handy. To cite just one example, Toyota officials boast that they did not lay off regular employees in Southeast Asia during the crisis – even though they had to suspend production at several factories. One reason they were able to fulfill their pledge of protecting jobs was that they dramatically expanded their program of sending overseas employees to Japan for training. In 1998, at the peak of the crisis, Toyota doubled the number of Southeast Asians in its training program (from 250 to 500), and doubled the amount of time spent in Japan (from an average of three months to an average of

---

[59] See *Nikkei Weekly*, October 19, 1998, p. 18; and December 21, 1998.

[60] See *Nikkei Weekly*, May 11, 1998, p. 19.

[61] See *Nihon Keizai Shinbun*, February 5, 1998.

[62] See *Nikkei Sangyô Shinbun*, April 6, 1998.

[63] See *Nikkei Weekly*, October 5, 1998, p. 18. Aishin Seiki, one of Toyota's most trusted suppliers in Japan, also got into the act by importing door locks from its affiliates in Thailand and Indonesia. *Nikkei Weekly*, October 26, 1998, p. 18. Asahi Glass did the same, importing auto glass for as many as 50,000 vehicles a year from its affiliate in Thailand. See *Nikkei Weekly*, January 11, 1999, p. 18.

[64] See *Nikkei Weekly*, September 21, 1998, p. 22.

[65] Mori Minako, "New Trends in ASEAN Strategies of Japanese-Affiliated Automobile Parts Manufacturers," *RIM: Pacific Business and Industries* (Sakura Institute of Research) 1, no. 43 (1999): 23.

six months).[66] The Japanese state helped finance this and other training programs through the Association for Overseas Technical Scholarships, an arm of MITI/METI.

For Japan's political elites, the economic crisis in Asia presented a difficult challenge but also a golden opportunity. "Our status in the region has increased, and so has our budget at home," boasted one official.[67] MITI/ METI, in particular, has used the crisis as a pretext to pursue aggressively its controversial scheme of implementing a regionwide industrial policy. It has convened "joint public-private sector dialogues" under the auspices of AMEICC in Bangkok to consider how it can work with state officials in each country to help "guide" investments that will contribute to the development of the entire region.

To promote economic recovery, Japan announced in 1998 that it would dramatically increase the flow of ODA loans and grants, as well as technical assistance, to its hardest-hit neighbors in Asia. On its face, the emergency plan to spend $80 billion over ten years seems undeniably generous. But on closer inspection, one finds that it includes a number of items designed to strengthen relational ties between the Japanese state and Japanese industry, as well as to help maintain interfirm and labor-management ties.

First, the aid package renews the controversial practice of "tying" – that is, providing financing for a project only on the condition that it is carried out by home-country firms. Asian countries hit by the crisis will receive a total of $6 billion in "special loans" over three years for equipment purchased from Japanese suppliers or for public works performed by Japanese contractors.[68]

Second, the package makes it possible to dispatch an unprecedented number of JICA experts to Asia, providing advice to host country officials on everything from industrial structure reform to trade finance. This advice, of course, tends to favor the interests of Japanese MNCs operating in those countries. And in the case of a new program proposed by the head of Nikkeiren (Japan Federation of Employers Associations), this advice will also serve the interests of some firms remaining in Japan. For the first time, the government is recruiting "white-collar experts" from Japan's private sector, particularly its financial institutions, to provide guidance to Asian governments on such matters as accounting and auditing. All of the volunteers – an estimated 1,000 each year – are between the ages of forty and sixty-nine; many, it turns out, have been rendered superfluous by the hard economic times in Japan. For this reason, says a JICA official, the program can help Japanese firms as well as Asian governments. "In most of these Asian countries, there is a serious shortage of administrators trained

---

[66] Fourin, *Jidôsha Chôsa Geppô* (Monthly report on the global automotive industry), no. 157 (1998): 6.

[67] Interview, Tokyo, July 23, 1999.

[68] *OECF Newsletter*, no. 73 (April–May 1999).

in fields such as financial management. On the other hand, in Japan, we now have an excess number of such people."[69]

Finally, the massive aid package included a significant amount of financing for Japanese firms in Asia, particularly the SMEs that make up an all-important supply base for machinery assemblers and that might otherwise be tempted to withdraw from the region. Some of this money goes to host governments, which in turn loan it to private interests. Malaysia, for example, is receiving such a "two-step" loan ($160 million in 1999) for SMEs, and especially Japanese suppliers, suffering from a credit crunch in that country. Much of the money, however, is channeled to Japanese firms through government-affiliated banks in Tokyo. For example, as of July 1999 the Export-Import Bank of Japan had agreed to provide $900 million in additional assistance to Japanese affiliates in Indonesia through what it calls "investment financing."[70]

Furthermore, these government-affiliated banks are now authorized not only to subsidize new overseas investment for plants and equipment but also to provide operating funds for Japanese SMEs in jeopardy of closing down existing facilities in Asia. The government makes loans to the parent companies in Japan, which are then expected to inject capital into their affiliates in Asia. In just the first three months of 1999, JFS loaned nearly $10 million to keep fourteen affiliates afloat.[71]

In addition, MITI/METI has tried to maintain investment in Asia by expanding its already generous program insuring foreign bank loans for the overseas activities of Japanese affiliates. In March 1998 the government announced it would begin to cover ordinary credit risks, such as the bankruptcy of an overseas affiliate borrowing money.[72] Then, a few months later, it announced it would relax the insurance program further by eliminating the requirement that Japanese parent firms participate in providing up-front guarantees for overseas loans made to their affiliates.[73]

The Japanese government has not tried to disguise the fact that its massive bailout plan for Asia is also designed to help Japanese industry. Indeed, when he announced his $30 billion piece of the package in 1998, Finance Minister Miyazawa Kiichi noted candidly that a substantial sum would go to Japanese SMEs. The government justified the expenditures in these terms:

Japanese companies, which have contributed greatly to the economies of these countries, are also facing difficulties due to the economic crisis. If this situation continues, it would be difficult to invigorate these economies with new economic activity, with

---

[69] Interview with JICA official, July 23, 1999, Tokyo.
[70] JICA handout, "JICA and Japan's Support to Cope with Asian Financial Crisis," Tokyo, July 22, 1999.
[71] Interview with manager, international section, JFS, Tokyo, July 5, 1999.
[72] *Nikkei Weekly*, March 9, 1998.
[73] *Yomiuri Shinbum*, July 11, 1998.

the strong possibility that many companies might have to pull out of the region. This would be damaging to the local economies, and could possibly have damaging effects on the bilateral relationships of these countries with Japan.[74]

Japanese Technonationalism

One of the themes repeated throughout this volume is that innovation occurs within a system composed not only of institutions but also of ideas. Put simply, ideas matter. But how should we evaluate the ideas that inform Japan's technoindustrial regime – or, more precisely, the ideas that articulate the regionalization of that regime? One way is to listen carefully to the words of pivotal players in the process. In a 1993 interview, Kôzuki Yatsugu, the former president of the Japanese Chamber of Commerce and Industry in Singapore, argued that Japan must regionalize carefully – or risk losing its technological autonomy. Parent firms, he advised, should not give up too much authority to their local affiliates. "In my personal opinion, we should keep the control in Japan. Once you lose that control, that power, it never comes back. It never returns. All you have to do is look at what happened to England in the late nineteenth century, or what is happening to the United States today."[75]

Kôzuki's view reflects what Samuels has identified as a long-standing ideology of technonationalism, a belief that a nation's security depends fundamentally on its overall technological capacity.[76] This ideology, used by Meiji elites to promote industrialization in the late nineteenth century, informed domestic institutions in the postwar period as Japan raced to catch up with the United States. More recently, this ideology has informed the corporate strategies of Japanese MNCs operating in Asia, where they have proven reluctant to set up overseas R&D facilities and to use indigenous suppliers, and where they have moved slowly to localize management. Instead, Japanese multinationals in this region have continued to rely on long-standing relational ties with conationals. As Itami puts it, "the East Asian networks of Japanese corporations are integrated extensions of domestic production systems."[77]

Let us first consider the use of subcontractors in Asia. JETRO reports that 47 percent of the nearly 900 Japanese manufacturing affiliates it surveyed in

---

[74] OECF (Overseas Economic Cooperation Fund), "Q&A on Asian Economic Crisis Support," *OECF Newsletter*, April–May, 1999, p. 7.

[75] Interview, Singapore, April 27, 1993. Quoted in Hatch and Yamamura, *Asia in Japan's Embrace*, p. 19.

[76] Richard Samuels, *"Rich Nation, Strong Army": National Security and the Technological Transformation of Japan* (Ithaca: Cornell University Press, 1994).

[77] Hiroyuki Itami, "Overview: The Structural Upgrading of East Asian Economies and Industrial Networks," in Institute of Developing Economies and JETRO, eds., *Can Asia Recover Its Vitality? Globalization and the Roles of Japanese and U.S. Corporations* (Tokyo: IDE, 1998), p. 21.

Southeast Asia in 1998 were relying on Japanese transplants for most of their locally purchased parts and materials.[78] And in certain industries, this figure is much higher. For example, 100 percent of Japanese automakers in Thailand and 88 percent of Japanese electronics manufacturers in Indonesia reported that they relied on Japanese suppliers for at least half of their local inputs. In a study commissioned by the government of Thailand, the Foreign Investment Advisory Service (FIAS) finds that Japanese affiliates in Asia's electronics industry "tend to bring their own subcontractors from Japan or create their own satellite subcontractors, neither of which generates significant backward linkages with domestic firms."[79] Likewise, Okamoto expresses concern that export-oriented production by Japanese electronic firms in Southeast Asia is carried out in "enclaves" that are well connected to Japanese subcontractors in the region but rather poorly connected to truly local firms.[80]

The automobile industry is no different. Kumon visited dozens of Japanese car and truck manufacturers in Asia and found that, in parts purchasing, they have a "high dependency on Japanese or Japanese-affiliated suppliers."[81] Ueno reports that up to 70 percent of the "local" suppliers used by Japanese assemblers in the ASEAN-4 are, in reality, Japanese transplants.[82] And FIAS argues that Japanese automakers in that country deliberately avoid Thai suppliers: "One local producer claims he was excluded from the OEM market by a Japanese assembler until he could prove, by using a Japanese testing company, that his components were of higher quality than those Japanese components being used by the assembler at that time."[83]

Now let us consider progress (or lack of progress) toward the hiring of local management staff. Japanese MNCs must pay much higher salaries and benefits to their expatriate managers than to their local managers at overseas affil-

---

[78] JETRO, *Shinshutsu Kigyô Jittai Chôsa Ajia-hen* (A survey of investing firms: Ajia edition) (Tokyo: JETRO, 1999). In fact, JETRO does not actually "report" any such figure. But one can calculate it rather quickly by using the raw data for five different countries (Thailand, Malaysia, Singapore, Indonesia, and the Philippines) on five different pages: 63, 108, 151, 198, 242.

[79] Foreign Investment Advisory Service (FIAS), "Impediments to Backward Linkages and BUILD, Thailand's National Linkage Program," a report submitted to Thailand's Board of Investment, Washington D.C., September 1991, p. 41.

[80] Okamoto Yumiko, "Shuyô Sangyô no Taigai Chokusetsu Tôshi no Dôkô: Denshi/Denki Sangyô," *NIRA Seisaku Kenkyû* 9, no. 10 (1996): 20.

[81] Kumon Hiroshi, "The Automotive Assembly Industry," in Itagaki Hiroshi, ed., *The Japanese Production System: Hybrid Factories in East Asia* (Hampshire: MacMillan Business, 1997), p. 161.

[82] Ueno Kaori, "ASEAN Sangyô Kyôryoku Keikaku (AICO) to Nikkei Jidôsha Meikaa no Chinai Senryaku" (The ASEAN industrial cooperation [AICO] scheme and the regional strategies of Japanese automakers), in *Tokubetsu Keizai Chôsa Repôto: Heisei 8-nendo* (Tokyo: JETRO, 1997), pp. 27–38.

[83] FIAS, 1991, p. 62

iates – in some cases, as much as ten times higher. Furthermore, they receive relentless criticism from host government officials for using Japanese rather than local staff at their operations in Asia. Given these two constraints, one would expect to find a steady reduction in the share of these expatriate managers.

But there has been no real progress on this front – despite frequent promises by parent companies that they will "localize" (*genchika*) their Asian operations. Japanese expats held more than 13 percent of the management positions at Japanese manufacturing affiliates in the region in 1995 – a small decrease from 1989, when they held 15 percent of the positions.[84] This phenomenon is evident not only in wholly owned subsidiaries but also in joint ventures in which the Japanese partner owns less than 50 percent of the stock. "In places like Indonesia and the Philippines, where we do not have a majority of the equity," says Yokoi Akira, vice-president for international affairs at Toyota, "we are still able aggressively to send in our own management team and maintain control."[85] Even in those rare instances in which an Asian manager ends up in charge of production, finance, or some other important division in a Japanese subsidiary or joint venture, he often is paired with an expatriate manager, who serves as a "big brother" or adviser.

The net result is that regionalization has not led to a serious "hollowing out" of the Japanese economy. Manufacturing continues to account for nearly one-quarter of nominal GDP in Japan – a higher share than in almost all other mature or "postindustrial" economies, including the United Kingdom (19 percent), France (18 percent), and the United States (17 percent). By expanding into Asia with the help of existing relational ties, Japanese MNCs have reduced both production costs and job losses at home. And they have limited technology "leakage" to potential rivals in Asia.

Indeed, it is instructive to note that, in 1995, intrafirm technology licensing (from parent to affiliate) began to account for more than half of the total technology exports from Japan to Asia.[86] Although intra*network* exports are not counted, and thus defy quantification, one can surmise that such exports account for much of the remainder. This means, then, that Japanese technology licensing to Asia is rarely conducted in the "unrelational" spot market.

The Costs of Continuity

If its manufacturing base is not "hollowing out," and its technological resources are not "leaking" out, then Japan must be benefiting from the preservation – via

---

[84] MITI, *Kaigai Jigyô Katsudô Kihon Chôsa* (Basic survey on overseas business activities), various years.

[85] See "Ajia no Jidôsha Sangyô: Zadankai," *Asahi Shinbun*, November 27, 1996, p. 15.

[86] See Management and Coordination Agency, *Kagaku Gijutsu Kenkyû Chôsa* (Survey on R&D), Tokyo, various years.

regionalization – of its existing technoindustrial regime, right? Wrong. The costs of strong ties begin to outweigh the benefits in a developed or "mature" economy like Japan, because firms no longer can simply adopt existing technology and transfer it to related firms; they now must pursue radical innovation. That is, they must acquire and develop new ideas, new information in an environment of technological uncertainty. But firms in a highly relational regime are handicapped in such an environment; they are bound together by strong ties and thus are less receptive to market signals and creative inputs that could contribute to technical breakthroughs or radical innovation.

Japan sits today on the cutting edge of the global technology frontier. It is a fully developed economy whose manufacturing firms, to compete, must develop new technologies and introduce new products. But because these firms commit themselves to long-term, reciprocal relationships, they often cannot freely take such bold steps. Relationalism, which in the past had yielded net gains through lower transaction costs, now generates net losses through higher opportunity costs.

A cursory glance at R&D data suggests that Japan is holding its own as a technological powerhouse in the global economy. Indeed, it spent 3.06 percent of its GDP on research and development in 1998 – more than the United States (2.59 percent) and other industrialized economies. And this represented an increase from 1990, when Japan's R&D/GDP ratio was 2.85 percent.[87] But this statistic obscures the fact that Japan is lagging further and further behind in basic research – precisely the area where it most needs to focus.[88]

In the mid-1980s, the public and private sectors in Japan spent about 13 percent of their R&D budgets on basic research – about the same as in the United States but lower than in Germany and France (about 20 percent). In the late 1990s, the share of overall R&D expenditures allocated to basic research remained about the same in Japan, but increased in the United States (to about 16 percent) as well as in Germany and France (to about 22 percent).[89]

Japan's performance in this critical area would have fallen even further behind had it not been for a massive and steady increase in government spending under the 1996 Science and Technology Basic Plan.[90] Japanese producers have slashed basic research expenditures, choosing instead to dedicate resources to the development of new applications with old technologies.

---

[87] National Science Foundation, "National Patterns of R&D Resources," 2000, available on the web at <http://www.nsf.gov/sbe/srs/nsf01309/start.htm>.

[88] One should also note that this statistic is a ratio. The numerator is the value of R&D expenditures, which actually rose at a slightly faster clip in the United States than in Japan in the 1990s; and the denominator is the GDP, which hardly budged at all in Japan but climbed sharply in the United States. Given this fact, we should not be surprised to see Japan's R&D/GDP ratio increase relative to the U.S. ratio.

[89] Science and Technology Agency, *Kagaku Gijutsu Hakusho, Heisei 12-nen* (White paper on science and technology) (Tokyo 2000), pp. 141–42.

[90] See Hiroshi Inose, "Boosting the Basic," *Look Japan*, March 1997, p. 22.

In one survey, the Society for the Promotion of Machine Industries found that most Japanese firms were content to continue utilizing existing know-how. Fewer than 27 percent of firms were planning to innovate.[91]

Research and development "intensity"(R&D expenditures as a percentage of total sales) actually *declined* in the manufacturing sector during the late 1980s and early 1990s, according to Watanabe and Hemmert.[92] At the same time, they note, R&D's share in total manufacturing investment fell from 13.2 percent in 1987 to 8.9 percent in 1994. The two researchers trace this slowdown in R&D activity to the heady bubble years, when manufacturers focused on expanding production capacity – in Japan as well as overseas – rather than innovating. In the 1990s, then, firms had to try to compete without the benefit of innovations that could or should have been made in the late 1980s. "In other words," Watanabe and Hemmert assert, "the long-lasting virtuous circle between capital investment and technological advance appears to be on the verge of collapse."[93]

Although some have suggested that Japanese academics are beginning to collaborate regularly with manufacturers on basic research, the results continue to disappoint. Japan has more than twice as many scientists and engineers as Germany, and nearly four times the number in France, but the productivity of their research is quite low. Boyer has shown that Japan in the mid-1990s produced half as many research articles – on a per capita basis – as Germany, and only about one-third as many as France.[94] And the research environment does not seem to be improving. Since 1985 the number of scientists and engineers leaving Japan to pursue research elsewhere has exceeded the number of scientists and engineers coming to Japan. And the gap is growing wider each year; in 1995 the "brain drain" was equivalent to a net loss of 110,000 people.[95]

For Japanese firms, this has translated into reduced competitiveness. In the first half of the 1990s, value added by manufacturers of general machinery and precision instruments fell 20 percent; value added by manufacturers

[91] Society for the Promotion of Machine Industries (Kikai Shinkô Kyôkai), Engineering Industries of Japan: Moving toward New Operations, New Products, no. 32 (1998): 10.
[92] Chihiro Watanabe and Martin Hemmert, "The Interaction between Technology and Economy: Has the 'Virtuous Cycle' of Japan's Technological Innovation System Collapsed?" in Martin Hemmert and Christian Oberlander, *Technology and Innovation in Japan: Policy and Management for the Twenty-first Century* (London: Routledge, 1998), pp. 37–57.
[93] Ibid., p. 53.
[94] Robert Boyer, "Will the Japanese and the German Innovation Systems Cope with the Challenges of the Twenty-first Century?" paper presented to the Economic Research Center, Nagoya University, Nagoya, Autumn 1998.
[95] See Science and Technology Agency, *Kagaku Gijutsu no Shinkô ni kansuru Nenji Hôkoku, Hensei 8 Nendo* (Annual report on the promotion of science and technology), Tokyo, 1996, pp. 61–62. Of the scientists and engineers leaving Japan, most are headed to the United States or Europe. And most of those coming to Japan hail from Asia.
[96] MITI, *Kôkôgyô Shisû Nenpô* (Annual report on manufacturing and mining indices), various years.

of transportation equipment fell 13 percent.[96] Of the four major machinery industries, only electronics managed to achieve growth. But this was due primarily to a temporary surge in domestic demand for computer and telecommunication equipment in the early 1990s; indeed, the industry's fortunes quickly soured in the second half of the 1990s as demand collapsed. Profits in these machinery industries plummeted nearly 60 percent in the first half of the decade, then recovered a little in 1996 – only to fall sharply again.

For Japan as a whole, this means sluggish economic growth today and into the near future as Japanese firms move too slowly to upgrade their technological capabilities. From 1991 through 1999, Japan's economy managed to grow (on average) by only 1.3 percent a year, less than any other industrialized economy in the world. And at the end of what has come to be called the "lost decade" of the 1990s, it just barely avoided the dubious distinction of being the only economy since the global depression of the 1930s to experience three consecutive years of contraction.

The Japan Center for Economic Research expects the pain to get worse before it gets better; it estimates that the Japanese economy will barely hold its own until 2005, then slow by an average rate of 0.1 percent a year until 2015, and slow even more (0.2 percent a year) until 2025.[97] Exports, which had provided a welcome boost at various times in the past, no longer can do the trick. Japanese exports, as it turns out, are heavily concentrated in sectors with low growth intensity; Legewie reports that, in 1992, only 5 percent of those exports belonged to product groups that had enjoyed high performance.[98] Rather than exports, it was extraordinary government spending on public works – enough to push the budget deficit up to 9.4 percent of GDP in fiscal year 2000 – that kept the economy from collapsing in the 1990s.

In the race to develop state-of-the-art technology, how did Japan, which only a decade earlier looked like a sure winner, manage to fall behind? Some blame the Japanese system of higher education, which they say fails to promote independent scholarly research at a sufficiently advanced level.[99] Others, including the Japanese government, blame Japanese culture in general, saying it is conformist and thus stifles creativity.[100] But these explanations fall short because they cannot tell us why success in Japan's case so quickly turned

---

[97] See the JCER webpage at <http://www.jcer.or.jp/eng/eco-for/97long.htm>.

[98] Jôchen Legewie, "Foreign Direct Investment, Trade, and Employment: The Role of Asia within the Discussion of Industrial Hollowing Out in Japan," Working Paper 97/1, Deutsches Institut für Japanstudien (DIJ), Tokyo, 1997, pp. 24–25.

[99] See, for example, Olaf Karthaus, "Polymer Education in Germany," *Kôbunshi* 45, no. 10 (1996): 733. He laments the comparatively low quality of chemistry training in general, and polymer science in particular, in Japan.

[100] See the Ministry of Labor, *Chiteki Sôzôgata Rôdô to Jinji Kanri* (Knowledge-creating work and personnel management) (Tokyo: Rôdô Daijin Kanbô, 1996), pp. 90–91. The ministry assails Japan's "risk-averse institutional culture."

to failure. The answer has more to do with the institutions – or, more specifically, the network structures – that make up relationalism in Japan.

State-industry cooperation, which worked so well when public and private technocrats could see the technological road ahead, now impedes the important signaling function of the market, which provides "bottom-up" information on consumer needs and wants to producers. Interfirm linkages, while facilitating the diffusion of already developed technology through established networks, nonetheless limit opportunities for acquiring new ideas for product, process, and organizational innovation. At the same time, intrafirm linkages between labor and management, which had promoted teamwork and thus served to protect the firm's investment in human capital, now inhibit risktaking in an environment of technological uncertainty.

In the aggregate, these relational ties form a national system of innovation that is ill-equipped to cope with such uncertainty. This system is founded on what Rtischev and Cole call "organizational continuity"; that is, it works well when the status quo is stable but "less well when there are fundamental and frequent changes in industry standards and dominant designs."[101] Okimoto and Nishi make virtually the same argument. Japan's system of innovation, they argue,

is not designed to encourage bold new conceptualizing, radical departures from the prevailing orthodoxy, and freewheeling exploration of territories unmapped by known theories. Instead, Japanese organization is geared to operate on the basis of caution, conservatism, and incremental change. It filters out bold new ideas if those ideas cannot be readily proved. It can be accommodating in such areas as hardware, because hardware is predictable and susceptible to design proof; but radical, new concepts seldom pass through the intricate mechanism of consensual deliberation.[102]

A growing body of literature suggests that, for many countries, small and medium-sized enterprises represent a vital source of new technology, especially "breakthrough" innovations.[103] In the United States, for example, Okimoto and Saxonhouse found that SMEs produce a relatively large number of patents

---

[101] Dimitry Rtischev and Robert E. Cole, "The Role of Organizational Discontinuity in High Technology: Insights from a U.S.-Japan Comparison," a paper presented at a conference on Business Venture Creation and New Human Resource Management in Japan, Europe and the U.S.A, sponsored by Deutsches Institut für Japanstudien (DIJ), Tokyo, October 1998, p. 3.

[102] Daniel Okimoto and Yoshio Nishi, "R&D Organization in Japanese and American Semiconductor Firms," in Masahiko Aoki and Ronald Dore, eds., *The Japanese Firm: The Sources of Competitive Strength* (Oxford: Oxford University Press, 1996), p. 203.

[103] Bonin puts it this way: "When the process of innovation is broken down into phases, it appears that small firms have an advantage in the initial stages of invention, as well as an advantage for less expensive, but much more 'radical' inventions." See Bernard Bonin, "Oligopoly, Innovation, and Firm Competitiveness," in Jorge Nosi, ed., *Technology and National Competitiveness: Oligopoly, Technological Innovation, and International Competition* (Montreal: McGill-Queen's University Press, 1991), p. 276.

with a relatively small amount of investment in R&D; in Japan, however, they found that SMEs are not as productive in generating new technology. Of thirty-four major technological innovations achieved over a twenty-year period in postwar Japan, SMEs accounted for only two.[104] This finding is confirmed by the Small and Medium Enterprise Agency, which reports that 70.6 percent of manufacturing subcontractors in Japan have never filed a patent. It concludes that "technical development activity in the small-manufacturing sector has fallen to a low ebb."[105]

In the 1950s and 1960s, Japanese SMEs tended to depend heavily on large firms for technology, as well as for capital and markets. In spite of this, some – even many – prospered, growing into large, independent, innovative firms with names like Canon and Kyocera. But nowadays, when the economy has matured and growth has slowed overall, powerful upstarts like these are few and far between. If anything, small manufacturing firms in Japan today are more likely to *shrink* than to grow in size.[106] Kiyonari Tadao, the president of Hosei University, notes that "microenterprises" (tiny start-up ventures) are popping up virtually everywhere in the industrialized world with the exception of Japan, "where such small businesses are rapidly declining in number."[107]

Figure 2.2 tells this story. The rate at which Japanese entrepreneurs launch new firms has fallen sharply since the early 1970s, when 7 percent of all firms were start-ups. In the early 1990s, the start-up rate fell below the closure rate for the first time in the postwar period; this means, of course, that Japanese firms are unable to hold their own and are, in the aggregate, declining in number. Today, the start-up rate is less than 4 percent (and even lower for manufacturing) – well below the U.S. start-up rate of about 14 percent.

Contrary to journalist accounts, Japan has not yet spawned a "venture vanguard" of young, restless, highly educated, and computer-savvy entrepreneurs like the dot.com generation in the United States.[108] According to the Japanese government's Research Group on New Business Creation,

---

[104] Daniel I. Okimoto and Gary Saxonhouse, "Technology and the Future of the Economy," in Kozo Yamamura and Yasukichi Yasuba, eds., *The Political Economy of Japan,* vol. 1, *The Domestic Transformation* (Stanford: Stanford University Press, 1987), p. 399. For a very different view of SMEs and innovation in Japan, see David Friedman, *The Misunderstood Miracle: Industrial Development and Political Change in Japan* (Ithaca: Cornell University Press, 1988).

[105] Small and Medium Enterprise Agency, *Chûshô Kigyô Hakusho, Heisei 8-nenban* (Small business in Japan) (Tokyo: MOF Printing Bureau, 1996).

[106] See Ibid. In the 1988–90 period, 7 percent of SMEs shrank substantially in size (as measured by number of employees) and nearly 8 percent grew substantially. But in the 1991–93 period, almost 9 percent of SMEs shrank and only 6 percent grew.

[107] Tadao Kiyonari, "Japan's Small Businesses Need Bigger Hand," *Nikkei Weekly,* July 14, 1997.

[108] These journalist accounts include Peter Landers, "Venture Vanguard: Small Firms Aim to Re-Ignite Japan's Entrepreneurial Spirit," *Far Eastern Economic Review,* July 31, 1997; and Kazunari Yokota, "Start-Ups Find Ways to Vault into Mainstream Economy," *Nikkei Weekly,* November 8, 1999.

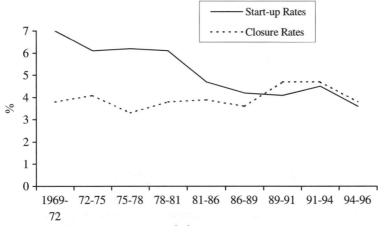

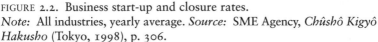

FIGURE 2.2. Business start-up and closure rates.
Note: All industries, yearly average. *Source:* SME Agency, *Chûshô Kigyô Hakusho* (Tokyo, 1998), p. 306.

which conducted a survey of more than 1,000 microenterprises identified in 1998 by the *Nihon Keizai Shinbun* as new, fast-paced, and innovating, the typical venture businessman in Japan is fifty-five; does not have a technical background in science or engineering (64 percent of the presidents of these venture firms did not); and, in a surprising number of cases (36 percent), may not even have graduated from a four-year college.[109] Only 12.5 percent of these firms are involved in information technology.[110]

A legacy of relationalism, these new start-ups increasingly tend to be affiliated in some way with a large firm. Figure 2.3 documents this ongoing trend. Among start-ups created since 1991, only 8.7 percent can be classified as truly independent (by contrast, nearly half of the start-ups founded in the early 1950s were independent). All of the other firms created in the 1990s are

[109] Research Group on New Business Creation, *Nihon no Benchaakigyô to Kigyôsha ni kansuru Chôsa Kenkyû* (A survey on start-up firms and their founders in Japan), NISTEP Report no. 61, National Institute of Science and Technology Policy, Tokyo, March 1999. Respondents to this survey came from a directory of 2,400 venture firms listed in Nihon Keizai Shinbunsha, 1998-*nenban Nikkei Benchaabijinesu Nenkan* (The 1998 Nikkei venture business yearbook) (Tokyo, 1998), which focuses on firms that possess their own technology or know-how, have enjoyed high growth, and are relatively young.

[110] A different study by the Nikko Research Center found that eight of the top ten firms engaged in information processing and information services were established by large manufacturers of information hardware (such as Hitachi) or large users of information software (such as Nomura Securities). The two independent firms in this key industry were established in the 1960s. See Nikko Research Center, *Analysis of Japanese Industries for Investors* (Tokyo: Nikko Research Center, 1999), pp. 32–41.

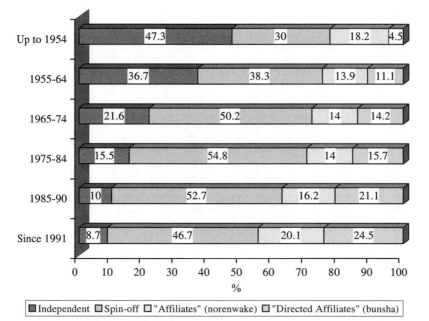

FIGURE 2.3. Character of start-ups in different periods.
Note: Like *keiretsu* subcontractors, "affiliates" and "directed affiliates" are not formally or legally members of the parent firm's corporate group.
Source: SME Agency, *Chûshô Kigyô Hakusho* (Tokyo, 1997), p. 320.

tied to a parent firm: 46.7 percent can be classified as "spin-offs," in which an employee retires from an existing firm to start his own; 20.1 percent are "affiliates" (*norenwake*), a pattern in which an employee retires from a firm but intends to maintain a business relationship with his former employer; and 24.5 percent are "directed affiliates" (*bunsha*), a pattern in which an employee sets up a new firm under the direction of his old employer.

   With this in mind, one can safely conclude that relationalism is imposing heavy costs on the Japanese economy, an economy in which potential entrepreneurs struggle just to line up qualified suppliers and talented managers. And regionalization is merely preserving the status quo.

3

Crisis and Innovation in Japan

A New Future through Technoentrepreneurship?

D. H. Whittaker

The 1990s have been called Japan's lost decade. The decade began with the collapse of Japan's "bubble" as share prices plunged 40 percent in 1990, followed by a sharp decline in land prices. The heady spiral of the late 1980s "bubble economy" now became a vicious circle of bad debts and declining asset values. A string of high-profile corporate failures followed, and the decade closed without a resolution of Japan's financial crisis. Nor was the crisis limited to the financial sector. Major construction companies that had rashly offered developers collateral or guarantees during the bubble boom were kept alive only by massive injections of public funds in the form of stimulus packages.

Eventually, malaise hit Japan's dynamic manufacturing heartland. After a period of massive investment in the late 1980s a substantial cyclical adjustment was to be expected, but at the same time the cumulative hollowing-out effects of foreign direct investment (FDI) and difficulties in reorienting domestic operations toward higher-value-added, knowledge-intensive goods and services began to be felt, particularly in the small and medium-sized enterprise (SME) sector. Large trade surpluses continued, with new opportunities for equipment exports to power the growth in East Asian manufacturing prior to 1997, but there were now growing signs that many Japanese companies were falling behind in the fast-moving, fiercely competitive, global "new economy" that was emerging.

As companies set about restructuring, insecurity spread, and consumers kept their wallets shut. Exhortations to spend by politicians and bureaucrats were to no avail. On the contrary, their inability to deal with the country's crises – and a string of high-profile scandals – undermined their credibility and, with it, faith in Japan's future. The loss of confidence was palpable. People began to talk about "system fatigue" and "system failure," and calls for root-and-branch reform mounted. Now all Japan's woes were bundled into a box marked "system" – the same box to which all its strengths had been assigned a decade earlier.

What were the causes of Japan's crisis? Were they linked to those of the 1997 Asian financial crisis? Were they "systemic," curable only by a thoroughgoing dismantling of the "Japanese system"? More pointedly, what has been done to address Japan's crises? This chapter explores these issues, particularly the last of these questions, by focusing on attempts to nurture and rekindle "technoentrepreneurship." The chapter also considers whether these attempts are being carried out under the spirit of technonationalism, or whether there is a shift toward a more technoglobalist perspective.

The focus on technoentrepreneurship is deliberate. Popularized versions of Japan's developmental state model (held responsible first for Japan's economic miracle and more recently for its crisis) frequently present an oversimplified view of business-state relations in Japan and devalue the role of entrepreneurship. Samuels notes that such models "rest on four often contradictory assumptions": harmony among interests in society; state independence and state control; state strength, and often prescience; and the inexorability of development.[1] His "reciprocal consent" model sees different and sometimes competing interests, a distinction between jurisdiction and control, negotiation and compact, and choices and contingency. Regarding entrepreneurship, the issue is not just recognizing its contribution but also different sources or types. Most attention has focused on large firms and their links to the state through industrial policy, but as Morris-Suzuki shows, in addition to this central dynamic, a peripheral dynamic featuring small firms and local communities has been vital in Japan's industrialization and technological transformation.[2]

Together, Samuels's "reciprocal consent" and Morris-Suzuki's "social networks" point to diverse sources of innovation as well as problems, which must be examined when considering prospects for technoentrepreneurship. Concretely, after looking at Japan's financial crisis and changes in the financial sector, this chapter examines the crisis and response in the large-firm (technology champion) sector as well as the small-firm sector, science and technology policy and the changing role of universities, and "competitive government." A third criticism of much developmental state writing is that it focuses almost entirely on "pie" creation and either ignores or oversimplifies distributional issues. The section on competitive government considers this dimension.

Japan is seen as a paradigmatic technonationalist country. Samuels defines this as "the belief that technology is a fundamental element in national security, that it must be indigenized, diffused and nurtured in order to make a country

---

[1] Richard Samuels, *The Business of the Japanese State* (Ithaca: Cornell University Press, 1988), p. 19.
[2] T. Morris-Suzuki, *The Technological Transformation of Japan* (Cambridge: Cambridge University Press, 1994).

rich and strong."[3] While it is hard to imagine this belief disappearing, contested visions and competing ideologies might weaken its effectiveness. "Rich" and "strong" might be emphasized to different degrees, by different groups. The "ism" might weaken, and technoglobalism, particularly in its corporate-interests-first form, might either supplement it, or be used to pursue it. The concluding section considers these possibilities.

Japan's Financial Crisis

As in the Asian financial crisis countries, Japan's financial crisis was preceded by a program of financial liberalization, and some dubious policy choices, although Japan's crisis itself was not triggered by a sharp reversal of fund flows and currency turmoil. From the late 1970s Japan came under strong pressure to stimulate domestic demand as its trade surpluses mounted. Monetary policy was relaxed in 1983 and again in 1985, setting in train an investment spree that should have been reined in long before 1989, by which time Japan's asset bubble had grown to enormous proportions.[4]

The "lost decade" of the 1990s began with share prices plunging 40 percent, followed by a sharp decline in land prices. The heady ascent of the late 1980s now became a vicious spiral of bad debts and declining asset values. As the bubble collapse gradually turned into a full-blown crisis, with a string of financial institution failures of increasing magnitude, criticism mounted over prevarication and mismanagement by the financial authorities. In part the indecision was linked to the belief that an upturn in the economy would eventually take care of many of the problems; in part it was also linked to questions over how the blame – and hence the pain – for imprudent loans should be apportioned.

Stronger banks, already struggling to meet Bank for International Settlements (BIS) capital requirements, became increasingly reluctant to bail out weaker institutions in traditional "convoy system" manner. Three failures in November 1997, including the first "city bank" (Hokkaido Takushoku) and, a week later, the fourth largest securities company (Yamaichi), highlighted this reluctance. Coming hard on the heels of the Asian financial crisis, these failures marked a turning point in views on reconstructing the financial sector. The subsequent injection of public funds was small and shown to be ill-judged when the Long Term Credit Bank (LTCB) went bankrupt shortly after, but in June 1998 a Financial Reconstruction Commission was set up,

---

[3] Richard Samuels, *"Rich Nation, Strong Army": National Security and the Technological Transformation of Japan* (Ithaca: Cornell University Press, 1994), x. Technonationalism may be a shared belief, but pursuit of it involves "contested visions and subordinated preferences."

[4] D.H. Whittaker and Y. Kurosawa, "Japan's Crisis: Evolution and Implications," *Cambridge Journal of Economics* (Special Issue on the Asian Crisis) 22, no. 6 (1998): 761–71.

and a massive financial stabilization package was put in place.[5] The decade closed without a resolution of this crisis, as the deflationary spiral continued to throw up new "bad" loans and depressed share prices undermined attempts to improve capital adequacy ratios.

Restructuring in the financial sector was partly stimulated by Japan's "big bang" financial deregulation program. First, a string of mergers among leading city banks was announced. These mergers would have been considered unthinkable a few years earlier, as they crossed traditional *zaibatsu-keiretsu* boundaries (such as Sumitomo with Sakura [Mitsui], IBJ with DKB and Fuji). At the same time, there were mergers among related financial institutions and eventually life insurers.[6] These mergers, which created four big financial groups, may not mark the collapse of the main bank system, as the credit squeeze has forced companies to strengthen ties with main banks, but it does mark the beginning of a new chapter in Japan's financial system.

Second, there has been a conspicuous increase in participation – ownership, activities, and influence – in Japan's financial markets by foreign financial institutions. In some cases this has been achieved by picking up the pieces of failed Japanese institutions, such as Merrill Lynch of Yamaichi and Ripplewood Holding of the LTCB.[7] Seven of Japan's life insurance companies were also absorbed by foreign insurers by early 2001. In some cases participation was actively sought by Japanese institutions struggling to survive in a rapidly changing and competitive environment. Foreign institutions are seen to have more competitive financial products and management know-how, and tie-ups with them are sometimes seen as preferable to tie-ups with rival domestic institutions. The trend has also been encouraged by the dissatisfaction of individual savers, customers, and policy holders with poor products and services of domestic institutions. Increased participation by foreign institutions also marks a new chapter in Japan's financial sector in terms of openness, which many believe will spur – is spurring – fundamental changes to Japanese capitalism.

Third, there has been a reduction in cross-shareholding, a practice in which companies with business relations also hold a portion of each others' shares. Speculation over the demise of this practice goes back to the 1980s, but sales of mutual shares increased markedly from about 1997, as banks set

---

[5] The total stabilization package represented the equivalent of 12 percent of Japan's GDP: T. Sakaiya, mimeograph of speech at Sorbonne University, January 7, 1999.

[6] On the announcement of the Sumitomo-Sakura merger, the Asahi Shinbun, October 15, 1999, commented: "The merger of these former zaibatsu banks heralds the end of the era of postwar Japanese corporate society." The four financial groups were Mitsubishi-Tokyo, Mitsui-Sumitomo, Sanwa-Tokai, and Mizuho (IBJ-DKB-Fuji).

[7] U.S. equity funds have begun to acquire a significant stake in the market for corporate restructuring in Japan. Ripplewood also acquired Nippon Columbia from Hitachi, and Niles Parts Co. from Nissan, and the failed Seagaia resort complex.

about improving their capital adequacy ratios and clearing up their bad debt problems. In addition to banks, life insurance companies, trading companies, and restructuring businesses have also been selling such shares to the tune of $20 billion per year. The introduction of market-value-based asset accounting from 2001 (cross-held shares from 2002) accelerated the sell-off.[8]

At the same time, foreign participation in Japanese stock markets has risen; foreign companies and individuals owned 18.8 percent of Tokyo Stock Exchange–listed shares by value in 2000, up from 8.1 percent in 1994, and they are now often the major traders on a day-to-day basis. As a consequence, listed companies have become more mindful of share prices, capital efficiency, and investor relations. It would still be premature to forecast the end of cross shareholding,[9] but the increasing volatility of the stock market, and the importance attached to it, also mark a new chapter in Japanese corporate society.

Japan's financial system was undoubtedly very effective in providing stable funds for industrial development. But the wealth generated and the transition from the late 1980s were much less effectively managed, resulting in Japan's financial crisis. Underutilized funds in Japan ultimately fueled bubbles elsewhere in East Asia: loans by Japanese institutions to Asia surged to $265 billion in 1996 from just $40 billion in early 1994. In this sense, Japan contributed to the Asian crisis.[10]

Japan's Technology Champions

The Japanese "system" should not be understood as a static set of practices; it has evolved according to endogenous and exogenous pressures over the past hundred years. Perhaps the irony is that its recognition as a "model"

---

[8] *Nikkei shinbun*, September 8, 2000. Some businesses, such as Hitachi, Mitsubishi Heavy Industry, and Sumitomo Chemical, introduced such accounting practices from mid-2000. The move is part of a drive to introduce "global standards" and transparency in accounting practices in Japan.

[9] T. Inagami and Rengo Soken, *Gendai Nihon no koporeto gabanesu* (Corporate governance in contemporary Japan) (Tokyo: Toyo keizai, 2000). Their 1999 corporate governance survey of listed company executives found an average "stable" shareholding ratio of 53.8 percent of shares issued (most surveys cite around 40–50 percent), with main banks, employee shareholding associations, other Japanese financial institutions, and key customers figuring prominently; 61.3 percent thought that the current ratio was "about right," 22.9 percent thought it desirable to reduce the ratio, and 12.9 percent to increase it.

[10] Subsequently, too, Japan's domestic malaise limited its ability to absorb exports from the crisis countries, delaying their recovery. Conversely, while Japanese exports to East Asia were negatively affected, Japanese manufacturers with FDI operations were able to insulate themselves from the worst effects through internal balancing, and their medium-term strategies regarding where to locate production were not fundamentally changed. M. Takii and M. Fukushima, *Ajia tsuka kiki* (Asia currency crisis) (Tokyo: JETRO, 1998). Japan's global trade surplus actually rose by almost 30 percent in 1998, but subsequently declined.

(in the normative sense), and the worldwide attention it gained in the 1980s, may well have reduced the incentives to address these pressures just when they needed serious attention; if failure leads to success, the reverse is also true.[11] This becomes apparent when we look at Japan's large manufacturing "technology champion" sector.

In the early 1990s Japan's postbubble recession seemed to be largely confined to the financial sector, and the vitality of its manufacturing appeared largely intact. There were, to be sure, pessimists who argued that the relocation of manufacturing operations abroad was causing a hollowing out of domestic industry, that as the most productive operations were being relocated, Japan would be left with a high-wage, low-productivity domestic economy. Others argued that large manufacturers were resting on their laurels and failing to keep up with rapidly changing markets, and that there was a conspicuous shortage of entrepreneurial start-up firms.[12] But by and large, Japan's manufacturers continued to operate in profit, stratospheric trade surpluses continued, and the performance of this sector made Japan's recession bearable. In terms of technology, too, despite alarm in some quarters about U.S. domination of new high-tech industries, surpluses in technology trade expanded rapidly, and the structure of Japan's exports showed a steadily increasing share of capital goods.[13]

Such optimism evaporated in 1998. Gloomy news of the Asian financial crisis, along with Japan's financial crisis, bureaucratic scandals, and political maneuvering, was joined by reports of mounting losses in the manufacturing sector, factory closures, downsizing, and rising unemployment. Subsequent developments to some extent mirror changes in the financial sector; consolidation and restructuring, increased foreign participation and

---

[11] A similar argument is made by Y. Funabashi, citing Cees va Lede (chairman of Akzo Nobel Arnhem), who argues that the recent vogue for acclaiming Holland as a new model is a "kiss of death." Belief in models creates rigidity in thought and inhibits responsiveness to major changes. *Asahi shinbun,* April 20, 2000.

[12] See, for example, some of the contributions in Japan Commission on Industrial Performance (JCIP), ed., *Made in Japan: Revitalizing Japanese Manufacturing for Economic Growth* (Cambridge, Mass.: MIT Press, 1997). As the title suggests, this book was a response to the MIT Productivity Commission's *Made in America.* It was published in Japanese in 1994.

[13] Imports of technology (licenses, blueprints, etc.) in 1997 were valued at ¥438 billion, largely unchanged from 1992, when exports began to surpass imports, while exports had almost doubled to ¥831 billion (<http://www.stat.go.jp/o53313.htm>, accessed October 18, 1999). Export figures include licensing arrangements with foreign subsidiaries, and should be treated with some caution, but the United States was the largest importer of Japanese technology, and Japan's technology balance of payments (BOP) with the United States moved into surplus in 1996–97. Japan's patent account balance moved into surplus in 2001. *Nikkei Weekly,* April 3, 2001. Japanese sources accounted for 20.7 percent of U.S. patents in 1990, 17.7 percent in 1999. (U.S. sources rose marginally, from 55.1 percent to 55.5 percent): U.S. Patent and Trademark Office (USPTO) online figures.

rationalization of trading relations. The automobile industry not only saw Renault acquire a 37 percent stake in the troubled Nissan, DaimlerChrysler raise its stake in Mitsubishi Motors to 34 percent, Ford in Mazda to 34 percent, and GM in Isuzu to 49 percent and in Suzuki to 20 percent (January 2001 figures), but a string of new collaborative alliances that had upstream and downstream knock-on effects. Nissan's restructuring plan called for not just the closure of several factories but a halving of the number of suppliers. Restructuring in the automobile industry probably accelerated restructuring in the steel industry, with consolidation around the giant New Japan Steel on the one hand and Kawasaki-NKK on the other. In the electronics and semiconductors sector a trickle of sector-specific alliances between erstwhile competitors in 2000 became a veritable torrent in 2001 and 2002. In October 2000 Sony took the hitherto inconceivable step of selling two of its domestic factories to leading U.S. contract manufacturer Solectron. NEC sold its NEC Ibaraki subsidiary to Solectron a year later.

Globalization of production networks, global alliances to reduce development and marketing costs, and intensifying competition are clearly factors behind these developments, but they fail to explain fully the difficulties faced by many manufacturing companies, or why the global dominance some industries enjoyed in the 1980s was eroded in the 1990s. There was, of course, a problem of overinvestment (and overrecruiting) during the bubble years, but that was not all. To risk a broad generalization, past success led to failure in at least three ways. (It is a generalization because in some capital-goods sectors Japanese dominance in world markets strengthened in the 1990s.)

First, success generates wealth, and, as Porter argues, in the "wealth-driven stage" of corporate development stewards replace entrepreneurs in senior management positions, reducing the drive to innovate.[14] The Japanese manifestation of this change was the "large-firm malaise" of the 1990s. In retrospect, the beginnings of this transition can be traced to the turbulence of the 1970s, when ambitious new projects were reined in and decision making began to gravitate upward to overburdened senior executive committee meetings.

Second, the response to that turbulence was aggressive process and product innovation and the introduction of microelectronics-based technology, which, combined with cooperative industrial relations and wage restraint (from 1975), propelled Japan's machine industries onto the global stage, even as it subsequently began to lose its low-wage advantage. The success of this strategy established the pattern for reacting to future problems into the 1990s, a

---

[14] "Stewards ascend to senior management positions in place of entrepreneurs and company builders. Belief in competition falls not only in companies but in unions, which both lose the taste for risk-taking. The compulsion to innovate diminishes as the willingness to violate norms and bear disapproval falls." M. Porter, *The Comparative Advantage of Nations* (Basingstoke: Macmillan, 1990), p. 556.

tendency reinforced by international attention and acclaim. As Baba observed, however, new sources of competitiveness were emerging, from outside Japan.[15] Whatever might be said about brutal downsizing methods, the focus by U.S. and some European manufacturers on raising white-collar productivity and using information technology to achieve it (in addition to learning from Japan) shrank the productivity gap that Japanese companies had earlier opened.

Third, indirect workers in Japanese companies expanded rapidly during the 1970s, and while white-collar productivity – and creativity – was recognized as a problem, few concerted efforts were made to improve it. To address it fundamentally would probably have required major reforms in personnel management, potentially threatening industrial relations stability (by differentiating between white-collar and blue-collar workers), which was also beginning to attract worldwide attention. The combined effect of these three factors created an inertia toward new conceptions of innovation as long as profits were still being made.

Companies that gave the world "just in time" manufacturing, *kaizen*, and the like now had to import enterprise resource planning (ERP) systems from abroad and hire foreign consultants to advise on business process reengineering (BPR) and outsourcing in the late 1990s. Such ironies might be related not just to the success of the Japanese system but also to the fact that it is a production-oriented system, which has placed greatest emphasis on value creation through production.

The Case of the Giant Hitachi

A case study lends empirical weight to these comments.[16] Although no single company can be considered representative of the whole Japanese manufacturing sector, Hitachi is a major bedrock presence, ranked third globally in terms of sales in the electric, electronic, and computer industries by *Fortune* in 1997 (after GE and IBM), with consolidated sales in the financial year 1997–98 of $64 billion. The core company Hitachi Ltd. had around 70,000 employees, but employees of the 1,000+ Hitachi Group companies totaled around 330,000. Founded in 1910, the company became a giant through a combination of entrepreneurship (including a strong commitment to R&D and technology development) in a growth economy, internal organization characterized by a rigorous and decentralized factory profit center system, top-down and bottom-up improvement processes, and

---

[15] "The era for manufacturing is coming to an end in which competitiveness is determined by superiority of shop floor technologies. The principles forming a new type of competitiveness have appeared from outside Japan." Y. Baba, "Manufacturing Technologies," in JCIP, *Made in Japan*, p. 221.

[16] This section draws on extensive interviews on restructuring and HRM reforms at Hitachi, 1996–2001, a fuller presentation of which is forthcoming.

(after the landmark Hitachi Dispute of 1950) an employment system characterized by welfare corporatism.[17] Having never made a loss since its postwar listing in 1949, however, the company announced a massive projected loss for the financial year 1998–99 of over $2 billion. Reacting to the announcement, the leading economic newspaper commented: "Japan's economic woes have now reached the major electric machine companies which support the nation's very economic foundations. The picture of this gigantic battleship Hitachi, losing its way, unable to take effective measures before this massive loss materialized, is the very picture of Japan today."[18]

Why could the company, which was reputed to be able to weather any recession, not take effective measures before the loss materialized? What went wrong, and what measures have been since taken to set things right? Certainly the situation was not helped by the "silicon cycle"; semiconductors generated half Hitachi's profits in 1995 and half its losses in 1998. Nor was it helped by recession within Japan and fallout from the Asian financial crisis. But operating and after-tax profits had been declining since the 1970s, and it was clear to all that the problems were more fundamental. In general terms, the problems were those referred to earlier; Hitachi had become a victim of its own success. It had lost its erstwhile vigor, decision making had become too slow, and it was now an "also-ran" in too many markets, a situation that prompted "Neutron Jack" Welch's famous restructuring of GE in the early 1980s. As competition had intensified, Hitachi had begun to be outmaneuvered not only by smaller, more focused manufacturers in Japan but also by the combination of de facto standard technology generators within Silicon Valley on the one hand and upgrading manufacturers in Taiwan and Korea.

Hitachi's 1998 loss was turned into a crisis – intensified by the sense of crisis elsewhere in the economy – through which a broad consensus was generated for more radical reform than previously attempted. The reforms, however, were different from those of GE. Hitachi attempted "downsizing" to speed up decision making and improve responsiveness to market conditions without massive layoffs (organization reforms), to increase profitability and ROE without sacrificing the interests of other stakeholders (corporate governance reforms), and to improve white-collar productivity without precipitous delayering (human resource and business process reforms). Let us look at these briefly in turn.

In June 1998 Hitachi announced that it would take advantage of changes in the Commercial Code and Antimonopoly Law to institute a holding company structure. Unlike Toshiba it would not separate most of its operating divisions into legally separate companies, but mature operations would be spun out as

[17] R. Dore, *British Factory – Japanese Factory* (London: Allen and Unwin; Berkeley: University of California Press, 1973).
[18] *Nikkei shinbun*, September 4, 1998. The actual loss for the year, including special write-offs, was $3 billion.

separate companies, and the divisions being retained would concentrate on information business. Headquarters staff would be slashed, and board members would be limited to those responsible for corporate planning. The level of investment requiring corporate approval would be raised by a factor of ten.

Analysts believed that this attempt to cure "large-firm malaise" was vague and lacked strategic vision. Organization reform was one thing; they wanted to see evidence of strategic focus, and plans for exit from nonprofitable areas. The media, too, became scathing when the projected losses were announced in September. In October the company announced that its operating units would be organized into eleven virtual companies, each with a CEO, one of which would be spun out immediately. In effect, it was trying to create a number of smaller companies, each of around 6,000 employees, with authority and ability to respond rapidly to changes in markets and technology, and crucially with the potential to set separate pay and conditions, but without losing the benefits of access to the larger company's resources. Still the skeptics were not convinced.

On April 1, 1999, a new president told new recruits that he would eschew time-consuming *nemawashi* and *ringi* consensus building in favor of "real time" decisions. He told CEOs of the new business groups that he did not want to deal with things they should be deciding. Within weeks the fortnightly top Management Meeting was said to be dealing with a fraction of the business of its forerunner, the Senior Executive Meeting. Internal skeptics began to think that change was possible. For external skeptics the "i.e.Hitachi Plan" was unveiled in November 1999, setting out in some detail how strategic focus in information and electronics ("i.e.") would be achieved (including the investment of some $500 million in a new Internet-based solutions business; $3 billion in acquisitions, equity participation, and alliances; and $2 billion in existing information technology business), and how exit from unprofitable business would be carried out. It was an aggressive plan that focused on business expansion rather than employee reduction.

Included in the plan was the pledge to raise ROE from 1.2 percent in 1999 to 7.5 percent by 2003, and subsequently to 8 percent. Declared the president at the press conference: "Our priority is to imagine ourselves in the shoes of shareholders. We must change our mindset."[19] Behind growing attention to ROE and investor relations (IR) were legal changes making it easier for disgruntled minority shareholders to sue corporate managers and a decline in stable shareholding: a reluctance by Japanese investors to invest in the stock market paralleled a growing participation by foreign investors in Japan's stock markets.[20] In 1989 foreign investors owned 10 percent of Hitachi's shares; in

[19] Cited in *Financial Times*, November 11, 1999.
[20] Also significant was the growing influence in the business media of the financial perspective of business performance; progressive companies aimed for higher profitability, if necessary at the expense of sales growth.

1997 the figure was 27 percent and by 2000, more than 30 percent. Eight percent was considered the minimum level to achieve global standards in ROE. But it was also considered the minimum level needed for management purposes, to restore the company to health and ensure future development.

Changing mind-sets meant forging more active relations with investors, improving information disclosure, and paying greater attention to profitability, but it did not mean – as was made clear in internal communications – disregarding the interests of other stakeholders. The executive stock option scheme introduced in 2000 was also designed to change mind-sets but not to bring about wholesale conversion to shareholder capitalism.

Human resource management (HRM) reforms began in 1998 with the introduction of a new system designed to stimulate the productivity and creativity of the company's "knowledge workers."[21] Personnel managers were particularly keen to move away from what they described as "management based on time (worked)" and "management based on seniority," and to give greater recognition to achievement. They introduced a new qualification system, designed to make the criteria for promotion transparent; a new wage system, which retained a 40 percent base component but emphasized results in the remaining 60 percent; and a new work system with more flexible working patterns. Subsequently a package of family-friendly measures was introduced and welfare schemes were reformed to offer greater choice, modifying but not eliminating the communitarian basis of employment relations. Employment relations are moving from a corporate community model toward a more explicit reciprocation model, while maintaining some community features.

Hitachi was also beginning to raise its payback to individual researchers as a result of technology license income.[22] Such moves by leading Japanese companies in 1997–99 reflected a growing propatent mood in Japan, the growing contribution of license fees to corporate income, and a desire to keep leading researchers and their know-how.

The organization reforms highlighted the issue of leadership within the company – "it was like trying to find 11 CEOs all at once" – and the need to rethink staff development. They also raised questions about what jobs should be done where, which led to a business process reform movement in 2000 targeting personnel, procurement, and accounting functions, underpinned by IT investment. The BPR movement marked not only an attempt to link the other pillars of reform together but also a rethinking of indirect functions and work. From "support staff," indirect employees were to become value-enhancing professionals.

---

[21] In the 1960s, when its former HRM system was put into place, more than half the employees were production workers; by the mid 1990s this proportion was less than 25 percent. The proportion of graduates had increased from 10 percent to more than 30 percent.

[22] In 1997 it raised the upper limit from ca. $50,000 per year to ca. $100,000. The top amount actually paid to a researcher in 1998 was ca. $75,000. *Nikkei shinbun*, July 28, 1997; May 12, 1998.

A further stage of this reform process will see the spinning out of some of these tasks into separate companies to provide specialist services for Hitachi Group companies. This will add to the growing prominence of service companies within the group and the transition "from manufacturer to solutions provider." The creation of Hitachi Capital in October 2000 (from the merger of Hitachi Credit and Hitachi Lease) also symbolizes this transition. Again, while it is tempting to draw parallels with GE, the president of this company is adamant he will not follow GE Capital's business plan; his job is to support manufacture and improve investment efficiency, and growth will be mainly organic.[23]

How successful will these reforms be? The answer is important because the continued dynamism or otherwise of giants like Hitachi will have a major impact on the generation and diffusion of technology in Japan in the coming years. There is a tendency by some in the United States and United Kingdom to judge restructuring and reforms in Japan according to an Anglo-Saxon yardstick, or rather an Anglo-Saxonization yardstick, and to dismiss anything else as cosmetic. Rather, we should see these reforms as drawing some inspiration from the United States, but attempting to extend rather than abandon the traditional productionist model, and transform rather than abandon the corporate community in which it is based. Indeed, from 2001 prominent Japanese manufacturers began to reaffirm their production orientation, albeit a reformed version.

Time (measured in years rather than months) will tell how successful the reforms are in terms of restoring entrepreneurial vigor and in forging a new system. The prospects of tapping hitherto neglected areas of productivity appear positive, but concentration on information and electronics promises more intense competition with companies like NEC. A new semiconductor slump, IT, and global economic downturn in 2001 resulted in a loss in 2001 even greater than that of 1998. The reforms are mainly directed at Hitachi's domestic operations, and Hitachi still has a long way to go before it can be considered a global company (despite having about 300 subsidiaries outside Japan, alliances with major foreign companies, and a number of R&D facilities abroad). The long-term objective of 50 percent of sales outside Japan (compared with a 1998–99 figure of 21 percent) announced in the "i.e.Hitachi Plan" suggests a future round of reforms in this direction, the opening salvo of which may have been English competency requirements for managerial promotion announced in 2001. It was envisioned that a substantial chunk of the earlier-noted ¥300 billion earmarked for acquisitions, equity participation, and alliances would be spent abroad.

[23] M. Hanabusa, interviewed in *Nikkei Business*, June 5, 2000. GE Capital accounted for two-thirds of GE's 100 or so acquisitions (worth a cumulative $51 billion) between 1997 and 2000. It also accounted for more than 40 percent of GE's profits (<www. FT.com>, July 31, 2000).

The "i.e.Hitachi Plan" also announced the objective of increasing patent activity overseas, and increasing intellectual property sales. In 1999 Hitachi's net patent income came to ¥32.2 billion, which was less than 1 percent of turnover but represented a substantial chunk of profits.[24] Can Hitachi create de facto technology standards that will significantly boost this kind of income? Again, time will tell, but it is clear to corporate managers that the objective is important, and its realization depends not simply on stimulating the creativity and productivity of their own employees but on forging various kinds of alliance, not only within Japan but increasingly with partners outside Japan.[25]

Hitachi might be considered a champion of technonationalism in terms of its origins and early growth. Although this ideology might not have disappeared, other potent forces animate corporate managers today, including pride in their company and a sense of responsibility to stakeholders, particularly to employees and those who created and built the company. Fulfilling these responsibilities might require the acquisition and development of technology, but it also requires a wide range of cross-border alliances and cooperation.

New Entrepreneurial Champions?

Some 80 percent of Japanese R&D takes place in the private sector, and most of this takes place in large firms.[26] Although the research labs of large companies might generate most fundamental new technologies, however, small firms also play a crucial role in new technology development, application, and diffusion into new markets. This has been true in key periods of Japan's industrial history and has been particularly true in the United States and United Kingdom in the recent upswing of economic activity based on new technologies. Indeed, the United States lead in many new technologies has been extended by mechanisms that accelerate the incubation and growth of small firms so that they create standards to which others must work. Commentators have pointed to the lack of this dynamic as a contributing factor in Japan's lost decade, arguing that unless this dynamic can be generated, Japan will not regain its economic vigor.

---

[24] *Nikkei Weekly*, April 30, 2001.

[25] At the tenth anniversary of its semiconductor collaboration with The University of Cambridge, for instance, Hitachi announced a possible breakthrough in the race for a single-electron memory device, with the goal of commercialization by 2005. *Financial Times*, May 18, 1999. In February 2001 Hitachi also signed an agreement for technological exchanges with IMEC in Belgium.

[26] In 1997 SMEs (in terms of employees, less than 300 in manufacturing, and less than 50 in other sectors) accounted for only 5.5 percent of corporate R&D according to a government survey. Those which engaged in R&D devoted an average of 1.9 percent of turnover to it, versus 3.5 percent for large firms. See Chusho kigyo cho, ed., *Chusho kigyo hakusho* (SME white paper) (Tokyo: Okurasho insatsu kyoku, 1999), p. 220. These figures undoubtedly underestimate the extent of R&D in small firms, much of which is not listed as a separate activity.

The irony here is that, while small firms hardly feature in most formulations of the "Japanese model," Japan had, and still has, the highest proportion of small and medium-sized enterprises and employment in them of any major industrialized country, SME resurgence in the United States and United Kingdom notwithstanding. (See Table 3.1 for their presence in high-tech manufacturing.) They were traditionally considered a problem – too small, too many, an impediment to modernization – and were long synonymous with "subcontractor" in a dual structure, although a substantial number of them were not subcontractors.[27] Even today SMEs tend to be lumped together in the protected sector and seen as a brake on attempts to create a more open and market-based economy.

In reality the SME sector has always been very mixed, with dynamic, entrepreneurial SMEs as well as static, livelihood businesses.[28] Change and transition have produced winners as well as losers – this has been part of the upgrading dynamic in the SME sector. The "new SME problem" of the 1990s is the breakdown of this Darwinian dynamic. Start-up rates declined steadily from the late 1960s and, from around 1989, were exceeded by closure rates in most sectors of the economy (see Figure 3.1). These rates, moreover, were lower than in the United States,[29] and a rising proportion of start-ups were subsidiaries of large firms rather than independent companies.

Factors behind the decline in start-ups include greater sophistication and the need for more resources; it became difficult to accumulate the necessary financial, technological, and human resources. Also, however, "stability-oriented social consciousness, as represented by progression through a single firm rather than founding a firm and developing it, has been one factor in stagnating start-up activity," despite a "reserve army" of over a million would-be founders.[30] Such "stability-oriented social consciousness" may be declining but to date has

---

[27] The proportion of manufacturing SMEs reliant on subcontracting for all or part of their income was less than half in the early 1960s, peaked in 1981 at 65.5 percent, and dropped back to 47.9 percent by 1998. Chusho kigyo cho, *Chusho kigyo hakusho* (SME white paper) (Tokyo: Okurasho insatsu kyoku, 2000), p. 408. Even when their subcontracting contribution came to be celebrated in the 1980s, the impetus for quality and technological upgrading was seen to come from "parent" firms.

[28] D.H. Whittaker, *Small Firms in the Japanese Economy* (Cambridge: Cambridge University Press, 1997).

[29] Chusho kigyo cho, *Chusho kigyo hakusho* (SME white paper) (Tokyo: Okurasho insatsu kyoku, 1998), pp. 306–7; Kokumin kin'yu koko, ed., *Shinki kaigyo hakusho* (White paper on start-ups) (Tokyo: Chusho kigyo risachi senta, 1998), p. 210. Between 1994 and 1996 annual start-up rates in Japan were estimated at 3.5 percent of total stock, while closure rates were estimated at 3.7 percent. By contrast, start-up rates in the United States in 1994 were estimated at almost 14 percent, with closures at less than 12 percent. The figures are not directly comparable, however, because the method of calculation differs, and the Japanese method understates both start-ups and closures. Moreover, the larger Japanese "stock" base should also be noted, but seldom is.

[30] S. Kamata, *Chusho kigyo no sogyo to koyo mondai* (SME start-up and employment problems), *Nihon rodo kenkyu zasshi*, no. 425 (1995): 4.

TABLE 3.1. *Small-Firm Employment Share in High-Tech Manufacturing Industries in Japan, the United States, and the United Kingdom (%)*

	Japan (1996)	United States (1997)	United Kingdom (1998)
Chemicals	19	10	9
Pharmaceuticals	13	9	5
Metalworking, textile, and special purpose machinery	46	42	39
Special purpose machinery	45	32	35
Ordnance	9	10	5
Office machinery and computers	20	9	15
Electricity distributing, generating, and control equipment	32	16	16
Electronic components and other equipment	20	16	17
Radio, TV communication, and related equipment	14	12	11
Medical instruments	44	20	41
Instruments for checking, testing, navigating, industrial control, and other purposes	20	15	16
Optical instruments	37	13	28
Aerospace	21	4	5
ALL MANUFACTURING	45	22	25

Notes: U.K. figures are for businesses with 1–49 employees, Japanese figures for 4–49, and U.S. figures for 0–99. Definition of "high tech" based on R. Butchart, "A New UK Definition of High Technology Industries," *Economic Trends*, no. 400 (February 1987); and D. Heckler, "High Technology Employment: A Broader View," in *Monthly Labor Review*, June 1999.

Sources: Japan: Ministry of International Trade and Industry, *Kogyo tokei*; United States: Small Business Administration online figures; United Kingdom: Department of Trade and Industry, *SME Statistics for the UK*.

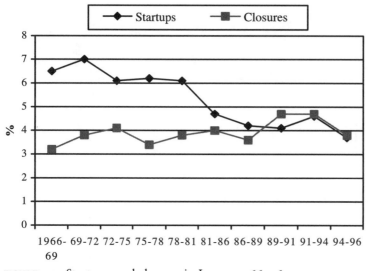

FIGURE 3.1. Start-ups and closures in Japan, 1966–96.

Notes: Establishment base, all sectors excluding primary; start-up (closure)

$$\text{rates} = \frac{\text{no. of start-ups (closures) during period}}{\text{no. of establishments at beginning of period}} \times \frac{1}{\text{years during period}} \times 100.$$

Source: Chusho kigyo cho, ed., *Chusho kigyo hakusho* (SME White Paper) (Tokyo, 1999), p. 219.

been replaced more by apprehension of losing a job or being transferred permanently to a small subsidiary than the actual step of starting a business.

As for rising closure rates, on the face of it these appear to be caused by factors such as deregulation and large firms' moving their production bases offshore and concentrating their orders in a smaller number of middle-sized subcontractors. An additional factor, however, has been generational change as 1950s and 1960s founders retire with no successor. Where there are successors, some have lost the entrepreneurial drive of their parents, but some inject new innovative vigor by introducing new technology, launching a new product, or diversifying into a new field.

This points to a second SME upgrading dynamic – upgrading by existing SMEs, which have an established human resource base, a track record for borrowing money, and an income base to support diversification. Existing business are able to benefit from long-term relationships whereas start-ups are often handicapped by them. Nintendo, whose Pokémon captured the hearts and minds of children (and wallets of parents) worldwide, is the ultimate expression of this dynamic: it was founded as a trump card company in 1889. If this second dynamic is alive and well, the decline of the Darwinian (birth and death) dynamic gives less cause for worry. But is it?

The decline in subcontracting rates was accelerated in the late 1980s when large firms began to concentrate their orders into a smaller number of medium-sized firms. At the same time, however, increasing numbers of

SMEs strategically attempted to diversify order sources or quit subcontracting because the traditional advantages – steady orders, not needing functions such as marketing – began to be outweighed by continuous pressures to cut prices and adapt to "parent" company demands. Although some built a strong technological platform, rising closure rates pointed to polarization within the sector. More recent surveys point to the continuation of this transition; those SMEs with either the least, or the most, subcontracting dependence on a specific "parent" report the greatest growth or stability of orders, whereas those in the middle suffer.[31] Some SMEs, therefore, have succeeded in joining the ranks of independent product makers or specialist process businesses; some are thriving through dependent subcontracting, while others are struggling.

Not surprisingly, Japan's financial crisis affected small firms, especially from late 1997, when city banks and regional banks reduced their SME loans sharply in order to improve their own financial health and reduce risk. Extra loans from government financial institutions and credit banks, as well as special loans and credit guarantees, however, softened the impact and kept the number of bankruptcies in 1998 to 1985 levels (in terms of numbers, but not value).

A serious challenge is internationalization. If this is difficult for giants like Hitachi, it is even more difficult for SMEs. To give one example, die and mold makers in Ota Ward, Tokyo, are renowned for their high-technological levels, which contribute to the competitiveness of Japanese manufacturing. Although they have been forced to look for new order sources or diversify in the face of rationalization by large companies, much of this has been done within the context of domestic markets. By contrast, Taiwanese die and mold makers may not boast the same technological levels – though these are rapidly rising – but they have been aggressively seeking orders, not just from Japan and Chinese-speaking Asia but from the United States, South America, and Europe.[32]

Moreover, those SMEs which set up production bases in East Asia (where most of their FDI is concentrated) were more severely hit by the Asian financial crisis than were large firms. Between late 1997 and 1998, SMEs shed 21.4 percent of their employees in ASEAN and NIEs subsidiaries, whereas

---

[31] Survey reported in Chusho kigyo cho, (SME white paper 2000), 409. According to another survey, "escaping from subcontracting" was the third most common reason for SMEs to carry out R&D after "to produce competitive products" and "to make products not made by other companies," and ahead of "at the request/demand of clients." The proportion responding to this option jumped markedly in the 1990s, moreover; see ibid., 145.

[32] Interviews of die and mold makers in Japan and Taiwan in 1996. From 1991 to 1996 die and mold exports from Taiwan more than doubled (and the *proportion* of overall production exported almost doubled as well; Taiwan Mold and Die Industry Association mimeograph, Taipei); from Japan they rose by 17 percent (proportionately by slightly more, as overall production declined; JDMIA mimeo).

large firms shed only 6.6 percent, reflecting their relative ability to absorb the turbulence internally. Subsequent FDI by SMEs also plummeted.[33]

Still, there are strong expectations that existing SMEs will emerge from the trials of the 1990s and beyond even stronger and, moreover, that the former Darwinian dynamic can be rekindled. At the close of the decade, there were significant developments toward this end. Changes to the listing conditions of the over-the-counter (OTC) market in 1995 failed to produce a decisive surge, but in November 1999 a new Market for High Growth and Emerging Stocks (MOTHERS) was created by the Tokyo Stock Exchange, and in June 2000 NASDAQ Japan was opened in a joint venture between Softbank and the Osaka Stock Exchange.[34] Large funds were amassed from both abroad and domestic sources in anticipation of a boom in initial public offerings (IPOs).

Media attention focused particularly on the monthly parties of "Bit Valley," attended by hundreds of young would-be entrepreneurs in their twenties and thirties, shunning the "salaryman" way of life or escaping from it: students, venture capitalists, consultants, and representatives of large computer firms.[35] A significant number of people involved in the Bit Valley phenomenon had lived abroad, particularly in the United States, and, critically, a growing band of serial entrepreneurs were themselves becoming actively involved in incubating and accelerating the growth of new businesses. In the words of a former NTT and DDI manager turned serial entrepreneur and professor, 1999 marked the beginning of a fundamental change in Japan toward an (SME) entrepreneurial-driven economy.[36]

Time will tell if he is right. A more cautious view – warranted in view of the past history of premature obituaries for Japan's large firms on the one hand and proclamations of a new entrepreneurial dawn on the other[37] and, more obviously, in view of the past-2000 economic and technology stock market turbulence – would be that future entrepreneurial dynamism will be a combination of restructured large firms and their small firm progeny,

[33] MITI survey, cited in Chusho kigyo cho, (SME white paper 2000), 400.

[34] The OTC (renamed Jasdaq) and Nasdaq Japan plan to integrate their operations in 2003.

[35] "Bit Valley" is derived from the English translation of Shibuya (literally "bitter valley"), center of a burgeoning cluster of 400–500 net companies (as of early 2000).

[36] S. Senmoto, interviewed in *Aera*, December 27, 1999–January 3, 2000, p. 29. Also *Asahi Shinbun*, October 10, 1999.

[37] Dual structure critic Nakamura pointed to the large numbers of leading specialist medium-sized businesses (*chuken kigyo*) in the 1960s, and in 1970 to the sprouting of a new kind of knowledge-intensive, innovative small business, which he and his colleagues dubbed "venture business." His claim that the age of large firms was over, and that Japan's future belonged to such businesses, proved premature, however. Large firms went on to give the world JIT, etc., while the venture businesses were the casualties of the 1970s economic turbulence. There was a similar boom and fizzle in the 1980s, and to some extent in the 1990s. H. Nakamura, *Daikibo jidai no owari* (End of the age of large scale) (Tokyo: Daiyamondo sha, 1970); "Japan Science and Technology Policy: Retooling for the Future," Report 98-06, National Science Foundation, Tokyo office report, April 7, 1998.

diversifying SMEs, and entrepreneurial businesses and start-ups, as well as the evolving relationships between them. This is particularly true in high-tech industries, where small firms actually lost ground to large firms in the 1990s, in both manufacturing and services.

Creating a Science and Technology Policy

Asserting the importance of entrepreneurship in Japanese economic development does not mean denying the role of government policy. Science and technology (S&T) cannot produce economic growth without entrepreneurship (a common lament in the United Kingdom); however, entrepreneurship for a major economy ultimately (and increasingly) needs a pool of scientific and technological knowledge from which to draw. Few would deny that the Japanese government and particularly the Ministry of International Trade and Industry (MITI) has, at least in the past, played an important role in making available to entrepreneurial businesses such a pool of knowledge, whether by assisting transfer from abroad or by encouraging its generation and diffusion in Japan.

The problem is the overwhelming prominence this was given in the "Japanese model" of innovation in the 1980s, often in an oversimplified form. Ironically, as in the corporate model (in fact, linked to the corporate model), success in the turbulent 1970s masked nascent problems and made it difficult to address them fundamentally until the late 1990s. Equally ironic, Japan's earlier success provoked a reaction in other countries, notably the United States, and the results of this reaction ultimately provided a new model for change for Japan. (This was happening as MITI was being forced to espouse technoglobalism by opening its programs to foreign participation.) In 2001 Japan got its equivalent of the (U.S.) National Science and Technology Council (NSTC), and inhibiting rigidities in business-state interaction were addressed under reforms inspired by the Bayh-Dole Act in the United States.

This interpretation does not see a linear decline in the relevance of industrial and S&T policy, to be solved simply by deregulation. Major companies certainly do not see things in this way. While government money constitutes only 1–2 percent of Hitachi's overall R&D budget, for instance, R&D managers contend that if anything its value has increased since the late 1990s. In a difficult business environment it has not only enabled them to maintain and expand research in key information technology (IT) areas – through participation, for instance, in semiconductor consortia like Asuka and Mirai – but to move into new research areas like genome informatics and micromachines, as well as medical and welfare-related equipment. Research consortia, in fact, have become increasingly important for the survival of the once-dominant Japanese semiconductor industry. They do, however, believe that change is necessary, and some of their senior managers have been on the commissions drawing up plans for reform.

The reasons for this are historical. By the 1980s Japan's leading manufacturers had emerged as powerful competitors in technology-intensive goods, creating not just massive trade surpluses but accusations that they had been free-riding on basic technologies developed abroad under the orchestration of MITI. Diminishing opportunities for "catch-up" development, continued economic development, and disarming such accusations required Japan to place greater emphasis on basic S&T development. Difficulties in this transition have been charted by Callon.[38] It resulted in jurisdictional conflict, for instance between MITI and the Ministry of Education, intensified by bureaucratic rigidities and technological change itself.[39] It led to both a proliferation of projects – partly in order to hedge technological bets, partly as a result of interministerial rivalry – and a lengthening of program time spans, increasing vulnerability to technological obsolescence. And the increased size and competitiveness of technology champions like Hitachi reduced the relative importance to them of government R&D funding and their willingness to contribute to R&D consortia pursuing increasingly risky basic research under problematic conditions.[40]

Heightened by successes in the 1970s and fanfare accompanying projects like the Fifth Generation "thinking machine," expectations were often not met. Domestic criticism in the 1990s mounted over the S&T budget, the debilitating effects of interministerial rivalry, rigidities and red tape in research programs, and the weak contribution of universities. Passage of the Science and Technology Basic Law in November 1995 marked the beginning of a significant policy response. The enabling first Science and Technology Basic Plan of 1996 declared the objective of doubling government R&D investment from the 1992 level as soon as possible, with 2000–1 as the target financial year. A former chairman of the Science and Technology Council of Japan hailed the announcement as a major turning point for Japan.[41] Apart from ¥17 trillion of investment, the Basic Plan addressed a number of qualitative concerns as well. It called for a more competitive funding and evaluation process, more university-industry research cooperation, less encumbered by restrictions, and greater postdoctoral researcher support.

These qualitative concerns were long-standing, and the continued lack of coordination of S&T policy at the highest level, and the resulting inability to allocate funds strategically according to nationally set priorities, were seen as fundamental obstacles still needing to be addressed. The need for further

[38] S. Callon, *Divided Sun: MITI and the Breakdown of Japanese High-Tech Industrial Policy, 1975–1993* (Stanford: Stanford University Press, 1995).
[39] The increasing overlap between computers and telecommunications resulted in turf wars between MITI and the Ministry of Posts and Telecommunications (MPT), graphically depicted in T. Ebato's novel *Shosetsu Tsusansho* (Tokyo: Tokuma shoten, 1989).
[40] Callon, *Divided Sun.*
[41] M. Ito, quoted in National Science Foundation, Tokyo Office report, April 7, 1998.

reform was underlined by problems with national projects like the H-II rocket, and the failure, despite cumulative capital investment of over $2 billion by 2000, of Key Technology Promotion Center projects to generate patent income.

In January 2001 a new Science and Technology Policy Council was launched, situated in the new cabinet office and hence above individual ministries. Its twenty-eight councilors included fourteen politicians, seven bureaucrats, and seven members from the private sector (academics and business leaders, headed by the Nobel Laureate Shirakawa), and it had a staff of sixty, mostly bureaucrats but also private-sector participants. This was to be the "control tower" ensuring "joined-up" policy making and implementation. The second Basic Plan envisaged an expenditure of ¥24 trillion over five years from 2001, bringing S&T expenditure up to the target 1 percent of GDP, focusing on the four areas of IT, life sciences, environment, and new materials–nanotechnology.

Much of the inspiration for the "national strategy" reforms came from the United States.[42] A second area of reforms drew inspiration from the United Kingdom, where chunks of the civil service were spun out as agencies by Mrs. Thatcher in 1988. The agencies had set budgets and performance targets, but they were given considerable freedom over how to attain those targets. In Japan, the 2001 Independent Administrative Body Law placed national research institutes and national universities under an agency structure, including the fifteen research institutes under the new Ministry of Economy, Trade and Industry (successor to MITI). Agency directors were supposedly given considerable discretion over designing strategy to meet targets, securing and allocating resources, and pursuing efficiency. New fixed-life centers and thematic programs in line with nationally set objectives were established. Funding was to be allocated competitively, and participation from the private sector was to be solicited both on boards of governors and through active project management.

In addition, a Japanese version of the 1980 Bayh-Dole Act was passed in 1999, making it easier to trade intellectual property rights (IPR) derived from publicly funded research. Companies had long felt IPR regulations to be a sticking point in pursuing partnerships with national research institutes and universities, and indeed in R&D consortia, and compromise in the form of joint ownership did little to assuage this perception. Removal of this obstacle, and other rigidities under the administrative bodies (such as greater flexibility in setting and spending budgets), might well see a surge in new partnerships.

Universities have not played a prominent role in Japan's efforts to strengthen its basic S&T knowledge base and technoentrepreneurship. There are historical reasons for this, including caution because of the prewar association of

---

[42] The revamping of Key Technology Promotion Center activities, along with the switch from capital investment to subsidy funding, also draws its inspiration from U.S. practice. *Nikkei shinbun*, August 25, 2000.

university research with Japan's military-industrial complex, as well as a lack of funding. Expansion of higher education in the 1960s produced a remarkable growth in science and technology graduates, who fed the booming (large-company) corporate central research laboratories and development centers, but the expansion was not funded sufficiently to maintain spending, and hence standards, on the research side. Subsequent budgetary restraint, especially in the 1980s, exacerbated the situation. University spending as a proportion of national R&D expenditure declined from 20 percent in 1978 to just 11.6 percent in 1990, and within this figure, the proportion spent on basic research declined from 57.3 percent to 52.9 percent.[43] As research facilities in universities declined, the tendency toward R&D concentration in corporate-sector labs intensified. In 1997 universities accounted for a minuscule proportion (0.3 percent) of patent applications in Japan.

Such statistics conceal a more complex picture. Because of constraints in collaborative arrangements and intellectual property rights, university researchers have sometimes given their research findings to companies in return for donations to their labs.[44] Such relationships have tended to be multifaceted, but, on balance, red tape inhibited the development of university-industry collaboration, and major companies sometimes found it easier and more fruitful to pursue such collaboration with universities abroad, which were more aggressively pursuing links with industry.[45]

In 1998 a new law was passed to encourage technology transfer from university to industry. As noted, Bayh-Dole-type legislation was enacted the following year. A further step will be the change of status of national universities under the agency structure, which will be effected in 2004. Universities, like national research institutes, will acquire effective control over the management of their technological resources, including those developed with government funds, while their faculty members, no longer strictly national civil servants, will be freed from many of the former restrictions on commercial activities.

---

[43] In national research institutes, the picture was similar: the proportion of R&D spending declined from 27.5 to 21.7 percent over the same time and, within this, basic research expenditure from 18.5 to 14.2 percent. K.T. Lee, "Managing Basic Research in Japan: Towards a Japanese System of Breakthrough Innovation?" (Ph.D. dissertation, University of Cambridge, 1997), pp. 161–88. The figures are for natural science only. See S. Kobayashi, "Education System in Raising Human Capital," in JCIP, *Made in Japan*, for a historical overview.

[44] Before it set up its technology-licensing office, inventions at Tokyo Institute of Technology allegedly resulted in 230 corporate patents in one year (presumably 1997), only 20 of which were reported to the institute's evaluation committee. In 1999, after the TLO had been established, the number of inventions reported to the committee jumped to 230. *Nikkei Weekly*, January 8, 2001.

[45] In fiscal 1999 Japanese companies are said to have spent ¥154 billion on research in overseas institutions, compared with ¥73 billion for domestic institutions. *Nikkei Weekly*, August 6, 2001.

By late 2001 twenty-five universities had set up technology-licensing offices (TLOs), with the objectives of auditing salable and patentable research, assisting in patent acquisition, marketing the technology, and allocating revenues. In addition, there has been a rush by universities, in partnership with public and private organizations, to set up business incubators. Courses on entrepreneurship and business plan competitions are booming (and are particularly attractive in view of difficulties with graduate employment: roughly 20 percent of graduates in 2000 reportedly failed to find a job). Internships and short-term project placements, too, are on the rise.[46] These developments mark the beginnings of a process evident in the United States and United Kingdom: the designation of wealth creation – through links with business, technology creation and commercialization, and entrepreneur incubation – as a major objective of university activities, alongside teaching and research.

One effect may be to open up research conducted in Japanese universities to foreign companies. In October 2000, in the first such deal, Australian materials company Silex Systems Ltd. acquired worldwide patents for a new semiconductor material technology from Keio University and its inventor Itoh. Itoh said: "We first tried Japanese companies, but they said the technology wasn't proven enough to have commercial potential. But when I contacted the Silex people, they immediately flew to Japan and made the decision quickly."[47]

Attempts are being made to make Japanese universities more attractive to foreign students. Consternation that Japan is missing the benefits the United States gains from attracting ambitious students from around the world, and keeping some of them, is evident. The number of foreign students studying at Japanese universities plateaued in the mid- to late 1990s at just over 50,000, but the government announced at the Okinawa Summit in July 2000 that it would seek to double this figure to 100,000. Visa requirements were also relaxed for IT specialists. Without more generous scholarships, however, it is hard to imagine that Japan will become the favored destination for top Asian students, or that these will stay on to produce an "IC" (Indian and Chinese engineers and entrepreneurs) Silicon Valley effect. This is related less to barriers created by nationalism and more to a range of interlocking factors such as the structure of university education, job placement networks, corporate recruiting, and subsequent career development. The same might be said about attempts to nurture U.S.-inspired innovation institutions in general.[48]

---

[46] M. Mizuno, "Technology Licensing: Collaboration between University and Industry," discussion paper for APEC Conference, January 21, 2000.

[47] Quoted in *Nikkei Weekly*, January 8, 2001.

[48] R. Dore, *Market Capitalism, Welfare Capitalism: Japan and Germany versus the Anglo Saxons* (Oxford: Oxford University Press, 2000).

We should also note growing fears in Japan that the public education system is failing in basic education, one of the state's greatest contributions to industrialization. To the worry that schools stifle creativity, new fears have emerged of a wholesale decline in academic standards, or dumbing down, which many attribute to the Education Ministry's more relaxed policies of the 1990s (*yutori kyoiku*).[49] Critics fear that these policies may become even more entrenched in forthcoming revisions to key legislation on education. Basic education is set to become a key focus of debate and reform in the coming years.

Competitive Government

Recent changes to S&T policy and its implementation, designed to strengthen Japan's S&T generation capabilities, have as a backdrop changes in the state itself. As noted earlier, criticism mounted about how the Ministry of Finance (MOF) handled the postbubble financial turmoil, which reached a crescendo in late 1997–98 with the emergence of full-scale crisis. The bureaucrats in the MOF appeared unable to judge the real situation of institutions they were supposed to supervise. It was also widely reported that they accepted lavish hospitality from financial institutions. Perceptions that MOF's obsession with fiscal prudence choked off a recovery in the making added to these criticisms, as did the snail's pace of administrative reform in general. Bureaucrats came to be seen as primarily concerned with protecting vested interests, a cause of rather than a solution to Japan's woes.

This backdrop prompted two thrusts of reform. On the one hand there was a welter of legislation, some of which has already been noted. In the context of technoentrepreneurship, we might also note the Industrial Regeneration Law, introduced in October 1999 to promote corporate refocusing through, for instance, mergers and acquisitions and management buyouts. In addition, various laws were passed by the November 1999 "SME Diet" to promote entrepreneurial business. These had the aim of doubling the number of start-ups within five years, raising IPO levels to those of the United States, and facilitating winding down and bankruptcy. The means used to devise these laws were familiar. Deliberation councils came up with recommendations, bureaucrats drafted legislation, and politicians enacted it. But they were characterized by three factors: their sheer volume, foreign (U.S. and U.K.) inspiration, and growing calls for competition and evaluation in the policy process itself. Ironically, however, many of the foreign policies used for inspiration were not evaluated in a similar way, resulting in the impression of frenetic change for change's sake.

On the other hand, there were efforts to reform the state itself. The most striking expression involved proposals drawn up by the Administration

---

[49] E.g., the lead article of *Nikkei Business*, June 5, 2000: "Undermining Japan: the Collapse of Academic Standards."

Reform Council under the Hashimoto government in 1997 and eventually implemented in January 2001. Features included strengthening the prime minister and cabinet function in order to provide more effective leadership; restructuring the ministries and improving ministerial coordination through a new cabinet office; introducing an agency structure to make policy implementation more efficient; and streamlining central government by reducing national civil servants by 25 percent by 2010.[50] The objective of these reforms was ostensibly to bring about shifts "from the public sector to the private sector" and "from the central government to the local governments."

In the new environment, the state should not only be implementing measures to foster technoentrepreneurship in the business world; it should also be turning a critical eye on itself, making itself more efficient and competitive. Both of these thrusts can be seen in the "e-Japan" campaign to make Japan the world's most advanced IT nation within five years. The campaign was launched at the close of the decade amid growing fears that Japan was missing out on the IT revolution, even falling behind some of the more nimble Asian states like Taiwan, Singapore, and Korea. In 2000 the IT Strategy Council established four priorities: the creation of an ultra-high-speed network infrastructure and competition policies, facilitation of e-commerce, nurturing of high-quality human resources, and digital e-government.

This e-government initiative was not the first. In 1994 plans were made for a local area network (LAN) for each ministry, and for each bureaucrat to be equipped with a personal computer. As in private industry, however, it was not clear why each individual had to have a computer, and work processes were not redesigned to improve efficiency. Critically, efficiency across ministries was not tackled. In preparations for the budget, forms from the various ministries had to be retyped for the MOF system, different forms continued to be needed for export permission (MITI) and customs-tax (MOF), and so on. Six years later, and with the benefit of observing the effects of legislation in the United States,[51] a new attempt was made. A bridge certification (digital authentication) authority linking key ministries was to be established by 2001, with all central ministries linked by 2003. By this date, too, central and local governments should be linked, more than 10,000 application and notification forms should be made available electronically, public procurement (except for public works) should be done

---

[50] "Central Government Reform of Japan," brochure of the Headquarters for the Administrative Reform of the Central Government (Tokyo, 1999), p. 2. Also <http://www.kantei.go.jp/jp/cyuo-syocho/>. Politicians had seized the moment to effect a shift of power in their direction, away from the bureaucrats.

[51] E.g., the Federal Acquisition Streamlining Act, 1994; Paperwork Reduction Act, 1995; Federal Financial Management Improvement Act, 1996; Information Technology Management Reform Act, 1996; and Government Paperwork Elimination Act, 1998.

electronically, and new security technology developed. Industry observers, however, are not at all optimistic that these goals can be achieved.[52]

The problem is not just bureaucratic sectionalism but also political leadership. The 2001 state reforms in theory gave politicians decisive control over policy formulation and implementation but – and this is a dangerous irony – as a group they have shown themselves least capable of reform. Despite a decade of scandal, turbulence, tactical coalitions, and indeed electoral reform, factional and "vote gathering machine" politics continued to hold sway, frequently under the children of an earlier generation of political leaders. Can those (so far) unable to reform themselves undertake the job they have given themselves?

Concluding Discussion

Problems relating to entrepreneurship and governance in Japan built up over the past two decades. Adherence to hitherto successful formulas in the face of a rapidly changing environment delayed transitions, intensifying the problems. The bursting of Japan's economic bubble in 1990 is often taken as a turning point, but in fact the Asian financial crisis of the 1997–98 may be more decisive. Japan's financial crisis deepened sharply in 1997, management problems in manufacturing intensified, and the Yamaichi shock gave a new significance to share price and corporate governance issues. The Asian financial crisis added to the sense of vulnerability, and MOF's ability to rehabilitate the financial sector and steer the economy was called into question. By contrast, the U.S. economy appeared to be romping away, setting new records for sustained growth, and performing particularly impressively in the development, commercialization, and standardization of new technologies. Japan, it was feared, was missing the "new economy" boat, and bold reforms were necessary to catch it.

There were various responses: first, a willingness to embrace new ideas embodied in inward investment and direct foreign management. Statistics tell this story. The ratio of the stock of inward FDI to outward FDI rose from 9.7 percent in 1998 to 18.5 percent in 1999 (compared with 35.7 percent for Germany, 70.3 percent for the United Kingdom, and 102.5 percent for the United States at the end of 1998). But in terms of flows, the ratio jumped from 13.2 percent in 1998 to 53.7 percent in 1999.[53] The rush in 1999 was headed by French companies, which in addition to Renault included L'Oreal (cosmetics), Carrefour (retail), Axa Life (insurance), to name a few. The jump in inward investment reflected not just a grudging willingness that foreigners might play a useful role in rebuilding failing institutions, but a growing

---

[52] H. Shirai, K. Jono, and K. Ishii, *Denshi seifu* (Digital government) (Tokyo: Tokyo keizai, 2000).

[53] S. Kaji, "Japan's Lost Decade: Lessons for the Future," seminar at Chatham House, London, September 26, 2000.

acceptance that the importation of foreign management could stimulate and accelerate transition in Japan and that, as a result, investment friction would decline and Japan would become more open and "normal" (which presupposes, of course, acceptance of the view that Japan has not been "normal"). Another notable entry has been Wal-Mart, which in 2002 acquired a stake in Japan's fourth largest supermarket operator, Seiyu.

Second, at the policy level there was a flurry of new policy initiatives, many drawing inspiration from policies in the United States and United Kingdom, which were seen as having moved more swiftly to address economic stagnation problems in the 1980s. Here a growing mistrust of bureaucrats to deliver solutions in the public interest also increased the attractiveness of United States and United Kingdom concepts of accountability and government competitiveness.

Third, at the corporate level (in manufacturing at least) management models were imported more dialectically. They stimulated debate on reform and possible solutions to problems that had been building up, but there was also a reluctance to abandon practices that had generated past competitiveness. At both levels, numerical goals inspired and justified by Western standards were used to overcome inertia to reallocating resources. (These included goals of S&T spending as 1 percent of GDP, doubling start-ups in five years, 8 percent ROE, and doubling spending on employee training.)

At an ideological level there was a swing from faith in social contract institutions and practices toward market-based solutions, often led by U.S.-trained academics and an increasingly receptive media. This swing was less pronounced or shorter-lived in manufacturing companies, where past productivity coalitions remained more intact. There were, not surprisingly, countercurrents, some inspired by the Asian financial crisis, which warned of the dangers of unfettered global capitalism, hasty financial deregulation, and ideology-driven market reforms.[54] Books such as *The End of Market-ism* rejected not reform itself, but the way it was being carried out in Japan.[55] Predominantly, however, the ideological air space of the late 1990s belonged to the Anglo-Saxon-inspired reformers.

That said, the extent of swing in terms of real institutional change should not be overemphasized, in part because of systemic interlock. Relational contracting or long-term employment, for instance, might be criticized, weakened, or applied more selectively, but not abandoned. Indeed, they might be selectively exported, as Hatch argues in this volume (though this is not the same as technonationalism in my view).

Neither was nationalism dormant. As Dore argues, even those calling for a dismantling of "the barriers within," far-reaching market reforms, the tonic of individualism, and English as an official second language (notably the Prime

[54] The Enron scandal in the United States will also feed this countercurrent to some extent.
[55] R. Sawa, *Shijoshugi no shuen* (The end of market-ism) (Tokyo: Iwanami shoten, 2000).

Minister's Commission on Japan's Goals in the 21st Century) based their arguments on what was good for the nation.[56] Though clearly different from exclusive or aggressive variants, this was a form of nationalism nonetheless.[57] Conversely, however, even the nationalist governor of Tokyo (coauthor of *The Japan That Can Say No*) argued that independence from the United States must not be equated with isolationism, and expressed support for opening Japan up to large-scale immigration and "mixed blood," which would eventually produce a new Japanese culture.[58] The difference between Anglo-Saxon-inspired reformers and nationalist positions, therefore, was a matter of degree, reflecting the shared perception that Japan needed to change, while rejecting autarky.

Regarding technonationalism, it is inconceivable that policy makers and business leaders in Japan will stop believing that technology is a fundamental element in national security, that it must be indigenized, diffused, and nurtured in order to make a nation rich and strong,[59] although for many (now rich) citizens the importance attached to making the country strong has diminished. But like nationalism, technonationalism has been predominantly outward-looking, even technoglobalist in expression.

The interplay of technonationalism and technoglobalism, in various nuances, will have an increasingly important regional dimension in coming years. Investment in China has grown, spurred by attempts by manufacturers to remain competitive. Service sector investment in Asia is also growing. Conversely, within Japan the late 1990s saw the beginnings of a rediscovery of Asia. Beyond ethnic cuisine, an Asian business presence is becoming more apparent, notably in high-tech – including IT – sectors.

The Asian financial crisis prompted a flurry of reforms in many Asian countries, but also a questioning of the medicine handed out through the International Monetary Fund (IMF). Japan's proposal for an Asian Monetary Fund in the wake of the crisis was squashed by the United States, but has subsequently been resurrected in a revised form under the Chiang Mai Initiative, which envisages a regional currency stabilization system

---

[56] R. Dore, "Puresuteju o hakichigaeruna" (Don't mix up prestige), *Ronso*, January 2001, pp. 30–37.

[57] For Brown's account of the oscillation between types of nationalism in Japan, and his contrast of "new" postwar Japanese nationalism with "aggressive" prewar and wartime nationalism, see Delmer M. Brown, *Nationalism in Japan: An Introductory Historical Analysis* (Berkeley: University of California Press, 1955).

[58] S. Ishihara and S. Tahara, *Katsu Nippon* (Winning Japan) (Tokyo: Bungei shunju, 2000), pp. 80, 238.

[59] This belief, in fact, has gained ground in many countries. Economic growth or well-being is increasingly understood to derive from the mobilization and use of technological resources. In an age of "globalization," innovative practices abroad are more visible than ever, prompting benchmarking and fueling debates on competitiveness, which elected governments ignore at their peril. Nowhere is this more evident than in the United Kingdom, where it features Foresight exercises, targeted science and technology funding, initiatives to foster technoentrepreneurship, clusters around universities, and mobilization of social science for these ends.

based on bilateral agreements. Leaders from the "ASEAN plus three" (China, South Korea, and Japan) countries agreed in November 2000 to consider holding regular summits toward creating a unified market. Strains between the "plus three" over symbols of Japan's past nationalism subsequently intervened, but at the November 2001 summit they agreed to ministerial level meetings and cooperation on a range of issues, including fighting terrorism. However regional integration develops – and it is likely to be slow – Japan's engagement with Asia will differ from that under aggressive nationalism in the past. For one thing, China in the twenty-first century will be very different from China in the 1930s.

4

Crisis, Reform, and National Innovation in South Korea

Linsu Kim

The greatest strengths in South Korea's national innovation system in earlier decades became its most serious liabilities in the 1990s, as South Korea failed to adapt to the rapidly changing political and economic environment. This chapter first assesses the impact of the Asian economic crisis of 1997 on South Korea's national innovation system. The crisis resulted in numerous negative consequences in the short term but also provided a rare opportunity for long-term reform. The chapter then discusses how South Korea has progressed in reengineering the various aspects of the technonational innovation system that has bearing on the future competitiveness of its economy. South Korea will make major changes to accommodate to multinationalization, but increasing globalism will be a means toward a nationalist end.

Beyond Technonationalism

South Korea's phenomenal economic growth in the 1960s and the 1970s, during the first two decades of its industrialization, may be attributed to its strong system for national innovation. But major strengths in the early decades have become liabilities in more recent times, as South Korea failed to adjust to rapidly changing political and economic circumstances. This failure, together with mismanagement of the financial sector and foreign investor panic, led to the onset of a major economic crisis in 1997. It is yet premature to assess the full impact of the crisis, as it is still unfolding and national economic performance appeared to take another downturn in 2001, in tandem with the slowing U.S. and global economies. The Asian crisis undoubtedly affected painfully the economic and social life of South Koreans. Yet, despite the negative effects of the crisis, as widely reported in the news media, the crisis could also turn out to be a "blessing in disguise" if policy makers and managers can use it as an opening to transform South Korea's outmoded economic and innovation systems, and to bring these systems more in line with requirements of the new millennium.

South Korea has made significant strides in reengineering various critical elements in its innovation system. The government, financial, domestic support, and corporate sectors have undergone a series of restructuring programs with noteworthy results. Research and development activities at corporations and universities also produced significant results after the onset of the crisis, and workers' attitudes have improved noticeably. But South Korea still has a long way to go; experiences in such countries as New Zealand, Sweden, and the United Kingdom show that, even with consistent efforts, it takes a decade or more to see the substantial results of major reforms.

This chapter poses several critical questions. Is South Korea making major changes to accommodate global finance and markets in the aftermath of the Asian economic crises? Is it possible for a small country like South Korea to sustain its technonationalism in the face of increasing domination of innovation by larger, more technologically advanced nations? Is South Korea abandoning technonationalism in the wake of the Asian crisis and moving toward a more technohybrid or technoglobal system of innovation and corporate structure?

South Korea is evidently making major changes to accommodate a more highly integrated international economy. Both the government and large firms are actively seeking foreign investment to attract new capital, new technology, and new management know-how. They are seeking to develop broader links with advanced industrialized countries. There can be no doubt that the Asian economic crisis resulted in a major increase in foreign direct investment in South Korea. But do these changes signal a move toward technoglobalism? The answer is definitely no. South Korea is willing to work more closely with multinationals to accommodate increasing globalization, but it will try to use every means to retain its own system of technological innovation and industrial production, perhaps moving toward technohybrid solutions. The government, for example, intends to increase public R&D funding from 3.47 percent of the total government budget in 1999 to 5.0 percent within a few years, indicating its determination to reinforce basic and mission-oriented applied research.

After the Asian economic crisis, the government launched a new initiative called the 21st Century Frontier Technology R&D Program, indicating South Korea's efforts to produce cutting-edge technologies on its own. The industrial sector also has similar goals. Although the Asian crisis caused a major setback in industrial R&D in South Korea and uncovered many problems in several sectors, they are only temporary phenomena. It might take many more years before the financially troubled *chaebol* (family-controlled corporate groupings) can again take up their R&D activities, but other firms drastically intensified R&D activities after the onset of the Asian crisis to strengthen their international competitiveness. Samsung Electronics, for instance, ascended from seventeenth in 1997 to fourth in 1999 in terms of U.S. patent registration, which is often viewed as a measure of international competitiveness.

South Korea may be the only country among newly industrialized economies in which many firms market their products under their own brands, a sign of its determination to survive on its own. In short, increasing globalism in South Korea is a means toward a nationalist end.

From 1962 to 1997 South Korea achieved remarkable economic growth, an average of nearly 8 percent per year. This success is largely the result of a strong national innovation system, which functioned effectively from the 1960s through the 1980s. A national innovation system reflects the strengths or weaknesses of a nation in sustaining its competitiveness through innovation by its firms in interaction with other firms and supporting institutions. But in 1997 South Korea faced a full-blown economic crisis. Unlike previous economic disruptions, which were the result of exogenous forces, the 1997–98 crisis stemmed from fundamental structural weaknesses in the institutions that support national innovation in South Korea. The government of Korea had consolidated sufficient power to pick "winners," and mobilized and allocated resources for ambitious developmental goals. This approach eventually led, however, to corruption and collusion between the state and big businesses, and mismanagement of the financial sector resulted, with serious resource misallocation. The *chaebol* relied heavily on state protection, which resulted in diversification by big businesses beyond their financial and technological capabilities. Lack of transparency and accountability in the economic system was also a serious problem. As a result, the balance in trade declined from a surplus of $7.6 billion in 1987 to a deficit of $20.6 billion in 1998, and foreign debt increased from $31.7 billion in 1990 to $156 billion in 1997. Recognizing the weakness of the Korean economy and its declining competitiveness, foreign investors withdrew from South Korea in 1997, compounding the Asian economic crisis.

Greek mythology provides an interesting paradox that is still relevant to modern-day industry. The fabled Icarus constructed powerful wings that enabled him to fly so high, so close to the sun that his artificially waxed wings melted and he plunged to his death.[1] The paradox also applies to South Korea. The greatest strengths in South Korea's innovation system in the past became its most serious liabilities in recent years.[2] South Korea's core competence throughout the 1980s became its core rigidity in the 1990s.[3]

After the Asian economic crisis and the subsequent bailout by the International Monetary Fund (IMF), the new government, the first one in South Korean history to be installed through a democratic process, launched

---

[1] Danny Miller, *The Icarus Paradox: How Exceptional Companies Bring about Their Own Downfall* (New York: Harper Business, 1990).

[2] Linsu Kim, *Imitation to Innovation: The Dynamics of Korea's Technological Learning* (Boston: Harvard Business School Press, 1997).

[3] Dorothy Leonard-Barton, *Wellspring of Knowledge* (Boston: Harvard Business School Press, 1995).

major domestic reforms in four areas: the public sector, the financial sector, the *chaebol*, and the labor market. Most of the reform programs had long been discussed but never implemented because of inertia and resistance from stakeholders. Several months prior to the crisis, a major study of the South Korean economy by Booz, Allen, and Hamilton made two interesting points.[4] The first is that many good studies were already available in South Korea, diagnosing and prescribing the problems of its economy. The second was that none of them had been implemented. The crisis, however, provided South Korea with a rare opportunity to carry out reform prgrams aggressively. The crisis was painful in the short term but may turn out to have been a "blessing in disguise" in the long term.

There is no one best way to describe the different innovation systems that characterize countries of diverse sizes, stages of economic development, and historical experiences.[5] There are, however, many common features among different definitions.[6] That is, firms should be at the center of a nation's innovation system because they are the organizations that translate technological resources, which the system generates, into innovations. With firms in the center, an innovation system can be seen as a set of interactions among five sectors under four critical environments. The former encompasses the industrial, global, domestic support, financial, and education sectors. The four critical environments include: market and technology, government and policy, labor market, and socioculture.

This chapter first discusses the impact of the Asian economic crisis on South Korea's system of innovation. It then describes South Korea's attempts to reengineer that system to improve the performance of the various sectors and create a more conducive environment for innovative activities. The Asian crisis has undoubtedly resulted in tremendous economic and social consequences in South Korea in terms of rising bankruptcies, unemployment, and a dwindling standard of living. It also affected the various aspects of South Korea's innovation system that will influence the future competitiveness of the economy.

Government and Policy Environment

South Korea has been recognized as one of a few relatively successful developmental states.[7] In 1961 a military coup consolidated sufficient state power

---

[4] Booz, Allen, and Hamilton, *Korea Report* (Seoul: Maeil Economic Daily, 1997).

[5] Richard R. Nelson, *National Innovation Systems: A Comparative Analysis* (New York: Oxford University Press, 1993).

[6] Chris Freeman, "National System of Innovation in Historical Perspective," *Cambridge Journal of Economics* 25 (1995): 1737–58; Beng-Ake Lundvale, *National Systems of Innovation: Towards a Theory of Innovation and Interactive Learning* (London: Pinter, 1992); and Nelson, *National Innovation Systems*.

[7] Peter Evans, *Embedded Autonomy: States and Industrial Transformation* (Princeton: Princeton University Press, 1995).

to mobilize and allocate resources for ambitious developmental goals. The state achieved autonomy from vested interests and was able to formulate and implement strategies and policies for rapid economic development in the 1960s and 1970s.

In the subsequent decades, however, the government changed little in response to radical transformation of the social and economic environment. The military government did make structural changes at the ministerial level more than forty-eight times before 1997, as well as many more incremental changes in operating systems and deregulation. Despite these efforts, the government sector continued to expand and became increasingly rigid. The agricultural civil service, for example, grew 500 percent despite a 33 percent decrease in the farming population over the past thirty years. The government continued to function as a developmental state, hindering the development of a free-market economy by authoritative dictates, frequent intervention in the market, and unnecessary regulations. Nontransparent policies and inaccessible administration nurtured collusion between the government and the *chaebol*, leading to political corruption. The *chaebol* were unable to launch large-scale projects without the support of powerful politicians.

Moreover, the government had to rescue many financially troubled *chaebol* under political pressures. In return, illegal contributions to politicians and bribery of bureaucrats became widespread in South Korean society. The result was serious misallocation of resources, leading to the erosion of competitiveness. In addition, the concentration of power in the central government stifled the development of local government authority. As a result, the competitiveness of the South Korean government sector as a whole was ranked thirty-fourth, management efficiency forty-fourth, and the degree of its intervention at the bottom of forty-six countries in the 1997 study.[8]

After the Asian economic crisis, the elected administration of Kim Dae Jung targeted government reform as one of its highest priorities. Upon inauguration, the administration took several extraordinary measures intended to improve productivity in the government sector. First, the new administration established a permanent government body, the Government Reform Office (GRO) headed by an assistant minister, with the explicit mandate to reform the public sector. This office, with a powerful link to budget mechanisms, is designed to carry out reform as an institutionalized continuous process of self-innovation, in contrast to the transient, ad hoc changes in the past. Second, the administration invited nineteen private consulting organizations to help determine the appropriate scope and function of all central government ministries as well as selected local governments, and to review their current work and management systems. This is something that had previously been unimaginable in a society where the civil service occupied the top of the social hierarchy. Third, the

[8] IMD (Institute of Management Development), *World Competitiveness Report: 1997* (Lausanne, 1998).

postcrisis reform drive differed markedly from previous attempts in terms of its scope, comprehensiveness, and intensity.

It is premature to evaluate the outcome of government reform over the past three years (1998–2001), but the downsizing of both central and local governments has resulted in savings of approximately $3 billion. Some of the central government functions have also been transferred to local governments, outsourced or privatized, or transformed into executive agencies. In addition, the new administration introduced an open career system (20 percent of high-level positions open to the private sector), a performance-based management system, and various measures to improve flexibility and efficiency in public finance and eliminated half of more than 11,000 regulations.[9] In short, the government has implemented more reform programs in two years than had been implemented in the previous fifty years. As a result, the Institute of Management Development (IMD) ranking of competitiveness in the government sector has ascended from thirty-fourth to twenty-sixth in two years.[10] Such reform efforts have, however, lost their momentum owing partly to economic recovery in the succeeding years and partly to political corruption surrounding the ruling party.

The Asian crisis also triggered the government to restructure its administrative apparatus for coordinating public science and technology efforts. A separate Ministry of Science and Technology appears ostensibly to be an ideal structural arrangement to focus efforts on science and technology (S&T), but it has, in fact, no power to function adequately in bringing about effective coordination across different ministries. As a result, its ability to formulate and implement S&T policy has been decoupled from the nation's economic and social development programs. To put S&T at the center stage of Korea's developmental effort, it was necessary to integrate S&T policy across different industries and agencies into the nation's economic policy at the highest level. Accordingly, the government established the National Science and Technology Council to be chaired by the president of the nation. Unlike a similar council chaired by the statutory prime minister in the past, the new organization is expected to bring about effective coordination among fourteen different ministries in the government that are active in science and technology. In addition, the government elevated the status of the minister of education to become a deputy prime minister, integrating various ministries concerned with the development of human resources and science and technology. The efficacy of the Council and the deputy prime minister remains to be seen.

[9] Linsu Kim, "Public Sector Reform in Korea," paper presented at the International Conference on Public Sector Reform: Challenges and Vision for the 21st Century, organized jointly by OECD and KIPF, Seoul, June 22–23, 2000.

[10] IMD (Institute of Management Development), *World Competitiveness Report: 1999* (Lausanne, 2000).

In pursuing further reform, the government faces new challenges. First, concerted efforts should be made to change organizational culture within government, so that it may be compatible with the logic of the new organization and management systems that have been introduced over the past three years. Organizational culture is, of course, harder to change than are management systems. No management system can be implemented effectively without support from a compatible culture. Second, in the wake of rapid economic recovery, civil servants are less willing than before to accept painful reform. This makes it difficult to reengineer South Korea's innovation system, although economic events in 2001 have certainly undermined the recovery.

The Financial Sector

The financial sector has long been a tool of collusion between the government and the *chaebol*, resulting in major resource misallocation and huge nonperforming loans, particularly after the Heavy and Chemical Industry program in the 1970s. This has long been recognized as one of the most serious problems in the South Korean economy. But moral hazards on the part of technocrats and politicians have kept the sector from correcting the problems. Such weak financial infrastructure, including poor prudential oversight, allowed excessive foreign borrowing on the short term, leading to panic by foreign investors after the onset of the Asian financial crisis.

The Asian crisis enabled the government of Kim Dae Jung to take bold steps and to introduce a major reform program in the financial sector. At the outset of the crisis, the National Assembly passed legislation to reform the financial system. The law, among other things, has created two public agencies – the Financial Supervisory Commission (FSC), to review, design, and supervise the financial system, and the Korea Asset Management Corporation (KAMCO), to buy nonperforming loans to recapitalize financial institutions. The Bank of Korea was made independent of the government. The FSC not only has regulatory powers but also operates instruments of financial reform. It closed 16 merchant banks, 5 commercial banks, and over 700 secondary financial institutions, giving a shocking signal to the public that even banking institutions can fail. The government rescued the "relatively better managed" remaining financial institutions by turning nonperforming loans into equity so that they in turn could negotiate with corporate borrowers. Several large commercial banks have merged into three giant banks. One large commercial bank has been sold to foreign interests, and another is under negotiation with foreigners. Foreign equity participation in the banks, both large and small, is expected to introduce more modern market-oriented banking techniques, accountability, and transparency in operations. This should result in a more rational allocation of financial resources.

A major concern in the financial sector is that the injection of public funds to rescue banking institutions has resulted in a drastic increase in government ownership of large commercial banks and investment trust companies. The result is that the government now has decisive power in the financial sector. Government intervention in Korea's banking system was necessary to achieve stability following the initial 1997–98 crisis period. The government plans to privatize its ownership by 2002 to enable commercial banks to operate on the basis of market principles. But its intervention might have the unintended effect of retarding reforms if bank managers continue to hesitate to make decisions without a nod from the appropriate government official.

Chaebol Restructuring

Multisector, family-controlled business groups were dominant in prewar Japan and are prevalent in many Asian countries today. But nowhere have they been so consistently aggressive in diversifying businesses and developing technological capabilities as in South Korea. The South Korean government deliberately created and nurtured *chaebol* to use them as locomotives for rapid economic development. These *chaebol* were the backbone of industrialization in the labor-intensive industries during the early decades. They also played a major role in expediting technological learning in industry, upgrading South Korea's technological capabilities, and globalizing South Korean business. They consequently generated the lion's share of production and exports from South Korea.

Behind the successful story of the *chaebol*, there are, however, serious divergences from free-market principles. Collusion with powerful government forces resulted in resource misallocation and economic inefficiency at the macroeconomic level. The concentration of economic power in the hands of a small number of *chaebol* also resulted in monopolistic exploitation at the microeconomic level.[11] The *chaebol* also stifled the healthy growth of small and medium-sized enterprises.

Overdiversification, extremely high debt-to-equity ratios, and the subsidization of unprofitable businesses made many *chaebol* vulnerable to the fluctuation of the international economic environment. Several minor *chaebol* including the Hanbo, Sammi, Jinro, Haitai, Halla, New Core, and Kia were in receivership prior to the onset of the Asian crisis, giving a serious if unheeded warning of just how vulnerable South Korean industry was.

At the onset of the Asian crisis, which hit the remaining *chaebol*, the administration of Kim Dae Jung set five principles of corporate restructuring:

[11] Linsu Kim, "Korea's National Innovation System in Transition," in Linsu Kim and Richard Nelson, eds., *Technology, Learning and Innovation: Experiences of Newly Industrializing Economies* (Cambridge: Cambridge University Press, 2000), pp. 335–60.

downscope to focus on core businesses, reduce debt-to-equity ratios to below 200 percent by the end of 1999, dismantle cross-credit guarantees among subsidiaries, maintain management transparency, and provide greater management accountability.

The government has three techniques to force the *chaebol* to comply with its directives: threats to undertake a comprehensive tax audit, the legal prosecution of family owners, and withdrawal of credits to debt-ridden firms.[12] To meet the mandate to downscope and reduce the debt-to-equity ratio for core businesses, *chaebol* had to sell off many of their unprofitable businesses to foreign firms. Hyundai, for instance, decided to focus on five core businesses: automobiles, electronics, construction, heavy industry, and financial services. Hyundai has, however, been dismantled recently; automobiles and heavy industry, managed by other siblings of its founder, have literally become independent of the *chaebol*. Its construction, electronics, and financial service businesses are in deep financial trouble. Samsung concentrated on four core businesses: electronics, finance, trade, and services. LG announced that its main business segments would be chemicals and energy, electronics and telecommunications, services, and finances. Daewoo went into receivership in the middle of its restructuring. Other smaller *chaebol* were also in the process of a major restructuring of their businesses.

The dominance of the *chaebol* prevented the development and healthy growth of small and medium-sized enterprises (SMEs). In the early 1980s the government belatedly began promoting SMEs by establishing SME sanctuaries and by requiring banks to comply with a compulsory lending ratio program. Such programs had little effect on the industrial structure in South Korea, and the imbalance between the large and small sectors has mostly remained. As a result, end-product-assembling *chaebol* rely heavily on Japan for technology-intensive parts and components, which constrain innovation in both large and small firms.

The Asian crisis appears to have catalyzed industrial restructuring in South Korea. Downscoping and downsizing in the *chaebol* and the recent promotion of venture businesses by the government prompted a major surge of high-technology venture firms in South Korea. Their number increased from a mere 100 before the Asian crisis to 5,000 in two years by the end of 1999. In spring 2000, more venture firms emerged at the rate of 500 per month, reaching more than 7,000 by June 2000, a significant change by any standard. The recent recession of information-technology-related sectors worldwide has resulted in a dramatic collapse of many newborn ventures in Korea.

---

[12] Lawrence Krause, "The Aftermath of the Asian Financial Crisis for South Korea," paper presented at the East West Center, Honolulu, January 2000.

Global Networks

South Korean firms have developed extensive global networks with foreign firms that have provided capital goods, licensed technology, and original equipment manufacturing (OEM) orders. These networks have been a major source of technological learning for South Korean firms. But South Korea has not relied heavily on inward foreign direct investment (FDI) for technological learning. The proportion of FDI to total external borrowing was only 6 percent in South Korea compared with 92 percent in Singapore, 45 percent in Taiwan, and 21 percent in Brazil.[13] As a result, unlike other newly industrialized countries, the contribution of FDI to the growth of the South Korean GDP in 1972–80 amounted to only 1.3 percent, while its contribution to total and manufacturing value-added was only 1.1 percent and 4.8 percent respectively in 1971 and 4.5 percent and 14.2 percent, respectively, in 1980.[14]

In contrast to the generally accepted wisdom, foreign direct investment (FDI) in South Korea does not contribute much to local capability formation. Whereas it definitely transfers production and management capabilities to ensure efficient production of foreign-designed products, it does not transfer engineering and innovation capabilities. A comparative analysis of technological learning processes and market performance between Hyundai Motors, an independent domestic firm, and Daewoo Motors, a joint venture with GM – the largest company with the largest R&D expenditures in the world – is illustrative. Hyundai licensed technologies from multiple sources and took the responsibility to integrate them into a workable mass-production system, entailing a major risk. This approach forced and motivated Hyundai to assimilate foreign technologies as rapidly as possible throughout the process.

In addition, Hyundai invested heavily in R&D in an effort to accumulate design and innovation capabilities. As a result, Hyundai developed its first indigenous car, the "Pony," with 90 percent local content in 1975. Hyundai quickly improved quality in subsequent years through serious R&D activities, making South Korea the second nation in Asia with its own automobile. As a result, Hyundai's local market share in passenger cars increased from 19.2 percent in 1970 to 73.9 percent in 1979. Hyundai exported 62,592 cars to Europe, the Middle East, and Asia, accounting for 67 percent of South Korea's total auto exports in 1976–80 and 97 percent of total passenger car exports from South Korea in 1983–86.[15]

---

[13] KEB (Korea Exchange Bank), "Direct Foreign Investment in Korea," *Monthly Review* (October 1987): 18–19.

[14] Dong-Sae Cha, *Weija Doip Hyokwa Boonsuk* (The effects of foreign direct investment) (Seoul: KIET Press, 1983).

[15] Linsu Kim, "Crisis Construction and Organizational Learning: Dynamics of Capability Building in Catching-up at Hyundai Motor," *Organization Science* 9, no. 4 (July–August 1998): 506–21.

Many have predicted that none of the independent Korean automakers will survive the global shakeout of the 1990s. However, Hyundai is determined to become a leading automaker on its own. To this end the company has established R&D centers in Korea, Japan, the United States, and Germany and has developed extensive R&D alliances with leading local universities. These developments are part of a plan to shift its strategy from exporting low-quality, low-priced, low-margin subcompact cars largely to the developing world to a strategy of exporting high-quality, competitively priced, high-margin larger cars targeted primarily to the U.S. market. As a result, Hyundai, together with its subsidiary Kia, sold 853,000 cars in the United States in 2000 compared with 333,000 cars in 1999, ranging from subcompacts to full-sized cars, generating sales of $14.5 billion and a net profit of $530 million. Furthermore, Hyundai is betting billions of dollars on a green car breakthrough. A recent development of fuel cell electric cars enabled Hyundai to join the California Fuel Cell Partnership.

In contrast, constrained by GM's global objectives, Daewoo relied heavily on GM for technology sourcing, instead of developing its own technological capability and designing its own products. Technology transfer in the form of joint ventures is apt to lead to a passive attitude on the part of the recipient in the learning process, as the supplier guarantees the performance of the transferred technology. The investment in product and process improvement undertaken by Daewoo between 1976 and 1981 was only one-fifth as great as that undertaken by Hyundai, although its production capacity, on average, was approximately 70 percent as large. As a result, although their products were comparable in engine size and price, Daewoo was operating at 19.5 percent of capacity compared with 67.3 percent for Hyundai in 1982. The differential in labor productivity was just as stark – only 2.61 cars per head at Daewoo compared with 8.55 at Hyundai. Conflicts between the two partners continued to plague the joint venture, giving the smaller Kia a chance to outpace Daewoo. The 1992 divorce from GM finally freed Daewoo to set its own global strategic direction and navigate at its own ambitious pace, recapturing the second position after Hyundai. A recent mismanagement, however, resulted in a serious financial crisis not only at Daewoo Motors but also at other Daewoo subsidiaries.

The semiconductor industry presents a similar story. Multinational corporations transferred production technology but not design or innovation capabilities. Signetics, Fairchild, Motorola, Control Data, AMI, and Toshiba began assembling discrete devices in South Korea in the 1960s and 1970s in order to take advantage of cheap local labor. Operations involved simple packaging processes: bonded assembly operations by wholly owned South Korean subsidiaries of foreign corporations with all parts and components imported from the parent companies and reexported back to the consignors. The assembly operations required only about six months' training of unskilled workers, transferring little design or engineering capability to South Korea. It was the largest domestic companies – Samsung, Hyundai, and LG – that marshaled investment to enter very large scale integrated (VLSI) chip design and production on their own. Leading foreign producers refused to license VLSI technology to the South Korean *chaebol*. But the *chaebol* were able to locate a number of distressed small semiconductor companies in the United States that were ready to sell what the *chaebol* needed most – chip designs and processes – in attempts to fuel cash for survival. To master the licensed technologies, Samsung set up an R&D outpost in Silicon Valley in 1983 and hired five South Korean – American Ph.D.s in electronics engineering with semiconductor design experience at IBM, Honeywell, Zilog, Intel, and National Semiconductors. The outpost also provided opportunities for engineers in South Korea to participate in training and research in the United States, enabling them to learn about VLSI technology.[16]

The Asian economic crisis has, however, forced South Korean firms to pursue FDI in an attempt to mitigate pressing short-term cash flow problems. In addition to peripheral businesses, core businesses went on the chopping block. Consequently, in contrast to China and the Southeast Asian countries, some of which sustained a sharp plunge in FDI after the Asian crisis (e.g., Singapore, 24.8 percent; Taiwan and Malaysia, 19 percent), South Korea saw a substantial increase in FDI. For example, FDI inflow in manufacturing drastically increased from $2.3 billion in 1997 to $8 billion in 1998 and to $15.5 billion in 1999. The lion's share of the new FDI is associated with merger and acquisition of South Korean firms by foreign-based multinationals. Hewlett-Packard purchased a 45 percent stake in its South Korean subsidiary from its joint-venture partner, Samsung Electronics, for $36 million. Dow Chemical took over Ulsan Pacific Chemical by purchasing a 20 percent stake. Phillips purchased a 50 percent stake in LG's highly profitable flat-panel display business for $1.4 billion. Volvo purchased Samsung's construction machinery division for $730 million. In short, the South Korean economy will be more closely linked with foreign multinationals than in the past, but recent foreign investments may not transfer new technology, as they have mainly taken the form of acquisition of existing South Korean firms. They may, however, transfer management know-how and improve transparency and accountability.

Some multinational companies (MNCs) have established local R&D centers in South Korea. Thirty-nine MNCs, or 1.4 percent of the total number of MNCs operating in South Korea in manufacturing, have so far established R&D centers in South Korea. Thirty-three, or 82 percent, of them were established in the 1990s when South Korea had developed a significant R&D base. The R&D centers of multinationals, however, account for less than 1 percent of the total number of corporate R&D centers. Most of the R&D centers that multinationals operate in South Korea are involved in adapting their products

---

[16] Kim, *Imitation to Innovation*.

to the local market, indicating that local R&D activities by multinationals are insignificant compared with those of domestic firms in South Korea.

More recent foreign investors such as Motorola and Lucent Technologies came to South Korea to tap South Korea's leading-edge technologies in semiconductor memory chips, flat-panel displays, and code division multiple access (CDMA) mobile telecommunications – areas in which South Korea is ahead of Japan and the United States. Motorola acquired a South Korean venture firm, Appeal Technology, to gain access to sophisticated design and innovation capabilities and to source one of the most compact mobile telephone sets for global marketing. Lucent Technologies is in the process of establishing an R&D center in South Korea to gain access to significant capabilities in telecommunications technologies.[17]

Domestic Industrial R&D Activities

As South Korea underwent structural adjustments and entered progressively more technology-intensive industries, R&D investment became imperative to sustain its competitiveness in international markets. As a result, R&D investment has seen a quantum jump in the past decades. Table 4.1 shows that the total R&D investment increased from W.10.6 billion ($28.6 million) in 1971 to W.3.349 trillion ($4.7 billion) in 1990, and to W.12.858 trillion ($12.8 billion) by 1997. Although the South Korean economy recorded one of the world's fastest growth rates, R&D expenditure rose even faster than GDP. Research and development as percentage of GDP increased from 0.32 percent to 2.69 during the same period, surpassing that of many West European countries.

The government has launched various programs to induce the private sector to set up formal R&D laboratories. Spurred partly by these programs and partly by increasing competition in the international market, the number of corporate R&D laboratories increased from 1 in 1970 to 3,060 in 1997, reflecting the seriousness with which South Korean firms have pursued high-technology development. The *chaebol* have dominated R&D activities, with the twenty largest domestic firms accounting for 71.8 percent of total corporate R&D in South Korea.

Over time, there has been significant change in the composition of R&D investment in South Korea. The government played a major role in R&D activities in early years of industrialization, when the private sector faltered in R&D despite the government's encouragement. More recently, domestic firms have assumed an increasingly larger role in the country's R&D efforts in response partly to increasing international competition and partly to a policy environment supportive of private R&D activities. In 1963 the private sector accounted for only 2 percent of the nation's total R&D expenditure.

[17] Kim, "Public Sector Reform in Korea."

TABLE 4.1. *Research and Development Expenditures, 1965–98*

	1965	1970	1975	1980	1985	1990	1995	1998
R&D expenditure (W million)	2.1	10.5	42.7	282.5	1,237.1	3,349.9	9,440.6	11,336.6
Government	1.9	9.2	30.3	180.0	306.8	651.0	1,780.9	3,051.8
Private sector	0.2	1.3	12.3	102.5	930.3	2,698.9	7,659.7	8,276.4
Government vs. private	61:39	97:03	71:29	64:36	25:75	19:81	19:81	27:73
R&D/GNP	0.26	0.38	0.42	0.77	1.58	1.95	2.51	2.52
Manufacturing sector								
R&D expenditure (W million)	NA	NA	16.7[a]	76.0	688.6	2,134.7	5,809.9	6,439.2
Percentage of sales	NA	NA	0.36[a]	0.50	1.51	1.96	2.72	2.64
Number of researchers (total)[b]	2,135	5,628	10,275	18,434	41,473	70,503	128,315	129,767
Govt. research institutes	1,671	2,458	3,086	4,598	7,542	10,434	15,007	12,587
Universities	352	2,011	4,534	8,695	14,935	21,332	44,683	51,162
Private sector	112	1,159	2,655	5,141	18,996	38,737	68,625	66,018
R&D expenditure per researcher (W 1,000)	967	1,874	4,152	15,325	27,853	47,514	73,574	87,361
Researcher per 10,000 population	0.7	1.7	2.9	4.8	10.1	16.4	28.6	27.9
Number of corporate R&D centers	0	1[c]	12	54	183	966	2,270	3,760

[a] For 1976.
[b] The figure does not include research assistants, technicians, and other supporting personnel.
[c] For 1971.

Source: Ministry of Science and Technology.

This had risen to over 80 percent by 1994, which is one of the highest among both advanced and newly industrialized countries.

The R&D growth rate has also been one of the highest in the world. For instance, the average annual growth rate of R&D investment per GDP in 1981 through 1991 for South Korea was 24.2 percent compared with 22.3 percent for Singapore, 15.8 percent for Taiwan, 11.4 percent for Spain, and 7.4 percent for Japan. The average annual growth rate of business R&D per GDP is also the highest in South Korea, 31.6 percent, compared with 23.8 percent in Singapore, 16.5 percent in Taiwan, 14.0 percent in Spain, and 8.8 percent in Japan.[18]

In addition to intensified in-house R&D, South Korean firms began exporting their R&D activities. For instance, LG Electronics has developed a network of R&D laboratories in Tokyo; Sunnyvale, California; Chicago; and sites in Germany and Ireland. These R&D centers monitor technological change at the frontier, seek opportunities to develop strategic alliances with foreign firms, and develop the state-of-the-art products through advanced R&D. In Sunnyvale, LG Technology plays a pivotal role in designing the latest personal computers, display terminals, and high-resolution monitors, while the LG North American Laboratory in Chicago concentrates on HDTV, digital VCR, and telecommunications equipment. Samsung, Daewoo, and Hyundai Electronics have developed equally extensive and far-flung R&D networks. Samsung has R&D facilities in San Jose, Maryland, and Boston in the United States; Tokyo, Osaka, and Sendai in Japan; as well as London, Frankfurt, and Moscow. Daewoo has two in France, one in the United Kingdom, and one in Russia. Hyundai has R&D facilities in San Jose, Frankfurt, Singapore, and Taipei.

Other important indicators of South Korea's rapid growth in industrial R&D are patent registrations in South Korea and abroad. Patent activities in South Korea have significantly jumped in the past two decades compared with activities in the previous two, increasing a mere 48 percent in the first fourteen years (1965–78), but almost tripling in the next eleven years (1979–89) and almost tripling again in the next four years (1989–93). This reflects the increasing importance of intellectual property rights in the face of declining reverse engineering. The gap is still great when compared with advanced countries, but South Korea is catching up rapidly. Furthermore, the share of South Koreans in local patent registration also increased from 11.4 percent in 1980 to 58.9 percent by 1997, indicating rising technology activities.

U.S. patent registration is often used as one indicator of international competitiveness. The number of U.S. patents granted to South Koreans is far less than to Taiwanese, let alone that granted to applicants in the advanced

---

[18] DIST (Department of Industry, Science and Technology, Australia), *Australian Science and Innovation Resources Brief 1994* (Canberra: Australian Government Publishing Service, 1994), p. 21.

countries. The cumulative number of U.S. patents granted to South Koreans between 1969 and 1992 is only 1,751, compared with 4,978 to Taiwanese. But South Korea jumped from thirty-fifth in terms of the number of patents in the United States with 5 patents in 1969 to eleventh with 538 patents in 1992 – with an average annual growth rate of 43.32 percent.[19] This growth rate is the highest among countries in the NTIS report.

The onset of the Asian crisis of 1997, however, appears to have exerted a significant influence over industrial R&D activities in South Korea. To improve short-term liquidity, the large *chaebol* reduced their R&D activities by about 13 percent during the year following the onset of the crisis, but the government increased its R&D budget, raising its share in total R&D from 23 percent in 1997 to 27 percent in 1998. However, South Korea's total R&D decreased from W.12.185 trillion ($12.8 billion) in 1997 down to W.11.336 trillion ($9.5 billion) in 1998.[20] The disproportionate drop in terms of U.S. currency is caused by the devaluation of the South Korean currency during the crisis. The downsizing of R&D activities by the *chaebol*, together with the government's promotion of venture businesses, led to a major surge of technology-based small firms in South Korea. As a result, contrary to general expectations, the number of corporate R&D centers increased from 3,060 in 1997 to 5,200 in 1999. Small and medium-sized enterprises account for 95 percent of this increase.

Despite decrease in R&D investment, R&D output in terms of patents increased significantly, indicating the improved quality of R&D activities. The number of patents granted more than tripled in two years after the onset of the Asian crisis from 24,579 in 1997 to 80,642 in 1999. The share granted to South Koreans also increased from 58.9 percent to 69.4 percent during the same period. South Korea is now fifth in the world in 1999 in terms of the number of industrial property applications, following Japan, the United States, China, and Germany. In terms of industrial property applications by local residents per population, South Korea ranks second, with Japan taking first.

The number of U.S. patents granted to South Koreans almost doubled in two years from 1,891 in 1997 to 3,679 in 1999, ascending from seventh in the world to sixth, behind Japan, Germany, Taiwan, France, and the United Kingdom. Samsung Electronics, one of the most R&D-intensive firms in South Korea, almost tripled its U.S. patents granted, from 582 in 1997 to 1,545 in 1999, ascending from seventeenth to fourth, just behind IBM,

[19] NTIS (National Technical Information Service), *Industrial Patent Activity in the United States: Part I Time Series Profile by Company and Country of Origin, 1969–1992* (Washington, D.C.: Patent and Trademark Office, July 1993), A1-1.
[20] Linsu Kim, "National Technology Policy: The Korean experience," in Mukul G. Asher, David Newman, and Thomas P. Snyder, eds., *Public Policy in Asia: Implications for Business and Government* (Westport, Conn.: Quorum Books, 2002), pp. 283–94.

NEC, and Cannon. Such a rise is significant compared with the 49 percent increase in the total number of U.S. patents granted to nonresidents during the same period, suggesting that South Korea has been gaining rapidly in technological competitiveness.

Education

South Korea is a land in which natural resources are comparatively scarce. Accordingly, the government and South Korean families have invested heavily in education, drastically expanding educational institutions in terms of quantity during the early decades of industrialization, when the country was very poor. Unlike most developing countries, South Korea's expansion was well balanced at all levels prior to launching the industrialization drive. This produced a vast quantity of human resources with enough initial capacity to make sense of mature technologies transferred from abroad in the 1960s and 1970s. In more recent decades, however, the government did not focus on developing the quality of educational institutions, which caused a major bottleneck in South Korea's technological learning. The problem of underinvestment is most acute at the university level. All but a few universities have remained primarily undergraduate-teaching-oriented rather than research-oriented institutions. The government has belatedly recognized this problem and contemplated ideas of making a major educational reform, but little reform was implemented prior to 1997.

Nevertheless, university research did expand significantly in the 1990s. R&D expenditure by universities rose by a factor of five in eight years from W.244.3 billion ($341.2 million) in 1990 to W.1.27 trillion ($1.6 billion) in 1998. The number of university researchers more than doubled from 21,332 to 51,162 during the same period. In addition, emulating the U.S. experience, the government also introduced in 1989 a scheme to establish Science Research Centers (SRCs) and Engineering Research Centers (ERCs) in the nation's leading universities. The number of SRCs and ERCs increased from thirteen in 1990 to eighty-four by 2000. These centers receive research grants from the government for nine years.

As a result, the number of scientific publications per year by South Koreans as quoted in the Science Citation Index (SCI) increased steadily from 27 in 1973 to 171 in 1980. After 1980, the pace accelerated to 1,227 in 1988, and to 3,910 in 1994. In 1999 it had drastically increased to 10,918. The number of publications has climbed from thirty-seventh in the world in 1988, to twenty-fourth in 1994, and to sixteenth in 1999.

The Asian crisis prompted the South Korean government to formulate an ambitious education reform program, called Brain Korea 21, to transform a dozen of the leading Korean universities into first-class research-oriented institutions. The government earmarked W.1.6 trillion (about $1.4 billion) to invest over seven years to implement the program. Despite strong resistance from lower-tier universities, the government is determined to push the program forward. It is still premature to estimate the outcome of the program, but once properly implemented, the quality of scientists and engineers graduating from South Korean universities is expected to be much higher.

In addition, leading universities have established technology parks and venture "incubating" centers as a means to establish joint research with leading firms and to foster technology-based small businesses spinning off from university R&D laboratories. The implication is that universities will play an increasingly important role in South Korea's pursuit of high-technology industries in the future, a model that is familiar in the United States.

Domestic Support Infrastructure

In the absence of research in universities in recent years, the government took the initiative to establish a Government Research Institute (GRI) by recruiting overseas-trained South Korean scientists and engineers. Government Research Institute accounted for 83.9 percent of the nation's total R&D expenditures and 43.7 percent of the nation's pool of researchers in 1970, reflecting their dominant role in R&D activities in the early years.

To keep pace with increasing industrial sophistication and diversity, the government established several specialized GRIs (e.g., chemical, machinery, electronics, ocean, standardization, nuclear energy, biotechnology, system engineering, aerospace) to serve the growing needs of the private sector. Government Research Institutes began to play an important role in strengthening the bargaining power of local enterprises. This helped to acquire increasingly sophisticated foreign technology and to slash the price of foreign imports by developing competing local technologies. But most importantly, the GRIs generated experienced researchers for corporate R&D centers and played a dominant role in undertaking various national R&D projects through the mid-1990s.

In the face of the rapid expansion of private R&D activities, however, and increasing intensity of university R&D, the role of GRIs has decreased compared to universities and corporate R&D centers over time for two reasons. First, GRIs are far less dynamic than corporate R&D centers. The former are under the bureaucratic control of the government, whose many rules and regulations tend to stifle creativity. In contrast, the latter dynamically responds to market and technological changes for survival. Second, GRIs face difficulties in retaining competent researchers, as these researchers move either to academic institutions for prestige and freedom or to corporate R&D laboratories for better economic incentives. Reform of GRIs to redefine their roles has been discussed for some time. In the past, inertia and the labor union of GRI members have made it difficult to implement reforms.

But the Asian economic crisis enabled the government to introduce a major restructuring of GRIs. As part of public-sector reform, the government introduced three research councils, modeled on aspects of the German and British systems, and reorganized GRIs under the jurisdiction of these councils, eliminating direct control by government ministries. It might take some time before the new structure functions properly, but the changes are expected to result in increased administrative freedom and a major reorientation of the GRIs to address new missions.

A critical problem remains unresolved. Government has largely been so preoccupied with mission-oriented projects that it has failed to develop effective infrastructure to support small and medium-sized enterprises. The technical extension networks developed in the 1980s have not proved adequate to help SMEs grow technologically. South Korea belatedly established a few industry-specific R&D institutes for SMEs in the 1990s, but their effectiveness remains to be proved.

Corporate Governance and Management

In addition to focusing on core businesses and reduction in debt-to-equity ratio, the *chaebol* face serious problems in the area of corporate governance. In the environment where the state was the major source of constraints and contingencies, family owners of the *chaebol* developed a "conservation-of-power rationality."[21] They sought collusion with powerful politicians and technocrats in order to enter lucrative businesses and to maximize the predictability of business and political environments. Few family businesses could have grown into a *chaebol* without such political patronage in South Korea. Because family owners were more concerned with garnering outside influence than they were with generating internal capability in making their companies profitable, boards of directors and minority shareholders have had little power to curb the family owners' mismanagement. Moral hazards were prevalent.

In response to the Asian crisis, the government introduced measures to change corporate governance of the *chaebol*. Listed companies must appoint outside directors to strengthen the independence of the board of directors in supervising top management. Within the first year, 752 listed companies had assigned outside directors. But many companies hired their friends to the board. In the future, it will be difficult for the company to do so, as institutional investors and minority shareholders will have the right to recommend outside directors.

Another important arena is the improvement of management style in order to enhance effectiveness. With so much of the firm's success resting on the top manager's personal skills, South Korean firms naturally adopted a top-down management style. This management imperative, combined with the rule of military government over three decades, fostered a management

---

[21] Burton Klein, *Dynamic Economics* (Cambridge, Mass.: Harvard University Press, 1997).

that resembled a military bureaucracy – hierarchical and centrally controlled but relatively less formalized. The notion of Confucian traditions and its familism fits comfortably with the hierarchical style of family-centered conglomerates. Unlike highly formalized bureaucratic organizations, South Korean firms could adapt to changes once a decision was made at the top by the "commanding general." These organizations were quite compatible with and efficient in the imitative reverse-engineering and production-oriented tasks of the 1960s and 1970s.

Many *chaebol* have recognized the imperative to transform themselves into innovation-oriented organizations. This requires more decentralized, self-contained, strategic business units that can respond quickly to changing markets and technologies; an organizational climate that nurtures creative individuals and effective teamwork; efficient lateral communication and coordination across functions; and bottom-up communications to identify and respond quickly to market opportunities and threats. In the past, there was much rhetoric on these issues but little action.

The economic crises of the late 1990s have, however, forced the *chaebol* to reform their organizations and management to be compatible with new needs. Although many *chaebol* are making major efforts to transform their organizational structures and management styles, it will take time to demonstrate results. The *chaebol* find that although the formal organizational structure and management system can be changed overnight, altering the behavior of managers and employees to be compatible with the new system is far more difficult and time-consuming.

Labor Movement and Sociocultural Factors

Another important element that influences the dynamics of technology development is the labor market and sociocultural environment, which sets the stage for individual behavior and social interaction in South Korea. Although the formal ban on unions was lifted in the early 1960s, the legal framework in which unions were permitted to function was so restrictive that it virtually eliminated the possibility of organizing any genuine independent unions through 1987. In addition, the government used various means to suppress the labor movement in the name of industrial peace and rapid economic development. As a result, workers became exceedingly docile.

Following the democratization decree in 1987, the labor movement suddenly exploded in disorderly, violent, and in many cases unlawful ways. But due to deteriorating social and economic conditions, the once militant unions became relatively more mature and evolved into more responsible forces in the 1990s. Nevertheless, a series of labor strikes have resulted in significant changes in the social and organizational climate. There have been shifts in the power structure, and workers have become far less submissive in recent years. One survey shows, for example, that workers who agreed to obey supervisors' directions dropped from 90.6 percent in 1979 to 65.3 percent in 1991.[22]

Many cultural and situational factors have affected South Korea's work ethic.[23] After a decade of labor unrest, the work ethic and labor force discipline have deteriorated significantly. Constant demands for higher wages have also pushed South Korea's real wage to more than 91 percent in terms of U.S. dollars, which was 2.8 times that of productivity, eroding South Korea's competitiveness in international markets. In addition, the new generation brought up in affluence appears less willing to work hard compared with the older generation.

The Asian crisis has, however, exerted a major impact on labor in South Korea. Facing the bankruptcy of banks and *chaebol*, the drastic downsizing of surviving companies, consequent high unemployment, and the reduction of the purchasing power of the average surviving worker by 30–40 percent, labor unions had to shift from a militant strategy to one that involves more bargaining and compromise. Workers have become more willing to work harder than they were before the crisis.

Conclusion

Is it possible for a small, weak country like South Korea to survive and retain its technonationalism in a globalizing economy? South Korea is not a small country like the Scandinavian or the Benelux countries. Its population size approaches that of France and United Kingdom. If North and South Korea were to unite, the resulting population would increase to well over 70 million, approaching that of Germany. It is the perception of policy makers and managers in Korea that such a large country cannot prosper only as a production locale of (and at the whim of) multinational companies, and that South Korea should have its own global strategy to determine its own destiny. Japan could not have advanced as much, it is argued, if it had followed Singapore's strategy.

Can South Korea succeed in the race of innovation and production increasingly dominated by larger technologically advanced countries? The answer is, It remains to be seen. Like Japan, the South Korean government is determined to revamp its educational systems and strengthen its basic research capability. Leading universities will be transformed from undergraduate-oriented teaching schools into graduate-oriented research institutions. It might take a decade or longer to bring them up to the level of advanced OECD countries, but changes will definitely be accelerated in

---

[22] Yoo-Keun Shin and Heung-Gook Kim, "Individualism and Collectivism in Korean Industry," in Gene Yoon and Sang-Chin Choi, eds., *Psychology of the Korean People: Collectivism and Individualism* (Seoul: Dong-A Publishing, 1994), pp. 189–208.

[23] Kim, *Imitation to Innovation*.

the future. Large firms will undoubtedly strengthen their R&D activities, as they move closer to the world frontier. In this process, South Korea will become a fully modern advanced industrial country.

These efforts, however, may not be sufficient to sustain South Korean technonationalism, giving way to an intermediate or hybrid configuration. The worst-case scenario is that South Korea might excel in a few sectors and become a smart follower in many others. History tells that smart followers often outperform pioneers in the long run.[24] Even through technoglobalistic participation in innovation and production systems dominated by industrially advanced countries, smart partners can engage in more sophisticated technological activities and enjoy a greater degree of control and autonomy than otherwise. And given local absorptive capacity, the diffusion of learning to local firms through such participation will undoubtedly take place.

[24] Steven P. Schnaars, *Managing Imitation Strategy: How Later Entrants Seize Markets from Pioneers* (New York: Free Press, 1994).

5

From National Champions to Global Partners

Crisis, Globalization, and the Korean Auto Industry

John Ravenhill

The Asian Crisis and Korean Economic Nationalism

Of the five Asian economies most severely affected by the financial crises of 1997–98, the Republic of Korea has undergone the most fundamental institutional transformation. For some observers, the Korean response to the crises was all the more surprising because its long-term economic record had been far superior to that of the other crisis economies – Indonesia, Malaysia, the Philippines, and Thailand. Compared with the other four countries, Korea had sustained a higher rate of economic growth (an average of close to 8 percent) for a longer period (more than three decades).[1]

Korean growth, unlike that of the Southeast Asian economies, had been based primarily on the nurturing of domestically owned and controlled companies. The Korean developmental trajectory emulated the technonationalist strategy of Japan. A measure of the success of this strategy was that Korean corporations became household names in the West in consumer electronics, automobiles, and domestic appliances. A Korean company, Daewoo, was the only company not based in Europe, Japan, or the United States that ranked in the mid-1990s in the top fifty of the world's multinationals.[2] Korean firms had logged an impressive number of patents in industrialized economies (see Chapter 4 in this volume). Korea alone of the "Gang of Four" East Asian newly industrializing economies had gained admission to the Organization for Economic Cooperation and Development (OECD), the "rich man's club."

The crisis that rocked the Korean economy in 1997–98, however, was more than just a financial crisis. It was a systemic crisis – the direct consequence

---

[1] Of the four Southeast Asian countries, often referred to as "second-tier newly industrializing economies," Malaysia and Thailand grew most rapidly, averaging growth of 4.2 percent annually between 1960 and 1985.

[2] Ranked by value of foreign assets. *World Investment Report: Trends and Determinants* (Geneva: UNCTAD, 1998).

of a developmental strategy that had encouraged corporations to rely excessively on bank lending, to diversify outside their areas of core competence, and to seek market share rather than profitability. Specialization in sectors in which worldwide surplus capacity was growing, difficulties in penetrating the markets of industrialized economies, and excessive debt burdens severely depressed the profitability of the giant Korean corporations that technonationalist policies of promoting national champions had fostered. Even during the boom years of 1994 and 1995, the peak of the business cycle, all the *chaebol* (family-controlled corporate groupings) ranked between eleventh and thirtieth in size had earned a negative return on their assets.

For the largest corporations, the rapid growth in semiconductor exports in the mid-1990s partly masked the fragile state of finances. In 1995 the top three semiconductor companies (Samsung Electronics, Hyundai Electronics, and LG Semiconductors) reportedly contributed 70 percent of the *total* net profits of Korea's top thirty *chaebol*.[3] With the collapse of semiconductor prices in 1996, these companies too became vulnerable. Ever increasing levels of investment had sustained high rates of economic growth but these had been accompanied by declining productivity of capital and "almost vanishing corporate profitability."[4] Several prominent *chaebol* filed for bankruptcy even before the full force of the financial crisis hit Korea in November 1997.

The automobile industry reflected the accomplishments and weaknesses of Korea's overall economic performance and its technonationalist mode of innovation and development. On the eve of the crisis, Korea had become the world's fourth largest producer of automobiles, having overtaken European giants such as France and the United Kingdom. Production had grown by a factor of more than 20 from 120,000 units in 1980 to 2.85 millions in 1996 (see Figure 5.1). This rapid growth of output was generated by domestically owned firms – a significant achievement given the barriers to entry in an industry characterized by economies of scale and by rapidly changing product and process technologies. Faced with these barriers, less developed economies typically have depended substantially on subsidiaries of multinational corporations for entry into automobile

---

[3] International Monetary Fund, "Republic of Korea: Selected Issues," Staff Country Report 98/74, International Monetary Fund, Washington, D.C., August 1998, pp. 5–6. See Greg Noble and John Ravenhill, "The Good, the Bad and the Ugly? Korea, Taiwan and the Asian Financial Crisis," in Greg Nobel and John Ravenhill, eds., *The Asian Financial Crises and the Global Financial Architecture* (Cambridge: Cambridge University Press, 2000), pp. 90–91, on which this paragraph is based. The poor performance of Korean corporations stands in marked contrast to that of the manufacturing sector in Taiwan, where profitability improved from already higher levels through the 1990s.
[4] Eduardo Borensztein and Jong-Wha Lee, "Credit Allocation and Financial Crisis in Korea," Research Department Working Paper WP/99/20, International Monetary Fund, Washington, D.C., February 1999, p. 7.

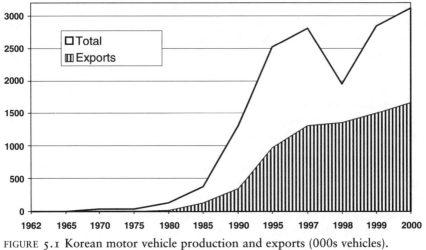

FIGURE 5.1 Korean motor vehicle production and exports (000s vehicles).
Source: Korea Automobile Manufacturers Association (http://www.kama.or.kr/).

production.[5] Moreover, Korea alone among the industrializing economies had established itself by the late 1980s as a major exporter of autos, with close to half of total domestic production destined for export markets. Again, and many would assert not coincidentally, this success had been achieved by Korean companies exporting for the most part under their own brand names. The Hyundai Excel became the best-selling import model in the U.S. market in 1987. Korean imports outsold those from Japan in the Australian market. Korean companies also assembled annually more than three quarters of a million cars in foreign plants: cars produced overseas by Korean companies, for instance, had the largest share of the auto markets in India and Poland.[6]

Yet, even before the financial crisis, the weaknesses of the Korean auto industry were apparent. Auto companies had achieved export success primarily through competing on price. Korean companies specialized in small,

[5] On the experience in Southeast Asia, see Richard F. Doner, *Driving a Bargain: Automobile Industrialization and Japanese Firms in Southeast Asia* (Berkeley: University of California Press, 1991); on Mexico, see Douglas C. Bennett and Kenneth E. Sharpe, *Transnational Corporations versus the State: The Political Economy of the Mexican Auto Industry* (Princeton: Princeton University Press, 1985).

[6] Again, this record stands in marked contrast to other less developed economies that had attempted a technonationalist approach in the automobile industry. Contrast Korea's record, for instance, with that of India. The only other country that might credibly claim to have enjoyed some success in creating a national auto champion that penetrated international markets is Malaysia – but the scale of production and exports of Malaysia's two national car companies is much smaller than that of Korean companies.

inexpensive cars where profit margins were razor thin or negative.[7] They experienced great difficulties in penetrating and sustaining their shares of the car markets of Western Europe and the United States. Protectionist barriers played a role, especially in Western Europe. But more important was the negative brand image that Korean cars acquired when exporting began in earnest in the late 1980s and early 1990s.[8] Consumers frequently perceived Korean cars as cheap, technologically backward, and (judging by the poor performance of some models in crash tests) nasty. Although quality control improved significantly in the mid-1990s, the legacy of the negative brand image lived on. Korean cars were comparable with the Honda Civics of the 1970s. Korean companies had yet to make the transition that the Japanese companies achieved in the 1980s to reap success based on a reputation for quality rather than on price alone.

Rapid expansion of production capacity in the 1990s created enormous structural problems for the Korean assemblers. As in the semiconductor industry, Korean auto companies had become such large players that their decisions affected both local and global markets. In particular, they contributed to a growing problem of surplus capacity in the global automobile industry.[9] At home, bringing more production on line led to a fall in the capacity utilization rate to 70 percent. The scramble to create new capacity came at a high price – in terms of both increasing indebtedness and the actual price paid for new plants. The debt burden of Korean auto companies escalated rapidly in the 1990s as they took advantage of the easy access to loans afforded by a flawed process of financial liberalization. To cite an

---

[7] Daewoo, for instance, was estimated to be losing $30 million annually in India. *Business Week*, August 30, 1999.

[8] Exports to the United States surged in 1986–88 but fell by more than a half by 1990. Concerns over quality (reflected in the rapid depreciation of cars imported from Korea) were a significant factor. In 1987, when Japanese imports averaged 0.6 defects per vehicle, Hyundai Excels averaged 3.1. See James P. Womack, Daniel T. Jones, and Daniel Roos, *The Machine That Changed the World: The Story of Lean Production – How Japan's Secret Weapon in the Global Auto Wars Will Revolutionize Western Industry* (New York: HarperCollins, 1991), p. 262. Quality concerns were not alleviated by the problems with cars produced at Hyundai's Br mont, Quebec, plant, which opened in 1989 (a plant that turned into an economic as well as i public relations disaster for Hyundai, the company eventually closing it after incurring lo es of more than a billion dollars). Also acting against Korean exports at the end of the 1980s was the appreciation of the won against the yen and the dollar.

[9] Korean companies not only substantially increased their domestic production capacity but also invested in massive new capacity overseas. Daewoo, for instance, built a plant capable of producing 200,000 vehicles a year in Uzbekistan, and a plant with a similar capacity in Poland. Surplus capacity in the global auto industry in the second half of the 1990s has been estimated to be close to one-third of overall production capacity. The problem of surplus capacity has remained relatively unexplored in the study of global political economy since the pioneering work of Susan Strange and Roger Tooze, *The International Politics of Surplus Capacity: Competition for Market Shares in the World Recession* (London: Allen & Unwin, 1981).

extreme example: at the end of 1996 the debt-to-equity ratio of Ssangyong Motors, a company that specializes mainly in four-wheel-drive vehicles, stood at 10,496 percent.[10] Meanwhile, Samsung Motors was widely believed to have paid substantially above a "fair" market price for the $2.5 billion plant that it created in the mid-1990s with technology licensed from Nissan.[11]

From Technonationalism to Technoglobalism?

Even before the financial crisis caused a collapse in domestic demand in 1998, Korean auto companies were in trouble. Ssangyong and Kia were reported to have made no profits in their auto operations throughout the 1990s. Some analysts suggested that Daewoo Motors has never made a profit if its results are assessed by any normal accounting standards. The lack of financial transparency within the *chaebol* precrisis and the practice of cross-subsidization of subsidiaries make an accurate judgment on such issues impossible. In its investigation of Daewoo, the government's Financial Supervisory Committee uncovered some evidence of the scale of the *chaebol's* economic problems and unorthodox financial management. It found 23 trillion won ($18 billion) in accounting errors on Daewoo's books.[12] Auditors estimated the company's debts to be nearly double those anticipated when it first went into receivership.

A mischievous leaked report from Samsung in June 1997 suggested that Kia and Ssangyong would not be able to continue as independent auto producers.[13] Within a month, as investor confidence crumbled, Kia had to seek a bailout from creditors. The motor industry, alone responsible for close to 5 percent of Korea's GDP and 6 percent of exports, subsequently figured prominently in Korea's financial crisis. Government indecision over what to do with Kia – first refusing to intervene, then nationalizing the company in October 1997, and then conducting two unsuccessful auctions to dispose of its assets – did much to weaken confidence in the country's economic management at a critical moment when the contagion effect of the Asian

[10] Ssangyong had invested more than $2.5 billions in new production lines and component plants following the initialization of its alliance with Mercedes-Benz in 1992. Ssangyong had anticipated that it would become a significant exporter of luxury vehicles based on Mercedes-Benz technologies, but this optimism proved ill-founded. The average debt ratio for auto producers increased from 416 percent in 1995 to 530 percent in the following year, substantially above the average of 300 percent for all manufacturing companies. *Korea Herald,* May 10, 1997.

[11] In addition, the licensing agreement provided that Samsung would pay Nissan up to 1.9 percent of the factory price of each car produced in the plant's first five years of operation. *Wall Street Journal,* August 25, 1997.

[12] *Korea Times,* July 21, 2000.

[13] The report was widely viewed as a cynical attempt by Samsung to stake a claim for acquiring Kia. Three years earlier, it had launched a hostile takeover bid for Kia, an almost unprecedented move in the Korean corporate world.

financial crisis first hit Korea.[14] Two years later, the bankruptcy of Daewoo Motors cast an enormous shadow over efforts to restructure Korea's financial system.

At the same time that the Korean economy was experiencing convulsions, the global auto industry was undergoing its most fundamental consolidation since the 1920s. Former national champions such as Saab, Volvo, Jaguar, Rolls Royce, Land Rover, Audi, Skoda, and Seat were taken over in the 1990s by General Motors, Ford, or Volkswagen. The merger between Daimler Benz and Chrysler was then the world's largest industrial merger. Renault acquired a one-third stake in Nissan, DaimlerChrysler a similar stake in Mitsubishi. General Motors meanwhile bought 20 percent of Fiat. Several factors have driven this rush to consolidate. Global overcapacity – production capacity is over 70 million units in an industry where demand is under 52 million units a year (and capacity is expected to be double world demand by 2002) – has produced intense downward pressure on prices. Companies are frantic to realize synergies especially in component sourcing through global supply chains, through sharing production platforms, and through joint research and development ventures. Industry analysts forecast that only producers with a capacity to manufacture more than 4 million cars annually would survive in the new competitive environment. None of the Korean producers – even after the crisis-induced mergers – comes close to this figure. Hyundai-Kia has the largest annual production capacity, 2.8 million vehicles.

Imperatives of market and product diversification also drove the flurry of merger activity. With little expansion anticipated in the mature markets of North America and Western Europe, companies sought to create a global presence and especially to penetrate markets in Asia where much of the increase in world demand in the first part of the twenty-first century is expected to occur.[15] They are also under pressure, particularly from the new fleet emission standards in the European Union, to provide a full range of vehicles across all market segments within the one company grouping. DaimlerChrysler, for instance, requires a smaller vehicle with low emissions to offset the emissions from the larger cars in which it has traditionally specialized. Korean producers, with their specialism in producing small, low-cost vehicles, became potentially attractive targets for acquisition by the global alliances.

Disentangling the medium-term effects of the problems of the Korean industry from the pressures emanating from the globalization of auto production is

---

[14] Standard and Poor's DRI, "Developments in Asia: An Overview 2000"<http://www.just-auto.com/features_details.asp?art=255.>, accessed September 8, 2000. The government decision in October 1997 to bail out Kia caused Standard and Poor's to downgrade Korea's credit rating, a move that in turn precipitated the run on the Korean won.

[15] Standard and Poor's (2000) projects total demand in Asia (excluding Japan) to reach 14.8 million units in 2010, or 20 percent of global demand (in contrast to 11 percent in 1999).

difficult. Even in the absence of the financial crisis, it is debatable whether Korean companies could have sustained their rapid expansion of domestic production capacity at a time of global overproduction. The domestic car market was already saturated, and the government was under increasing international pressure to open it to imports.[16] Any sustained expansion of domestic output would have depended on winning new export markets. The car companies were already in financial difficulties precrisis. It is possible but unlikely that they could have muddled through in an environment where they could turn to the state to bail them out financially.[17] The onset of the financial crisis removed this possibility, however.

As economic conditions deteriorated and debt servicing became impossible, first Kia, then Ssangyong, then Samsung Motors, and finally Daewoo Motors, the flagship of Korea's third largest *chaebol*, sought protection from creditors. The Korean government faced an unenviable choice. The options boiled down to two nationalist approaches and a globalist alternative. The first nationalist approach was to attempt to bail out the companies. But such a move would have been problematic at a time when the financial system was in need of substantial recapitalization, and the government under intense international pressure to reduce its role in the economy. The second was to allow another Korean company to take over the bankrupt car firms. This was the preference of economic nationalists but an option opposed by liberal economists because of the potential for creating a monopolistic domestic industry. The globalist option was to permit foreign auto producers to purchase the assets of the bankrupt Korean national champions.

The eventual outcome appeared a clear victory for the economic rationalists over the economic nationalists, for technoglobalism over technonationalism. In the middle of 2001, the expectation is that foreign corporations eventually will control three of the Korean producers (Daewoo, Samsung, and Ssangyong). Meanwhile DaimlerChrysler has a 10 percent shareholding in Hyundai Motors (50 percent in its heavy division), the only former national champion that will not be under foreign control. As suggested in Chapter 1, the financial crisis opened the way for foreigners to acquire valuable assets in Korea at fire sale prices. Renault purchased 70 percent of Samsung Motors, on which the Samsung *chaebol* had lavished more than $5 billion since 1994 to create production and research facilities and dealerships, for a cash

---

[16] In the two full years before the onset of the crisis, the domestic car market grew by 1.7 percent (1995) and 8 percent (1996); from 1990 to 1994 the average annual growth rate had been 12 percent.

[17] Kia, it should be remembered, went bankrupt before the onset of the crisis. Some informed observers were already questioning Daewoo's viability in the mid-1990s. See, for instance, Gregory W. Noble, "Trojan Horse and Boomerang: Two-Tiered Investment in the Asian Auto Complex," Berkeley Roundtable on International Economics, University of California, Working Paper No. 90, November 1996.

payment of only $100 million.[18] Similarly, General Motors and its alliance partners will acquire 67 percent of most of the domestic and overseas assets of Daewoo Motors for an outlay of only $400 million.[19]

The recent history of the Korean auto industry thus appears to be a simple story: a transition from an industry created by a developmental state, which followed a strategy of technonationalism, to an industry incorporated into global production networks and substantially foreign-owned. In the aftermath of the financial crisis, technoglobalism apparently supplanted technonationalism. The golden era of the developmental state in Korea had long since passed. A strategy of promoting technological autonomy no longer appeared viable where access to the latest technologies, to markets, and to economies of scale and scope had become defining characteristics of viable competitors in a globalized industry.

The reality of the matter is somewhat more complex. The success of the technonationalist approach is more questionable than some accounts of the Korean auto industry suggest; the triumph of technoglobalism involved a significant struggle between agencies of the state and may yet be incomplete.

The Development of the Korean Auto Industry: How Statist? How Autonomous?

'The initiative to enter new manufacturing branches has come primarily from the public sphere. . . . every major shift in industrial diversification in the decade of the 1960s and 1970s was instigated by the state.'[20]

---

[18] In addition, Renault assumed $250 million of Samsung's debt and agreed to pay a further $270 million out of the future profits of the plant. Because Samsung Motors depended on Nissan's technology, Renault (with its controlling interest in Nissan) was the only likely foreign purchaser of its assets.

[19] The memorandum of understanding between General Motors and Daewoo Motors' creditors signed in September 2001 provided for the acquisition of Daewoo plants in Changwon (annual production capacity, 240,000 units) and Gunsan (320,000 units), its research and development center and maintenance division, overseas assembly plants in Vietnam and Egypt, but excluded its oldest domestic plant at Bupyeong, renowned for its worker activism. The sum agreed to by GM contrasts with the $7 billion that the Ford Motor Company was reported to be considering bidding for Daewoo's assets in mid-2000 and the preliminary bid of $6 billion that GM made in 1999; it was even substantially less than the $1 to $1.2 billion that analysts were forecasting in the days before the announcement of the sale. See, for instance, *Korea Herald*, September 21, 2001. The new joint-venture company established by the agreement will assume only $320 million of debt (owed by the overseas plants). It is widely expected that creditors (primarily the state-owned Korean Development Bank) will eventually write off the other debts of Daewoo Motor, estimated at $17 billion (since the company sought protection in August 1999, creditors are believed to have injected $2.3 billions to prevent it from collapsing). See "GM-Daewoo: Third-Time Extremely Lucky?"<http://just-auto.com/features_detail.asp?art= 572>, accessed September 27, 2001.

[20] Alice H. Amsden, *Asia's Next Giant: South Korea and Late Industrialization* (New York: Oxford University Press, 1989), p. 80.

The centrality of the state in establishing and nurturing the automobile industry in Korea is beyond dispute. The Automotive Industry Promotion Law, promulgated in 1962, part of the First Five Year Development Plan, marked the birth of the modern automobile industry in Korea.[21] The Ministry of Trade and Industry was given discretion to determine which companies could participate in the industry. The plan brought the full panoply of industrial policy instruments to bear in support of auto production. Imports of cars were prohibited – a ban that was not to be lifted for a quarter of a century. The government provided subsidized loans and tax incentives for investments and export subsidies, including export promotion loans, that enabled Korean cars to be sold in foreign markets at less than half the domestic market price. Imported components were exempted from tariffs.

The auto industry became a central part of the government's Heavy and Chemical Industries drive in 1973, nominated for its critical backward linkages to the steel and machine engineering industries and for its potential strategic importance. Eventually, the government, under pressure from trading partners, finally lifted its ban on imports. However, it continued to discriminate against imported cars by levying differential rates of taxation dependent on engine size. And potential purchasers of imported cars were discouraged by the none-too-subtle threat that they would be subjected to a tax audit. Even at the end of the 1990s, more than a decade after the government lifted its ban on imports, Korean companies enjoyed the luxury of a de facto sanctuary in the domestic market, one of Asia's largest: imports contributed only 0.8 percent of total vehicle registrations.[22]

The apparent success of the Korean state in fostering an internationally competitive industry, however, masks decades of meandering policies, failed directives, and bureaucratic squabbling. Many of the issues that were to come to the fore during the crisis of 1997–98 are familiar to observers of the Korean auto industry: disputes between economic nationalists and economic rationalists in state agencies over whether to promote national champions or to rely on market forces; failed state efforts to coerce companies into mergers; and indecision and frequent policy reversals by successive governments.

The Automotive Industry Promotion Law of 1962 may have successfully launched the Korean industry, but the context was one of rent seeking and political corruption. The government's strategy in the early 1960s was the "unitarization" of the automobile industry, the creation of one producer with the objective of generating economies of scale. The original producer favored

---

[21] Linsu Kim, *Imitation to Innovation: The Dynamics of Korea's Technological Learning* (Boston: Harvard Business School Press, 1997), p. 107.

[22] In 2000 imports of all motor vehicles totaled 11,168; motor vehicle registrations in Korea in that year totalled 1,441,628. Source: Data on the Korean Automobile Manufacturers Association webpage<http://www.kama.or.kr>.

by the government was the Sammi Corporation, but the mantle was shifted to Saenara Motors after the latter allegedly made financial contributions to the political party that the military government had recently established.[23] Saenara, which was assembling a Nissan Bluebird kit, collapsed in the following year. In turn, Shinjin Motors replaced it as the designated producer. This company's bid to enter the industry was again allegedly successful because of its financial contributions to politicians.[24] Shinjin began by assembling kits provided by Mitsubishi, and then switched its foreign partnership a year later to Toyota. But this alliance was also short-lived; Toyota withdrew from Korea in 1972 following the announcement by the People's Republic of China (PRC) that it would not permit any company that had connections with Taiwan or South Korea to operate in China. Shinjin then turned to General Motors, launching a new joint venture as General Motors Korea (GMK).[25]

The weakness of the strategy of having a single assembler soon became obvious. The monopolist was able to earn significant rents in the market – and the foreign partner, Toyota, appeared to be gaining the lion's share of these. In 1967 the government responded to complaints, emanating among others from domestic parts producers that were excluded from the Shinjin venture, by licensing two other producers for the motor vehicle industry: Hyundai and Asia Motors. Kia entered as a fourth producer in 1971.[26] A government attempt, meanwhile, to enhance local content by establishing a single engine plant through a partnership among all four assemblers failed. The 1960s thereby laid the foundations for problems that would continually beset the Korean industry: fragmentation (with consequent low-volume production runs) and excess capacity.

The government's next major effort to rationalize and promote the industry came as part of the Heavy and Chemical Industries Project, proclaimed in January 1973. The automobile industry, designated as strategic for the economy's future, was targeted to move from import substitution to export-led growth. To realize economies of scale, producers were required to submit plans for a "people's car," the specifications, timetable, and costing of which were laid down by the government. The government approved plans from three of the assemblers – Hyundai, GMK, and Kia – and excluded Asia Motors from car manufacturing.

---

[23] Seok-Jin Lew, "Bringing Capital Back In: A Case Study of the South Korean Automobile Industrialization" (Ph.D. dissertation, Yale University, 1992), p. 135.

[24] Ibid., p. 138.

[25] The new partnership immediately encountered difficulties when the domestic market collapsed following the first round of oil price rises in 1973. Its losses led to GMK being placed under the management of the Industrial Bank; the name of the joint venture was changed to Saehan Motor Corporation. In 1978 Daewoo bought the Industrial Bank's shares in the venture, and in 1983 Saehan Motors was renamed the Daewoo Motor Corporation (which continued as a fifty-fifty joint venture with General Motors until 1992).

[26] Hyundai originally had a joint venture with Ford, Asia with Renault, and Kia with Mazda.

Hyundai had already developed plans for a Korean car before the government announced its directive (raising the question of where the initiative for the "people's car" actually originated). Both it and Kia thrived with the production of new small models as the Korean economy quickly bounced back from the first Organization of the Petroleum Exporting Countries (OPEC)-induced recession. Hyundai's Pony model was the first indigenous Korean car; Kia's entry was the Mazda-designed Brisa. Local content in both these cars reached 85 percent.[27] In contrast, GMK continued to assemble unpopular larger cars with a high share of imported content and went into receivership.

By July 1978 the government was sufficiently confident in the industry that it set a future annual production goal of 2 million units.[28] Its encouragement led the companies to engage in substantial new investment. The timing, however, was abysmal: the investments were made on the eve of the second round of oil price rises and another severe recession in the Korean economy. The domestic market collapsed in 1980, as did Hyundai's nascent export business when Japanese competitors lowered export prices in an attempt to maintain market share.[29] Korea's auto assemblers were producing at only one-quarter of their capacity.

The government's response was a familiar one: a call for the rationalization of the industry. But on this occasion, the voices making this call were louder and more persistent, a reflection of the growing power of economic rationalists in the Economic Planning Board (EPB). By the end of the 1970s, it was clear that many officials and several agencies shared the World Bank's skepticism about the government's promotion of the automobile industry. Earlier optimism that the global automobile industry would experience a similar life cycle to textiles and footwear and be transferred to countries with low-cost labor appeared misplaced. Although the industry was in some senses mature, it was also undergoing constant renewal. The advent of front-wheel-drive cars led to the development of radically different technologies for engines and transmissions. Meanwhile, the application of assembly-line robots had undermined much of the cost advantage of low-wage economies. Moreover, innovations in the assembly process in Japan had generated marked improvements in product quality that were difficult for new entrants to the industry to attain. Skeptics suggested that the Korean industry's prospects inevitably would be poor because of the relatively small size of the domestic market and because of its inability to compete on price and especially on quality in export markets.

---

[27] Young-Suk Hyun and Jinjoo Lee, "Hyundai Motor Company: Self-Reliance Strategy and Growing Challenges," in Dong-Ki Kim and Linsu Kim, eds., *Management behind Industrialization: Readings in Korean Business* (Seoul: Korea University Press, 1989), p. 520.

[28] Lew, "Bringing Capital Back In," p. 194.

[29] Womack, Jones, and Roos, *The Machine That Changed the World*, p. 261.

The debate over the future of the industry provides insights into the different approaches to development favored within various branches of the government. A consensus existed that consolidation of the industry was imperative, preferably under the auspices of a single assembler (a report commissioned for the Economic Planning Board and the World Bank concluded that the domestic market could support only one producer). Rather than promoting a national champion, however, the Economic Planning Board favored a joint venture in which substantial foreign participation would strengthen the technological base of the industry. In contrast, the Ministry of Trade and Industry preferred to promote a single domestically owned company. The EPB initially appeared to prevail: the original government proposal sought to exclude the most successful domestic producer, Hyundai, from the industry altogether in favor of the Daewoo-GM joint venture.[30] The government gave Hyundai the choice of specializing in autos or in power generation equipment; the expectation was that its management would choose the power sector. Clearly, it underestimated the commitment of Hyundai's chairman to the auto industry for the company rejected the power generation sector. The government then encouraged Hyundai and GM to enter into a joint venture but negotiations broke down over GM's insistence on a 50 percent stake in any new venture. Anxious not to offend its U.S. patron or to signal an apparently hostile attitude to foreign investors, the government backed down on rationalization and announced that it would revise its policy to license two producers in the industry.[31] Kia would be excluded from auto production but compensated by being given the principal responsibility for truck and bus manufacture (in 1976, Kia had acquired Asia Motors, which specialized in heavy vehicles).

The attempted consolidation of the industry in 1980–81 showed again the limits of state capacity to impose change when significant private-sector resistance existed. The number of assemblers was reduced from three to two but even the elimination of Kia from the industry proved short-lived. In 1982 Kia began to plan for a new passenger car model; at the end of the following year it reached agreement with Mazda on the development of a new model, at which point Mazda took a 10 percent equity holding in Kia.[32] In late 1984 the government decided to allow Kia to reenter auto production, a decision announced in the following year.[33] Once again, the

---

[30] As discussed in more detail later, Hyundai had been the company that had moved furthest in the local accumulation of technological capability.

[31] The policy reversal was announced just after an official visit by President Chun Doo Hwan to the United States in February 1981.

[32] The new model was the Kia Pride, rebadged as the Ford Festiva in the United States. Ford took a 10 percent stake in Kia in 1986 in return for marketing Kia's cars in North America.

[33] The government compensated Daewoo and Hyundai by permitting them to reenter the production of small trucks and buses, thereby also encouraging overcapacity in that segment of the industry.

government appeared to be following rather than leading the private sector in the automotive industry.[34]

On one issue the government remained resolute throughout the 1980s: a determination to exclude the country's second largest *chaebol*, Samsung, from automobile production. Samsung originally proposed to enter the industry in 1984 in alliance with Chrysler, a proposal that prompted the government to announce its decision to readmit Kia to auto production. In 1989 Samsung gained a foothold in the industry by being granted permission to produce heavy commercial vehicles in a joint venture with Nissan. The government, however, rejected its second application to manufacture cars in the following year. The subsequent debate over Samsung's efforts to enter the industry illustrates many of the contradictions faced by the Korean state in its efforts to promote economic liberalization in a market dominated by oligopolies.

A long-standing goal of the government was to attempt to force the *chaebol* to specialize in only a few sectors to reduce the problem of overcapacity. Moreover, increased specialization was expected to realize not only economies of scale but also a more rapid acquisition of technological expertise through a concentration of research and development expenditures. In March 1991 the government adopted a new approach on this issue. It required the top thirty *chaebol* to nominate three of their subsidiaries as "core businesses" and provided favored access to bank loans for their activities in these sectors. But by the early 1990s the largest *chaebol*, with their worldwide networks and their own financial institutions, no longer depended on privileged access to domestic bank loans.[35] Financial liberalization was to reduce further the significance of this policy instrument that had been so important in the state's direction of industry in the 1960s and 1970s. Access to finance would certainly not be a factor preventing Samsung's entry into auto production.

Samsung, ironically, was able to use the arguments of the economic rationalists to support its bid to enter the auto industry, a move that would further weaken efforts at rationalization. The government of Kim Young Sam, the country's first civilian president for more than thirty years, adopted *segyehwa* (globalization) as the guiding principle for its economic strategy.[36] Samsung was quick to argue that the new state agendas of liberalization and globalization were incompatible with state directions that prohibited companies from entering the industries of their choice. Samsung's renewed application for entry into car production in 1992 exposed continuing differences

---

[34] Lew, "Bringing the Capital Back In," pp. 56–57.

[35] And, in any event, given the opaqueness of *chaebol* accounting practices, companies could easily switch bank lending for government-preferred purposes to the "noncore" activities they wished to develop. On the changing relationship between state and *chaebol*, see Kim, *Imitation to Innovation.*

[36] Samuel S. Kim ed., *Korea's Globalization* (Cambridge: Cambridge University Press, 2000).

within the bureaucracy. The Ministry of Commerce and Industry (MCI) announced its opposition to the proposal on the grounds that it would create overcapacity, excess competition, prevent the realization of economies of scale, and that exit from the industry for any participant would incur enormous costs. For others, however, three decades of government direction of the sector had produced unsatisfactory results. Their argument was that the market should be allowed to determine the viability of Samsung and its domestic competitors in the industry. Moreover, trade liberalization would also expose domestic producers to increased international competition. The market would eventually produce the desired rationalization.

Political factors eventually proved decisive. Samsung, with a good nose for politics, had proposed to locate its auto plant in Pusan, the hometown of President Kim Young Sam, an area badly affected by the offshore migration of the athletic footwear industry.[37] The Blue House (Korea's presidential residence) eventually sided with the Fair Trade Commission and the Economic Planning Board against the MCI, existing automobile producers, and public opinion, and in November 1994 announced its authorization of Samsung's joint venture with Nissan.[38]

The inability of the state to force rationalization on the auto industry points both to the limits of state power in Korea and to some of the weaknesses of the technonationalist approach that prevailed in this sector.[39] A balanced perspective on the state's role in the evolution of the Korean car industry is required. On the one hand, the considerable achievements of Korea's auto industry, listed in the introduction to this chapter, should not be underestimated. The Korean success in creating national champions in the auto industry that were able to conquer export markets stands in marked contrast to the experience of all other late industrializers, including the country with which Korea is often compared, Taiwan.[40] As with the development of the Japanese auto industry, state policies to direct capital to the sector, to encourage localization, to limit the entry of foreign producers,

---

[37] It had previously located its commercial vehicle plant in the home area of the president at that time, Roh Tae Woo.

[38] For further details, see Chung-in Moon, "Democratization and Globalization as Ideological and Political Foundations of Economic Policy," in Jongryn Mo and Chung-in Moon, eds., *Democracy and the Korean Economy* (Stanford, Calif.: Hoover Institution Press, 1999), pp. 23–25; and Seok-Jin Lew, "Democratization and Government Intervention in the Economy: Insights on the Decision-Making Process from the Automobile Industrial Policies," in Jongryn Mo and Chung-in Moon, eds., *Democracy and the Korean Economy* (Stanford, Calif.: Hoover Institution Press), pp. 158–65.

[39] The Korean state, of course, was not alone in failing to rationalize its auto industry. MITI's similar failure in Japan is often cited to contest the statist perspective on Japan's rapid industrialization.

[40] On the failure of Taiwan's auto strategy, see Noble, "Trojan Horse and Boomerang," and Walter Arnold, "Bureaucratic Politics, State Capacity, and Taiwan's Automobile Industrial Policy," *Modern China* 15, no. 2 (April 1989): 178–214.

and to preserve the domestic market for local firms played a decisive role in providing a supportive environment for the local industry.[41] On the other hand, notwithstanding the capacity to provide a supportive environment for domestic producers, state policies toward the auto sector were inconsistent, subject to rent seeking, and seemingly incapable of producing the rationalization required if Korean companies were to become profitable, internationally competitive producers. State policies more often responded to private-sector initiative than provided effective direction.[42] And with the weakening of state control that accompanied liberalization in the 1990s, the problem of fragmentation in the industry was intensified.[43] The failure of state policy to provide effective coordination in the industry laid the foundations for the crises of the second half of the 1990s.

Opening the Korean Auto Sector

The decision of the Kia Group in July 1997 to seek bankruptcy protection vividly illustrated the vulnerabilities of the Korean auto sector. Kia was the seventh largest *chaebol*. Although it had diversified into eleven industrial sectors, vehicle manufacture remained its core business. It had the second largest production capacity after Hyundai Motors (1.2 million cars annually) and was a significant exporter (over 250,000 units each year). Together with its heavy vehicles subsidiary, Asia Motors, it had close to 7,500 subcontractors with a total of more than 600,000 employees.[44] By most accounts, the Kia Group – unusual for a *chaebol* in that it was no longer under family control – had been comparatively well managed until the early 1990s. Its subsequent efforts to diversify into construction and steel, coupled with the overcapacity problems in the auto industry, became its undoing. By July 1997 the Kia Group had accumulated debts in excess of $10.7 billion. Kia Motors alone had debts of more than $6 billion; it had to spend more than 9 percent of its sales revenues on interest payments, a percentage the industry regarded as unsustainable.[45]

---

[41] On the effectiveness of state policies to limit the role played by foreign capital in Korea, see Russell Mardon, "The State and the Effective Control of Foreign Capital: The Case of South Korea," *World Politics* 43, no. 1 (October 1990): 111–37.

[42] Robert Wade, *Governing the Market: Economic Theory and the Role of Government in East Asian Industrialization* (Princeton: Princeton University Press, 1990). In Wade's terminology, the Korean state provided strong "followership."

[43] Ha-Joon Chang, Hong-Jae Park, and Chul Gyue Yoo, "Interpreting the Korean Crisis: Financial Liberalisation, Industrial Policy and Corporate Governance," *Cambridge Journal of Economics* 22, no. 6 (November 1998): 735–46. Chang, Park, and Yoo attribute the problems of overcapacity and lack of coordination in Korea's leading industrial sectors to the weakening of state power in the 1980s and 1990s.

[44] *Korea Herald*, July 22, 1997.

[45] "Car Crash," *Asia Week*, August 1, 1997. Kia's CEO, Kim Sun Hong, was arrested in May 1998 and charged with embezzling $37 million, which he had allegedly used to bribe politicians. In October that year, he was sentenced to seven years' imprisonment.

Contending views within the bureaucracy produced paralysis as to how to respond to Kia's bankruptcy and to that of several other *chaebol* outside the auto sector. On the one hand, economic rationalists argued that the market should determine the outcome and be permitted to deliver its own restructuring of Korean industry. On the other, advocates of planning saw the problems of the corporate sector as at least temporarily reversing the secular shift in the balance of power between the government and the private sector: a new opportunity was available for the government to force rationalization in key industries and to promote stronger national champions. While the government dallied in its response to Kia's problems, Ssangyong Motors also went bankrupt. Here a swift (technonationalist) solution was forthcoming: Daewoo took over its rival by assuming a 53.5 percent stake in the company. The cost, however, was a further 2 trillion won ($1.8 billion) in debt for Daewoo, which was to contribute to its own failure in the following year.

After several months of indecision, the Kim Young Sam government's initial approach to resolving Kia's problems was firmly in the technonationalist tradition. It announced in October 1997 that it would place Kia Motors and Asia Motors under court receivership and that the state-run Korea Development Bank's loans to Kia would be converted to equity, making the bank, with 30 percent of its total equity, Kia's largest shareholder.[46] The Minister of Finance and Economy asserted that the government had no intention of allowing Kia to be taken over by a third party but would run the company as a successful state enterprise.[47]

The deepening of the economic crisis (with the collapse of the won in the following month), however, and the election of the opposition leader, Kim Dae Jung, as president led to a reversal of policy. The currency crisis strengthened the hands of the economic rationalists and opened the way for the international financial institutions and bilateral creditors to exert significant external pressure for a reduced role for the state. The government eventually agreed to auction off Kia's assets. The manner in which the government conducted the auction, however, raised doubts about the new government's willingness to permit the takeover of Korean assets by foreign companies.

The initial auction attracted bids from the other three Korean auto producers, Hyundai, Daewoo, and Samsung, and from Kia's U.S. partner, Ford.[48] But two auction rounds were aborted because all bidders refused to take on the volume of Kia's debts that creditors (essentially the Korean state) required. Ford, which failed to participate in the second auction, alleged that

---

[46] *Korea Herald*, October 23, 1997.

[47] *Korea Herald*, October 27, 1997.

[48] Besides its direct shareholding in Kia, other ties between Ford and the Korean company came through Mazda, which also held shares in Kia, and was the principal foreign source of its technology. Ford imported 75,000 Kia vehicles each year, rebadged as the Festiva.

the process was less than transparent.[49] Accusations flew that the government conspired with Kia to inflate the value of its assets and to understate the size of its debts.[50] Foreign commentators saw delays in resolving the issue as a sign of the government's continuing reluctance to make the necessary painful decisions in economic restructuring.[51] Kia was eventually sold to the highest bidder, Hyundai, amid allegations that economic nationalism had prevailed over a more rational internationalist solution of selling the troubled automaker to Ford.[52] This first consolidation among Korean auto manufacturers produced a new problem: market domination. The Hyundai-Kia conglomerate controlled 72 percent of the Korean market.

The Kim Dae Jung government, meanwhile, had pressed the *chaebol* to consolidate their operations by engaging in asset swaps (the "Big Deal" program) and to reduce their debt to equity ratios to below 200 percent by the end of 1999. For the automobile sector, the principal issue was what was to become of Samsung Motors. With the collapse of the domestic market in Korea following the onset of the financial crisis, Samsung could hardly have faced a less auspicious climate for the start of its operations.[53] The corporation acknowledged that the relatively small capacity of its Pusan plant (80,000 vehicles) would preclude the development of a viable enterprise – hence its interest in taking over the much larger Kia Motors. But corporate hubris eventually gave way under pressure from the government, and Samsung agreed in September 1998 to exchange its auto operations for Daewoo's consumer electronics plants. Daewoo was supposed to take over the Samsung plant by mid-February 1999. The corporations, however, failed to reach agreement over the terms of the deal, particularly the insistence by Samsung that Daewoo continue to produce Samsung cars for at least two further years. Plant closure was not an option.[54] The deal was never consummated, overtaken by the financial

---

[49] "Creditor to Postpone Auction of Kia Motor: Bids Seen Too Low as Ford Protests Process," *International Herald Tribune*, August 31, 1998, citing Korea largest-circulation daily, *Chosun Ilbo*.

[50] The state was directly involved in the process through the state-owned Korea Development Bank, Kia's largest single creditor. After the first auction failed, creditors agreed to debt write-offs of more than $2.1 billion.

[51] For instance, "South Korean Cars: Eurekia," *Economist*, October 24, 1998.

[52] Kia's executives and workers reportedly favored a takeover by Ford, anticipating that Ford would use Kia as its principal agent for manufacturing and selling small cars in East Asia. They opposed a takeover by Hyundai, fearing that amalgamation would lead to job losses (which, indeed, it did for Kia's executives, most of whom were quickly replaced with Hyundai managers).

[53] Samsung Motor operated for eleven months, during which it sold about 30,000 cars. Each car sold was estimated to have lost the company $5,000. In 2000, Korean consumers voted Samsung's only model, the SM5, the worst car in its class for quality and performance. The car was also named the most unsafe in collision tests conducted by the government. "Renault's SM5 Named Worst Car of the Year," *Korea Herald*, December 29, 2000.

[54] The government, facing parliamentary elections later in the year, was keen to ensure that Samsung's Pusan operations continued in what was now the heart of opposition territory.

difficulties of Daewoo that led to its being placed in receivership in July 1999 and the decision in the following month to dismantle the group.

The failure of the Big Deal restructuring in autos left the government with little alternative than to sell the assets of the two bankrupt producers, Daewoo and Samsung. But to whom? Hyundai, following its absorption of Kia, already controlled close to three-quarters of the domestic market. To permit it to acquire Daewoo would have provided it with an almost complete monopoly. No other credible domestic purchaser existed. The car industry became a test of the government's commitment to encourage foreign direct investment in the Korean economy.

The sale of Samsung Motors to Renault was relatively noncontroversial in that no alternative bidder expressed an interest – although the bargain-basement price that Renault paid for the Samsung plant did generate criticism from the Korean press. Daewoo was an altogether different story. In opening the way for possible foreign purchase of the flagship arm of Korea's third largest corporation, the government faced opposition from a formidable nationalist coalition. A public opinion poll reported 87 percent of respondents opposed Daewoo's sale to a foreign bidder.[55] Public hostility to the sale was supported by some academics, the Federation of Korean Industries (the *chaebol*'s lobby group), the Korean Federation of Small Business, many civic groups, and the opposition Grand National Party. Daewoo's unions, concerned about job security, opposed a sale to a foreign company, as did its suppliers that were affiliates of the Korean Auto Industries Cooperation Association. Their fear was that a foreign company would confine Daewoo's future operations to the domestic market and cause a decline in demand for their products.[56]

On the other side, some of Daewoo's parts makers came out in favor of its sale to a foreign producer, fearing that a Hyundai monopoly of the domestic industry would leave them vulnerable.[57] So, too, did many economists. But of critical importance was the hostility to a Hyundai takeover within key agencies of the state. On record as opposing a Hyundai takeover of Daewoo were the Minister of Finance and Economy, the state-owned Korean Development Bank (Daewoo's largest creditor), the chairman of the Fair Trade Commission, and several research agencies including the Korea Development

[55] *Korea Herald,* June 12, 2000.
[56] *Korea Herald,* June 27, 2000.
[57] *Korea Herald,* June 29, 2000. Hyundai, unlike Daewoo, followed the Japanese model of subcontracting, establishing close relationships with a relatively small number of suppliers (who often produced solely for Hyundai). For discussion of the contrasts between Hyundai and Daewoo in subcontracting, see Alice H. Amsden and Linsu Kim, "A Comparative Analysis of Local and Transnational Corporations in the Korean Automobile Industry," in Dong-Ki Kim and Linsu Kim, eds., *Management behind Industrialization: Readings in Korean Business* (Seoul: Korea University Press, 1989), pp. 579–96; and Amsden, *Asia's Net Giant,* pp. 184–88.

TABLE 5.1. *Partners in the Korean Auto Industry Pre- and Postcrisis*

	Precrisis	Postcrisis
Daewoo		GM & Alliance Partners 67%[a]
		Daewoo creditors 33%[b]
Hyundai	Mitsubishi 4.8%	DaimlerChrysler 10%[c]
		Mitsubishi 4.8%
Kia	Ford 9.4%	Hyundai Group 51% (of which
	Mazda 6.7%	Hyundai Motors 40%)
	Hyundai Motor 5%	
Samsung	Pan Pacific Investments 31%	Renault 70.1%
		Samsung Group 19.9%
		Miscellaneous creditors 10%
Ssangyong	Daimler-Benz 2.4%	Daewoo 53.5%[d]

[a] According to press reports at the time of the signature of the Memorandum of Understanding between General Motors and Daewoo's creditors, GM will hold less than 50 percent of the equity in the restructured GM-Daewoo; the balance of the 67 percent will be held by GM's alliance partners.

[b] The state-owned Korea Development Bank is Daewoo's largest creditor.

[c] DaimlerChrysler was reported in January 2001 to be seeking to increase its shareholding in Hyundai Motors to 15 percent.

[d] Ssangyong's production facilities are to be sold separately by Daewoo's creditors. At the time final revisions to this chapter were completed (October 2001), this sale had not been effected.

Source: Compiled from various newspaper reports.

Institute and the Korea Institute for International Economic Policy. The government eventually kept its nerve on the sale. It offered Ford an exclusive opportunity to negotiate for the purchase of Daewoo Motors, following Ford's making the highest bid for its assets in an auction at the end of June 2000.[58] In September 2000, however, Ford announced that it would not proceed with the bid. The government turned to Daewoo's old partner, General Motors, which, after a year of negotiations with the Korean Development Bank, reached the agreement discussed earlier in this chapter.

The financial crisis hastened what was probably inevitable – a consolidation of the Korean industry (the Hyundai-Kia merger) and the entrance of foreign companies (DaimlerChrysler through its 10 percent holding in Hyundai, as well as Renault and the reentry of GM) (see Table 5.1). The

[58] The previous sale of Samsung to Renault had been viewed as improving Hyundai's chances of acquiring Daewoo by reducing concerns over a future monopoly. Hyundai had also entered into an alliance with DaimlerChrysler to purchase Daewoo, with DaimlerChrysler reported to be willing to finance 80 percent of a bid for Daewoo. DaimlerChrysler publicly had shown little interest in Daewoo; it was particularly enthusiastic, however, about an opportunity to purchase 50 percent of Hyundai's commercial vehicle operation.

crisis thereby achieved the rationalization the state had failed to accomplish in the previous three decades. The inability of the government to consolidate the industry pointed to the limits of state power in Korea when faced with an obdurate (and increasingly autonomous) private sector. And government followership at critical junctures in policy development suggested that the relationship between the state and auto producers was characterized as much by reciprocal consent as by state direction.[59]

The State and Technological Development in the Auto Industry

Linsu Kim has documented Korea's impressive record of technological learning.[60] The rapid development of the Korean auto industry and especially the increase in local content point to the skill of Korean companies and their engineers in acquiring, absorbing, applying, and improving on imported technologies. Technological capabilities varied substantially across companies, however. And the experience of Korean companies in their relations with foreign partners casts a worrying shadow over the future of the industry.

The state's role in the auto industry was confined for the most part to providing a supportive environment. As described earlier, the state brought to bear the full panoply of industrial policies in support of auto producers. Even in the 1980s it still provided subsidized loans and investment and other tax incentives to car producers. By requiring production of a people's car and specifying local content requirements, the state had also played a directive role. Unlike the prominent role that the state played in the semiconductor industry,[61] however, state agencies did not themselves acquire and develop relevant technologies that they subsequently passed on to the private sector. The state left the task of technology acquisition and development in the hands of the car companies.

The strategy for the acquisition of technology varied substantially from company to company. Hyundai set out deliberately to avoid dependence on any one partner, to maintain its managerial autonomy, and eventually to achieve technological autonomy through its own research and development. In its early days, after the termination of an unhappy alliance with Ford, Hyundai rejected alliances with Volkswagen, Renault, and Alfa Romeo because all sought participation in its management.[62] Although Mitsubishi became Hyundai's principal partner after taking a 10 percent stake in the Korean

---

[59] On reciprocal consent, see Richard J. Samuels, *The Business of the Japanese State* (Ithaca: Cornell University Press, 1987); on followership, see Wade, *Governing the Market*.

[60] Kim, *Imitation to Innovation*.

[61] See John A. Mathews, *Tiger Technologies* (Cambridge: Cambridge University Press, 1999); and the chapter by Keller and Pauly in this volume on the state's role in the development of Korea's semiconductor industry.

[62] Lew, "Bringing the Capital Back In," p. 41, n. 25.

company in 1981, Hyundai did not give up management control or its quest for alternative sources of technology. As Kim documents, Hyundai's success in technological development derived from its strategy of acquiring technologies in unpackaged form from multiple sources and integrating them in its own production.[63] In the period up to 1985, Hyundai licensed fifty-four foreign technologies from eight different countries.[64] And when no foreign supplier was willing to provide state-of-the-art engines, Hyundai eventually succeeded in developing its own. Through this strategy of fostering autonomy, Hyundai raised its local content more quickly than other Korean producers and was free to elaborate its own export strategy without external constraint.

The state may have encouraged Hyundai to avoid entangling alliances.[65] But whatever the state's rhetorical commitment to technonationalist strategies, it did nothing to prevent the other Korean auto companies from entering alliances that substantially impinged on their autonomy. Management participation by foreign partners imposed severe constraints on other Korean assemblers. The most egregious example is Daewoo, in which GM had a 50 percent share from Daewoo's entry into the industry in 1978 until the partnership was terminated in 1992. Management control of GMK rested with GM until 1982. Consequently, GM determined technological sourcing, which, not surprisingly, came entirely from within its corporate empire. In comparison with Hyundai, Daewoo invested little in product and process improvements with the consequence that its overall performance was far inferior to that of its more independent competitor.[66]

Even after 1982, when Daewoo took over management control of the joint venture, the affiliation still placed significant constraints on the Korean partner. Daewoo's principal products were derived from GM's Opel division; these were widely regarded in Korea as embodying obsolete technology. And decisions on export markets rested with GM. Its refusal to allow Daewoo to market in Eastern Europe was the catalyst for the termination of the partnership in 1992. Daewoo subsequently attempted to make up for lost time by adopting Hyundai's strategy of diversifying its sources of technology. It bought engines from GM's Australian subsidiary, General Motors Holden, and transmissions from Germany's ZF group and from Japan. It also established a product development center in Worthing in the United Kingdom,

---

[63] Eun Mee Kim, *Big Business, Strong State: Collusion and Conflict in South Korean Development,* 1960–1990 (Albany: State University of New York Press, 1997).

[64] Hyun and Lee, "Hyundai Motor Company."

[65] For discussion of this issue, see Lew, "Bringing the Capital Back In," p. 86, n. 16. Lew quotes a senior official who claims that the government convinced Hyundai not to enter into any agreements that would have impinged on its managerial autonomy. Other sources suggest, however, that Hyundai's management made an early decision not to enter into any alliance that constrained its freedom of action.

[66] For more details, see Amsden and Kim, "A Comparative Analysis of Local and Transnational Corporations in the Korean Automobile Industry."

which employed more than 300 workers, in an attempt to tap into European technological expertise. Although it had substantially improved its technological capabilities by the time of its demise, Daewoo still depended heavily on foreign suppliers for critical components.

Kia's record was in between the extremes occupied by Hyundai and Daewoo. As a company with long-standing experience in producing motorcycles and then trucks and buses, Kia succeeded in raising its local content substantially in the 1980s. Nonetheless, its principal export model depended wholly on Mazda's technology and, like Daewoo, it found its operations subject to the marketing decisions of a partner – in this instance, Ford. Displeasure with what it regarded as Ford's failure to promote its products adequately in the United States led Kia to attempt to establish its own dealer network there after 1993.

Finally, the most recent entrant to the Korean industry, Samsung Motors, had little opportunity to advance its technological competencies in the short period between its establishment and bankruptcy. It relied exclusively on technology supplied by its Japanese partner, Nissan.

The government's role in fostering technological autonomy and development was more significant in the auto parts industry, to which it gave subsidized finance. The emphasis was on building up the local industry through licensing and other partnerships with overseas firms in lieu of foreign direct investment. Dependence on foreign partners for technology nonetheless remained high. Between 1980 and 1986 Korean auto parts firms entered into 21 joint ventures and 160 technology licensing agreements, of which 60 percent were with Japanese companies.[67] The auto assemblers themselves have been more significant sources of knowledge for their component suppliers than has the government, as they worked closely with subcontractors on quality improvement and control.

In short, while the pursuit of technonationalist strategies in the auto industry had the desired result of promoting several national champions in this complex industrial sector, the policies were of limited effectiveness in fostering technological autonomy. In promoting consolidation of the industry at the beginning of the 1980s, the Korean state had attempted to exclude the one company, Hyundai, that had gone furthest in developing local technological competencies. As Richard Samuels suggested at the conference at which this chapter was first presented, the end product of three decades of government promotion of the auto industry in Korea was a "porous" technonationalism. The ongoing reliance on foreign firms for technology (and, in some cases, marketing channels) was far from the technonationalist ideal.

---

[67] Organisation for Economic Cooperation and Development, *Globalisation of Industrial Activities: Four Case Studies: Auto Parts, Chemicals, Construction, and Semiconductors* (Paris: Organisation for Economic Cooperation and Development, 1992), p. 53.

Conclusion

The Korean auto industry underwent profound change within the space of three years. The industry's structure was transformed from five national companies to one in which only a single company is still under Korean control – and even this company, Hyundai, now has 10 (possibly soon to be 15) percent foreign equity in its auto operations, and 50 percent in its commercial vehicle subsidiary. Whatever autonomy the Korean industry enjoyed before the financial crisis has to a significant extent disappeared. It is no longer a national industry.

What will be the future of Korean plants in an industry with substantial worldwide surplus capacity, an industry in which intense competition occurs not only between firms but also within them as individual plants seek to consolidate their roles as preferred production locations? What can Korean companies bring to the new alliances? Is there an advantage in the auto industry to the label "made in Korea"?

Unlike their counterparts in the electronics sector, Korean companies in the automobile industry have few cutting-edge technologies coveted by foreign partners. Hyundai may be a partial exception to this generalization but even its domestically designed engines, a breakthrough in technological autonomy for a Korean auto producer, are unlikely to be of interest to DaimlerChrysler except for cars produced in Korea. Hyundai's research and development budget remains low by international standards: expenditures are less than one-third of the level of those of Toyota.[68]

The rapid expansion of productive capacity in the 1990s, however, did furnish the Korean producers with state-of-the-art plants (some domestic and others located abroad) that are of interest to global companies seeking a low-cost production base for the Asian region (and a means of penetrating the Korean market itself, currently still the second largest Asian market after Japan).[69] Korea is strategically placed for producers to take advantage of the liberalization of the car market in China that is scheduled to occur following China's entry into the World Trade Organization (WTO).[70] Productivity and quality control in the Korean industry remain substantially below that of Japan, however; whether the new foreign owners will be able

---

[68] *Korea Herald*, February 10, 2000.

[69] Cars produced within Korea are also likely to face increased competition in the domestic market following the lifting of the ban on imports from Japan with the ending in July 1999 of the government's import source diversification scheme (essentially a measure aimed at curtailing Japanese imports). Japanese companies previously could export to Korea only cars from their American transplants. The entry of GM and DaimlerChrysler into Korean production may facilitate imports from the United States, especially of components, and reduce the ongoing complaints from the USTR to the Korean government about the allegedly closed nature of the Korean market.

[70] China's auto tariffs are scheduled to drop from 100 percent to 25 percent over five years as part of the WTO accession deal. Korean cars are currently produced at lower cost than those manufactured by joint ventures in China; see *Business Week*, January 24, 2000.

to bring their Korean plants up to world-best practice remains to be seen. The best hope for the remaining national champion, Hyundai-Kia, will be to establish a reputation for inexpensive but reliable cars – not necessarily vehicles at the technological edge but ones that provide good value for money for the average motorist.

For Samsung, the future appears clear-cut. Renault will use the plant to produce Nissan cars for the Korean market, with some possibilities of export to other parts of Asia in the future, although this will depend on its plans for Nissan plants within Japan. For Daewoo, the outlook is far less clear, not least because GM had not completed the negotiations for its acquisition at the time this chapter went to the publishers. Daewoo's models have a particularly poor reputation for quality in the United States so it is unlikely that GM would continue to export them to that market, least of all under the Daewoo badge. And Daewoo's East European plants are likely to lose their linkage with Korea, as they were not part of the package acquired by GM and its partners. The concerns of the economic nationalists that a foreign-owned Daewoo may be confined by its new owners to producing primarily for the domestic market may yet be realized. The name of the game in recent rationalizations has been cost cutting through plant closures and downsizing (evident, for instance, in GM's actions in Europe, and especially in Renault's restructuring of Nissan's operations). Plant closures and job losses among the Korean auto assemblers have been politically unacceptable to date but will be an unavoidable if uncomfortable consequence of internationalizing the domestic industry.[71]

The most intriguing issue is the future of Hyundai in its partnership with DaimlerChrysler. Hyundai can fill a significant gap in the DaimlerChrysler product range as a producer of small cars. Besides providing an instrument for launching (an unsuccessful) joint bid for Daewoo, another intention behind the DaimlerChrysler alliance with Hyundai was the coproduction of a subcompact "world car." Hyundai is scheduled to produce from the first half of 2002 from 300,000 to 350,000 units domestically, and a further 100,000 to 150,000 in a new Chinese plant, a significant portion of the total worldwide production of this new vehicle of between 750,000 and 1 million units. Production at these levels would still leave Hyundai with significant capacity to produce its own models. The partnership with DaimlerChrysler may provide new marketing possibilities for its own models through badge engineering arrangements.[72]

---

[71] This sensitivity surfaced again during the negotiations between Daewoo's creditors and GM. GM refused to take over Daewoo's thirty-year-old plant at Bupyeong; the government refused to allow its closure. The compromise was that the new GM-Daewoo would commit to purchase cars produced at Bupyeong for six years and would have an option to purchase the plant at the end of that period.

[72] For instance, in July 2000 Hyundai announced that its Atoz model would be rebadged for sale under the Dodge label in Mexico, thereby opening up a new market to the Korean producer. The Mexican market had previously been closed to Korean companies because they

Joint ventures between Korean companies and foreign partners have an unhappy history, however. Foreign partners have refused to supply their Korean associates with state-of-the-art technologies and have restricted their overseas marketing. The unwillingness of American and Japanese companies to supply contemporary technologies may have its roots in fears that they would lose control of them in ventures where they were minority partners, especially in a country with a notorious lack of respect for intellectual property rights. With Renault and GM having majority control of Samsung and Daewoo respectively, this issue may be resolved for these companies. For Hyundai in its relationship with DaimlerChrysler, it may still prove problematic – as may marketing arrangements for the new world car.

A critical question for the long-term prosperity of the industry in Korea is the future of the parts industry. Worldwide, the auto components industry has experienced the same consolidation and restructuring as car assemblers, in part because suppliers are being squeezed in an increasingly oligopolistic industry. The emphasis has again been on economies of scope and economies of scale with first-tier suppliers increasingly expected to sell complete modules – on a global basis. The assemblers have moved to reduce the number of these tier-one suppliers, which they have cut in half in the last several years.[73]

Much of the Korean components industry is not well prepared for this new era of global competition. The vast majority of parts companies are small and traditionally tied to one assembler.[74] Exports of parts did grow substantially in the second half of the 1990s but were used almost exclusively to service the after-sales market for the growing number of Korean cars on foreign roads. These exports come overwhelmingly from a small number of firms. The economic crisis in Korea in the second half of the 1990s exacerbated the pressures from global consolidation on the domestic auto parts industry. The bankruptcies of four of the five domestic assemblers had flow-on effects for many of their suppliers that were unable to withstand the nonpayment of invoices. Although an exact figure is impossible to establish, estimates are that between 300 and 500 small and medium-sized enterprises exited the auto parts industry following the bankruptcies of the assem-

---

had no local production facilities; see *Korea Herald*, July 13, 2000. Contrary to the expectations of many foreign observers of the Korean industry, Hyundai has succeeded in turning around Kia's performance in a remarkably short period. Domestic sales in 1999 were up 125 percent on the previous year; for the first time in a decade, Kia Motors made a net profit. This was helped by creditors writing off or converting to equity most of its debts, so that the ratio of interest payments to sales revenue was slashed to 1.6 percent. Moreover, the company shed one-third of its previous workforce of 44,000.

[73] "The Automotive Sector: Driving a Hard Bargain," *Acquisitions Monthly*, July 1998 <http://www.acquisitions-monthly.co.uk/magazine/html/july_1998_cover_story.htm>.

[74] Samsung had to create a supplier network from scratch as Hyundai and Daewoo prohibited their subcontractors from supplying the new entrant to the industry. Renault has stated publicly that it has not undertaken to support the existing Samsung components suppliers.

blers. Ongoing uncertainty about Daewoo's future continues to cause financial problems for its suppliers.

The financial crisis has dramatically changed the ownership structure of some of the larger Korean parts companies. Bankruptcies among some of the largest conglomerates forced divestment of some of their auto components manufacturing. It opened the way for foreign investors to acquire significant shareholdings in Korean components producers – often at fire sale prices (the advantage of low stock market prices being compounded by a favorable exchange rate). More than 100 parts suppliers are estimated to have transferred 50 percent or more of their equity to foreign investors since the crisis began. Some of the most prominent mergers and acquisitions include the breakup of the Halla *chaebol*'s Mando subsidiary, one of Korea's best-known and largest parts makers, when the parent company went bankrupt; Hanwha Machinery Corporation's sale of a majority of its rolling bearing activities to FAG, the leading German-based producer of bearings; and the purchase of Halla Climate Control, Korea's single largest auto parts exporter outside of the assembly companies, by the Ford spinoff Visteon. Denationalization has been as prominent in the components industry as in auto assembly.

As with the assemblers, the future of the foreign majority-owned components makers in Korea will depend on how they fit into the global plans of their new owners. For these (larger) companies, their new links with the global giants in auto parts production will be their primary source of technology. The smaller companies that survive the industry's upheaval are likely to be the principal beneficiaries of government initiatives to improve the national innovation system, analyzed by Linsu Kim in his contribution to this volume.

What do the Korean financial crisis and more specifically the recent developments in the automobile industry tell us about the pursuit of technonationalist strategies in a globalized economy? Two schools of thought dominated early explanations of the Korean economic crisis of the second half of the 1990s: one I label the "I told you so" approach; the other, a "diehard statist approach."

The "I told you so" approach summarizes the views of most professional economists about Korean economic development. For years, they had criticized those elements of the technonationalist approach associated with sectoral industrial policies that, in Alice Amsden's words, had deliberately set out to get prices wrong.[75] At best, such policies had merely offset other distortions arising from state intervention. At worst, they had generated a fundamental misallocation of resources. Korea's economic success was attributable to sound macroeconomic policies, to investment in education and infrastructure, and to the government's emphasis on export-led growth.

[75] Amsden, *Asia's Next Giant*.

Ongoing government intervention in the financial system created moral-hazard problems that in turn encouraged further misallocation of resources.[76]

The "diehard statists" occupy the other end of the spectrum. Their argument is that the Korean financial crisis developed not because Korea was statist but because it had not been statist enough. In particular, in the process of economic liberalization that had begun in the late 1980s, the state had given up its capacity to coordinate the process of economic development. The consequence was the explosion of surplus capacity in various sectors of manufacturing in the 1990s, and an ill-conceived process of financial sector liberalization that encouraged corporations to rely excessively on short-term international loans.[77]

Both approaches offer some insights into the origins of the financial crisis, but both also suffer from blinkered vision. For the neoclassical economists, this tunnel vision is expressed in the denial that technonationalist policies that took the form of sectoral interventions ever made any significant contribution to Korea's rapid industrialization. The reality, however, was that the government mounted its Heavy and Chemical Industry push, which rapidly transformed the structure of the Korean economy, against the advice of the World Bank (which at the time was advocating additional investment in textiles where it saw Korea's comparative advantage as continuing to lie). It is difficult to believe that the Korean economy would have acquired the industrial prowess it came to enjoy within a remarkably short period of time had it not been for the technonationalist policies the Korean state pursued.

The problem with the diehard statist approach lies not so much in its analysis of one of the reasons for the economic crisis of the second half of the 1990s – a decline in the capacity of the state to coordinate economic activities – but rather in an apparent belief that the Korean state in the 1990s could have continued to play a role similar to that of the previous three decades. The world had moved on. So, too, had the relationship between Korean private-sector actors and the state. The *chaebol* enjoyed a substantial degree of financial autonomy, thereby depriving the state of one of its principal instruments of control. And as corporations moved closer to the

---

[76] Ross H. McLeod and Ross Garnaut, *East Asia in Crisis: From Being a Miracle to Needing One?* (London: Routledge, 1998), is representative of this analysis of the crises. Anne O. Krueger, *Foreign Trade Regimes and Economic Development: Liberalization Attempts and Consequences* (New York: National Bureau of Economic Research, 1978), provides the classic statement of the neoclassical economists' case against Korean policies.

[77] Robert Wade and Frank Veneroso (1998), Chang, Park, and Yoo (1998), and Weiss (1999, 2000) are representative of this approach. Robert Wade and Frank Veneroso, "The Asian Crisis: The High Debt Model versus the Wall Street–Treasury–IMF Complex," *New Left Review*, no. 228 (March – April 1998): 3–23; Chang, Park, and Yoo, "Interpreting the Korean Crisis"; Linda Weiss, "Developmental States in Transition: Adapting, Dismantling, Innovating, Not 'Normalising'" *Pacific Review* 14, no. 1 (2000): 21–56, and "State Power and the Asian Crisis," *New Political Economy* 4, no. 3 (1999): 317–42.

technological frontier, the capacity of state institutions to play a significant role in the acquisition and development of technologies was much reduced.

The analysis in this chapter points to a third explanation of the crisis: an obsolescing technonationalism. This argument highlights the declining efficacy of technonationalist policies in an increasingly globalized economy. The starting point is that the technonationalist strategies adopted to promote the Korean industry did work, albeit not as perfectly as intended, at a specific stage in the evolution of the Korean economy and of the postwar geopolitical and economic systems.[78] State policies that channeled capital to favored companies, excluded imports and foreign firms from the domestic market, and provided substantial funding to subsidize exports were significant factors in the success of the domestic auto industry. The capacity of the Korean state to pursue such strategies of aggressive technonationalism was grounded in a particular geopolitical context and in an international trading regime that, at the time, was invested with limited powers of monitoring and enforcement. It was also a function of the state's control over key resources, particularly its capacity to allocate scarce financial resources to favored companies.

The contexts have changed dramatically. It was no coincidence that Korean auto companies had encountered severe difficulties in the 1990s even before the onset of the financial crisis. Korean companies faced a world in which the global industry was consolidating at an unprecedented rate. Economies of scale and scope were becoming ever more important. It was also a world in which the Korean government was under intense pressure from major trading partners and the multilateral economic organizations to open up the closed domestic auto market. Korea suffers from its position as a medium-sized economy: too large for its actions to escape the critical scrutiny of trading partners yet not of a size such as that of China to have any realistic expectation of being able to dictate any of the rules of the international trade game.

The initial response of Korean car companies to the new competitive context was to embark on a scramble to achieve scale economies through a reckless program of expansion. This policy may have succeeded in an earlier era when the state had both the will and the capacity to bail them out. The approach, however, was an unlikely one in the new environment where membership in the OECD and the WTO added to pressures from trading partners for liberalization of the Korean economy. External factors placed unprecedented constraints on the autonomy of government policy making.

More than the external context had changed, however. The domestic environment was no longer conducive to the pursuit of technonationalist

---

[78] For further consideration of the significance of context in the success of industrial policies in East Asia, see Trevor Matthews and John Ravenhill, "Strategic Trade Policy: The East Asian Experience," in Andrew MacIntyre, ed., *Business and Government in Industrialising East Asia* (Ithaca: Cornell University Press, 1994), pp. 29–90.

policies. Although the Korean public remained supportive, as did several major lobby groups including Korea's powerful trade unions, the agencies of the state were divided as never before. By the early 1990s, the economic rationalists had gained the upper hand – even though it took the financial crisis and the advent of a new administration, whose leader, President Kim Dae Jung, previously had enjoyed few ties to Korea's large companies, to make the decisive break with the technonationalist past and open up the economy to foreign investment. Rather than risk the political consequences of the unemployment that would have resulted from the closure of Daewoo and Samsung's auto plants, the Korean state was willing to sell their assets to foreign corporations at fire sale prices and to write off their debts at the expense of Korean taxpayers.

The internationalization of the Korean economy has occurred prematurely for Korea's car companies. Korean auto companies, for all their progress over the previous quarter of a century, had not succeeded in joining the leaders of the pack, unlike their counterparts in the semiconductor industry. Only Hyundai Motors had developed a significant degree of technological independence – and, in the markets of industrialized economies, even its products still bore the stigma of negative brand association. Whether Hyundai or Daewoo, with its strategy of concentrating on emerging country markets, could have enhanced their technological autonomy in more favorable circumstances is a moot point. Not only did they face intricate technological challenges but the auto industry – unlike electronics, where the Information Technology Agreement has essentially brought free trade to the sector – remained a substantially imbalanced playing field, in which various formal and informal barriers, particularly in the markets of the European Union and Japan, continued to restrict the access of foreign producers.

The Korean state may continue to reinforce with various official barriers the obstacles posed to foreign penetration of the domestic car market by the nationalist urge to "buy Korean." By rejigging elements of the national innovation system, as discussed by Linsu Kim in Chapter 4, the Korean state can enhance the supportive environment for auto producers. But most of the technonationalist armory that it previously was able to deploy in support of national champions is now bare.

6

Crisis and Adaptation in Taiwan and South Korea

The Political Economy of Semiconductors

William W. Keller and Louis W. Pauly

Widely cited by comparative political economists as paradigmatic cases of the developmental state, South Korea and Taiwan constructed vibrant but vulnerable national economies during the latter decades of the twentieth century. Seeking to enter the leading ranks in the world economy, both were committed to moving indigenous industries rapidly up the technological value chain. In the contemporary period, no industry better exemplifies this effort than the one that develops and produces semiconductors – core elements in burgeoning global telecommunications, computer, and computer equipment industries. Notoriously cyclical, the industry poses complex challenges for business and government.

Two Approaches to Innovation in the Semiconductor Industry

This chapter examines the question of whether continuity or change is more characteristic of the semiconductor industries of South Korea and Taiwan. Each developed a distinctive strategic approach to achieving its national aspirations in this critical industry. The regional financial shock of 1997–98 brought these differences more fully into view, as did the global downturn in the information technology industries in 2001–2. Taiwan and Korea have long pursued industrial policies structured to advance national strategies in this sector. We argue,

Fieldwork for this chapter was partially supported by the MIT-Japan Program and by the Social Sciences and Humanities Research Council of Canada. We very much appreciate advice and assistance provided by Larry Sumney of the Semiconductor Research Corporation and also by Roger Mathus of the Semiconductor Industry Association who accompanied us during fieldwork undertaken first in 1996 and later in the winter of 1999–2000. We are grateful to many industry executives and government officials in South Korea and Taiwan for taking the time to meet with us and for providing various data. Several of the paragraphs in this chapter draw on our article, "Crisis and Adaptation in East Asian Innovation Systems: The Case of the Semiconductor Industry in Taiwan and South Korea," *Business and Politics* 2, no. 3 (November 2000): 327–52. Detailed comparative statistical analysis is included therein.

however, that Taiwan's more flexible and pragmatic approach, the core of its "foundry" model of chip production, enabled it to weather the financial crisis of the late 1990s, and even to find new opportunities.

By way of contrast, Korea's more rigid approach as it pursued an "integrated device manufacturing" (IDM) model left its industry more fragile and under pressure. Semiconductor manufacturers in both countries have recently made adjustments in their long-term strategies. But Taiwan's strategy has moved much closer to the "technohybrid" middle, introduced in Chapter 1, as part of the "technonational-technoglobal" continuum. To be sure, recognizably national goals and aspirations remain in Taiwan's industrial strategy for semiconductors. As Morris Chang, the pioneering leader of Taiwan's semiconductor industry, suggested in the fall of 2001, "As long as corporate enterprise and the government continue to work together, Taiwan will maintain its competitive edge."[1] Strong incentives for pragmatic flexibility and financial prudence have been provided both by persistent weakness in Japan and by gathering strength in China. For its part, Korea remains on the more overtly technonational side of the spectrum, especially as it seeks to rationalize and defend massive, and mainly debt-financed, historical investments.

Technological Innovation in Taiwan and Korea

After the concept of a national innovation system was first introduced into studies of the process of industrial development, it was widely understood to vary by the nature of the corporate-political networks at its core. These networks were shaped by history and culture as much as by specific strategies for inserting local factors of production into competitive international markets. The concept is still useful, even though much related research is now focused on the dynamics of innovation, either at the sectoral level or at regional levels above or below the nation-state as conventionally understood.[2] The more the concept was elaborated, however, the more obvious it became that interpretive subtlety was required. For example, cases like Taiwan and South Korea, once seen as quite similar, are now understood to

[1] "TSMC announces expansion program of NT$700 billion," *Taipei Times*, October 26, 2001.

[2] Daniele Archibugi and Mario Pianta, *The Technological Specialization of Advanced Countries* (Boston: Kluwer and the Commission of the European Communities, 1992); Giovanni Dosi et al., *Technical Change and Economic Theory* (London: Pinter, 1988); M.C. Harris and G.E. Moore, eds., *Linking Trade and Technology Policies* (Washington, D.C.: National Academy Press, 1992); T.H. Lee, and P.P. Reid, eds., *National Interests in an Age of Global Technology* (Washington, D.C.: National Academy Press, 1991); Bengt-Åke Lundvall, *National Systems of Innovation* (New York: St. Martin's Press, 1992); David C. Mowery and N. Rosenberg, *Technology and the Pursuit of Economic Growth* (Cambridge: Cambridge University Press, 1989); David C. Mowery, *Science and Technology Policy in Interdependent Economies* (Boston: Kluwer, 1994); Richard Nelson, ed., *National Innovation*

differ significantly in the character of the ideology that informs their approaches to industrial policy and technological innovation.

In the light of their contemporary histories, it is possible in both cases to trace the outlines of intentional policies guided early on by a shared ideology accurately characterized by the term technonationalism. Over time, and in key industrial sectors, however, those policies have diverged considerably, and their ideological underpinnings have become more difficult to compare – especially as Taiwan's hybrid development and insertion into multinational design and production networks deepened. The semiconductor industry provides an excellent template for bringing those divergent pathways to light and for probing the extent to which common ideological foundations may still support those pathways.

Despite vast changes in their national economies during the past decade, certain continuities are apparent in the financial and industrial systems of Korea and Taiwan. Before the financial crisis of the late 1990s, fundamental movement toward fully open capital markets and widely diversified patterns of corporate ownership looked like a very long-run proposition in both countries, but especially in Korea. In high-technology sectors now at the center of national developmental strategies, indigenous control, privileged access to public funding and public financial guarantees, and the availability of direct or indirect state subsidies all remained in evidence, especially at the crucial early stages of new product and process development. Nowhere was this clearer than in the semiconductor and related high-technology industries. The legacy of state strategies aimed at industrial success persisted well into an era when those industries had matured to the point where they seemed capable of financing and carrying out next-generation research and development in-house.

By the late 1990s both Korean and Taiwanese corporate planners in this sector could assume that only the most dramatic events in external markets, a national calamity or the most egregious of internal managerial mistakes, could threaten the continuity of their high-end electronics industries. It seemed that the sector, if not individual firms themselves, could not fail, save for the overarching failure of the political and financial systems within which they remained embedded. To be sure, this left the Korean and Taiwanese

Systems (New York: Oxford University Press, 1993); Richard J. Samuels, *"Rich Nation, Strong Army": National Security and the Technological Transformation of Japan* (Ithaca: Cornell University Press, 1994); Michael Hobday, *Innovation in East Asia* (Aldershot: Edward Elgar, 1995); Suzanne Berger and Ronald Dore, eds., *National Diversity and Global Capitalism* (Ithaca: Cornell University Press, 1996); Paul N. Doremus, William W. Keller, Louis W. Pauly, and Simon Reich, *The Myth of the Global Corporation* (Princeton: Princeton University Press, 1998); Richard Whitley, *Divergent Capitalisms* (Oxford: Oxford University Press, 1999); and Dieter Ernst and John Ravenhill, "Globalization, Convergence, and the Transformation of International Production Networks in Electronics in East Asia," *Business and Politics* 1, no. 1 (April 1999): 35–62.

governments with what economists call a significant "moral hazard" problem. With a new degree of confidence concerning their durability, firms could find themselves tempted not to make the most efficient use of their resources on a day-to-day basis. They could also be tempted to overinvest. Events in the late 1990s, as it turned out, made clear that such overinvestment did in fact occur, especially in Korea – but also in Taiwan – and especially in the standard memory chip (DRAM) side of the business.

The financial crisis that swept the East Asian region in the late 1990s did reshape the competitive landscape for the semiconductor industry. But the difficult challenge is to separate such effects from the impact of other forces simultaneously influencing international markets for semiconductor products. In short, throughout the late 1990s and into the new century, the Taiwanese industry accelerated its evolution toward a disaggregated "foundry" model – one based on its firms' organizing themselves mainly to produce customized chips for customers from around the world, customers who supplied the chip designs but retained their intellectual property rights.

Conversely, its Korean counterpart consolidated around the IDM model, which aimed to dominate global markets in certain products and then to expand out from there. The foundry model in Taiwan called for flexibility, and a remarkable expansion and deepening of alliance arrangements with foreign customers, mainly Japanese. In practice, it translated itself into a hybrid industrial structure that balanced classic national aspirations with an acceptance of the vulnerability entailed by not necessarily controlling intellectual property rights at the core of the production process. The IDM model, by way of contrast, coalesced around an enforced domestic duopoly, which aimed in clear technonational terms to control an entire value chain in a key sector and to accommodate the implied consequence of extreme financial vulnerability.

The regional financial crisis of 1997–98 tested both models, as did a coincident downturn in global semiconductor markets. A quick upturn followed by yet another downturn early in the next decade tested them once again. Although both models were technonationalist, the Korean IDM strategy emphasized a classic internally oriented approach to issues of corporate control and to the targeting of key niches in the world's electronics markets. The Taiwanese foundry model, conversely, rested on more cautious financial and strategic management, even at the cost of sharing important aspects of corporate control, which suggested a relatively more technoglobal vision of the future of those markets and of Taiwan's place within them. The following overviews give an indication of how the two models fared in recent years and how they continued to adjust.

Origins of the Taiwanese Foundries
In 1990 it was possible to paint a vivid picture of the system of industrial innovation and financing that initially propelled Taiwan up the technological

ladder.[3] A publicly owned and tightly controlled banking system originally channeled financial flows to high-priority industries. Foreign know-how was deliberately sought, both through joint ventures and other forms of direct collaboration with multinational firms, and by sending future scientists and technicians abroad, often to the United States, for extended periods of university education and subsequent experience in U.S. industry. Local firms benefited from opaque systems of preferential financing designed not to raise hackles over "unfair" competitive advantages abroad or at home. Government research laboratories substituted for private initiatives until targeted industries reached a level of internal expertise and staying power capable of competing with foreign rivals, at least in specific niches if not across the board. But the strategy was never inward-looking. To be sure, national advantages were sought and nimbleness was prized. Planning took on a technoglobal cast as early successes in such heavy industries as shipbuilding came to be viewed as untenable over the long term. Policy liberalization, including a gradual opening to external financial markets, was carefully guided.[4]

The industrial structure of Taiwan in the contemporary period has been deeply marked by an obvious and intricate network of ties between a party-dominated state apparatus and a private sector gradually gaining in scale and autonomy. From the 1950s through the 1970s, a paternalistic, disciplined, and Kuomintang Party–dominated government crafted the development of the national economy. At the base of that economy was a large state-owned sector, encompassing all industries deemed to be strategic. A decentralized private sector emerged from that base that was composed of myriad family-owned small and medium-sized firms.

The state-owned sector in industrializing Taiwan included energy, public utilities, agricultural-related industries, steel, shipbuilding, heavy machinery, construction, defense-related industries, insurance, banking, and financial services.[5] Since the late 1970s, private enterprise was deliberately encouraged by the state in other sectors. Significant opportunity existed for the personal enrichment of entrepreneurs and their families, and a flexible, highly competitive labor market moved Taiwan's approach to industrial transformation to a new phase.

In the wake of the oil crisis of the 1970s, the old system of state and party guidance of key industrial sectors began to erode. Traditional forms of

---

[3] Robert Wade, *Governing the Market* (Princeton: Princeton University Press, 1990). See also John A. Mathews et al., *Tiger Technology* (Cambridge: Cambridge University Press, 2000).

[4] Steve Chan and Cal Clark, *Flexibility, Foresight, and Fortune in Taiwan's Development* (London: Routledge, 1992); Alice Amsden, "Taiwan in International Perspective," in N.T. Wang, ed., *Taiwan's Enterprises in Global Perspective* (Armonk, N.Y.: M. E. Sharpe, 1992).

[5] Yun-han Chu, "The Realignment of Business-Government Relations and Regime Transition in Taiwan," in Andrew MacIntyre, ed., *Business and Government in Industrialising Asia* (Ithaca: Cornell University Press, 1994), p. 118.

protectionism were gradually dismantled and the national currency was allowed to appreciate considerably. A decisive turn in strategic direction came during the 1980s as planners moved their sights away from smokestack industries toward high technology. A high-level Science and Technology Advisory Group was established by the government to oversee policies and programs that would necessarily cross conventional ministerial jurisdictions. The group hired foreign consultants to advise the cabinet on the design and implementation of a new National Science and Technology (NST) Program.

The NST Program stimulated and subsidized research and development projects in a wide variety of promising world-market-oriented sectors. It supported the establishment of new state laboratories and parastatal research organizations under various ministries. Most important, many of those research facilities were explicitly mandated to support the private sector in areas targeted by a new Strategic Industries Program. Semiconductors and microelectronics topped the list. Others included materials science, precision engineering, biomedicine, specialty chemicals, nuclear energy, and aerospace – all of which could be seen as resting on the building blocks provided by an ultimate commitment to semiconductor production. Technological achievements and capabilities in national labs were transferred for commercial application either directly to private firms or to new semipublic joint ventures, ventures that were in any event characterized by a high degree of entrepreneurial energy.[6] A decided preference for equity over debt financially underpinned those ventures.[7]

Moreover, the Kuomintang Party established its own Central Finance Committee, which participated in virtually all state-sponsored joint ventures in high technology. Through such organizations, party- and state-trained personnel moved into positions in the private sector, and in a mixed sector involving state, party, and private entrepreneurs. The semiconductor industry constituted a perfect example of the latter combination, where effectively subsidized start-up funding, equity-based deferred compensation arrangements, and opportunistic labor-recruitment and training policies kick-started firms like Taiwan Semiconductor Manufacturing Co. (TSMC) and United Microelectronics Co. (UMC). The technology and the people who created it were quite literally spun off from government national laboratories, as government technologists became private-sector employees. National champions

---

[6] Ibid., p. 123. See also Kenneth L. Kraemer et al., "Entrepreneurship, Flexibility, and Policy Coordination: Taiwan's Computer Industry," *Information Society* 12 (1996): 215–49.

[7] Where average debt-equity ratios in Korea grew from 300 percent in the early 1970s to 400 percent a decade later and to 500 percent in 1997, comparable ratios in Taiwan stayed near, and often below, 100 percent over the same extended period. See D. M. Leipziger, "Industrial Restructuring in Korea," *World Development* 16 (1988): 128; and Mark R. Stone, "Corporate Debt Restructuring in East Asia," *IMF Paper in Policy Analysis and Assessment*, PPAA/98/13 (October 1998): 18.

like TSMC and UMC also benefited from basic infrastructural assistance through incentives such as government-industry science parks and guaranteed electricity contracts.

Origins of the South Korean Integrated Device Manufacturers

The path to leading-edge industrial innovation in South Korea has been quite different.[8] The overarching framework may clearly be labeled technonational, one that is rooted in a long-run strategy to compete with Japan. Its core contained a credit-based, tightly regulated financial system that encouraged high debt burdens in firms induced to grow very rapidly and, at least until they achieved stability and dominance, to orient themselves toward market share in lieu of profitability. That system intimately linked state agencies and strategic industries throughout the 1960s and 1970s.[9] Their collaborative industrialization strategy rested on import substitution and a redirection of capital toward industries capable of generating exports. It initially focused on textiles, shipbuilding, heavy manufacturing (steel, chemicals), and overseas construction. By the end of the 1970s electronic products and a large-scale automobile sector were added to the mix. Higher-end electronic products, especially certain kinds of semiconductors, began to be intensively developed in the 1980s.

An explicit national planning apparatus channeled export-generated financial surpluses and borrowed financial resources toward Korea's industrial conglomerates, the *chaebol*. Behind such institutions as development banks was a paternalist and relatively lean government backed by a strong military. The success of the *chaebol* in international markets, moreover, was aided and abetted by the willingness of the United States to tolerate a competitive exchange rate, a high level of imports from Korea, and opaque markets within Korea – a tolerance conditioned by the exigencies of the Cold War.

Pressures for change in these arrangements began to build in the late 1970s.[10] Industrial planners and *chaebol* executives alike had miscalculated on several fronts. Growth slowed in some markets on which Korean exporters depended. Protectionist pressures reemerged abroad, not least in

---

[8] See, e.g., Jung-en Woo (Meredith Woo Cumings), *Race to the Swift: State and Finance in Korean Industrialization* (New York: Columbia University Press, 1991); Alice Amsden, *Asia's Next Giant: South Korea and Late Industrialization* (New York: Oxford University Press, 1989).

[9] Byung-Nak Song, *The Rise of the Korean Economy* (Oxford: Oxford University Press, 1990); Kae H. Chung and Hak Cho Lee, *Korean Managerial Dynamics* (New York: Praeger, 1989).

[10] Chung-in Moon, "Changing Patterns of Business-Government Relations in South Korea," in Andrew Macintyre, ed., *Business and Government in Industrialising Asia* (Ithaca: Cornell University Press, 1994); also see Karl Fields, *Enterprise and the State in Korea and Taiwan* (Ithaca: Cornell University Press, 1995).

the United States. Korean manufacturers found that other neighboring states had emulated their own strategies. The rate of economic expansion in Korea plummeted and pent-up inflationary pressures surged. The country's relatively narrow sectoral base and highly leveraged corporate balance sheets could not withstand the shock. After a period of economic turmoil, the national government collapsed in a military coup.

The subsequent regime of President Chun Doo Hwan moved not to liberalize the system but to tighten its apparatus of control. Largely symbolic moves to rein in the rising autonomy of the *chaebol* ensued. The real change in government industrial planning was to emphasize macroeconomic stability and to foster a push toward industrial diversification. Credit conditions were tightened, both to dampen inflationary pressures and to force restructuring of industries facing surplus capacity. A further move up the technology ladder ensued. By the 1980s, semiconductors, electronic consumer products, other finished manufactured goods, and high-quality automobiles were at the top of the value-added pyramid. Unmediated "market" signals did not guide this transformation. Twenty-six of the largest *chaebol*, for example, were simply ordered by government planners to sell off 166 subsidiaries (out of a total of 631) and large tracts of real estate. Extraordinary state powers were deployed to enforce compliance, ranging from selective credit concessions and personal and corporate tax audits to physical intimidation by security agencies. Between 1985 and 1988 nearly eighty firms were "merged" into healthier ones on terms exceptionally attractive to the latter, including loans that carried five- to thirty-year grace periods. Direct public subsidies were sometimes granted to compensate for anticipated losses, and companies were able to negotiate loans well below market rate, sometimes as low as 2 percent. Simultaneously, the government took various steps to deregulate the financial system and to open it up to new competitors. These measures had the ironic effect of shoring up domestic cartels, even though they were ostensibly designed to respond to American calls for market liberalization and the reduction of the *chaebol* power. Formerly forbidden from owning financial institutions, the *chaebol* could now do so. Deregulation also expanded direct access to foreign sources of capital. Before the 1980s ended, the sales of the thirty largest *chaebol* would account for 95 percent of South Korea's gross national product.[11]

In the early 1990s the governments of Chun's successors, Roh Tae Woo and Kim Young Sam, again faced pressures to reduce the role of the *chaebol* in the national economy and to diversify further the national industrial base. Predictably, in the face of mixed economic pictures in leading export markets, the drive toward deconcentration and liberalization did not always fit comfortably with the enduring national goal of enhancing the external competitiveness of key sectors. The tension between those objectives throughout

---

[11] *Business Korea,* November 1989, p. 21.

the 1990s lay at the center both of industrial restructuring in Korea and widely reported corruption scandals. Beneath those tensions, in turn, lay one constant: the mutual recognition by both government and *chaebol* leaders that the success of sectors capable of generating foreign exchange remained of vital importance for the nation. Semiconductors, especially memory chips (DRAMs), were at the core of the sector most prominently meeting that test. Their main producers were embedded within the electronics arms of the Hyundai, Samsung, and Lucky Goldstar *chaebol*.

In the late 1990s, during the presidency of Kim Dae Jung, many Korean corporations tried to reduce their historical dependence on bank debt while increasing both their debt to nonbank financial institutions and their reliance on bond markets.[12] There was, however, no corresponding shift toward a reliance on equity markets. The major corporate groups continued to be characterized by high levels of cross-shareholding and cross-lending. In consequence, and as in the case of Japan, the risk of large-scale takeover by other firms, hostile or not, was virtually nonexistent in Korea before 1997 – not surprising, given a long-standing aversion to sharing control over indigenous industries. Political tensions and controversy concerning industrial concentration notwithstanding, the prospects for major reform and restructuring among the *chaebol* at the leading technological edge looked remote just before the 1997–98 financial crisis hit.

During the 1990s the most dramatic change in new investment within Korea had come in the electronics sector. From a low base, Korean firms were increasing their electronic machinery imports by 50 percent per year midway through the decade, signifying a massive industrial retooling. Semiconductors and related industries were priority sectors. Firms were eligible for "policy loans," which could lower the cost of borrowing to 5 percent per annum when market rates ranged between 12 and 15 percent. The government also channeled subsidies directly to designated industries through the National Investment Fund. Such financing supported massive imports of new technology, but as licensing agreements became more expensive and difficult to arrange, and as the industry matured, a shift toward internal technology development began to occur. The initial venue developed inside government research institutes, but it did not take long until almost all applied research and even most basic research relevant to semiconductors moved inside *chaebol* companies themselves.[13] The question of whether such an overtly

---

[12] See the chapter by Linsu Kim in this volume.

[13] Research institutes channeled development funding mainly to next-generation products, especially in the memory field. Approximately $63 million was available in 1996 for the flagship Next Generation Project, with half coming directly from various ministries and the other half from matching grants from private industry. At the center of the enterprise until the precommercial phase of development was complete was the Korean Semiconductor Research Institute.

technonational approach to innovation in such fast-changing sectors could be sustained became urgent in the late 1990s.[14]

Building Capacity in Taiwan

The 1997–98 regional crisis did not injure the Taiwan semiconductor industry in any significant way. It did, however, provide new opportunities and an additional impetus to move forward with a distinctive set of strategic plans. Industry revenues fell 2.9 percent from $10.1 billion in 1997 to $9.8 billion in 1998, but then rose the next year to $14.1 billion, an astonishing increase of 43.5 percent. Throughout the crisis, Taiwan continued to export chips to Europe and the United States, its traditional markets. Its companies were prudently managed, matching low debt loads with highly efficient systems of production, and developing selective equity-based (not debt-based) technology alliances. This resulted in very high levels of retained earnings, once the silicon cycle turned up again in 1999. As a senior executive in one company put it, "During the crisis the Taiwan foundry model proved itself. The Korean IDM model showed its deficiencies."[15]

After the crisis, the consensus view within Taiwanese semiconductor companies was that the foundry marked the most promising road to the future. Foundries achieve scale economies that the developers of new chips can achieve only with massive investments in production. They do so by efficiently filling orders for chips that can be customized in flexible facilities capable of manufacturing related products, even for rival firms. In foundry production, manufacturers do not need to design or control the core technology in order to succeed. Instead, they must be able to protect technologies controlled by others and master the process techniques necessary to achieve world-class levels of quality and efficiency. Although economic value is certainly still harnessed in the early stages of research and product design, the foundry model assumes that considerable value is now being added at crucial later stages in a production process capable of disaggregation.

Strategists within the industry expect the foundries of the future to take the form of associations of affiliated companies. The financial complexity and expense of developing new technologies, and then of commercializing them, militated in this direction. To a considerable extent, the underlying contention was that the latter part of the business had become a commodity-like operation. As one outspoken company vice-president put it, "The Taiwan

---

[14] Relevant in this regard is Dieter Ernst, "What Are the Limits of the Korean Model? The Korean Electronics Industry under Pressure," *BRIE Research Paper*, June 1994; and Chung-in Moon, "In the Shadow of Broken Cheers: The Dynamics of Globalization in South Korea," in Aseem Prakash and Jeffrey A. Hart, eds., *Responding to Globalization* (London: Routledge, 2000), pp. 65–94.

[15] Interview, Taipei, November 8, 1999.

foundry producing even the latest semiconductors simply provides a high-tech service. On the basis of available raw materials and efficient production skills, they operate like McDonald's does."[16]

In the long run, the foundry model may well turn out to have been a means to another end. Early in the twenty-first century, however, it reflected the contemporary phase of a long-term and highly successful national strategy, a strategy that willingly embraced the kind of vulnerability implied by deepening interdependence with non-Taiwanese companies. During the depth of the oil crisis in the 1970s, as noted earlier, a plan emerged within Taiwan's government to diversify the island's economy and quite consciously not to follow neighboring countries in the intensive development of heavy industries. The Industrial Technology Research Institute (ITRI) played a key role in designing practicable strategies for implementing the overall vision. Born in Shanghai, Morris Chang, the director of ITRI and chairman of the TSMC, came to Taiwan after an illustrious career in the electronics industry in North America. Chang pioneered what came to be known as the foundry model in Taiwan and soon became a national hero. Less well understood is how the model actually works.

In the early days, much depended on the foundries being able to achieve capacity utilization rates near 100 percent, as well as on their ability to expand capacity quickly to meet anticipated future demand, even during industry downturns. Even now, when such demand is delayed, foundries appear often to find it necessary to keep fabrication facilities (fabs) in action by ramping up production of basic DRAMs. Globally, this can have the effect of deepening the silicon cycle. At such times, not surprisingly, allegations of dumping are commonly leveled, either directly at the foundries or at local electronic appliance assemblers. In 1997–98, in order to maintain full production in rapidly changing circumstances, design libraries built up in the foundries facilitated rapid adjustment on production lines from DRAMs to logic chips and then back to DRAMs again.[17]

Once the industry began to mature in the 1980s, and strategic responsibility moved decisively from research institutes to company boardrooms, the character of the industry work force came widely to be seen as the ultimate source of competitive advantage in Taiwan's foundries. As one company leader put it, "Our people are more dedicated. This does not mean that they work harder. The Koreans and the Japanese work very hard too. But our workers will sacrifice everything for the company. If there is a problem at 3 A.M. on the line, they will race in to fix it and keep the line moving." Under pressure, "an instinct for survival" constantly reasserts itself.[18] That may be so, but by the mid-1990s it had also become clear that skilled engineers at the top Taiwan

[16] Interview, Taipei, November 9, 1999.
[17] Interview, Taipei, November 15, 1999.
[18] Ibid.

firms could make more money – after annual bonuses, sometimes much more – than they could elsewhere, including the United States.[19] Employee dedication in Taiwan may have traditionally rested on other factors, but there was no reason in recent years to discount the impact of financial incentives.

In truth, much more than employee dedication underpins the foundry model as Taiwan has elaborated it. The aftermath of a severe earthquake in 1999 reminded everyone of the extent of the government's commitment to an industry critically dependent on large and stable supplies of electricity. Immediately after the earthquake cut such supplies to Taiwan's main foundries, the most optimistic outlook was for a two-week period of recovery, and even then all that was expected was a partial resumption of production. In fact, within one week the foundries were producing again at 90 percent of capacity.[20]

Taiwan accounted for 12 to 15 percent of global integrated-circuit production at the turn of the century, a number expected to grow rapidly. But this depended on the successful management of significant new risks. The foundries promised that "fabless," even so-called "chipless" companies could become global players in their own niches. Those companies would, however, have to bet that the foundries could meet their demands for product not just in troughs in the silicon cycle but especially at the peaks.[21] It also meant betting that one could trust the foundries not to share vital technological secrets and not to seek ways to compete more directly with their customers. Such considerations were hardly abstract, for as foundries increased their share of global production and their access to advanced semiconductor designs, they entered into strategic alliances with some of those customers. Could they be expected to treat allies the same as other customers, especially when they had to ration production space when they were at full capacity? Building trust therefore soon came to be seen as crucial; this, in turn, again depended on flexibility and an exceptional degree of efficiency. The test of the latter was the continuous reduction of production costs, which would translate into pricing disincentives for customers to go it alone.

The strategic importance of reliability came to be underlined in the late 1990s in a way that a technonationalist might have found paradoxical. The big Taiwan producers began opening production facilities abroad. Even in North America, it turned out not only that customer concerns about the vulnerability of supply (e.g., from earthquakes) could thereby be assuaged but even that production costs could be lowered. The bigger story in this regard, however, involved strategic investments by Taiwan's semiconductor manufacturers in China, a matter to which we return later.

---

[19] At TSMC, average bonuses in 1999 were widely reported to be around 600 percent of salary.

[20] *Business Week*, October 11, 1999.

[21] See "Foundry Execution Problems," *Pathfinder Focus* 9, no. 12 (2000): 8–9.

As elsewhere, the future of Taiwan's semiconductor industry depends very much on continuous expenditures in research and development, an area in which the country's universities have played only a small part to date. As in Korea, universities have long been valued mainly for their ability to turn out capable engineers, not for their ability to conduct basic or applied silicon research. There is, however, a clear understanding of the future role of universities in grounding basic research and pushing the national innovation system ahead. As noted, in the pioneering days of the industry, the applied impetus came from government research labs. That baton has now clearly been passed to R&D facilities within the leading firms themselves. At the same time, governmental resources are being pumped into related sectors and more broadly to the universities. Hsinchu Science-Based Industrial Park, where the leading fabs are located, was built around the National Tsing Hua University and the National Chiao Tung University. As was the case in Korea, the Taiwanese semiconductor firms valued the universities more because of their future personnel needs than for new ideas. Within those firms, however, there is every expectation that the national universities will increasingly be able to provide high-quality graduates. There will remain room at the top of the strategic and technological ladder for recruits from U.S. universities, but many fewer U.S.-trained engineers and scientists are expected to be needed in the future.

Engineers continue to repatriate to Taiwan in large numbers, mainly from the United States, and often after acquiring several years of experience in top U.S. semiconductor companies. Between 1994 and 1999, approximately 1,963 foreign-trained Taiwanese semiconductor technologists have returned to take jobs in Hsinchu Park.[22] In the previous five years, 1989 to 1993, the number of returnees was 1,139 for a total of 3,102 in ten years. The number of doctoral level employees at the Hsinchu Park, for example, reflects these increases as well as the overall increases of science and engineering graduates from Taiwan's universities. Over the five-year period 1993–98, the number of Ph.D.s in Hsinchu Park, where more than 80 percent of Taiwan's integrated-circuit-related industries are located, increased by more than a factor of four from 244 to 985, while the number of masters-level employees increased from 2,314 to 10,033 for the same period.[23]

The quality of Taiwan's leading science and engineering universities has improved rapidly in recent years, a source of great pride among both government officials and industry executives. Unpublished data from the U.S. National Science Foundation support this view. The number of

---

[22] Hsinchu Science-Based Industrial Park Administration, "Personnel Data," "November 1999. For an analysis of links to Silicon Valley, see Annalee Sayenian and Jinn-Yu Hsu, "The Silicon Valley–Hsinchu Connection: Technical Communities and Industrial Upgrading," *Industrial and Corporate Change*, forthcoming.

[23] For further information on Hsinchu Park, see <http://www.sipa.gov.tw/seconde/hsip/hsi11000_08.htm>.

semiconductor-related Ph.Ds. awarded to Taiwanese nationals by U.S. universities fell steadily from a high of 296 in 1995 to 173 in 1998, a drop of 42 percent.[24] There was a time-honored tradition of Taiwanese engineers studying in the United States or working for U.S. companies for a few years, and then returning home. The U.S. university system is still seen as both unique and accessible for top-level researchers. It is no longer the case, however, that access translates into desire. As one executive put it, "Electrical engineers trained in Taiwan are more capable than those trained in the United States; in any case, they are good enough."[25]

By the late 1990s Taiwan's leading semiconductor companies believed that they could either develop all the technology they needed internally, through licensing agreements, or through alliances. Opportunities along the latter line, as it happened, began to present themselves ever more frequently, especially as Japanese firms sought to counteract the effects of deepening economic turmoil in their home markets. Such alliances deserve a central place in any analysis of how Taiwan's foundries bolster the sense of trust on which they depend and the incentives to keep their production costs ultra-competitive. The evident preference is to build new production sites, both in Taiwan and internationally, through the use of shared equity arrange-ments and guaranteed purchase contracts, both of which keep recurring debt obligations as low as possible.

The strategic alliances between Taiwanese foundries and Japanese IDMs seem particularly important for the future. Fujitsu, Toshiba, Oki, NKK, Sanyo, Matsushita, and Mitsubishi Electric have all teamed up with a Taiwanese manufacturer.[26] Such alliances sometimes provide supplemen-tary equity resources to help build the next generation of fabs, but, more important, they reduce the financial risk associated with their construction by providing guaranteed chip-purchase contracts. Asked to reflect on the possibility that Japanese partners would be very careful to retain control even over the kinds of process technologies that could prove important for the future of the foundries, one Taiwanese executive simply asserted, "If the Japanese cannot beat you, they will share with you before they give up."[27]

In Taiwan, an ambitious national strategy is clearly still evolving in semi-conductors and semiconductor-related industries, a strategy that envisages a disaggregated but synergistic industrial infrastructure underpinning firms themselves integrated into globally disaggregated industries. According to an April 1999 study, more than 200 integrated circuit companies are now

---

[24] NSF, Sciences Resources Studies Division, *Survey of Earned Doctorates,* special tabulation, R. Lehming, January 29, 2000.

[25] Interview, Taipei, November 15, 1999. The Chinese phrase for "good enough" can also be translated as "just right," which is widely taken to imply an emphasis on profitability in the here and now, not on the expensive frontiers of semiconductor research.

[26] *Agence France Presse,* June 28, 1999.

[27] Interview, Taipei, November 15, 1999.

in operation, software development capabilities are expanding rapidly, and ambitious planning is underway for critically important backward as well as forward linkages in key foreign markets. Companies are proliferating in the cognate chip-making fields of design, mask, fabrication, packaging, testing substrate, leadframe, wafer, and chemicals. This industrial infrastructure is being fostered by government and industry jointly in information technology parks, especially at Hsinchu and Tainan. Both private investors and the national government have recently also focused efforts on stimulating chip design as an industry of the future.[28] Relatedly, government and industry are targeting the software industry.[29]

In some sense, the leading foundries are in this regard themselves considered infrastructural. The belief that the semiconductor manufacturing business is now a mature one is widely shared. Big investments continue to be made to keep the core of the business in Taiwan. In October 2001, for example, TSMC announced plans for $20 billion in new investment in Tainan and Hsinchu for six new fabs. Simultaneously, its chairman stressed the company's commitment to build new production facilities in China.[30] Even if Morris Chang had not still occupied that position, such a commitment seems necessarily to imply the endurance of an overarching national strategy. In light of the expanding and flexible framework of the semiconductor foundries, other industries may be expected to arise.

Of the three hypothetical levels of intellectual property in this sector – chip architecture and design, intermediate-stage building blocks, and standard cells – Taiwan today can boast world-class expertise only in the latter. The

---

[28] In the long run, the deepening of indigenous design capability could pose profound challenges for the contemporary foundry model. Keeping customer designs proprietary is difficult at the best of times. The customer must be assured that innovations are not leaked to competitors whose chips may even be produced on the same line in the same foundry. Even more important, they must have complete confidence that the foundries themselves will not copy their designs. All of this was relatively easy to accomplish when there existed a relatively low design capability in the Taiwanese semiconductor industry as a whole. But as one senior executive of a Taiwanese DRAM producer, himself recently returned to Taiwan after a long career in Silicon Valley, forecast: "Today most intellectual property in the Taiwan industry is coming from the Valley. In five years, it will come from here." Interview, Taipei, November 15, 1999.

[29] One major project is the "government assisted, privately funded" Nankang Software Park. The 4.1 hectare Phase I, twelve kilometers east of Taipei city center, opened in the summer of 1999. In January 2000 twenty-seven companies were based in the park, with a total of 1,800 employees. C.N. Liu, "Software Development in Asian Pacific Region: The Case of the Nankang Software Park Project," unpublished manuscript. Data provided by park officials, Taipei January 2000. For further information, see <http://softwarepark.centurydev.com.tw>.

[30] In making the announcement, Morris Chang stated: "As long as corporate enterprise and the government continue to work together, Taiwan will maintain its competitive edge.... TSMC is determined to construct fabs in China and other major markets around the world. Taiwan, where TSMC was founded, will remain a vital base for TSMC's future investments." *Taipei Times*, October 26, 2001.

belief that the expertise thereby developed will simply remain at that level, however, is becoming implausible. The big Taiwan foundries are already capable of producing central processing units (not yet highest end) and are constantly improving first-class design libraries and library tools. The foundries are gearing up for the next-generation "system-on-a-chip" era by producing to world standard most of the separate component parts; they are also building in the production compatibility necessary to "put all of the pieces together" quickly. Internal R&D horizons are now being pushed out to ten years by the leading firms. It is true that the production of semiconductor equipment machinery is not in sight within Taiwan itself, but the capital required to acquire it is ready at hand. The present version of Taiwan's foundry model, therefore, is unlikely to be the last. One company executive told us that "there are very few really good ideas that have originated in Taiwan," but this is quickly becoming a minority view. A more accurate assessment might be that once a good idea surfaces, wherever it originates, it can now be quickly taken up and developed in Taiwan or within networks shaped by regional and global industrial alliances. In the near-term future, however, it is likely that "good ideas" will begin to emerge in Taiwan. In this regard, for example, industry sources estimate the number of indigenous design houses to have increased from 75 in 1995 to more than 150 in 2000.[31]

In Korea, we encountered a significant degree of skepticism concerning Taiwan's foundry model and its future implications. Korean competitors view the model as effective only in good economic times, and necessary only if a firm is starting from scratch with no owned technology.[32] In the long run, licensing designs is viewed as a recipe for profit dilution and technological dependency. The possibility that foundries can ever develop a serious R&D capability is therefore routinely discounted. The model is seen to preclude locally controlled leaps to the next level of technology.

In Taiwan, such skeptical observations are not vehemently rejected. Although very large bets are being placed on the proposition that the skeptics are wrong, the managerial spin is very subtle. Prudence and conservative financial management are everywhere in evidence. Pragmatism seems to have the upper hand, and for this reason perhaps the foundry model appears more and more a strategic hybrid. Whatever may turn out to be the ultimate vulnerabilities of the foundry model, it looked at the turn of the twenty-first century to be succeeding.

Crisis and Adaptation in South Korea

The 1997–98 financial crisis passed through the South Korean semiconductor industry with amazing swiftness. Although the pain it inflicted left a

---

[31] Interview, Taipei, November 15, 2001.
[32] Interviews, Taipei, November 8, 1999.

legacy of general economic problems, the semiconductor industry itself adjusted far more quickly than many observers had expected. This occurred in sharp contrast to the automobile industry, discussed in Chapter 5 of this volume. Indeed, the bulk of the adjustment in semiconductors seemed primarily occasioned by the periodically recurring global drop in chip prices, the so-called silicon cycle. This time its downturn coincided with (and deepened) an unusual and truly national liquidity crisis. After one major organizational shift within the industry, however, old patterns of control reasserted themselves. Talk of major *chaebol* reform, at least in this sector, proved empty as revenues turned sharply upward in 1999. A new downturn commencing two years later revived reform efforts, but a decisive break from past practices still looked like a remote possibility.

Whatever its source, the 1997–98 crisis was the proximate cause for the forced takeover of LG Semicon by Hyundai Electronics. At the end of a painful process of negotiation, President Kim Dae Jung summoned both company CEOs to his office and explicitly demanded a merger. The widespread view was that Hyundai "won" in the semiconductor sector, but that the Lucky Goldstar *chaebol* would be granted some concession in another area. The combined Hyundai-LG (renamed Hynix Semiconductor Inc. in March 2001) had strengths, based on production economies of scale as well as complementary research expertise and technology assets, but it also had significant financial weakness caused by excessive debts. It was now the world's largest DRAM maker, although Samsung Electronics retained its edge as the innovator and financial leader in the sector. Samsung saw Hynix as a formidable competitor once the two corporate cultures had coalesced and if the merged entity's financial problems were successfully addressed. The latter task was to prove more difficult than expected in 1998 and intensive discussions were soon to commence on various mechanisms to relieve Hynix's financial pressures, including foreign alliances. Both firms, nevertheless, continued to pursue similar global strategies as IDMs.

One significant change involving the industry as a new decade opened was in the educational profile of its top-level staff. In particular, the flow of South Korean engineering and technology graduate students to the United States slowed appreciably. Indeed, there was a significant fall in the number of Korean nationals receiving semiconductor-related Ph.D.s from U.S. universities, from a high of 185 in 1994 to 116 in 1998, a drop of 37 percent.[33] Beyond a generational shift in student interests toward careers in such fields as software development and finance, there were two practical reasons for this change. First, Korean employers now perceived that the educational

---

[33] NSF, Sciences Resources Studies Division, *Survey of Earned Doctorates*. As used in this report, the term "semiconductor-related" includes the following fields: electrical, electronics, communications and computer engineering; computer science; information science and systems; systems engineering; and operations research.

opportunities in Korea at places like Seoul National University (SNU) and the Korean Advanced Institute of Science and Technology (KAIST) were quickly approaching – if not yet equal to – U.S. analogs. The second and less important reason was that within certain limits set by the Korean government, some engineering students who stayed in Korea for their Ph.D. training could be exempted from military conscription.[34] The question of whether quality could be maintained in high-level research remained an open one; the same sort of concern worried close industry observers in the wake of the 1997–98 crisis, when layoffs and perceptions of instability appeared to discourage first-rate engineering students from planning careers in the industry.[35]

These developments were important because applied research was increasingly undertaken within Korean semiconductor firms themselves, and commensurate programs had not developed in Korean universities. Those universities made enormous strides in the 1990s in educating greater numbers of electrical engineers and improving the quality of training, but they had never been known for fostering innovation at the leading edge. In general, companies invested in local universities to gain access to their graduates, not to obtain research that might be useful in their businesses. There were a few exceptions, but those were concentrated mainly on training student-engineers in computer-assisted design (CAD).[36]

In the wake of the financial crisis, the Korean government initiated an effort to reshape university-level research in important respects. The goal was to place 10 Korean universities among the top 100 research universities worldwide, a goal that the semiconductor firms supported, mainly because of their recruiting needs, but also because they were interested in selected fundamental research projects. In June 1999 the government began moving its official funding for electronics research from government research institutes to the universities. It also created high-level research councils in the Office of the Prime Minister, ultimately responsible to the president of Korea. Based on a combination of British and German models, the Korean Research Councils for Fundamental Science & Technology, Industrial Science & Technology, and Public Science & Technology would in principle stand at arm's length both from government ministries and from universities. Their combined annual budgets were initially set at $300 million per year, of which 30–40 percent came directly from the budget ministry. The balance came from research grants that continued to be channeled through the industry and planning ministries. Over time, their architects hoped that the councils would set

---

[34] A total of 800 exemptions were granted in 1999.

[35] Interviews, Seoul, November 9 and 10, 1999.

[36] For example, the Integrated Circuit Design Education Center at KAIST was funded at the level of $3–6 million a year, while the Inter-University Semiconductor Research Center at SNU receives about $25 million per year. For further information, see <http://idec.kaist.ac.kr>, and <http://chips.snu.ac.kr>.

new priorities for public research in Korea, some of which might ultimately affect the fortunes of such sectors as semiconductors.[37]

Meanwhile, the two big Korean semiconductor companies, Hynix and Samsung, moved as aggressively as possible to expand their internal research capabilities and to wring new efficiencies out of older production facilities. Given the now duopolistic domestic environment, moreover, each company was more reluctant than ever to cooperate with the other, even in precompetitive research.[38] Because each believed that it had superior research and technology, mainly of an applied nature, this came as no surprise. Both companies were, however, pursuing plans to acquire Silicon Valley design houses, to hire experienced researchers in selected fields from U.S. companies, and to sustain relationships with professors at major research universities in the United States. (At one company, we directly encountered U.S. professors intensively engaged in product development on a consulting basis.)

With the rise of profitability at Samsung after 1999, key decision-making power that had flowed during the crisis to financial strategists started flowing back to engineer-managers. The company had a long-standing reputation, relative to its Korean peers, for financial prudence. Indeed, because of its comparatively low gearing ratios, it stayed profitable even during the financial crisis. At the same time, the firm managed to shed some $10 billion in consolidated debts between 1997 and 1999.[39] Burdened by a higher degree of leverage, Hynix faced greater pressure once the crisis passed; the upswing in the silicon cycle in 1999 was not sufficient to cure its financial disability.

In 1997–98 the downturn in the silicon cycle, compounded by the financial crisis, did shock Korean chip makers into reconsidering their traditional lack of product diversity, and their reluctance to develop strategic alliances with foreign firms. In 1999 both Samsung and Hynix began positioning themselves for aggressive development of nonmemory products, particularly for end products that involve system-on-a-chip (SOC) technologies. Samsung announced its intent to develop new products in home, mobile, and personal multimedia devices to complement current strengths in semiconductors and liquid-crystal displays.[40] Hynix followed a similar path, even

---

[37] Interviews with three council chairs, Seoul, November 11, 1999. Council boards are comprised of five ministry officials, five industry representatives, five representatives from government research institutes, and five academics.

[38] Hynix executives estimate that only 5–10 percent of their overall R&D budget is invested in projects at the precompetitive stage. Interview, Seoul, November 8, 1999. It is worth noting here that Hyundai held R&D fairly constant during the 1997–99 period at about 10 percent of sales, while Samsung spent about 6–8 percent of its annual sales receipts on R&D. Most of this focused on DRAMs, but in 1999 more attention began to be paid to SRAM, flash memories, and system-on-a-chip (SOC) technologies.

[39] *Business Week*, International Edition, December 20, 1999.

[40] *Korea Herald*, December 21, 1999; *Asiaweek*, November 12, 1999.

though its financial constraints increased after 2000.[41] Nevertheless, both companies remained heavily dependent on – and strategically committed to – DRAMs; in 2000 they still constituted 90 percent of Hynix's production and 85 percent of Samsung's.[42] Samsung, in particular, had acquired a great deal of intellectual property, but it had not yet achieved significant competence in design engineering, especially top-level engineering for the construction of new chip architectures. Still missing, moreover, was a fully thought-out national plan to build the kind of broadly based system of innovation symbolized by Silicon Valley or its analogs around the world, a plan within which the firms would surely fit.[43]

Although their own internal commitments to applied research promise new kinds of products in the future, the big firms appear to believe that Moore's Law – the famous rule of thumb in the industry about the logic density of silicon integrated circuits doubling roughly every year – is becoming obsolete. They seemed to be coming to the view that putting massive resources into forcing the geometry of the chip, as they and others have long done, may no longer be the best way to proceed. As one company executive put it, "After you get to 150 nanometers, it is very difficult to see how to make end products economically feasible. It might make more sense, therefore, to manufacture more products at 180 nanometers and more aggressively to seek economies elsewhere in the process of final product development and marketing."[44] Indeed, we encountered evidence of companies finding lucrative new markets in

---

[41] Hynix's debt load remained unsustainable, and when a new downturn came in global chip markets, the company's troubles deepened. In October 2001, creditors of Hynix agreed to freeze repayments of the company's debt while they put together a rescue package including about 1 trillion won in new funding. *Korea Herald*, October 19, 2001. Soon thereafter, highly contentions talks began on a potential strategic alliance with U.S. rival, Micron Technology. *Korea Herald*, December 4, 2001, March 15, 2002.

[42] Interviews, Seoul, November 9 and 10, 1999; and *Korea Herald,* December 6, 1999. Samsung announced in November 1999 its intention to increase investment in its nonmemory operations with the intent to expand annual sales by 40 percent by 2001. Hynix also planned to double its annual sales in nonmemory, with the long-term goal of reducing DRAMs to 65 to 70 percent of total chip production. Samsung's share of the global DRAM market rose to 16.8 percent in 1999, while Hynix's rose to 23.5 percent.

[43] Interviews, Seoul, November 8, 1999. The government's flagship program in this sector was the "2010 Project," which is aimed at building an integrated SOC. The project is located at the Inter-University Semiconductor Research Center at Seoul National University. From 1998 through 2003, it was to receive approximately $25 million per year with 40 percent coming from the government and 60 percent from industry.

[44] This was the consensus view in Taiwan as well, where one senior executive predicted that Moore's Law would be irrelevant in five years. Interview, Taipei, November 15, 1999. In March 2002, nevertheless, TSMC announced that it would be able to produce in Taiwan at the 90-nanometer level by year-end. Older technology could then, presumably, be moved to China. *Commercial Times* (Taipei), March 26, 2002; *Financial Times* (London), December 18, 2001. On the very real prospect of chip size shrinking even more dramatically, and the pace of innovation actually accelerating, see *New York Times,* February 4, 2002, p. B-1.

multimedia and optical sensing devices using "obsolete" 350-nanometer technology. The risk that truly revolutionary and rapidly commercializable new innovations in integrated circuitry would come along within the next decade or so was apparently being heavily discounted. At the dawn of the millennium, key strategists in the Korean industry saw themselves as operating within a rapidly maturing industry, where conventional strategies to catch up with and surpass foreign rivals would continue to suffice.

It would be unwise, however, to forget the capacity of Korea and its strategic industries to surprise. A lowering of expectations certainly occurred internally over the course of the crisis years. With a degree of exaggeration, perhaps, those reduced expectations were transmitted externally, and planners within Hynix and Samsung had an interest in keeping those expectations low. It remained likely, nevertheless, that any future surprises would not come in terms of raw technological breakthroughs. Rather, on the basis of improved sales and production efficiencies, they seemed more likely to come in the form of dramatic drops in costs and, in turn, in accelerated pricing cycles. Exploiting crises, lowering expectations, refocusing work forces, catching up with leading technologies, and outcompeting rivals when underlying technologies become stable are not new in Korean history.[45] In the electronics sector, the most important external rivals have usually been Japanese. In the face of a new crisis in 2001, therefore, few industry observers registered surprise when just such a pattern led the four biggest Japanese chipmakers to file their first antidumping complaint against Hynix and Samsung. The complaint alleged a deliberate attempt by the Koreans to put them out of the DRAM business by selling chips at half the cost of production.[46] Not too long ago, those same Japanese firms found themselves on the other side of similar complaints in the United States. Like the owl of Minerva, technonationalism may be most obvious at dusk.

Conclusion: Continuity and Change

We asked at the start of this chapter whether the past few years in Korea and Taiwan were characterized by continuity or change in the core financial

---

[45] On this theme, see Linsu Kim, "The Dynamics of Technological Learning in Semiconductors," *California Management Review* 39, no. 3 (Spring 1997): 86–100. In this regard, Japanese firms have long been both role models and targets. When asked to name his company's leading competitor, a senior Samsung official answered, without hesitation, NEC. Interview, Seoul, November 8, 1999.

[46] *Nihon Keizai Shimbun*, October 24, 2001. At this point, competitors perceived the Koreans to be flooding world markets as the Korean government struggled to prop up Hynix and as Samsung seized the moment concurrently to ratchet up to the next level its core chip production technology. (Samsung became the first company in the world to use 300-nanometer wafer [12-inch] technology, which promised new scale economies; see *Korea Herald*, October 30, 2001.)

and industrial structures underpinning the historic success of their high-technology industries. To the extent that semiconductors are representative, the answer clearly has to be both. The fortunes of the semiconductor industry have changed quite dramatically over time. The regional financial crisis of the late 1990s had relatively more severe effects in the overleveraged Korean industry. It changed the strategic context too for the Taiwanese industry, whose underlying corporate structures and strategies provided remarkably successful buffers from the most negative effects of the crisis. But the effects of the crisis were very difficult to separate from the larger effects of changes in global markets for semiconductor-related products, marked as they were by an upturn in the silicon cycle in 1999 and a downturn two years later.

In both cases, notable changes also occurred in the mechanisms through which next-generation processes and products are created. In short, in this sector the center of gravity in each national innovation system has shifted decisively from government to the private sector. Accordingly, heightened sensitivity to developments in global and regional markets is now evident in both the Korean and Taiwanese semiconductor industries. It would be misleading, however, not to emphasize the points of continuity between their unique histories and their present circumstances. These operate mainly at the level of ideology and deep structure. A simple evocation of the word "tech-nonationalist" does not do them justice. In both cases, there clearly remains an overriding strategic intent that can be understood only in national terms. Even under the rubric of "globalization," a word constantly used by senior executives and government officials in both countries, the objective is to defend and build upon the remarkable successes already achieved – for the nation – in the semiconductor and semiconductor-related industries.

Continuity is also evident in the quite strikingly diverse strategies designed and implemented in the two cases to maintain and expand global market positions in this sector. As in the past, the Korean strategy at the government level is to encourage, even force, consolidation and economies of scale with a commodity-type view of the industry's future. The developmental state continues to exist, but it is adapting to a changing national and international environment. Ministries and bureaucratic mind-sets have not disappeared, but a new generation of *chaebol* managers, a new class of young business innovators, and even independent-minded university professors are emerging as leaders of the next phase of Korea's industrial development. The prospects for their future success, however, continue to depend on their access to the levers of state power as Koreans have uniquely constructed and reconstructed them during the past few decades.

At the industry level, the consistent effort is to continue playing a low-cost-producer game, to encourage price-driven dependencies on the part of global customers, and to hope that underlying technologies in this sector are truly becoming stabilized. The risks of the strategy are encapsulated therein. Major near-to-medium term breakthroughs – such as leaps in chip miniaturization at the electron level or through biological processes – would threaten the very existence of the Korean industry, an industry that remains financially fragile in comparative terms. As in the past, no great leap forward in basic research within Korea itself seems imminent. In this sense, Korea's high-risk technonational strategy in this sector tracks the model classically associated with Japan.

In the Taiwan case, the continuity in industrial strategy is also striking, although its flexibility can make it seem that the true trajectory represents a discrete break from past patterns. The stimulation of basic research, the search for new competitive national advantages and fostering conditions, and the hopes for profitability in the promising sectors of the future remain the missions of government. Semiconductors are now seen as successfully "launched." Future organizational and product innovation in the sector is now commonly viewed as industry-led.

At the high end of the Taiwanese industry are the foundries, now embarked on an ambitious, potentially farsighted strategy pinned on alliances with leading electronics firms based in other countries. Key alliances have long existed, for example, with Philips and Siemens. Others exist with large U.S. companies like Motorola but, more important, with smaller chipless and fabless firms based in places like Research Triangle Park and Silicon Valley. Significant and sizable alliances are also now emerging between the Taiwan foundries and Japanese IDMs. Bold new investments by the foundries in Taiwan and in China would also seem to constitute a harbinger. Such alliances and investments typify a relatively more open model keyed on global market competitiveness that is well labeled "technohybrid."

Like the foundry strategy itself, the model may plausibly be interpreted as a means to an end, and not necessarily the end itself. What is that end? It has not yet been clearly elaborated, and there is no obvious master plan. But only one conclusion puts all of the disparate pieces of the current strategic and tactical puzzle together. The success of this key industry ties directly into the changing place of Taiwan in a region whose future will likely be profoundly reshaped, on the one hand, by the manner in which China inserts itself into world markets and, on the other hand, by the reshaping of Japanese industry in regional and global contexts. The foundry model has accommodated important vulnerabilities. Its success might therefore continue to be benchmarked against Taiwan's traditional objective of maximizing its degree of autonomy in a challenging regional environment and of enhancing its future room for maneuver.

7

China in Search of a Workable Model

Technology Development in the New Millennium

Barry Naughton and Adam Segal

Like other East Asian countries, China has been undergoing a process of liberalization and of opening to the world economy. During the past twenty years, economic reforms have slowly moved the country as a whole toward a more open, more market-oriented economy, and science and technology (S&T) policies and institutions have been reformed in a similar spirit. Policy makers gradually dismantled a highly centralized and hierarchical model of technological innovation and began replacing it with a more flexible and "bottom-up" system. Leaders at all levels have moved away from a research and development system dominated by central planning and state-owned enterprises to one that increasingly relies on individual innovation and entrepreneurship, while foreign direct investment (FDI) and multinational corporations both play larger roles in Chinese development plans. The openness to a diversity of actors crucially includes both outside actors – multinational corporations (MNCs) – and domestic non-state-owned corporations. China's entry into the World Trade Organization (WTO) promises to consolidate these trends.

At first glance then, China seems to be part of a larger project of the recasting of technology policy within the region. But ironically, in recent years, China's policy has also evolved in ways that bring it closer to technonationalism, at least in some senses of the word. Although the Chinese government's hand in technology development is now deployed in a lighter and, on balance, more sophisticated manner than in the past, its motivation is perhaps more explicitly nationalistic than it has been. In part, this is simply because nationalism, in its diverse manifestations, is today a more prominent and important force in China than in the recent past. Many in China today have a strong sense that China is resuming its "rightful" place in the world. Because of China's population, rapid economic growth, and tradition of cultural creativity, it is seen as destined to play a prominent role in the global economy. Moreover, now that socialism (and, a fortiori, communism) has lost most of its ideological and idealistic force in China, nationalism serves as an alternative to justify a continuing role for the government and the Chinese Communist Party (CCP) in economic and technology policy.

Economic reform has created a larger role for private businesses in the national economy, and nationalism now provides an underpinning for a government effort to articulate a new government-business partnership. Thus, in 1999 Jiang Zemin initiated the so-called "Three Representative" campaign, which declared the CCP the representative of the "most advanced" sectors of the economy and of the interests of the nation as a whole. This campaign seeks to delink the party from workers in state-owned enterprises (and the proletariat in general). Moreover, "advanced" economic sectors have increasingly been interpreted to include private entrepreneurs and nonstate firms. The language of technology policy justifies regime action. But it also, unwittingly, expresses the constraints under which the regime operates; the CCP cannot hope to stay in power unless it is seen to be creating a strong and modern China.

"Technonationalist" states – such as Japan and Korea through the 1990s – were willing to bear economic costs in order to maintain a high degree of technological and economic independence. Technonationalist policies in these countries were designed to create independent domestic capabilities in core or critical technologies, to support the establishment of domestic institutions that encouraged the diffusion of these technological capabilities across sectors, and to assist producers and users of these technologies.[1] The central point of this chapter is that policy makers in China are indeed forsaking some of the policy tools and institutions traditionally associated with technonationalism, especially its state-run variant; but China is not abandoning the project's larger goal of deepening domestic technological capabilities. If, as Chapter 1 of this volume suggests, we conceptualize technonationalism as an ideological orientation toward self-sustained autonomy and independence from other states, rather than a specific set of policies, China remains strongly technonationalist.[2]

Central planning may be scaled back and the level of support for state-owned enterprises curtailed, but fundamental strategic concerns remain. Chinese leaders continue to worry about autonomy and technological dependence on other countries, especially the United States. These worries express themselves in Chinese policies toward nonstate enterprises and MNCs, although the specific policy instruments may change. Indeed, Chinese planners act as if the old, coherent package of the Japanese-style technonationalist

---

[1] Richard Samuels, *"Rich Nation, Strong Army": National Security and Technological Transformation in Japan* (Ithaca: Cornell University Press, 1994).

[2] All economic nationalisms specify a direction for foreign economic policy away from an "other" and lead governments to interpret their economic dependence on some states as a security threat. See Rawi Abdelal, *Economic Nationalism after Empire: A Comparative Perspective on Nation, Economy, and Security in Post-Soviet Eurasia* (Ithaca: Cornell University Press, 2001).

policies are simply no longer viable or efficacious, and that they therefore have little choice but to select a few weakly related policies that promise some return in particular instances. If the current policies fail, other policies presumably wait in the wings; the overall pattern of technology development during the reform period has been one of restless change. Luckily for China, the size and diversity of the country might indeed make this a viable improvised strategy.

At least three reasons suggest that the dynamics for change in China's technology policy reflect uniquely Chinese factors and uniquely Chinese concerns. First, and most simply, China is bigger and more diverse than the other countries under study. As such, it has the option of maintaining two or more separate, competing, and not necessarily integrated approaches toward technology acquisition. The results are a national mosaic that varies both temporally and geographically. Policies first promoted at the local level may eventually be elevated to central policy. Localities may run competing technology development programs, or try to exploit opportunities implicit in national policies in ways that are not necessarily consistent with the spirit of national policy. The southern province of Guangdong is considerably more advanced than other Chinese regions in developing a technology policy based on human resource development and interfirm technology cooperation. Other regions may rely more on government-sponsored research and extension efforts.

With diverse outcomes in different localities, central policy makers can choose among existing policy experiments. Faced with challenges in different policy arenas and with the need to balance the interest of various state and nonstate actors, decision makers can look to regional outcomes to judge the ultimate feasibility of different policy packages. Regional decentralization thus aids policy innovation. The success of one province emboldens others, at both the regional and central level, to adopt the same or similar policies.

Within this general pattern of diversity and flexibility, there remains – precisely because of China's size – a hard core of continued central government sponsorship of R&D (largely for military purposes) and a strong central government role in setting the parameters of technology policy. It is not that decentralization and regionalization drives the entire system; rather, a degree of decentralization in interaction with a continued central government role creates one of the most crucial dynamics of the system.

Second, China is still in the process of reforming its economy, in particular the industrial management system, and the old science and technology system. The agreement with the United States on the terms of China's entry into the World Trade Organization provides a powerful impetus to further reforms and helps reshape the domestic economy. The Asian financial crisis had important effects on China's economy, and brought substantial costs, but the impact has been less than that of the successive phases of domestic reform. Whatever new system of innovation ultimately emerges in China, the scope and scale of that process will be significantly shaped by the trajectory of changes in the broader economic system.

Finally, and perhaps most important, China's technology acquisition policies interact with military and strategic issues in ways different from the other Asian economies. Because of its size and history, Chinese leaders act on the understanding that China will assume great power status some time in the near future. Larger than all the other East Asian countries put together by population (China is 65 percent of East Asian population), China's economic capabilities are still modest, accounting for only 10 percent of East Asian GDP.[3] Military capabilities lag still further behind, and relations with the United States, Japan, and Taiwan have recently soured over a range of political and technological issues. China is clearly *more* concerned with national defense and defense-related technological development today than a few years ago. In all states, certain sensitive areas or projects are simply circumscribed and kept out of the general liberalization stream. In China, because great-power pretensions are more significant, and strategic interactions (the "security dilemma") more immediate, these sensitive areas are likely to remain proportionately more important than in most other East Asian states. Areas directly related to security still remain tightly connected to central budgets, planning, and policy. More broadly, globalization combined with the perceived overwhelming predominance of the United States is seen to create important threats to national sovereignty. In response, a discussion on the nature of "economic security" has been prominent in Chinese media over the last several years.[4] These concerns temper and modify the general trend toward greater openness.

In addition, there has been an increasing willingness of the center to attach the language of technonationalism to policies that might also be consistent with technoglobalism. The central government has moved to diversify technology policies and relax controls over many areas of the economy. With the failures of more traditionally interventionist policies, and the success of relatively laissez-faire technological approaches such as that of the United States, central leaders are looking for new ways to enhance the nation's technological autonomy. This has meant the embrace of actors that before were ideologically suspect. What matters now for a national champion is not that it is state-, collective-, or privately owned, but that it is Chinese.

The existence of these strategic issues and of a core of state-led R&D activities along with the promotion of relatively laissez-faire technological approaches suggests that at times the language of technology policy may be

---

[3] Measured at exchange rates. Purchasing power parity calculations would promote China to a 36 percent share of East Asian GDP, about the same as Japan. Purchasing power parity calculations based on World Bank, *World Development Report 1996* (New York: Oxford University Press, 1996), pp. 188–89.

[4] For an example, see Ning Fang, Xiaodong Wang, and Qiang Song, *Quanqiuhua Yinyingxia de Zhongguo zhi Lu* (China's path under the influence of globalization) (Beijing: Zhongguo Shehui Kexue, 1999).

different from the logic of policies on the ground. But the two are not completely decoupled. The desire to be a modern, powerful country is deeply rooted, and the mastery of technology is a key symbol of success. No matter how closely Chinese technology policy comes to resemble that of its neighbors, it continues to reveal a historically rooted concern with technological autonomy. Chinese technonationalism remains regionally distinct because the Chinese are so clearly concerned about dependence on the United States.

The rest of this chapter illustrates these tensions with a discussion of contemporary Chinese technology policy, including several case study examples. We begin with an overview of Chinese technology policy from the start of the reforms until now. We describe technology policy in terms of three successive decades – a long 1980s (actually 1978 through 1991), a core 1990s period, and the millennial policies that emerged after the Asian crisis, clearly taking shape in 1999. This overview not only traces the most important secular trend – the evolution of a more market-friendly approach – but also shows that each shift in technology policy has been a reaction to the preceding phase, and reflects some dissatisfaction with what was achieved in an earlier phase. This perspective prepares us for contemporary technology policy, which, since about the time of the Asian financial crisis, has shifted to a distinctly stronger emphasis on small firms and on technological creativity, while simultaneously articulating a more clearly nationalistic rationale for the policy. It is not inconsequential that this shift occurred around the time of the Asian crisis, but, as we shall see, the change grows primarily out of domestic imperatives and the retrospective evaluation of technology policy over the previous two decades. In the following section, we examine some of the ways in which China's strategic pretensions affect its technology policy, and then conclude with an attempt to assess the complex crosscurrents in contemporary Chinese technology policy.

Reform through the Early 1990s

The reform process, begun in 1979, was a huge break from the past, but initially it also revealed the government's unquestioned assumption that it must continue to control the overall process of technology development. Marketization occurred rapidly, transforming the economy, but marketization was most rapid precisely in the most "low tech" parts of the economy: rural enterprises, agriculture, and petty commerce. High technology seemed to the majority of planners to fall into the area that most needed direct government involvement, and so the government's presence remained fairly strong in the higher-technology parts of the economy. Policy makers consistently stressed the need for two simultaneous processes: the absorption of advanced technologies from abroad and the development of the domestic capacity to absorb and digest technology, whatever its origins. The balance between the two – which we label technology import and technology development, respectively – has changed over time, but the two are intimately connected. Over time, policies focused on technology transfer from abroad have led to much greater roles for MNCs and foreign investment, whereas policies focused on developing an indigenous capability have gradually broadened from an exclusive focus on public research institutes and state-owned enterprises to one that embraces individual entrepreneurs and private (or semiprivate) firms. Neither of these processes, however, has been linear.

From the very beginning of the reform process, the need to accelerate the pace of technology import was put forward as a key argument for reform. In March 1978 – even before the triumph of the reformers in December of that year – Deng Xiaoping argued that "Profound changes have taken place and new leaps have been made in almost all areas. A whole range of new sciences and technologies is continuously emerging. . . . We have lost a lot of time as a result of the sabotage by Lin Biao and the Gang of Four. . . . Backwardness must be recognized before it can be changed."[5] Initially, lacking a coherent central government approach to technology, some control over technology import was decentralized to localities and parceled out to central government ministries. Localities generally were given authority to import technology under a certain financial ceiling. Feeling a sense of urgency to get into fast-developing new sectors, and acutely aware of their own limited ability to analyze and absorb technologies, local governments generally opted to import technology-embodying machinery and production lines. The result was a rush of machinery import – the central government gave away whatever bargaining power it might have had vis-à-vis foreign machinery suppliers.

As the 1980s proceeded, the central government reasserted its own important role in the technology import process. Seeking to shift the emphasis of technology import from new plant construction to the renovation of existing medium and large-sized state-owned enterprises, the government established an important role in brokering technology import projects. The State Economic Commission, which had responsibility for enterprise renovation, coordinated an approval process for 3,000 renovation projects, including 1,550 for machinery, 296 for conversion of defense industries, and 1,200 for light and textile industries, primarily with Japanese firms.[6]

Foreign investment also began to be encouraged but was still very much limited to various enclaves defined by the Chinese government. Local officials

---

[5] Deng Xiaoping, *Selected Works, 1975–1982* (Beijing: Foreign Language Press, 1984), pp. 103, 106. See also Barry Naughton, *Growing Out of the Plan: Chinese Economic Reform, 1978–1993* (Cambridge: Cambridge University Press, 1995), pp. 62–74.

[6] Jingping Ding, "Using Imported Technology to Transform Existing Enterprises in China," and Xiaojuan Jiang, "Chinese Government Policy towards Science and Technology and Its Influence on the Technical Development of Industrial Enterprises," both in Charles Feinstein and Christopher Howe, eds., *Chinese Technology Transfer in the 1990s: Current Experience, Historical Problems and International Perspectives* (Cheltenham: Edward Elgar, 1997), pp. 109–111, 142.

could approve individual cases of foreign investment (again under a given value ceiling), but foreign investors were generally denied access to the domestic market, were required to export, and had to balance their own foreign exchange needs. When access to the domestic market was granted, it generally followed an individual case-by-case determination by the relevant Chinese authorities that production involved technologies that China needed and could not replicate alone. Typically, this required extended negotiations with a Chinese ministry, which often arranged competing bids among different MNCs in an effort to pick a single foreign firm that would serve as the main technology partner. Thus, with respect to incoming FDI, the Chinese side tried very hard to set the terms of the technology bargain. It was precisely in "high-tech" fields where the influence of central government ministries remained strongest, and where the central government retained a significant degree of monopoly power confronting MNCs.

Telecommunications equipment provides an excellent example. The Ministry of Post and Telecommunications initially sought a technology partnership with AT&T (in the late 1970s and early 1980s) and subsequently with Nortel. AT&T – preoccupied with its impending judicially ordered breakup and a perceived need to focus on the domestic United States marketplace – declined to be elected. Nortel also dropped out of the competition. Both AT&T and Nortel were subsequently penalized for their lack of enthusiasm: they were placed in the "penalty box" and completely frozen out of competition for the domestic equipment market. They discovered that the ministry had a long memory and was quite unforgiving. Ultimately, the Chinese side was able to persuade ITT Belgium (subsequently acquired by Alcatel) to play the role of preferred partner. In exchange for substantial technology commitments, Alcatel was given not just market access guarantees for its Shanghai Bell joint-venture manufacturing facility but also the ability to sell imported telecommunications switches to Chinese clients. This policy, known as "combining direct import with technology acquisition," was implemented across a range of industrial sectors as a way to overcome the reluctance of multinationals to invest large sums of money and technology in the unproven China market. Monopoly control over market access was used to develop multidimensional bargains with foreign technology suppliers.

In domestic technology development policy, China also carried out significant initial decentralization, but gradually, during the mid-1980s, and particularly in 1985–86, developed a range of new indirect, long-term plans for the economy, trying to replace the old-style discredited highly centralized plans. One, the 863 Project (named for its approval date of March 1986) targeted industries in the areas of biotechnology, new materials, lasers, energy, information, robotics, and space. The program – which continues today – brings together specialists in many fields on cross-disciplinary products such as computer-integrated manufacturing systems. The 863 Project introduced the concept of peer review and a mixed method of project selection for the first time to technology plans in China, and researchers focused on predominantly (but not entirely) civilian technologies.[7]

Another new plan, the 1988 Torch Plan, hoped to develop China's high-technology manufacturing capabilities, focusing especially on R&D and the commercialization of new technologies in state-owned enterprises. Rather than having the central government arrange the delivery of commodities and allocating funds to research projects, the Torch Plan was the first large S&T plan originating from the center that was not prescriptive.[8] Central funding for the Torch Plan has been limited and administered by the Torch Development Center under the former State Science and Technology Commission (SSTC), which acts more like a fund raiser and broker than an investor itself. Initial SSTC investments totaled only 100 million RMB, but by 1992 investments reached 4.4 billion RMB (in U.S. dollars going from $40 million to about $800 million).[9] The Torch Plan also included the creation of high-technology development zones. Chinese policy makers intended to recreate the experiences of Silicon Valley, Route 128, and other science parks locally through a policy of locating universities and high technology firms in the same area and combining research and education with production. Subsequent elaborations described preferential policies in five areas: taxes, finance, imports and exports, pricing, and personnel policy.[10]

If we are to characterize policy through the 1980s succinctly, we may say that China was trying to carry out a form of technonationalism in which the chief agents were to be large state-owned enterprises (SOEs) and government research institutes. Chinese policy makers looked enviously to Japan and Korea and sought to replicate their perceived success, but with SOEs emerging as the Toshibas and Hyundais of China. Where MNCs were to play an important domestic role, they were to be partnered with strong domestic

---

[7] "High Tech R&D Program (Project 863) Surges Ahead," *Zhongguo Keji Luntan*, no. 5 (September 18, 1989): 8–10, in *Joint Publication Research Service – China Science and Technology* (hereafter, JPRS-CST), January 4, 1990, p. 1. On the organization of the 863 program, its roots in the past, and its difference from earlier defense-oriented critical technologies programs in China, see Evan Feigenbaum, "Soldiers, Weapons and Chinese Development Strategy: The Mao Era Military in China's Economic and Institutional Debate," *China Quarterly* 158 (June 1999): 285–313; and "Who's behind China's High Technology 'Revolution'? How Bomb Makers Remade Beijing's Priorities, Policies, and Institutions," *International Security* 24, no. 1 (Summer 1999): 95–126.

[8] Qin Shijun, "High Technology Industrialization in China: An Analysis of the Current Status," *Asian Survey* 32, no. 12 (1992): 1129.

[9] Deng Shoupeng, "The Torch Plan Facing the Nineties," *Renmin Ribao*, November 19, 1990, p. 3, in JPRS-CST, November 30, 1990, p. 25.

[10] The list is from the 1992 State Basic Policy for High-Tech Industrial Development Zones. Shao Zhengqiang, "Present Policy to Govern High, New Tech Industrial Development Zones," *Zhongguo Keji Luntan*, no. 4 (July 1992): 14–16, 54, in JPRS-CST, December 16, 1992, pp. 5–8.

SOEs. But Chinese capabilities at this time fell short of those in Japan or Korea a few decades earlier: government "technology brokers" had less familiarity with world trends, and Chinese corporations were still only partially liberated from the bureaucratic strictures of the planned economy.

By the late 1980s it became clear that there were inherent limitations to both technology import and technology development strategies. The 863 Project has had (and continues to have) limited success in bringing new products to market. Research institutions participating in the programs had few official connections with enterprises, and enterprises had few incentives to look to these institutions for new innovations.[11] Moreover, the government was too anxious to achieve dramatic results with limited resources in a short period. As a result, from 1988 to 1994 the average research fund for every 863 Project researcher was only about $5,000 because government funds were spread over an average 1,044 research programs annually.[12]

The Torch Plan made more progress in commercializing new technologies and supporting the growth of high-technology industries, but it also had problems. There were too many so-called high-tech industrial parks all over the country, some with only a few enterprises. Many firms that entered the parks did so only to take advantage of the preferential tax policies and export subsidies, and never developed any new technologies. Moreover, much of the program funding went to medium-sized and large state-owned enterprises rather than smaller, more technologically innovative firms.

The technology transfer policies of the 1980s were also perceived to be falling short by the early 1990s. Decentralized import of technology by local decision makers had numerous problems, and the overall record of absorption was not good.[13] At the central level, while the State Economic Commission (SEC) tried to act like MITI in Japan or the Economic Planning Board in Korea and coordinate technology imports to renovate older factories, the SEC lacked significant institutional capabilities. In many cases, ministries chose which technologies to import with little understanding of the technologies themselves, the needs of particular sectors within China, or the long-term implications of their choices. Ministry officials tended to chase after the "highest," most-advanced technologies. In Korea, by contrast, government research centers were more finely tuned to the needs of domestic enterprises, informing firms about the available technologies and thus enhancing their bargaining positions with the MNCs.

---

[11] CAS, "Accomplishments in High Technology Development Reviewed," *Xiandaihau,* January 23, 1990, pp. 10–12, in JPRS-CST, July 23, 1990, pp. 2–5.

[12] The average was 22,000 renminbi per researcher. Chen Chunbao, *Zhongguo Jishu Chanye Fazhan yu Waimaojingzhengli* (Development of high-tech industries in China and China's competitiveness in foreign trade) (China Northeast Caijing University Press, 1998), p. 64.

[13] Samuel P. S. Ho, "Technology Transfer to China during the 1980s – How Effective? Some Evidence from Jiangsu," *Pacific Affairs* 70, no. 1 (1997): 85–106. See also Xiaojuan, "Chinese Government Policy towards Science and Technology," n. 10.

The strategy of selective partnering with MNCs was not producing exceptional technological success. Delays and disputes plagued many of the big showcase projects. In a bilateral monopoly situation, both sides were capable of exploiting their position, and projects became increasingly complicated and delayed, and rarely resulted in rapid "leaps" in technological capability. A number of areas that had been designated the highest priority by the Chinese government displayed the slowest development. In the automobile industry, the large centrally controlled producers were authorized to seek joint-venture partners for passenger car production in the mid-1980s, but it took them a decade to get these ventures into production. In the meantime, locally run producers in Shanghai and Tianjin worked out quicker and more successful strategies, with the result that centrally run passenger car producers have never been profitable.[14] Expensive, high-profile projects to import semiconductor fabrication technology ran into repeated delays. The result was that the technology gap separating China from the rapidly advancing world technology frontier probably widened in the area of semiconductor fabrication.[15]

Furthermore, expanded marketization was undermining some of the presumptions embedded in the complex bargains the Chinese government sought with MNCs, bargains that were predicated on monopoly control of key sectors. For example, in telecommunications, in the early 1990s, Alcatel found that newly empowered local telecom authorities were unwilling to buy high-priced imported switches and aggressively sought alternative lower-price supplies. The bargain between the ministry and Alcatel had to be recast in order to save the project.

The limited success of the mainstream national approach to technology policy also contributed to divergent regional outcomes. Guangdong province, which had been allowed to carve out its own independent policies with respect to foreign participation in the economy (and thus, de facto, with respect to technology import) was having remarkable success. Guangdong allowed corporations much more independence in structuring their businesses internally and externally. Corporations in Guangdong could gain access to foreign firms much more easily (through Hong Kong) and had more freedom to craft

[14] Jin Chen and Takahiro Fujimoto, "Different Behaviors of Chinese Auto Makers in Technology Introduction and Assimilation," University of Tokyo Discussion Paper CIRJE-F-10, June 1998. Tomoo Marukawa, "WTO, Industrial Policy and China's Industrial Development," IDE-JETRO International Symposium, China Enters WTO: Pursuing Symbiosis with the Global Economy, Chiba, Japan, January 17, 2001.

[15] Yuan Zhijia, "Semiconductor Industry: Industrial Development under Government Initiative" (in Japanese), in Tomoo Marukawa, ed., *Iko-ki Chugoku no Sangyo Seiasaku* (China's industrial policy in transition) (Chiba: Institute of Developing Economies, 2000), pp. 407–37. See also the earlier discussion in Barry Naughton, *The China Circle: Economics and Technology in the PRC, Taiwan and Hong Kong* (Washington, D.C.: Brookings Institution, 1997), esp. p. 26.

cooperative business and technological relationships with foreign firms. In this environment, a new technological growth pole grew up in Guangdong by the mid-1990s. Ultimately, Guangdong's success was to pave the way for a shift in national policy.

Policy Shift: More Open, More Players

In the early 1990s, China underwent a significant shift to a more radical, less controlled version of technology policy. The change is most clearly marked with respect to technology import, because of the massive surge in foreign direct investment that emerged after Deng Xiaoping's "Southern Tour" in 1992. Although this political event triggered a much bolder approach to market transition overall, its impact was especially apparent with respect to foreign investment. In its wake, China became much more reliant on incoming FDI than Japan or Korea has ever been. The shift in 1992 was especially clear because the Tiananmen Incident of 1989–90 had caused three years of stagnation in FDI. During the period of stagnation, the key change was a reshuffling of foreign partners. Some MNCs reduced their involvement in China, and China faced potential isolation from Western partners. Meanwhile, though, other "contrarians" (such as Motorola in Tianjin) that were willing to make investment commitments in the aftermath of the Tiananmen incident emerged as competitors to first round technology partners.

Similar to Japan's experience in the 1950s and 1960s, the benefits of having multiple competing foreign technology sources began to seem increasingly obvious to the Chinese side. At the same time, the success of Guangdong's more open approach was becoming obvious. Export manufacturers from Hong Kong and Taiwan had been moving labor-intensive stages of production to the Chinese mainland. The scale of exports from foreign invested enterprises (FIEs) was increasing, surpassing 20 percent of total exports in 1992 (from only 1 percent in 1985). Even more striking, FIE exports, which had originally been predominantly clothing and toys, began to include a substantial share of electronics assembly and other production associated with high-technology sectors. These developments encouraged a dramatic liberalization of the investment regime in 1992–93. After 1992 FIEs had much more domestic-market access than before, and both they and FIE exporters faced a much more favorable policy regime. The result was a flood of foreign investment, much of it in medium- to high-technology sectors. Figure 7.1 shows the volume of three important flows associated with technology import.[16] The top line shows investment goods (nearly all of it machinery) imported as part of foreign investment projects; the middle line shows capital equipment imported by domestic firms and reported as

---

[16] *Zhongguo Duiqi Jingji Maoyi Baipishu* (China external economy and trade whitebook) (Beijing: Zhongguo Shehui Kexue, 1999), pp. 85–86, 131, and (2000), pp. 138, 368.

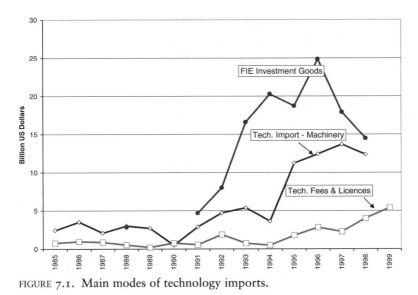

FIGURE 7.1. Main modes of technology imports.

technology import; and the bottom line shows funds expended for licenses and other technology fees. Clearly, there is no exact dollar equivalence between these different types of flows, each represented by data coming from different sources.[17] Equally clearly, though, while foreign investment was roughly equivalent to domestic-firm technology acquisition in importance through 1991, beginning in 1992, foreign investment quickly dominated domestic-machinery purchase, and almost certainly emerged as the dominant source of technology import through 1997. Investment poured into China.

The massive flow of foreign investment into China was in many respects an enormous success. As Figure 7.1 shows graphically, the overall pace of inward technology transfer stepped up dramatically after 1992. The reliance on FDI inflows – which since 1993 has surpassed 5 percent of GDP – was such that China in this respect came to resemble a Southeast

[17] In Figure 7.1, foreign invested enterprise (FIE) investment goods are taken from customs statistics, as reported in General Administration of Customs, *China's Custom's Statistics*, annual December issues. Annual figures are affected by the fact that imports of FIE investment goods were tax exempt through 1996, after which time tax exemptions were scaled back. As a result, there may be some overstatement for 1996 (as firms rushed to get in machinery before some tax exemptions expired) and some understatement for later years (because the incentive to report fully has diminished). Data on domestic enterprise technology acquisition are from State Statistical Bureau and State Science and Technology Commission, eds., *Zhongguo Keji Tongji Nianjian* (China Science and Technology Statistical Yearbook) (Beijing: Zhongguo Tongji, 1992), p. 329, and (1998), p. 200; MOFTEC, *Zhongguo Duiwai Jingji Maoyi Baibishu* (White book on China's foreign economics and trade) (Beijing: jingji Kexue, 1999), pp. 85–86, 131. Definitions of these series "drift" in different years as well and should be used only for a general assessment of large-scale trends.

Asian country more than a more traditionally technonationalist Northeast Asian country. MNCs were playing a dominant role in overall technology import. (The share of total exports produced by FIEs continued to grow as well, reaching 47 percent in 1999.)

As the approach to technology transfer shifted to a greater reliance on foreign investment, so technology policy targeted at indigenous capabilities expanded to include more forms of ownership. For the first time, the center took steps, albeit tentative, to promote and support nonstate technology enterprises. The 1993 "Decision on Several Problems Facing the Enthusiastic Promotion of Nongovernmental Technology Enterprises" recognized and encouraged these firms. The decision declared that nonstate enterprises would have a role in developing a new innovation system based on market-oriented technology firms as well as changing an S&T system dominated by public institutions to one that embraced organizations of various ownership structures.[18] These "nongovernmental" firms, often founded by entrepreneurial individuals from the Chinese Academy of Sciences or Beijing University, existed in a space between "private" and "public" ownership. Start-up capital came from friends or savings; the initial technology and office space were often located in state-funded research institutes.

Meanwhile, the inflow of FDI has also had significant implications for domestic firms. Nongovernmental companies like Legend Computer (discussed later), frequently excluded from bank lending, have been able to raise significant capital by forming joint ventures with foreign firms. Cooperation with foreign producers also allowed Legend access to an already established global network of foreign partners to market its joint-venture products. In addition, working with foreign enterprises allowed Legend to learn and experiment with new management structures.

In 1995 the Communist Party and the State Council also issued a "Decision on Accelerating S&T Development." While calling for the strengthening of government leadership in basic technology research, the decision accepted that the development of applied technologies should be left to the market. Scientific research institutes were to have full autonomy in choosing R&D projects, and they should try to form joint ventures with domestic and foreign partners. Moreover, the decision pointed out that nonstate companies were an important force in the high-tech field and worthy of encouragement. This point implicitly revised the previous priority given to large state-owned enterprises, while also implicitly recognizing that policy up through 1995 had continued to favor large state-owned enterprises.[19]

---

[18] "Guanyu Dali Tuidong Minying Keji Qiye Fazhan Ruogan Wenti de Jueding," in Xi'an Science and Technology Commission, *Keji Fagui Xuanbian* (Selected S&T laws and regulations) (Xi'an: Xi'an Kexue Jishu Weiyuanhui, 1996), pp. 390–98.

[19] There is an excellent discussion of this document at the U.S. Embassy website; see <http://www.usembassy-china.org.cn>.

The policies surrounding high-technology parks also became more highly attuned to the needs of nonstate enterprises. Within already established parks, local officials began creating small-business "incubators."[20] Officials in the Xi'an International Business Incubator, for example, established a venture capital fund for smaller firms and helped individual entrepreneurs apply for bank loans and Torch Program funding.

The success of Legend Computer illustrates the growing role and importance of these nongovernmental companies in the new economy. Legend was founded in 1984 by a group of scientists from the Institute of Computing Technology at the Chinese Academy of Sciences; the academy provided the initial start-up capital in the form of a 200,000 RMB loan.[21] The company's first product was a Chinese language card – an electronic card inserted in PCs to convert English keystrokes into Chinese characters – and in 1988 Legend introduced its own PC in the domestic market. By late 1996 Legend's PC was outselling all of its foreign and domestic competitors in the Chinese market. From 1993 to 1997 Legend's annual income almost quadrupled from 3.2 billion to 12 billion RMB (in U.S. dollars, tripling from circa $500 million to $1.5 billion).

Legend's organizational structure also came to resemble the modern enterprises that would underpin the "new innovation system" described in the 1993 decision. The company grew from 20 to 4,200 employees, and from one office to six departments, including offices for scientific development, finance, subsidiary companies, and production, as well as divisions for specific technologies including networks, software, and microelectronics.[22] In 1988 Legend established a holding company in Hong Kong and issued shares on the Hong Kong stock market.[23] In 2000 Legend officially ended its ambiguous "nongovernmental" status, formally becoming a joint-stock company, with the Institute of Computing Technology as one of the largest shareholders.[24]

Despite substantial successes, there were significant problems and tensions associated with the FDI-led program of technology acquisition. First, China found that in many sectors, MNCs moved rapidly and aggressively to establish strong market positions. Moreover, many MNCs proved quite capable

[20] Jing Junhai and Jin Hui, *Keji Qiye Chengzhang yu Qiye Fuhuaqi* (The growth of science and technology enterprises and business incubators) (Xi'an: Xibei Gongye Daxue Chubanshe, 1998).

[21] For a history of the Legend, see Chen Huihu, *Lianxiang Weishenma* (Why Legend) (Beijing: Beijing Daxue Chunbanshe, 1997).

[22] Lianxiang Jituan (Legend Corporation), company prospectus, no date. Interview, Legend Corporation, Beijing, June 26, 1997.

[23] "Sitong Gupiao Niandi Shangshi" (Stone to go on the stock market at the end of the year), *Keji Ribao* (S&T Daily), October 22, 1988.

[24] Hu Yanping, "Lianxiang/Jisuansuo – Ziji de Lihun Bieren de Piping" (Legend and the Computer Science Institute – our divorce, other people's criticism) <http://www.sina.com.cn/news/review/2000-01-18/15840.shtml>.

of maintaining effective control over proprietary technologies, either by resisting joint-venture partners and operating wholly owned subsidiaries or by structuring relations with partners to segment the technology. The latter was particularly easy when joint-venture partners were slow-moving traditionally structured state-owned enterprises.

There were many features of the Chinese system that limited the spillover benefits from FDI. An unsatisfactory level of intellectual property protection and doubts about the willingness of Chinese entities to abide by contractual agreements hampered China's efforts to receive and localize imported technology. Foreign companies were reluctant to engage Chinese enterprises as partners to develop their best technology for the Chinese market. In their eyes, there was a substantial risk that the Chinese partner would bring the product to market on its own or transfer the technology to other unauthorized partners.[25] Foreign investors had both the incentive and the ability to keep technological capabilities closely guarded within the firm.

Second, the trade and investment regime had characteristics that inadvertently discouraged technological learning. FIEs often operated in an externally oriented enclave economy, with limited links to the rest of the Chinese economy. FIEs were encouraged to export and to bring in advanced technologies. In order to facilitate the transplantation of export networks to China from elsewhere in East Asia, China adopted an extremely open export-processing regime, under which inputs could be imported duty-free, as long as production was exported. While this policy was effective in encouraging movement of producers to China, it also encouraged producers to maintain supply and sales links with external businesses, and thus inadvertently discouraged the growth of supply networks based on domestic Chinese firms.

An example of this is the hard disk drive (HDD) industry, which has grown rapidly in China in recent years. Chinese plants (all foreign-owned or joint ventures) now assemble hard disk drives (10 percent of world output in 1998), and also produce some of the components of HDDs, especially labor-intensive components such as heads. Yet all the components are imported, and all the heads and all the assembled disk drives are exported. Indeed, 100 percent of output is exported even though many of the heads are ultimately assembled into drives in China, and many of the drives are ultimately installed into personal computers in China.

Why are these drives exported and then reimported? Because for exporters to continue to operate under the liberal export-processing regime with minimal restrictions, they must export all output. Otherwise, imported inputs would be subject to duties, and value-added taxes (VATs) would be charged

---

[25] Keith Maskus and Sean Doughterty, "Intellectual Property Rights and Economic Development in China," Sino-U.S. Conference on Intellectual Property Rights and Economic Development, Chongqing, 1998.

on a portion of output value. Even local suppliers of low-technology inputs (cleaners and solvents, furniture, office supplies) are uncommon, and the HDD plants sit in a kind of splendid isolation in clean, greenfield technology parks. The supply and sales chains of these plants all lead across Chinese borders. Technology spillovers are, to date, quite modest or nonexistent.[26]

Thus, by the late 1990s Chinese policy makers were facing new dilemmas. The economy had become much more open to incoming investment and, in that sense, had swung out of the ambit of the government-steerage and technonationalist policies characteristic both of the planned economy and of Japan and Korea in earlier decades. Although the benefits of incoming FDI were considerable, there was a widespread sense that technological spillovers had been disappointing.[27] Perhaps this was inevitable. The policy swing that permitted the flood of investment had been sudden and had certainly not been calibrated with policies to foster technology absorption and diffusion. Moreover, Chinese capabilities in both the organizational and technological realm were growing but were still limited. Investment in the assimilation and absorption of purchased technology regularly ran behind what economists estimated was efficient.[28] There was clearly scope for more effective government action.

But in which direction? In this hybrid environment, government policies and institutions obstructed the type of technological spillovers that would occur in a pure market environment, because profitable activities such as outsourcing to local suppliers, subcontracting, and licensing were discouraged. And while government policies still attempted to squeeze technology concessions out of MNCs as a condition for operating in the Chinese market, these policies were neither systematic nor professional enough to provide really substantial technological benefits to the Chinese economy. In this environment, there were really two choices. The first was to move systematically to a technonationalist policy similar to the ones carried out by Japan and Korea in previous decades; the alternative was further liberalization.

In the case of movement toward a Japanese- or Korean-style industrial policy, China's gradually developing technological sophistication and administrative capability would be harnessed to a more systematic and sophisticated industrial policy. Incoming FDI might well be reduced, but more technological benefit would be squeezed out of each incoming dollar. Indeed, there were

---

[26] Industry interviews, Shenzhen, June 21, 1999; Wuxi, August 24, 1999.

[27] See, e.g., the discussion in Wang Chengxu, *Kejiao Xingguo* (Science and education for a prosperous China) (Beijing: China Taihai Press, 1998).

[28] Chinese economists have repeatedly raised the fact that Chinese organizations on average allocated resources for technology absorption equal to about 50 percent of technology purchase price, compared with 200–300 percent in Korea and Japan. See Jiangping Xu, "China's International Technology Transfer: The Current Situation, Problems and Future Prospects," in Charles Feinstein and Christopher Howe, eds., *Chinese Technology Transfer in the 1990s: Current Experience, Historical Problems and International Perspectives* (Cheltenham: Edward Elgar, 1997), p. 91.

initiatives in this direction. An automobile industrial policy in 1994 announced a moratorium on new producers (thus restricting incoming FDI). It also promised state support for the first producers who reached an annual 100,000 passenger car output, combining elements of a tournament with strong incentives to consolidate. The similarity to Japanese automobile industrial policy in the 1960s is overwhelming.[29] Minister Wu Jichuan, head of the telecommunications system, clearly favored an approach to telecommunications that stressed a vigorously nationalistic industrial policy. Yet, ultimately, these initiatives were not followed up. None of the other industrial policies promised in the wake of the automobile industry policy ever appeared. The ground was being laid for a different type of policy, and when the shift came, it was in the direction of greater liberalization.

New Millennium, New Technology Policy?

In the late 1990s the context for technology development changed once again. The impetus for the subsequent shifts in policy was both external and domestic. The Asian financial crisis deeply affected elite opinion by showing the limitations and weaknesses of the Korean-style model of large-enterprise-led, *chaebol*-dominated industrialization. For many Chinese, the *chaebol* had been an important model of what the most successful state-owned enterprises might become. Proposals to create 100 or more "enterprise groups" out of the stronger state firms have circulated for years. The revelation of extensive problems within the *chaebol* groups in the course of the financial crisis discredited policies to build up national champions out of SOEs and strengthened the hand of those like Premier Zhu Rongji who had been known to be skeptical about such programs.

Yet the Asian crisis, exploding in mid-1997, followed in the wake of a set of Chinese domestic policy changes that had already altered the economic context in which technology and industrial policy choices would be made. A series of reforms during 1993–95 had changed the institutional foundations of the economy. Tax reforms placed enterprises on a more nearly level playing field; labor reforms gave enterprises the right to lay off surplus workers; and financial reforms gave the banking system some insulation from pressures to prop up unsuccessful firms. As a result, the pace of credit creation and monetary growth slowed, and the economy began to move away from an inflationary shortage economy and toward a much more competitive economy.[30]

From the beginning of 1997 China's inflation rate dropped into the single digits, and Chinese economists proclaimed a successful "soft landing."

---

[29] Marukawa, *Iko-ki Chugoku no Sangyo Seiasaku*.

[30] For an earlier, more detailed, account, see Barry Naughton, "China: Domestic Restructuring and a New Role in Asia," in T. J. Pempel, ed., *The Politics of Asian Economic Crisis* (Ithaca: Cornell University Press, 1999), pp. 203–23. In this case, the Japanese analogy is to the Matsukata deflation.

Meanwhile, steady increases in production capacity – some created by FDI inflows – combined with consistent restraint in aggregate demand have led to enormous increases in the degree of competition in domestic markets. Increased competitiveness has been used to drive an impressive shrinkage of the public enterprise sector. Urban publicly owned industrial enterprises shed almost half of their labor force between 1992 and 1999, dropping from 81 million to 41 million total employees.[31] With these changes, the ability of the central and local governments to prop up public enterprises or subsidize their technological expenses has been severely curtailed.

Moreover, during the course of 1997 political changes were underway that strengthened central leaders like Zhu Rongji and ensured that they were better positioned politically to follow up on their promarket policies and on their skepticism toward the extensive promotion of "national champions." These political changes culminated in the 15th Party Congress in September 1997, and the installation of Zhu as premier in March 1998 – after several years in which he had been the de facto economic "czar" – shifted the balance of forces in the national government. Committed to the substantial downsizing of the state sector, Zhu helped initiate massive layoffs at SOEs and a significant shrinkage and restructuring of government organs. The number of ministries was reduced, and ministerial level personnel cut by 49 percent.

These reforms helped private and nongovernmental enterprises. The now weakened industrial ministries had advocated solutions that stressed protection and new resources for their subordinate enterprises. The Economics and Trade Commission favored engineering centers. Advisers at the State Science and Technology Commission (now renamed the Ministry of Science and Technology) had always supported policies that were favorable to start-ups, small firms, and venture capital.[32]

Moreover, the impact of the Asian crisis and the changed perception of the *chaebol* were just part of a broader shift in views about the nature of a successful economy that could be competitive internationally. The dramatic explosion of the Internet and related digital technologies in China has received significant coverage in the popular press, and it has also significantly influenced how Chinese leaders think about innovation. Small start-up companies appear to have been the engine of this wave of innovation in the West, and Chinese leaders are anxious not to miss out on the benefits of rapid technological change, as they had in the 1960s, 1970s, and 1980s. Especially significant has been the fact that many Chinese scientists and engineers have played a significant role in the most recent wave of innovation and are particularly prominent in Silicon Valley. The striking role of these entrepreneurial engineers has elicited policies designed *both* to reverse part

---

[31] *Zhongguo Tongji Zhaiyao* (China statistical abstract) (Beijing: Zhongguo Tongji, 2000), p. 38. This includes both state-owned industrial enterprises and urban collectives.

[32] We thank Wenkai He for bringing this point to our attention.

of China's serious brain drain and to make government policy more friendly to innovation and the creation of new businesses. Numerous localities have begun setting up special centers offering free rent and other benefits to lure young entrepreneurs home. Beijing, for example, has announced the establishment of a Silicon Valley recruitment center in a bid to attract students to return to China.[33] Taiwan's experience with initial brain drain leading to later technological prowess and creativity has been carefully studied.

These factors, as well as accumulating doubts about the previous policies, have led to important changes in the state's relationship to nonstate enterprises and innovation. First, and crucially, there has been a generous expansion of the type of Chinese domestic enterprises that are deemed worthy of support. Instead of favoring large SOEs, the government now supports virtually all technologically advanced enterprises, including small, private start-ups and technology-intensive spin-offs from schools and research institutes. This reflects the important ideological changes made at the 15th Party Congress in September 1997, which fully acknowledged the legitimacy, contribution, and equal rights of private enterprise for the first time. Simultaneously, it reflects an important shift of perception. Instead of seeing private firms as rivals with publicly owned enterprises, these firms are now viewed as "national" enterprises: nonstate firms can also be the national champions that compete with foreign firms.

Second, the nature of support has changed. Government ministries have been reduced in manpower and mandate, and nonstate firms were never subject to the same degree of government direction as SOEs were. Thus, the ability of the government to manage the process of selecting and importing technology directly has been substantially reduced. Instead, the government provides a kind of across-the-board support for domestic enterprises designated "high technology." This support can take the form of access to low-interest credit lines, preference in procurement decisions, or other kinds of regulatory preference or relief.

Third, China has gradually shifted the emphasis of technology absorption policies, encouraging the less tangible forms of technology transfer (i.e., licenses, consultancy, etc.) rather than "hardware" in the form of equipment imports. This shift in orientation, combined with delegation of decision making to more entrepreneurial organizations, may be yielding some results. As Figure 7.1 shows, intangible import of technology in 1998 and 1999 registered significant increases over previous years, whereas machinery imports declined, due to weak domestic demand.

In these circumstances, a new technology orientation has been shaping up and attempts to address some of the specific needs of the contemporary environment. Venture capital and private firms, in particular, have received unprecedented attention. This policy direction has been crystallized by a late 1999 decision that puts forth a set of practicable policies to foster

[33] "Beijing Targets High-Tech Ex-Pats," *South China Morning Post*, January 11, 2000.

domestic technology development.[34] In contrast to the vagueness in the 1993 and 1995 State Council Decision, the 1999 decision calls for concrete measures to foster high-tech industries and services:

- A fund to support S&T innovation by small and medium-sized enterprises.
- Preference for domestic high-tech products and equipment in government and enterprise procurement.
- A partial tax deduction for R&D expenditures.
- A tax exemption for all income from the transfer or development of new technologies and related consulting and technical services.
- A preferential 6 percent value-added tax rate for software products developed and produced in China.
- Complete deductibility of payroll expenditures for software development and manufacturing companies.
- Complete VAT exemption and subsidized credit for high-tech exports.
- Preferential tax treatment for imports of cutting-edge technologies and equipment not available in China.
- Listing new high-tech companies on the Shanghai and Shenzhen stock exchanges.

In addition, the state will support each year, through interest subsidies, a few technological restructuring projects by large and medium-sized state-owned enterprises that are deemed to be profitable and of strategic significance and merited on scientific grounds. Clearly, the Chinese government does not intend to take a "hands off" attitude toward technological development: it will continue to support favored firms aggressively.

Policies are also being altered to make it possible for technologically inventive entrepreneurs to reap large rewards for their contributions. The decision called for developing venture capital companies and funds; it was inspired by the great success of the alliance of S&T workers with venture capitalists in developed countries, especially in the U.S. high-tech industry. To stimulate venture capital, China has changed accounting regulations on how registered capital is calculated and begun to address problems of public sale of companies (or listing on stock markets) in order to provide an exit option for initial investors. Chinese Company Law formerly decreed that a maximum of 20 percent of an enterprise's registered capital could be granted for the contribution of intangible "technology." Originally developed to increase the bargaining power of Chinese firms negotiating with technology-rich MNCs, the 20 percent cap became part of domestic company law as well. The limit has already been abandoned in practice, although new regulations have not yet been issued. Plans for a "growth enterprise market," like NASDAQ in the United States, have been approved, but implementation

---

[34] The account in following pages is taken from the website of the State Council Development Research Center <http://www.drcnet.com.cn> or from <http://www.vcchina.com.cn>.

has been put off until after regulatory reforms that will restructure the existing Shanghai and Shenzhen stock markets.

Connected to this focus on nonstate actors in technological development is the belief that foreign direct investment will continue and even accelerate in the wake of China's entry into the WTO. In some respects, the focus of contemporary policy is less on maximizing the flow of technological capabilities into China than it is on maximizing the extent to which Chinese domestic firms will be able to master the technologies that are expected to flood into China. This may be realistic, and the pattern of government policy and firm response can be illustrated by recent events in the telecommunications equipment industry.

One of the most impressive Chinese firms to have emerged out of the recent liberalization is a telecommunications equipment manufacturer named Huawei. Huawei was started in an interior city but moved to the Shenzhen Special Economic Zone in order to take advantage of the greater freedom to source foreign components, travel abroad, and collaborate with foreign firms that the zone offered. Huawei is an entirely Chinese firm with a national reach. Its 1999 revenues reached $1.8 billion, almost entirely from selling switches and other infrastructure equipment to provincial telephone authorities (there are almost no consumer products). Huawei is an employee-owned corporation – not a "collective" but a joint-stock company with over 90 percent of its shares held by employees, including the founders and top managers. The right to purchase shares is carefully parceled out as an incentive device, but about 80 percent of employees own shares. Huawei has substantial capabilities: 85 percent of total employees have college degrees, and the average age is twenty-seven; in 1998 R&D expenditures were 18 percent of total revenues. Company's managers report that there is no government policy favoring them in procurement but readily acknowledge that Chinese network operators like to purchase from them for emotional and patriotic reasons.[35] Industry analysts in Beijing assert that provincial telecom operators have been told that in addition to whatever foreign-invested or foreign suppliers they use, they must also have at least one domestic Chinese supplier. The policy seems to be working: Huawei sold 6.5 million lines in 1998, for a 33 percent market share, and foreign companies respect it as a formidable competitor with strong technology and aggressive prices.

Similar policies, with more mixed outcomes, are in evidence in the mobile phone industry.[36] A number of Chinese firms have decided that assembly of mobile phone handsets is a business in which they can compete, particularly in the lower end of the market. The most aggressive entrants have typically not

---

[35] Company interviews, Shenzhen, June 20, 1999.
[36] Lester Gesteland, "Chinese Cell Phones Unpopular Despite Strong Official Backing," *China Online*, December 15, 1999; "Chinese Cell Phone Makers Poised to Take on the Foreign Giants,"*China Online*, December 6, 1999; and "The End of Price Wars in China's Cellular Phone Market," *China Online*, December 16, 1999, all at <www.chinaonline.com/industry/telecom/currentnews>.

been specialized telecommunications firms, which in the past would have been those selected for government assistance. Instead, the firms are those that manufacture consumer durables, especially color televisions. Prominent examples are at Konka and TCL, both diversified and successful consumer electronics firms. These companies purchase chips from Lucent and Siemens, respectively, so they do not seek to replicate core technologies but instead seek to leverage competitive advantage in assembly, design, and systems engineering into a competitive position in the market. These are not mere "assemblers" – both companies invest substantial sums into firm-level R&D and purchase of intellectual property rights from abroad. Government policy supports these firms through a series of channels. Direct financial subsidies are estimated to have reached 1.4 billion RMB ($169 million) in 1999, and regulatory favoritism is also evident. Foreign firms have to jump through a number of hoops to establish that their phones reach quality standards and that component imports are all legal. Domestic firms are generally untroubled by such regulatory obstacles.

These measures are still in their early stages and may not be effective. As of September 1999, the big four foreign producers (Nokia, Ericsson, Motorola, and Siemens) made 91 percent of mobile phone handsets sold in China. Chinese competition had brought down prices, without yet making dramatic inroads into market share. Perhaps more significant, though, Chinese policy is now to a significant extent shaped by market processes, while still attempting to shape market outcomes. The government did not choose the competitors, but elected to support aggressive competitors once they emerged. Moreover, the government dropped its scruples about supporting nonstate or mixed ownership firms. The broad categories of "domestic" firms are all deemed worthy of support.

The most successful parts of China's technological development in recent years appear to be precisely the areas where innovative domestic firms are closely related to FIEs but engage in complex relations of supply, cooperation, and competition. In electronics, for example, Chinese domestic firms have quickly found niches in which they could cooperate with MNCs. Although their initial entry has typically been in relatively low-tech, labor-intensive assembly phases, these firms have been in a position to move gradually but steadily into slightly higher technology stages of the complex electronics production chains. This seems to have led to rapid "indigenization" of technological competencies, even while government policy heretofore has stressed the "upgrading" of technological levels at FIEs, only to find that the competencies are bottled up in ventures controlled by foreign-based MNCs.[37]

---

[37] The precise contrast between indigenization and upgrading is from Greg Felker, "Malaysia's Industrial Technology Development: Firms, Policies, and Political Economy," in Greg Felker and K.S. Jomo, eds., *Malaysia's Industrial Technology Development* (London: Routledge, 1999). See also Barry Naughton, "Technological Development, Production Networks, and IPR: How the Global Revolution in Electronics Affects China's Optimal Technology Policy," National Bureau of Asian Research Working Paper, March 1999.

The shift in policy seems to recognize the successes that are being achieved by China's more entrepreneurial domestic firms and could position China well to take a larger share of the ongoing technological revolution.

A Big Emerging Market and Big Security Concerns

In the background of much of the preceding discussion about how China has veered from technonationalist toward technoglobalist policies while promoting an increasingly nationalistic discourse is the fact that China is the largest country in this study. What difference does it make that China is such a big country? First, China's technological development cannot be separated from military and strategic concerns. In the view of Chinese policy makers, China's earliest defense technology successes – the atomic and hydrogen bomb, and intercontinental ballistic missiles – were key to maintaining autonomy in relation to the states China viewed as the primary threats to its security, first the United States, then the Soviet Union. The link of technology to military needs and strategic goals is no less clear today. Even before the Kosovo and Taiwan Straits crises, the government increased spending for military research and development under the premise that the People's Liberation Army (PLA) must develop sophisticated weapons to maintain territorial integrity. These concerns have only been heightened by increased tensions with the United States over the past several years. In a recent Taiwan crisis, Jiang Zemin reportedly linked a "sound base in technology and national defense" to the success of the mainland's reunification enterprise.[38] Economic and foreign policy concerns may also overlap at the level of sanctions or the use of other economic weapons. In its purchase of twenty-eight aircraft valued at $1.8 billion from European consortium Airbus, China was seen as using checkbook diplomacy to drive home displeasure with U.S. policy over Taiwan.

As noted earlier, the Chinese self-perception is that it deserves a broad, well-lit place on the world stage. A recurrent theme in Chinese strategic writing is the idea that those with strength will (and should) use it; thus, weak states will be humiliated, and therefore military strength is indispensable.[39] Moreover, because people are forward-looking, it follows that existing powers – such as the United States – will resist the dilution of their current predominant position and try to block China's emergence. Chinese policy makers believe that they will be forced to develop a substantial degree of technological self-sufficiency because real technology dependency will inevitably provoke attempts by the United States and others to exploit that dependency when a backlash develops against China's rise. At the same time, though, Chinese

---

[38] Willy Wo-Lap Lam, "Jiang Boosts Defense Funding," *South China Morning Post*, December 1, 1999.

[39] For an interesting discussion, see Alastair I. Johnston, "Cultural Realism and Strategy in Maoist China," in Peter J. Katzenstein, ed., *The Culture of National Security: Norms and Identity in World Politics* (New York: Columbia University Press, 1996), 216–68.

military planners have absorbed many of the same lessons that Chinese economic planners have absorbed: the determinants of security are no longer to be found solely or even primarily in the big-ticket deterrent weapons but increasingly depend on sophistication in the information revolution. Yet such sophistication is hard to purchase with government dollars and requires a flexible and innovative civilian economy.[40] Undoubtedly, such views encourage more adaptable civilian technology policies; but at the same time, such a world view certainly will not foreswear government-directed technology initiatives, either. Although we do not discuss the military-technology complex in this chapter, there is no doubt that it retains an important role in China.

A second implication of China's large size is that the emerging scope of China's domestic market gives technology policy an additional element of leverage. In the first place, domestic Chinese firms could have substantial long-run advantages because of their intimate knowledge of the large and growing Chinese market. As that market increasingly comes to define its own technological standards – as has already happened, for example, with VCDs, a product in which China claims the bulk of the world market – Chinese firms will emerge in a better position in subsequent decades than they have experienced heretofore.

A more pointed implication is that the Chinese government can use the advantage of market size to influence the process of standard setting in the information economy. Like the rest of us, Chinese policy makers have taken note of the importance of market size and lock-in effects in determining which technological standards predominate – and of the fact that "ownership" of the dominant standards confers competitive advantage. This point may be best illustrated by the government's promotion of software companies working on Linux operating software and of its advocacy of domestic users adopting the operating system over Microsoft. Linux's open source code makes it easy for local users to modify and customize to local conditions. Moreover, China is currently unable to compete in the domestic market for Windows-related software. Chinese computer programmers and companies, however, could play a much bigger role in the Linux world.[41]

---

[40] For some of the most interesting examples of current Chinese thinking on military and technology issues, see Qiao Liang and Wang Xiangsui, *Chaoxianzhan: Dui Quanqiuhua Shidai Zhanzheng yu Zhanfa de Xiangding* (Unrestricted warfare: Thoughts on war and strategy in the era of globalization) (Beijing: Jiefangjun Wenyi, 1999); and Zhang Zhaozhong, *Xia Yige Mubiao Shi Shei?* (Who is the next target?) (Beijing: Zhongguo Qingnian, 1999). Excerpts from these works are translated on the U.S. Embassy website <www.usembassy-china.org.cn/english/sandt/unresw1.html>.

[41] G. Pierre Goad and Lorien Holland, "China Joins the Linux Bandwagon," *Far Eastern Economic Review*, February 24, 2000. Some important concrete steps have followed, including IBM's agreement to preinstall Redflag-Linux OS 2.0 in its large-scale S/390 computers in China. See "IBM, Redflag-Linux Team on Linux Development," *China Online*, August 24, 2000, reporting on an article from *Zhongguo Jingji Shibao*.

Promotion of Linux may also ease Chinese fears of dependence on Microsoft and the United States. The Chinese government suspects that Windows has "back doors" that allows the company or the United States to spy on users. In an editorial on "information colonialism," the *People's Liberation Army Daily* argued that China must develop its own software because "without information security, there is no national security in economics, politics, or military affairs."[42] According to one official, "maintaining independence and keeping the initiative over our own operating system will be the 'Two Bombs and One Satellite' (i.e., intercontinental missile) of the new era."[43]

A similar example may be unfolding with respect to mobile-phone standards. Globally, two digital telecommunications standards have been in competition since the mid-1990s. Worldwide, global system for mobile communication (GSM), the European standard, has maintained a lead over code division multiple access (CDMA), the U.S. standard, despite the technological superiority of CDMA, because GSM was first to market and has been supported by a steady stream of consumer-friendly product innovations. GSM is now well established in China, while CDMA has never quite been able to break into the Chinese market, despite successful demonstration projects as early as 1994 and the adoption of the CDMA standard by Korea in the fall of 1993.[44] The internal mechanics of Chinese decision making with regard to digital telecommunications standards remains opaque to even the best-informed industry observers, but one suspicion has seemed increasingly likely in recent months. The suspicion is that Chinese policy makers intentionally slowed down the introduction of CDMA because they were unwilling to support the emergence of still another globally dominant U.S.-based technological standard.

In this interpretation, Chinese policy makers were willing to delay China's adoption of so-called second-generation digital wireless standards in order to increase their influence over the configuration of the subsequent third-generation (3G) digital wireless standards, which were just becoming operational during the second half of 2000. This may not be wishful thinking: in early 2000 China surpassed Japan as the second-largest mobile phone market in the world, with 51.7 million users.[45] Although all 3G standards mix elements of GSM and CDMA, there is still competition between 3G standards that are

[42] Chen "Guanzhu 'Xinxi Zhimin Zhuyi' Xianxiang" (Concerning information colonialism), *Jiefangjun Ribao* (PLA Daily), February 8, 2000.

[43] "China to Ban Government Use of Windows," Reuters, January 6, 2000. Officials at the Ministry of Information Industry later denied the ban, but the point, and the worry, is the same.

[44] Barry Naughton and John Norton, *Qualcomm in China: A Telecommunications Licensing Negotiation Exercise in Two Parts,* rev. ed. (San Diego: University of California, San Diego Graduate School of International Relations and Pacific Studies, 2000).

[45] "China Succeeds Japan as Largest Cell Phone Market in Asia-Pacific Region,"*China Online,* August 23, 2000, reporting on *Zhongguo Xinwen She.*

backward-compatible with existing GSM operations (so-called wideband CDMA, or WCDMA) and those that are backward-compatible with existing CDMA operations (CDMA 2000), supported by European and U.S. firms, respectively. China's determination to play a role became clear when it announced its own 3G standard, called TD-SCDMA, for which it achieved approval by the International Telecommunications Union (ITU) in August 2000.[46] The standard was developed by a Chinese SOE, Datang Telecom, in conjunction with a research institute of the Ministry of Information Industry, with technical assistance from Siemens. The standard is, no surprise here, closer to WCDMA than to CDMA 2000, and promises backward compatibility with GSM operations. Industry technical experts consider it too little, too late, but do not rule out the possibility that it can have an impact on the overall standard-setting process.

What is of interest in this case is the way that technonationalism has been elevated to the global plane and given a strategic dimension, in the sense that behavioral interactions with other global players are incorporated. The contrast with Korea's strategy is significant: Korea moved aggressively to be an early adopter of CDMA, paying a high price in royalties and license fees, but successfully establishing an equipment industry with strong export competitiveness. Korean planners chose a fast-follower strategy, accepting (or gambling) that the technological superiority of CDMA would lead to U.S. predominance.[47] By contrast, China, even though its manufacturing capabilities are much weaker than those of Korea, has been emboldened to play a global strategic role because of its confidence in the current – and especially future – importance of the Chinese market.[48]

The promotion of technical standards in which Chinese producers may have a future advantage is a good example of how China's future technology policy may be technonationalist in spirit, even if specific policies diverge from those found in past technonationalist programs. The promotion of the open Linux operating system is motivated by both economic and security concerns. Government leaders hope that Chinese companies can play a dominant role in a new market, and reduce the country's dependence on U.S. multinationals. But many of the companies the government hopes will lead the charge are nonstate enterprises. Red Flag, for example, is

[46] "International Telecom Union Adopts China's TD-SCDMA 3G Mobile Standard," *China Online*, August 15, 2000, reporting on *Caijing Zazhi* (Finance magazine) report, August 11, 2000, at <www.chinaonline.com/topstories/000815/1/c00081107>.

[47] Korean critics of that decision now abound, and they point to China's stance as a tougher, more nationalistic policy that they feel Korea should have followed. In that sense, China's stance has relegitimated hardball policies to some sections of the Korean public.

[48] In the case of telecommunications standards, the exogenous technological trends may be pushing the competing standards together into a consolidated or hybrid standard. To the extent this turns out to be true, we expect China to become more enthusiastic about CDMA, and simply use its own standard as a bargaining point in discussions about royalties.

backed by the Chinese Academy of Sciences and the Founder Group, a company spun off from Beijing University. The government is no longer concerned that a company is from the public sector, just that it can compete on
international markets and that it is Chinese.

Conclusion

Notions of technonationalism are still relevant in China, even as it moves
toward reduced government steerage of the economy. China's size gives it a
strategic sensitivity, as it worries about the impact of its own size and
growth on the attitude of outside technology suppliers. But at the same
time, because of its size, China has an impact on global standard setting
that certainly can be used to its advantage. Moreover, the Chinese government is constantly casting about for factors that justify its continuing hold
on power and its extensive involvement in the economy. Chinese policy
makers long ago gave up on the idea that they could steer and shape the
entire economy. But world views that legitimate continued government
intervention in the economy – even if those interventions are selective –
serve a useful domestic political purpose. This is especially true when the
Chinese government actively promotes a view of itself as the strong defender
of China's national interests and pride. Ironically, under current conditions
such a world view can also be used to justify a much more market-oriented
policy toward domestic enterprise and domestic private ownership. China
must privatize precisely because only privatization can assure a strong national
economy. For all these reasons, technonationalism lives in China.

But the continuing vitality of technonationalist views in China also needs
to be seen in context. That context includes the failure of large government-
sponsored business groups to succeed on any significant scale. It includes an
increasingly broad-based view that the key actors in the next phase of technological development are likely to come from a rich entrepreneurial
seedbed rather than nurtured national champions. The future context will
also have to factor in compliance with WTO provisions that further limit
the ways the government can intervene in economic processes. In summary,
the future is likely to display the continuing salience of technonationalist
attitudes, but without the coherent, tightly integrated policy package that
supported technonationalism in Japan during the 1950s through 1980s.
China will select bits and pieces of preferential policies, designed to advance
technonationalist ideals within the context of a fiercely competitive and
fairly open domestic economy. Such policies will often seem to lack intellectual coherence and represent purely adaptive, opportunistic policies of
"muddling through." In the past, though, "muddling through" has been a
fairly effective approach for policy makers trying to cope with China's
diversity and dynamism. Perhaps it will be in the future as well.

8

Economic Crisis and Technological Trajectories

Hard Disk Drive Production in Southeast Asia

Richard F. Doner and Bryan Ritchie

Technology policies, and economic policies more generally, are means by which countries can maintain or increase their autonomy within the international political economy. Concretely, autonomy in this sense refers to a country's capacity to adapt to or insulate domestic industry from external shifts. An important component of this capacity for more advanced developing countries is the ability to sustain technological upgrading, independent of foreign control. This chapter explores three propositions. One is that, owing to increasingly international production structures, the range of growth-promoting technology strategies has narrowed for the developing countries of Southeast Asia over the past decade or so. The second is that the institutional and political challenges of pursuing indigenous technological development and industrial upgrading within the constraints of global production structures are significant. Finally, both policy strategies as well as institutional and political challenges surrounding industrial upgrading have been impacted by the region's recent financial crisis, albeit in different ways and to differing degrees.

Policy decisions made by political and economic elites have had an important influence on indigenous technological upgrading in Southeast Asia. The significance of such decisions is reflected in the ways in which the three countries explored in this chapter – Malaysia, Singapore, and Thailand – differ with regard to indigenous technological capacities. Within this decision-centered framework we employ, we self-consciously privilege the influence of institutional configurations on developmental outcomes. In doing so, however, we recognize that ideological preferences, material capabilities, and the talents and creativity of individual leaders have also impacted processes of technological development and economic growth in Asia.

With the exception of the Philippines, all of the market-based Southeast Asian countries were included in the World Bank's "High Performing Asian

Economies" along with the Northeast Asian newly industrialized countries (NICs).[1] Yet these countries pursued different degrees of autonomy through different kinds of technological trajectories. Each trajectory involved varying degrees of protection for indigenous firms and efforts to promote and diffuse indigenous technology.[2] And each trajectory implied both varying degrees of sector specificity in policy and different levels of institutional challenges. Finally, each set of policies and institutions reflected and reinforced a set of political arrangements.

Shifts in global production structures are raising the bar for sustained growth in two ways. First, growth now requires a greater emphasis on technological upgrading, especially for the market-based countries of Southeast Asia, which can no longer rely on cheap labor to attract new investment. Second, in the past, developing countries could pursue more purely technonationalist development strategies where upgrading of indigenous firms could occur through various types of "hothouse" modes prior to exposure to global competition,[3] and where absorption and diffusion of technology could be carefully managed over substantial periods of time. Now, protectionist options have diminished while technological pressures have steadily increased. Upgrading increasingly requires a more technoglobalist approach wherein firms become an active – indeed, a proactive – cog in a globalized production network. Autonomy requires that countries be able to garner and maintain new rents in globalized value chains.[4]

---

[1] World Bank, *The East Asian Miracle: Economic Growth and Public Policy* (New York: Oxford University Press for the World Bank, 1993).

[2] For useful reviews of differences among the NICs, see Poh-Kam Wong, "The Role of the State in Singapore's Industrial Development," paper presented at the conference on The Role of the State in East Asian Industrial Development: Reflections in the Light of the Asian Crisis, University of California, Berkeley, 2000; Gregory Noble, *Collective Action in East Asia: How Ruling Parties Shape Industrial Policy* (Ithaca: Cornell University Press, 1998).

[3] Greg Felker suggests two "traditional" approaches. One is to follow comparative advantage-type sectoral development, whether or not the state led or followed shifting comparative advantage. This typically involved import substitution industrialization (ISI) followed by export oriented industrialization (EOI) in consumer goods, ISI followed by EOI in intermediates, etc. See also Gary Gereffy and Donald L. Wyman, eds., *Manufacturing Miracles: Paths of Industrialization in Latin America and East Asia* (Princeton: Princeton University Press, 1990). A second approach was the "reverse product life-cycle" in which firms entered advanced industries but in mature product segments, then attempted to close the gap by entering production sooner and sooner in the product cycle. See also Michael Hobday, "Technological Learning in Singapore: A Test Case of Leapfrogging," *Journal of Development Studies* 30, no. 4 (1994): 831–58. Personal communication with Felker, August 2000.

[4] Raphael Kaplinsky, "Spreading the Gains from Globalisation: What Can Be Learned from Value Chain Analysis," unpublished manuscript, Institute of Development Studies, University of Sussex, 1999; Gary Gereffi and Tony Tam, "Industrial Upgrading through Organizational Chains: Dynamics of Rent, Learning and Mobility in the Global Economy," paper presented at the 93rd annual meeting of the American Sociological Association, San Francisco, August 21–25, 1998.

This does not deny the importance of openness and macroeconomic stability. But it highlights the need for a combination of generic and sector-specific policies that not only regulate markets but also promote them. Concretely, this translates into an active focus on the promotion of indigenous suppliers and technical personnel. But in dynamic industries, such policies involve extensive transaction costs, principal-agent problems, collective action dilemmas, and distributional difficulties. As such, their implementation requires strong local institutions and political supports. In our view, these policies and institutional capacities have been evident in Taiwan, but especially in the Singapore government's "facilitation of MNC-induced technological learning."[5]

This concept of "MNC-induced technological learning" implies a hybrid of technonationalism and technoglobalism based both on ends and means. With regard to ends, nationalism can be understood as an effort to increase autonomy by capturing new rents within globalized value chains. Such ends require the nationalist means of promoting indigenous firms and diffusing technology through indigenous personnel. But indigenous promotion and diffusion can occur through the medium of foreign firms induced to operate in the local economy in part by attractive financial incentives but also by the availability of capable firms and personnel. (See Chapter 6 by Keller and Pauly in this volume.) As John Dunning has noted, the creation of strong local capacities helps foreign producers to make better use of their own assets.[6]

This argument carries a certain irony: effective participation in a clearly more globalized production structure requires a more developed set of local institutional strengths. If there is pressure for convergence, it is toward enhanced local capacities that go well beyond what has been called the "second Washington consensus" on the importance of open trade and investment regimes, macroeconomic stability, and secure institutions such as property rights, corporate governance, and financial regulation.[7] However, owing to institutional histories and a range of political factors, some will succeed in developing such capabilities, and others will not.

We explore these arguments through a cross-national examination of the hard disk drive (HDD) industry in three Southeast Asian countries: Singapore,

[5] Poh-Kam Wong and Chee-Yuen Ng, "Re-Thinking the Development Paradigm: Lessons from Japan and the Four Asian NIEs," paper presented at the conference on The Role of the State in East Asian Industrial Development: Reflections in the Light of the Asian Crisis, University of California, Berkeley, 2000, p. 17.

[6] John H. Dunning, "Location and the Multinational Enterprise: A Neglected Factor?" *Journal of International Business Studies* 29, no. 1 (1998): 45–66. This model of "MNC-induced technological learning" differs in important ways from the Japanese experience. It does not involve efforts to replace MNCs or to position indigenous producers at the top of a value chain. And although Singapore is quite picky about the foreign firms it encourages to operate within the city-state, those firms have much more leeway in their operations than was traditionally the case in Japan.

[7] Shahik Burki Javed and Guillermo E. Perry, *Institutions Matter: Beyond the Washington Consensus* (Washington, D.C.: World Bank Latin American and Caribbean Studies, 1998).

Malaysia, and Thailand. The disk drive industry exhibits, albeit in a relatively extreme way, the pressures for high quality, low price, and rapid delivery within international production networks increasingly evident in a broad range of industries. Indeed, the CEO of one of the industry's leading firms calls disk drive production the "extreme sport" of manufacturing.[8] If there is any industry in which the benefits of local technological activism within global networks should be obvious, it is hard drives. Singapore, Malaysia, and Thailand have been the center of global disk drive production since the 1980s.[9] For each nation, the industry has become a key source of economic growth. Yet if each of the three has clearly succeeded in the industry, Singapore occupies a higher and, we suggest, more sustainable rung on the technological ladder than do Malaysia and Thailand. This is due to Singapore's conception of autonomy as the capacity for constant movement up and across value chains, a set of market-based industrial policies designed to overcome key market failures, and a concomitant set of institutional attributes. Neither Thailand nor Malaysia approaches Singapore's technological objectives and institutional capacity for implementation.

But if the disk drive industry is so demanding, how have Thailand and Malaysia done so well in it? Regional spillovers and generic policy convergence have been key. Malaysia and Thailand expanded as open, stable, and proximate locations for more labor- and less skill-intensive activities no longer feasible in Singapore. But these two countries were not simply export platforms for the low-end activities of disk drive producers. Agglomeration economies, in the form of pools of technical personnel and suppliers critical to the industry's dynamic performance, have emerged in both countries. These agglomerations are largely the result of corporate initiatives and externalities rather than Singapore-like public policies, although such policies have been somewhat evident in Malaysia's Penang.

The Malaysian and Thai cases thus imply that even the hard disk drive industry has room for countries lacking the interest and capacity for upgrading. But they also suggest limits to such room. Although the 1997 crisis did not significantly hit the hard drive industry, disk drive producers have moved to consolidate operations in the past five years into the lowest-cost and most efficient sites. As evidenced by Seagate's reduction of its Thai work force from over 70,000 to less than 35,000 workers in the past three years, and a concomitant reduction of its Malaysian work force by almost

---

[8] Comments of Steve Luczo, CEO, Seagate Technologies, Stanford Graduate School of Business, November 1999, cited in David McKendrick, Richard F. Doner, and Stephan Haggard, *From Silicon Valley to Singapore: The Competitive Advantage of Location in the Hard Disk Drive Industry* (Stanford: Stanford University Press, 2000), chap. 2.

[9] Indeed, there is strong evidence that the knowledge and skills found in these three countries combined constitute an important source of the industry's growth and the dominance of U.S. producers. McKendrick et al., *From Silicon Valley to Singapore*.

half, there is no guarantee that the industry will continue to generate the jobs and foreign exchange that it has in the past.

In addition, there is evidence that disk drive production in these two countries occupies a sort of enclave, providing few spillovers in terms of indigenous suppliers and technology development. The 1997 financial crisis highlighted just such weaknesses in the "real" economies – declining terms of trade, overcapacity, and lack of value added – as well as the more publicized problems in the financial realm. In the case of Thailand and Malaysia, these reflected technological weaknesses.[10] However, technological reform responses to the crisis have varied – strong and effective in Singapore, extensive but not necessarily effective in Thailand, and relatively weak in Malaysia.

Challenges of Globalized Production Networks

Until the 1990s, developing country firms in a range of industries could prosper by producing large volumes of standardized goods at price and quality levels below world standards, often for protected markets. Such a trajectory is less and less possible with liberalized trade in industries increasingly characterized by at least four features: reduced importance of cheap labor; final consumer markets that are both more fragmented and more demanding on price, quality, and delivery; shortened product cycles; and increasingly rapid technology change.

These pressures are evident even in a traditionally labor-intensive industry such as apparel. As market segments have become more fragmented and shifted away from price toward style and quality, "the size of production runs has steadily declined along with the time available for manufacturers to respond to market demand."[11] Southeast Asian apparel producers are now under increased pressure to improve price, quality, and delivery through better supply chain strategies, use of new technologies, and more extensive technical training.[12] Requirements for developing countries in the automobile industry are also becoming much more rigorous. As part of their shift away from production for protected domestic markets to global sourcing strategies, global automobile producers are concentrating on a smaller number of suppliers. Such suppliers must not only be linked to final buyers, they must also be capable of producing and even designing components

[10] Sanjaya Lall, "Thailand's Manufacturing Sector: The Current Crisis and Export Competitiveness," paper presented at the conference on Thailand's Dynamic Economic Recovery and Competitiveness, Bangkok, May 20–21, 1998.

[11] Jonathan Winterton and Ian M. Taplin, "Making Sense of Strategies for Survival: Clothing in High Wage Economies," in Ian M. Taplin and Jonathan Winterton, eds., *Rethinking Global Production: A Comparative Analysis of Restructuring in the Clothing Industry* (Brookfield, Vt.: Ashgate, 1997), pp. 189–98.

[12] Achara Pongvutitham, "Textile Exporters," *Nation* (Bangkok), May 28, 1999.

at world-class prices, quality, and delivery times. Requirements are so stringent that some express doubts as to whether developing country participation in the global auto industry is worth the investment.[13]

Such pressures are even more extreme in the disk drive industry. Firms must confront difficult and dynamic technologies in both product and process.[14] A disk drive is composed of a large number of highly advanced components and parts that must operate together in tolerances several orders of magnitude closer than those required in textile or auto manufacture. For example, to store and retrieve information, the disk drive's "read-write head" must move rapidly over a disk at a distance less than the thickness of oil on a person's skin while the disk is spinning at up to 15,000 revolutions per minute (rpm). Industry experts compare positioning the head over the disk to flying a Boeing 747 .025 inches above the ground while maintaining a course of flight directly over the center-dividing stripe on a road. These kinds of high speeds and almost unimaginably close tolerances indicate the daunting challenges of disk drive manufacture. For example, just a few specks of dust can cause the heads to touch the surface. If this impact is too severe, they will "crash," resulting in damage to the heads or data surface, lost data, and, in the most extreme cases, destruction of the drive. In addition, disk drive firms must contend with continuing pressures for price cuts from computer makers and with product cycles of less than a year. Failure to move large numbers of specific models to market precisely when buyers want them results in major losses. Successful firms are those capable of reducing costs, increasing yields, bringing out new products, and getting those products to market in high volumes just when they are in demand. Given these kinds of demands, how have Singapore, Malaysia, and Thailand succeeded in becoming key disk drive manufacturing sites?

Different National Capacities Constitute One Regional Industry

By the late 1990s, Southeast Asia – especially Singapore, Malaysia, and Thailand – accounted for roughly two-thirds of global disk drive production.[15] Foreign, mostly U.S., firms accounted for almost all HDD shipments and most major components such as read-write heads, disk media, and motors. But if foreign producers dominate the industry, its growth and the success of U.S.

---

[13] Kaplinsky, "Spreading the Gains from Globalisation," p. 24; John Humphrey, "Assembler-Supplier Relations in the Auto Industry: Globalization and National Development," unpublished manuscript, Institute of Development Studies, University of Sussex, 1998.

[14] For a review of disk drive components and technology, see McKendrick et al., *From Silicon Valley to Singapore*, chap. 2.

[15] The United States accounted for 4.6 percent, Japan 15.5 percent, "other Asia" (mostly South Korea) 5.7 percent, and Europe 10 percent. Peter Gourevitch, Roger Bohn, and David McKendrick, "Who Is Us? The Nationality of Production in the Hard Disk Drive Industry," Report 97–01, Data Storage Industry Globalization Project, University of California, San Diego, 1997. Unless noted, the rest of this review is drawn from McKendrick et al., *From Silicon Valley to Singapore*, esp. chap. 6.

firms in particular owe much to the "location-specific" assets found and developed in Southeast Asia. This is a regional as well as a national story.

Over time, the region came to constitute a network that offered two important advantages. First, assets found in different countries allowed firms to build redundancy into their production. Geographic redundancy in suppliers, managers, and technical personnel mitigated risks linked to exchange rates or other cost changes, labor shortages or plant-level problems in production. Redundancy allowed the industry to raise or lower production in specific locations depending on changing requirements.

Second and more critical for our purposes were gains from trade among differently endowed production sites (again, facilitated by common adherence to open-trade and -investment regimes). Southeast Asia provided a geographically proximate mix of location specific capabilities that allowed foreign firms to choose from a range of cross-national investment sites to meet shifting production needs. This portfolio of capabilities includes various combinations of skill-intensive, specialized services such as process engineering, clean-room services, product testing, and failure analysis; sophisticated technology- and capital-intensive production processes such as disk sputtering or ion milling of recording heads; specialized and precision metalworking such as casting, surface treatment, and machining; routine but still advanced high-volume manufacturing of products such as printed circuit boards; and labor-intensive subassemblies and final assembly of drives.

The heterogeneous nature of this network highlights the national part of our story. This range of capacities is spread across the region roughly in line with national levels of development. Singapore, Malaysia, and Thailand have all developed agglomeration economies of pools of technical labor and specialized suppliers. But Singapore is clearly more developed than its two neighbors. As the core of more skill-intensive operations and decision making, Singapore has led the industry, accounting for 45–50 percent of global HDD shipments between 1986 and 1996. Qualitatively, the city-state is also dominant as the leader in regional administration, process engineering, and product engineering. Historically, Singapore facilities ramped up and debugged drives developed in the United States and then handed the product off to Thailand or Malaysia. Seagate's Singapore facilities are the site of the first disk drive designed in Southeast Asia (the U-4). Singapore is also the production center for the industry's highest-performance products – the high-end server drives manufactured by Seagate and IBM. Thailand is the core of motor production, heads assembly, and the assembly of notebook or mobile drives. Malaysia straddles the two, mixing drive assembly, media production, heads machining, and printed circuit board assembly.[16] This hierarchy is far

---

[16] Malaysia's median position is deteriorating, however. With the closure of Seagate's Ipoh plant, only the Kedai plant manufactures drives. The remaining plant in Penang manufactures head gimble assemblies. Most of Seagate's low-end drives are manufactured in China while the mid- to high-end drives are manufactured in Singapore.

from rigid. For example, Thai and Malaysian facilities now ramp up products directly from the United States and Japan rather than receiving mature products for their end-of-life manufacture. And both Thai and Malaysian facilities support drive facilities in China. But overall, Singapore remains at the apex of this system.

It does so in part by virtue of its pool of indigenous technical personnel. Consider the manufacturing requirements for high-end server drives, produced only in Singapore.[17] The complexity of these drives means that their assembly demands more technical support for equipment in areas such as head positioning and head-disk assembly. In addition, the greater number of components, the more complex electronics, and greater variation in interfaces expand the possible sources of failure. Conducting failure analysis consequently requires that engineers understand how a drive works as well as how to produce it. Finally, server drives require a range of other specialized skills, such as development of advanced error correction code algorithms. Singapore's engineering capabilities in all of these areas exceed those of any other country in the region.

Singapore's position at the apex of the regional hierarchy is also a function of the best-developed cluster of suppliers, numbering over 100 firms. Certainly, many of these firms are foreign, especially in the more complex areas of read-write heads, disk media, and spindle motors. But the number of indigenous suppliers is significant. Local producers dominate in the key area of precision engineering services (machining, metal stamping, surface treatment, die casting), as well as in clean-room design and printed circuit board assembly (PCBA). Three local PCBA firms now rank among the global top ten electronic contract manufacturers. And several local precision engineering firms have expanded to Malaysia and China along with their final customers.

Disk drive production has expanded significantly in Malaysia and Thailand in part due to spillovers from neighboring Singapore. Numerous foreign disk drive firms opted to move operations out of Singapore for reasons of labor costs and availability. However, Malaysia and Thailand each developed their own agglomeration economies, albeit not nearly so extensive as Singapore's. Malaysia, especially the state of Penang, offered a growing pool of technical personnel that facilitated initial transfer of operations from Singapore and allowed joint problem solving between the two production sites. Over time, local expertise allowed Penang to undertake functions previously monopolized by Singapore. Seagate's Penang facility, for example, served as a stand-alone production facility for certain products and functioned as a transfer point for

---

[17] Server drives "are an order of magnitude more complex to make than are drives of an earlier generation: they have more disks, more heads, more complex electronics, greater variation in interfaces, and consequently lower yields. The coordination challenges are also more demanding. High-end server customers demand a small lot and different interface configurations, and components have less commonality. Because customers also pay a premium for these drives, they are even more demanding about service and delivery times." Poh-Kam Wong et al., "Singapore," in McKendrick et al., *From Silicon Valley to Singapore*, chap. 7, p. 167.

China. Implementing this strategy required the creation of a New Product Introduction Center. Although yields in Seagate's China facilities were actually higher than those in Penang, this was because the Penang engineering team, trained by Seagate expatriates, had already performed substantial failure analysis and debugging.[18]

A group of indigenous suppliers also developed in Penang, although not as broad or deep as Singapore's. Some of these firms were joint ventures with Singapore component producers who had moved to Malaysia. But many were local firms who had gotten their start in other electronics segments and used their engineering, design, and production capacities to diversify into the disk drive industry. For example, several local firms played a growing role in line modification, tooling, and automation for Komag, a U.S. media producer.[19]

Thailand's strengths lay largely in its pool of technical personnel. One measure of these strengths is the accumulation of local expertise within disk drive producer Seagate, the country's largest employer. As of 1999, Seagate employed 33,000 people, of whom all but 10 were Thai nationals.[20] Seagate's newest facility in northeast Thailand has only a few permanently assigned expatriates out of some 8,000 regular employees. Yet there are clear limits to the depth of Thai technical personnel. One producer of very high precision parts was forced to recruit the core of its new tool and die shop from a training institute in India after failing to find sufficiently qualified Thai machinists. The situation is considerably bleaker with regard to indigenous suppliers. As of summer 1999, a survey of disk drive producers and component and service providers turned up very few indigenous firms (and these were found largely in low-value-added areas).

Goals and Policies

In this section we explore the roots of the region's disk-drive-related hierarchy of capacities. After assessing cross-national variation in capacities in light of the three countries' broader goals in high-tech industries,[21] we then examine the policies through which these objectives have been pursued.

Goals and Performance

Acknowledging the vast literature on economic development, we can think of three different kinds of economic growth – static efficiency, structural

---

[18] See McKendrick et al., *From Silicon Valley to Singapore*, chap. 9, which also provides other examples.

[19] Ibid.

[20] This does not include expatriate employees temporarily assigned to Thailand for specific problems or new product launches.

[21] Countries, of course, vary with regard to their emphasis on high-tech sectors. Certainly Singapore is most aggressive in this regard, Thailand the least, and Malaysia in the middle. We are grateful to Greg Felker for emphasizing this point.

change, and upgrading – each of which translates into an approach to high-tech industries. Static efficiency involves maintaining productivity while expanding profitability and capacity utilization in an existing product range and/or economic role.[22] Structural change refers to intra- and intersectoral changes, including shifts from agriculture to manufacturing, diversification within agriculture and/or manufacturing, expansion from downstream products to upstream intermediates and capital goods, and moves from labor-intensive manufacturing to more capital- and technology-intensive production. In terms of high-tech industries, structural change tends to be extensive in the sense of vertically expanding or integrating the value chain within the national boundaries.

By contrast, what we are calling upgrading is more intensive, referring to the capacity for efficient use of new investments in order to generate higher value added. At one level, upgrading is indicated by firms' capacities to reduce prices, increase quality, and shorten delivery times not simply through increased inputs but through more productive use of such inputs. A key indicator is thus total factor productivity. At another level, upgrading is indicated by the capacity to move within a value chain into more sophisticated products and economic activities, for example, from simple assembly to original equipment manufacturing (OEM), original brand manufacturing (OBM), and finally to original design manufacturing (ODM).[23] These shifts in turn require capacities in areas such as research, product development and design, and marketing.

Upgrading requires the ability to promote intersectoral linkages and to develop technology. The former refers not simply to the creation and coexistence of upstream and downstream sectors but to dynamic complementarities in which upstream firms supply higher-quality and cheaper inputs that promote the competitiveness of downstream producers.[24] Technological development, although a vast topic, can be understood through three dimensions:[25] deepening, which is the capacity to perform progressively more demanding

---

[22] Economic roles refer to activities characterized by specific bundles of goods and services. One useful categorization of economic roles involves a continuum of activities ranging from assembly, to assembly and testing, to OEM (original equipment manufacture) production, to ODM (original design manufacture), to OBM (original brand manufacture). Role differences "imply different kinds of linkages to tangible inputs and intangible services." Gary Gereffi, "Intel Inside: A Global Commodity Chains Perspective on Costa Rica's Industrial Upgrading Options," memo prepared for SSRC-CODETI-FLASCO Roundtable on Industrial Upgrading, San Jose, Costa Rica, March 2001, p. 3.

[23] Gereffi and Tam, "Industrial Upgrading through Organizational Chains," p. 8, from which our discussion of upgrading is adapted and modified.

[24] Charles Gore, "The Rise and Fall of the Washington Consensus as a Paradigm for Developing Countries," *World Development* 28, no. 5 (2000): 797.

[25] Greg Felker and Charles Weiss Jr., "An Analytic Framework for Measuring Technological Development," in Denis Fred Simon, ed., *The Emerging Technological Trajectory of the Pacific Rim* (Armonk, N.Y.: M.E. Sharpe, 1994), pp. 384–400.

functions related to the production process (e.g., maintenance, quality control, product development, equipment design); proximity, which is the distance to an industry's most productive or sophisticated technology; and indigenization, which is the degree to which local personnel have mastered production, management, design, and innovative tasks.

Although for clarity's sake we have characterized the three types of economic growth as functioning distinctly and separately from one another, in reality there is significant overlap and fuzziness among them. It may be helpful to consider the types of growth as occupying points along a continuum of technological progress and development with static efficiency at the low end, structural change toward the upper middle, and upgrading requiring the most intensive levels of technological change and innovation. It is clear from this conception that multiple types of growth may be functioning simultaneously within the same economy, indeed, the same industry.

Nevertheless, in spite of inherent overlap, these categories are useful for characterizing the core objectives of the three countries under study. In high technology, Thailand tends toward static efficiency objectives within a structural shift to upstream and high-technology sectors. From 1985 to 1993, higher mid-level technology manufactured goods such as computer parts, electronics, and electronic appliances grew at 30 percent, whereas the growth of more labor-intensive products such as garments slowed to an average of 14 percent. By 1995 exports of higher mid-level tech products were roughly 40 percent greater than those of labor-intensive products.[26] But by 1996 exports stagnated and the current account deficit reached 8 percent. In one short decade Thailand had lost its comparative advantage in labor-intensive manufactured goods.

The country's lack of ability to manufacture as opposed to assemble higher mid-level technology products was becoming obvious. In a 1998 study, Lall concluded that, despite its intensive growth during the 1980s, Thailand's export structure was closer to that of the Philippines than the structures of Taiwan, Singapore, South Korea, or even Malaysia. Although the Thai export structure was more advanced than that of China or Indonesia, "it is not evident that Thailand is operating at much higher technological levels in the production process."[27] Indeed, the World Bank has emphasized the "rapid reduction in the growth rate of total factor productivity [TFP] since the late 1980s, and strikingly low levels of R&D in the private sector, one of the lowest in the region as a proportion of GDP."[28]

---

[26] Sussangkarn Chalongphop, "Thailand: Looking Ahead to 2020 in Light of Global and Regional Changes," *TDRI Quarterly Review* 12, no. 2 (1997): 7.

[27] Lall, "Thailand's Manufacturing Sector," p. 4.

[28] World Bank, *Thailand Economic Monitor* (June 2000): 42–43. There is, of course, extensive controversy on TFP estimates. Wong's review finds a consistent pattern of higher values for the Asian NICs than for the ASEAN-4, but notes that Thailand seems to be an exception in some of the studies. Wong, "The Role of the State in Singapore's Industrial Development," p. 11.

Thailand had remained an assembly platform whose cost advantage was likely to prove as temporary as its success in lower-technology exports. The underlying problem was Thailand's weak engineering base. The country's ability to absorb new technologies and to raise the capacities of indigenous firms was "far more limited than it was in the newly industrialized countries at a similar stage in their development." Thailand's more sophisticated manufactured exports came from foreign firms; its domestic firms, in contrast, are well protected, heavily oriented to the domestic market, and have much lower technical capabilities.[29] In sum, Thailand is characterized by a delinked dualism in which a foreign-dominated, technologically rich export sector functions alongside, but is largely detached from, the indigenous, technology-poor, import-competing sector.[30]

Like Thailand, Malaysia has undergone an impressive structural transformation. Between 1971 and 1993 the manufacturing share of GDP rose from 14 percent to 30.1 percent. In dollars, manufactured exports rose from $122 million in 1970 to $2.3 billion in 1980 to $20.7 billion in 1991 and then doubled again to $42 billion by 1994. The annual rate of growth over this period was 27.7 percent per year. The highest growth was recorded between 1970 and 1980 when exports grew at 34.2 percent.[31]

In addition to promoting structural shifts, Malaysia has placed greater emphasis on technological upgrading than has Thailand. Lall characterizes this emphasis as shifting from light (easy, traditional) to heavy (complex, capital-intensive) activities. During the 1980s the pace of industrial deepening accelerated as exports of semiconductors were quickly followed by electricals and electronics exports. By 1990 Malaysia was far ahead of Thailand with an advanced industrial structure only marginally lower than that of both Korea and Taiwan. With regard to electricals and electronics, Malaysia's industrial structure was higher even than that of most OECD countries.[32]

---

[29] Francis X. Coloco, "Thailand's International Competitiveness: A Framework for Increased Productivity," paper presented at the conference on Thailand's Dynamic Economic Recovery and Competitiveness, Bangkok, May 20–21, 1998, pp. 12–14.

[30] See Paopongsakorn Nipon and Belinda Fuller, "Thailand's Development Experience from the Economic System Perspective: Open Politics and Industrial Activism," in Toru Yanagihara and Susumu Sombommatsu, eds., *East Asian Development Experience: Economic System Approach and Its Applicability* (Tokyo: I.D.E., 1997), pp. 466–518; Paopongsakorn Nipon and Pawadee Tonguthai, "Technological Capability Building and the Sustainability of Export Success in Thailand's Textile and Electronics Industries," in Dieter Ernst, Tom Ganiatsos, and Lynne Mytelka, eds., *Technological Capabilities and Export Success in Asia* (London: Routledge, 1997), pp. 309–59; Greg B. Felker, "Upwardly Global? The State, Business and MNCs in Malaysia and Thailand's Technological Transformation" (Ph.D. dissertation, Princeton University, 1998).

[31] Sanjaya Lall, "Technology Policy and Competitiveness in Malaysia," in K. S. Jomo and Greg Felker, eds., *Technology, Competitiveness and the State* (London: Routledge, 1999), p. 153.

[32] Ibid., pp. 151–52.

Nevertheless, these statistics do not reveal the underlying weakness of the Malaysian industrial structure. First, much of the advanced electrical and electronics industries is concentrated in final assembly, incorporating little in the way of design, development, and other advanced technical and marketing skills. Second, many heavy industries in Malaysia depend on imported components and have very few local supply linkages. Third, the industrial structure lacks a local capital-goods industry, which could seriously hinder the machinery-manufacturing sector, normally considered the "hub" of technological diffusion and progress. Fourth, like Thailand, Malaysia is characterized by a strong dualism. That is, the large numbers of small and medium-sized enterprises (SMEs), which comprise the majority of industrial employment, are effectively disconnected from the high-technology production structure geared to export or to heavy industry.[33]

Unlike Thailand, however, by the 1990s Malaysia had developed a core of firms that specialize in technologically advanced electronic processes and products, such as highly advanced thin-film disk manufacture and semiconductor testing and assembly.[34] Moreover, a new group of fast-growing, large local firms is beginning to compete technologically in the world export market.[35] The most impressive developments, however, have occurred in Penang. Dynamic backward linkages from foreign semiconductor assemblers have generated a strong set of indigenous machine tool firms, several of which have gone on to produce for the disk drive industry.[36] Nonetheless, this is an exception that proves the importance of institutions and politics.

Singapore conforms most closely to the upgrading ideal. While the economy grew at an average annual rate of 8.3 percent during the period 1960–98, manufacturing expanded at an even faster rate of 9.9 percent. Along with this expansion, technological upgrading in manufacturing has been impressive. From roughly half the Organization of Economic Cooperation and Development (OECD) average in 1980, Singapore's labor productivity almost equaled OECD levels in 1994 and exceeded levels of the other Asian newly industrialized countries.[37] These achievements are qualified by Singapore's extensive reliance on foreign firms for the bulk of manufacturing output. The foreign presence is especially high in electronics where

---

[33] Ibid., p. 153.
[34] Michael Hobday, "Understanding Innovation in Eletronics in Malaysia," in K. S. Jomo, Greg Felker, and Rajah Rasiah, eds., *Industrial Technology Development in Malaysia* (London: Routledge, 1999), p. 100.
[35] Ibid., p. 82.
[36] Rajah Rasiah, "Politics, Institutions and Flexibility: Microelectronics Transnationals and Machine Tool Linkages in Malaysia," in Fredrick Deyo, Richard Doner, and Eric Hershberg, eds., *The Challenge of Flexible Production in East Asia* (Boulder, Colo.: Rowman and Littlefield, 2000).
[37] Wong, "The Role of the State in Singapore's Industrial Development," p. 15.

majority foreign-owned firms accounted for 56 percent of the number of firms and foreign equity accounted for 85 percent of the industry's total capital.[38] Yet, unlike Thailand and Malaysia (with the Penang exception), the presence of foreign firms has stimulated the emergence of indigenous electronics producers and related suppliers, at least thirty of which had annual sales of $100 million or more in 1997. Many of these firms were founded by former employees of multinational corporations (MNCs) and, unlike their Thai counterparts, all must face global competition because Singapore provides no protection against foreign competition.[39]

Policies

It is often difficult to determine whether cross-national differences in growth outcomes reflect variation in goals and preference intensities or in the ability to implement policies designed to achieve those goals. Comparing policies can shed light on the relative weight of goals and preferences because, at a minimum, the absence of upgrading-related policies suggests a lack of attention to such objectives. The three countries under study converged on generic, sector-neutral policies, reflecting their common belief that foreign direct investment (FDI) was critical for economic growth. With regard to high-tech exporting industries such as disk drives, each was characterized by free labor market policies, free trade regimes, solid physical infrastructure, macroeconomic stability, an open investment regime (full ownership rights, absence of local content or export requirements), and highly attractive incentives, especially tax exemptions.[40]

The three countries did differ on the degree to which they even formulated policies designed to promote indigenous capacities in high technology, especially electronics, and in the disk drive industry in particular. Our overall argument is that, prior to the 1997 crisis, Thailand's leadership was simply not that concerned with upgrading. Malaysia, in contrast, has paid systematic attention to upgrading and technology issues. But the intensity of this attention was offset by other, more redistributive concerns. Singapore's policy focus on technology has been the most systematic as redistributive concerns were compatible with efficiency goals. In each country, institutional systems built on precrisis policy decisions reflected these ideological preferences. But as the crisis deepened, ideology was trumped by the imperative to develop indigenous technological capacity. Where institutional systems meshed with crisis-induced new or modified developmental objectives, as in Singapore, processes of indigenous technological development were effectively implemented or accelerated. Conversely, in Malaysia and Thailand, where institutional structures did not meet new developmental imperatives, reform was slow and difficult.

---

[38] Ibid., p. 33.
[39] Ibid.
[40] McKendrick et al., *From Silicon Valley to Singapore*, chap. 10.

A 1996 report concluded that Thailand's science and technology environment "was characterized by mismatches in S&T human resource supply, very low levels of R&D activity, a private sector with strong manufacturing capability but weak research, development and engineering capability, and an information technology that is growing but remains insufficient."[41] This state of affairs is in large part a function of a policy regime and underlying set of beliefs that autonomy does not require extensive upgrading and technology development. The policy emphasis has been on quantitative growth in jobs and exports, often relying on cheap labor and/or protection. A Thai quality assurance director at one hard disk drive firm (Micropolis) summed up the impact of public policies in stating that Thai government incentives "are for investors, not technology developers." A Chinese manager at another firm (Magnecomp) said that when he worked in Hong Kong, his main focus was on engineering issues; in Thailand, he spent most of his time on personnel and regulatory issues.[42]

These weaknesses are evident in human resource development, local vendor-supplier development, and technology diffusion and absorption. Thailand's skill-development efforts are notoriously weak. The country's rapid economic growth since the mid-1980s resulted in significant shortages of technical personnel. The government responded in the 1990s with a skills development program based on a Singapore program and a set of tax exemption programs. In addition to fragmented implementation, neither of these was designed in close consultation with representatives from electronics or disk drive firms. A striking illustration of the government's lack of attention to human resource issues is that relevant officials showed no awareness of a certification program in basic disk drive competence initiated in Singapore by the International Disk Drive Equipment and Materials Association, until notified by foreign researchers (author interviews).

Thailand's weak supplier base reflects tariff and tax policies that discouraged subcontracting between foreign exporters and local producers, and vendor development programs that did little to support indigenous suppliers. Until the early 1990s, export-oriented reforms were grafted onto protection for local firms producing for the domestic market, which effectively discouraged them from supplying exporting firms. Tariff protection for upstream investors raised the costs of downstream firms using such inputs. Exporting firms, such as Seagate, could of course avoid these costs by importing cheaper inputs and obtaining duty rebates or not paying any tariffs by locating outside of congested Bangkok. But for indirect exporters – that is,

---

[41] Brooker Group, "Modalities of University-Industry Cooperation in the APEC Region," APEC Research Project for the Thai Minister of University Affairs, Bangkok, 1996, p. 96.
[42] Unless otherwise noted, this policy review draws directly from Richard F. Doner, with Peter Brimble, "Thailand's Hard Disk Drive Industry," Report 98-02, Data Storage Industry Globalization Project, University of California, San Diego, 1999, sec. 3.

firms producing in Thailand for sale to final exporters – the burden was heavy.[43] Reinforcing these tariff policies was a series of levies that encouraged vertical integration by exporters.[44]

In addition, Thailand's vendor development programs were close to non-existent until the late 1990s. A 1990 report found that Sharp and Seagate had tried but failed to find even simple metal and plastic injection-molded components from local firms.[45] Other firms in the disk drive industry (IBM, Fujitsu, ADFlex, and Nidec) also failed to find suppliers for more complex tools. The lack of a supplier base also became a concern since the influx of FDI in the late 1980s had expanded the current account deficit to 8.5 percent of GDP in 1990.[46] After a halfhearted effort to impose stronger local content criteria on new foreign investments in 1991, the Thailand Board of Investment (BOI) initiated a non-incentive-based vendor development program to encourage technology diffusion and subcontracting linkages between MNCs and local suppliers – the BOI Unit for Industrial Linkage Development program (BUILD). Despite positive responses from long-established firms such as Minibea, the program basically faded, even after it was upgraded to a "National Supplier Development Program" involving all major agencies responsible for small and medium-sized enterprise development. Part of the problem was the government's general neglect and ignorance of the country's SMEs. Indeed, government agencies could not even agree on a basic definition of SMEs until the financial crisis of 1997.[47]

Thailand also paid insufficient attention to technology diffusion and absorption. The investment regime has contributed little to technology promotion. Led by the BOI, it has tended to ignore what might be called the "quality" of investments. Instead of focusing on the potential for technological spillovers, the BOI emphasized numbers of firms promoted, the financial

---

[43] To remedy this problem, the government extended duty offsets to indirect exporters in the late 1980s. But despite progress, significant delays in document processes, leading to delays in rebates and added costs for imported raw materials, continued to occur. This resulted in significant cost not only for local SMEs but even for foreign-owned suppliers operating in Thailand. One Thai-based supplier of wire to Seagate's Thai facilities regularly sent its product to Singapore and then reexported it back to Thailand the same day to avoid the paperwork and related delays involved in tariff rebates for indirect exporters (author interviews).

[44] Examples include a business tax that imposed a higher burden on interfirm subcontracting than on in-house production. This was replaced by a value-added tax (VAT) in 1992, but the refund for exporters remains a slow process.

[45] Carl Dahlman and Peter Brimble, "Technology Strategy and Policy for International Competitiveness: A Case Study of Thailand," Industry and Energy Department Working Paper, Industry Series Paper no. 24, World Bank, Washington, D.C., April 1990.

[46] Laurids Lauridsen, "Financial Crisis, Structural Problems and Linkage Policy in Thailand in the 1990s," paper presented at the 7th International Conference on Thai Studies, the Netherlands, July 4–8, 1999, p. 3.

[47] Ramon C. Sevilla and Kusol Soonthornthada, "SME Policy in Thailand: Vision and Challenges," unpublished paper, Institute for Population and Social Research, Mahidon University, Thailand, 2000.

value of promoted investment, and numbers of jobs generated.[48] Institutions explicitly devoted to technology promotion have been weak and fragmented. The lack of linkages between universities and industry has been a concern for several years,[49] resulting in the loss of opportunities to diffuse and commercialize useful innovations.[50] Thailand has also been weak in both direct and indirect provision of diffusion-oriented technical services. Despite efforts to consolidate since the mid-1980s, Thailand's industrial-standards agency has been unable to move quickly to establish mutual recognition agreements with standards authorities in major export markets. There have also been problems with regard to testing laboratories and services, despite requests for an expansion of such services from both local and foreign firms.[51]

Thailand's inattention to high technology is reflected in the electronics industry. As late as 1997 an individual with more than twenty years experience in Silicon Valley said that "the industry was confused by the government's policies" and that Thai governments "had never had firm policies to develop the electronics industry despite its high potential."[52]

In contrast to the Thai case, Malaysia's weaknesses are not a function of public neglect of technology and upgrading. Beginning in the 1980s, science and technology policy became "progressively more institutionalized and integral to government development planning."[53] An Industrial Master Plan and Technology Action plan provided detailed surveys of the technical strengths and weaknesses of specific sectors and targeted several technology priority areas: electronics, biotechnology, information technology, advanced materials, and automated manufacturing.

---

[48] Larry Westphal, Kops Kri, Tayakirana: Kosal Petchsuwan, Harit Sutabutr, and Yongyuth Yuthavong, "The Development of Technological Capability in Manufacturing: A Macroscopic Approach to Policy Research," in Robert E. Evenson and Gustav Ranis, eds., *Science and Technology: Lessons for Development Policy* (Boulder, Colo.: Westview Press, 1990), p. 123.

[49] Brooker Group, "Modalities of University-Industry Cooperation in the APEC Region."

[50] A disk drive engineer in Bangkok contrasted the Thai situation with a case in Singapore involving the development of head cleaning technology. Read-Rite uses a water-based process, which obviously can introduce impurities. While in Singapore, this engineer learned of laser-based cleaning equipment developed by National University of Singapore (NUS) researchers. But the researchers were not able to make the shift from equipment that would clean a few heads to those cleaning millions. With support from Japanese investors, a spin-off resulted that did develop higher-volume equipment. Fujitsu is reportedly using the equipment and Read-Rite is considering it (interview by author, 1999).

[51] In 1987 Thailand's peak business association urged the government's major lab to accredit private laboratories to perform testing services, but only twenty-five firms were accredited by 1994. Felker, "Upwardly Global?"

[52] Priwan Yuthana, "Industry: Electronics Institute Planned: B20bn Fund Would Back New Ventures," *Bangkok Post*, August 4, 1997.

[53] Greg Felker, "Malaysia's Innovation System: Actors, Interest and Governance," in Jomo and Felker, *Technology, Competitiveness and the State*, p. 11, from which, unless otherwise noted, this review of Malaysian policy is drawn.

As early as the 1980s, Malaysia began to address shortages of technical personnel. After a disappointing response to a double tax deduction for training expenditures (1986), the government created a Human Resources Development Fund (HRDF) in 1993, which was a payroll levy and subsidy scheme in the early 1990s modeled on Singapore's Skill Development Fund. Simultaneously the government initiated reform efforts in higher education. These included an expansion of science and technology programs, permission for foreign universities to open Malaysian branch campuses, shortened degree requirements to speed the entry of engineering graduates into the work force, and incentives to encourage the state-owned telecommunication firm to set up a degree-granting institution. In a further effort to promote university-industry linkages, the government launched a project in 1997 to create a Malaysian Science and Technology University with assistance from the Massachusetts Institute of Technology (MIT).

Weakness in vocational education, for example in programs such as the National Apprentice Scheme and the Trade Skill Certification Courses, prompted the government to create joint training ventures with foreign governments and private firms. In the former case, the Malaysian government partnered with the French, German, and Japanese governments to set up technical training institutes. In the latter, the government supported the creation of industry-sponsored training centers. The forerunner of these industry-oriented training centers was the Penang Skills Development Centre, which was a cooperative initiative involving the Penang Development Corporation, local and foreign firms, and the local university. The venture was so successful that in 1994 the Malaysian government began providing fiscal incentives for Malaysia's other states to emulate Penang's example.

Yet in the final analysis, the return on these initiatives has been less than optimal. First, of the funds contributed to the HRDF, less than half were claimed for training expenses. Also troubling, only a tiny fraction of SMEs have registered with the HRDF or participate in its programs. Second, fragmentation and duplication are rife among university and vocational education institutions, at both state and federal levels. The lack of qualified instructors has been a clear impediment, especially for technical and engineering subjects. Third, linkages between academia and training institutes and the private sector remain scarce. Training centers established on the PSDC model have yet to achieve the same level of private firm participation as in Penang. Finally, as the economy shows signs of recovering, promising initiatives have lost government interest and support and faded away. For example, the effort to create the Malaysian Science and Technology University with MIT's help has been abandoned in favor of other initiatives.[54]

Malaysia also initiated ambitious programs as early as 1988 to promote subcontracting links between indigenous and foreign firms. The first program

---

[54] Interviews by author, Malaysia, October 2000–January 2001.

was a vendor-development effort, initiated by the government-owned auto firm Proton, to bring indigenous Malay (Bumiputera) suppliers into the formerly exclusively ethnic-Chinese autoparts industry. This was expanded in 1993 to the Vendor Development Programme through which large local firms and multinationals, in cooperation with state agencies and local banks, helped local firms with technical assistance, subsidized finance, and procurement contracts. More than fifty foreign firms signed on as "anchor companies," with the electrical and electronics industries accounting for the overwhelming majority of companies. Yet, as of 1995, the program had "yet to register a major impact on technology transfer through industrial sub-contracting networks."[55] Part of the problem involved lack of clear performance measurements and monitoring. Part reflected the weaknesses of the country's long-standing SME-assistance schemes. Again, however, Malaysia's state of Penang stands out as the exception. There, the Penang Development Corporation forged subcontracting linkages between foreign semiconductor firms and local machine tool firms resulting in several clusters of high-tech industries, including semiconductors and, as noted earlier, disk drives and related industries.

Finally, Malaysia has begun to promote actively the acquisition, transfer, and diffusion of new technology for foreign multinationals. Initially, Malaysia discriminated between FDI primarily on the basis of employment potential. But by the early 1990s it became increasingly clear that levels of technology in the private sector were low in the aggregate and that technology "spillovers" between foreign and local firms were minimal. In response, the government implemented incentives that rewarded firms for increasing R&D expenditures and improving the ratio of science and technical graduates to non-technical employees.[56] Yet it is unclear whether these incentives have had any real impact. Even after the financial crisis, levels of R&D in the foreign-dominated electrical and electronics sector is virtually nonexistent.[57]

The government has also attempted to stimulate technology creation by establishing specialized technology parks, essentially ready-made clusters of private research facilities and technology-intensive companies. These began in 1988 with the Technology Park Malaysia as an incubator program for microenterprises in information technology and electronics. It continued with the Kulim High-Technology Park in the northern state of Kedah, a facility with specialized infrastructure, public research institutes, technical universities, and special resources for SMEs. This facility now houses a number of disk drive and related component firms. The most ambitious project is the Multimedia Super Corridor, a multibillion dollar effort offering special facilities and incentives to promote the growth of information technology research and development. All of these efforts are buttressed by a range of financial

[55] Felker, "Malaysia's Innovation System," p. 19.
[56] Ibid., p. 16.
[57] Interview by author.

incentives for industrial R&D and by public standards, productivity, and research institutes devoted to offering special assistance for SMEs.

Singapore's technology development efforts, both in general and in relation to the hard disk drive industry, have been extensive and effective. In particular, the government emphasizes both quality and quantity in human resources. Given the city-state's small population, the government implemented a highly liberal and active policy of drawing on high-skilled, foreign personnel. Singapore's Economic Development Board (EDB) set up an International Manpower Division to attract foreign talent.[58] The distinctly "technoglobalist" nature of this personnel policy should be noted. For Singapore, if the reduction of external vulnerability requires foreign support, so be it (as reflected in the hiring of an expatriate to head the government Development Bank of Singapore).[59]

Public policies to improve the quality of labor devoted to high technology have been the most substantial in the region.[60] In the 1970s the government initiated efforts in vocational training, efforts that expanded to include a whole range of sectors and skill levels. The EDB established industrial training centers, actively seeking out foreign firms and institutions to cosponsor training programs. A Skills Development Fund based on a compulsory payroll tax was developed to train less-skilled workers. Companies can use this tax only by sending workers to approved training programs. Interviews with HDD producers and suppliers indicate that most if not all have used this program for worker training.[61] Direct public assistance went to workers pursuing training in specific technical skills, such as computer numerically controlled (CNC) machining. As required skills became more advanced, the government responded with new programs at the undergraduate and graduate levels in both the polytechnics and universities. Although these do not necessarily target the HDD industry, these programs have expanded the reservoir of disk drive manufacturing process-engineering skills.

Disk drive producers have also used other subsidized skill upgrading programs. In the mid-1990s, for example, several hard disk drive majors were using automation promotion incentives to adopt computer-integrated technologies and to send engineers abroad to be trained in advanced automation technologies. Finally, the government has recently collaborated with IDEMA, the international disk drive trade association, to provide specialized certification training for the industry.

---

[58] Wong and Ng, "Re-Thinking the Development Paradigm," p. 18.

[59] We are grateful to Greg Felker for this fact and for noting that when some people objected to this hiring, the government responded that Singapore could not afford nationalist protection (personal communication).

[60] Unless noted, this review of Singapore policies is drawn from McKendrick et al., *From Silicon Valley to Singapore*, chap. 7, written with Wong Poh-Kam.

[61] Ibid., p. 175.

Support for indigenous producers really developed following the recession of 1985. Several precision engineering firms serving the hard disk drive industry grew through a variety of public financial and technical assistance programs. The most important, at least for the hard disk drive industry, has been the Local Industry Upgrading Program (LIUP) launched by the EDB in 1986. Several features of this effort have contributed to its success. First, the EDB pays the salary of experienced multinational managers who identify and work with local suppliers with competitive potential. Second, the LIUP managers from different multinationals meet regularly at the EDB to combine their knowledge of problems facing local suppliers. In doing so, they leverage resources beyond their own firms even as they provide EDB officials with a full picture of supplier and multinational needs, thus allowing for a fine-tuning of the program. Finally, the LIUP has provided valuable preferential financing.

The third component of Singapore's technology efforts involves R&D promotion. The National Science and Technology Board (NSTB) has initiated a number of incentive schemes that, while open to foreign and local firms in and outside of the disk drive industry, have been used by all the disk drive majors in Singapore. Government research promotions have grown more extensive and more industry specific in the 1990s. In 1992 the NSTB set up the Magnetics Technology Center to provide technical support to the hard disk drive industry and stimulate a virtuous cycle of local R&D activities. Despite initially minimal achievements, the government expanded the Magnetics Technology Center into a Data Storage Institute (DSI) in 1996 to cover technology not just in magnetic storage but also optical and other storage technologies. The DSI has a staff of 144 and an annual budget of $28 million. Over time, it has drawn disk drive firms into collaborative agreements, leading to several approved patents and the establishment of at least one company in laser texturing of magnetic disks and laser microfabrication. Finally, the government provides direct financial support for corporate R&D. Such funding encouraged Seagate to create a design center in 1984. The center began doing design work in 1994, in part due to pressure and incentive funding from the EDB. By 1997 the firm's R&D staff grew to 140 and, in 1998, came out with the first disk drive designed in Southeast Asia (the low-cost U4).

Until the beginning of the crisis, the Singapore government directed most of its resources to encourage R&D in foreign MNCs. The 1997 crisis, however, placed into stark relief the top-heavy nature of the economy, making it apparent that small, technopreneurial firms were not being created. In response, the NSTB set aside $1 billion as seed capital to encourage spinoffs of indigenous technology firms from university incubators and the thirteen public research institutes.[62]

---

[62] Interview by author, Singapore, July 2000.

Several points emerge from the preceding account. First, Singapore's technology policies are the most extensive and industry-specific in the region. Second, these efforts are sustained over the long run, unless they are inconsistent with market performance.[63] Third, the policies are based on serving the needs of the industry, even as they reflect an effort to anticipate the kinds of skills and services Singapore requires to maintain its position in the high-value-added portion of the electronics value chain. Indeed, these policies reflect the belief that disk drives are an integral part of a broader electronics value chain. Fourth, the policies are designed to induce foreign firms to localize high-technology functions and to root them in dense, local institutions. Fifth, the policies are a reflection of Singapore's belief that local clusters or agglomerations constitute the best way to retain the country's position in electronics or any value chain. Sixth, the policies indicate that Singapore does not see a contradiction in pursuing national technological objectives through the simultaneous promotion of both local and foreign firms. As a result, these policies have effectively generated not only a pool of technical expertise and reliable suppliers; they have also begun to generate technological spillovers among drive producers, something that has not (to our knowledge) occurred elsewhere in the region.[64]

An early event in Singapore's electronics history illustrates the country's efforts to draw on foreign firms to develop local capacities. The government recruited Rollei, a German camera maker with strong machining capacities, to Singapore in the 1960s. In conjunction with the EDB, the firm set up an in-house precision engineering training institute, which succeeded in training twice as many precision engineers as Rollei needed for its operations in Singapore.[65] When Seagate established its Singapore operation, it asked the EDB for help in finding local producers of basic metal parts and components. Several of the suppliers were founded by Rollei alumni. Several years later, Seagate's motor division opted to set up a precision tool and die operation in Singapore in part because of a government-sponsored institute headed by a German formerly employed by Rollei.

---

[63] In 1996 Singapore Technologies, a government-owned, high-tech conglomerate, purchased a disk drive firm, Micropolis. The acquisition was a financial disaster and was liquidated in 1998 after significant losses.

[64] This involves mutual benchmarking as well as diffusion of process innovations. For example (the only one we have at this time), a disk drive official developed a way for drives to test themselves without specialized testers. Despite his patenting the technique, everyone in Singapore copied it and cut the amount of time sharply from the previous three days. McKendrick et al. *From Silicon Valley to Singapore*, p. 180.

[65] The firm's decision to close its operations in 1981 was a traumatic event for Singapore, which was not used to such departures. Instead of criticizing the firm, a senior government minister went on television to praise the firm for the skills it had developed and the toolmakers it had trained. And, in fact, several of its technicians went on to open their own precision engineering firms to service the new electronics MNCs.

Preferences, reflected through policies, are not the only determinant of technology development. After all, Thailand and Malaysia have initiated or considered training programs patterned after those in Singapore. Thailand attempted to strengthen its supporting industries as early as the late 1980s; Malaysia essentially copied the cluster and value-chain concept from Singapore for its Second Industrial Master Plan; and Penang consciously followed Singapore's policies of "MNC-induced technological learning." Yet only Penang has successfully emulated Singapore's achievements in using foreign producers to generate a strong local technology cluster.[66] Explaining differential capacities for implementing similar policies suggests the importance of variation in institutional strengths.

Institutional Capacities

Institutional Challenges of New Industrial Policies

Singapore's technology policies, viewed through the disk drive case, belie the dichotomy between state- and market-led policies. They illustrated the importance of basing sectoral interventions on market criteria and on general openness in trade and investment regimes; they also suggest that sector-specific measures do not necessarily lead to the subsidies, protection, and allocative inefficiency so often emphasized by critics of industrial policy. Indeed, in part for political economy reasons, a commitment to free investment and trade policies is critical for sectoral measures. These policies constitute a useful monitoring mechanism to ensure that business-government relations do not sink into rent seeking and that firms are exposed to global market pressures. Protectionism and the lack of competitive pressure was one key factor in the failure of Brazil to sustain its early effort in disk drive production.[67]

But, as recent research suggests, openness to both foreign trade and investment are not sufficient for the kinds of upgrading necessary for long-term growth.[68] "The trick in the successful cases has been to combine the opportunities offered by world markets with a domestic investment and institution-building strategy to stimulate the animal spirits of domestic entrepreneurs."[69] But endogenous growth theory suggests that simple "animal

---

[66] Richard F. Doner and Eric Hershberg, "Flexible Production and Political Decentralization: Elective Affinities in the Pursuit of Competitiveness?" *Studies in Comparative and International Development* 34, no. 1 (Winter 1999): 45–82.

[67] Brazil initiated local drive production by indigenous firms before HDD investment in any other developing country. For details, see McKendrick et al., *From Silicon Valley to Singapore,* chap. 10.

[68] Dani Rodrik, "Development Strategies for the Next Century," paper presented at the conference on Developing Economies in the 21st Century, Institute for Developing Economies, Chiba, Japan, January 26–27, 2000; Ashoka Mody, "Industrial Policy after the East Asian Crisis: From 'Outward-Orientation' to New Internal Capabilities?" unpublished manuscript, World Bank, Washington, D.C., November 15, 1998, pp. 13–14, 25.

[69] Rodrik, "Development Strategies for the Next Century," p. 8.

spirits," even when new technology is available "off the shelf" (rarely the case), are themselves insufficient to generate growth in an entire sector or economy. This is especially true given the need to expand product variety, to improve product quality, and to reduce costs as outlined here.[70] Traditional objectives of capital formation, job growth, and foreign exchange earnings are thus now supplemented by efforts not just to exploit current relative cost advantages but also "to promote investment and learning in economic activities where comparative advantage can realistically be expected to lie in the immediate future as the economy develops and as other late industrializing countries catch up."[71]

These goals require policy instruments focused on areas typically plagued by market failures: human resource development, technology diffusion, supplier linkages, and advanced infrastructure.[72] Such instruments involve a combination of sector-specific and sector-neutral policies.[73] This combination is driven by two factors. First, firms typically benefit from both generic and more industry- or product-specific services in areas such as training or advanced infrastructure and logistics. Second, the very definition of "sector" is now questioned, as successful countries view their economies as sets of value chains. The capacity for sustained growth thus requires going beyond support for discrete industries to "fostering the growth of dynamic industrial 'clusters' of complementary assembly, component production, producer-services, skill-development and technology support."[74]

These kinds of public policies are more difficult to implement than either sector-neutral or sectoral protectionist policies. The latter can – to exaggerate only slightly – be promulgated by the government with the stroke of a pen.[75] By contrast, the formulation and implementation of industry-specific policies such as training and supplier development require that governments directly mobilize and draw on the specialized knowledge of private actors, including the sharing of proprietary knowledge that can expose firms to risks of opportunism. Moreover, these informational requirements are highly dynamic; policies appropriate to one stage of the industry's growth may not be germane at another.[76]

---

[70] Paul Romer, "Endogenous Technological Change," *Journal of Political Economy* 98, no. 5 (1990): S71–S102.

[71] Gore, "The Rise and Fall of the Washington Consensus as a Paradigm for Developing Countries," p. 797.

[72] Mody, "Industrial Policy after the East Asian Crisis"; Hans J. Peters, "Thailand's Trade and Infrastructure," paper presented to the conference on Thailand's Dynamic Econmic Recovery and Competitiveness, Bangkok, May 20–21, 1998.

[73] Gore, "The Rise and Fall of the Washington Consensus as a Paradigm for Developing Countries," p. 797.

[74] Jomo and Felker, *Technology, Competitiveness and the State*, p. 4.

[75] McKendrick et al., *From Silicon Valley to Singapore*, chap. 10.

[76] The challenges have been captured by the New Institutional Economics literature. Christopher Clague, "The New Institutional Economics and Economic Development," in Clague, ed.,

Such problems typically defy resolution through simple arm's-length or parametric interventions common to generic, "base line" policies. They are rather "institution-intensive,"[77] requiring arrangements that facilitate information sharing, mutual monitoring, implementation of collective goals, and compensating losers while empowering winners. What kinds of institutions? Competition-promoting policies require enhanced rather than minimalist states. Only states with expertise, flexibility, and some degree of autonomy can appreciate, much less implement, sector-specific policies that promote private-sector efficiency. But states cannot pursue such policies absent extensive contact with those most directly involved in the market. Systematic public-private consultation can improve information for public-sector decisions, broaden ownership and enhance the credibility of such policies, improve accountability and transparency, and expand resources for policy implementation. And finally, such public-private sector exchanges can benefit from business itself being organized (although bilateral consultations with specific firms may be more suitable for policies involving highly proprietary information).[78]

Variation in Institutional Capacities

The three Southeast Asian countries differ significantly with regard to institutional capacities. Singapore's ability to implement as well as to formulate effective policies is a function of a network of well-coordinated agencies led by the Economic Development Board. These agencies benefit from strong political backing and insulation from democratic constraints by Singapore's

---

Institutions and Economic Development (Baltimore: Johns Hopkins University Press, 1997), pp. 1–13. First, transaction costs – the costs of searching, bargaining, and enforcing deals – increase with the number of actors involved, the information intensity of policy, and the extent of policy adjustment required to meet shifting industry requirements over time. Second, principal-agent problems become more acute when policy making and implementation involve more layers of government and larger numbers of private actors. Third, collective action problems grow with the involvement of larger numbers of actors, each of which may be tempted to "cheat" – to free-ride on the efforts and information provided by others. The tendency of firms to poach skilled workers from others rather than to contribute to training programs, whether in-house or industry-wide, is an obvious instance of such problems. And finally, because the resolution of differences within value chains typically results in winners and losers, growth-promoting measures can be undermined by distributive problems. These can in turn contribute to time inconsistency on the part of political leaders who, because of political reactions, might discount the future gains of growth-promoting measures.

[77] Clague, "The New Institutional Economics and Economic Development," p. 3.

[78] Business associations can help to limit the pursuit of particularistic benefits by individual firms and facilitate the provision of critical industry-specific information from – and among – firms. However, the degree to which associations pursue such productive objectives seems to depend on their exposure to market pressures and the imposition of selective benefits by state officials. Richard F. Doner and Ben Schneider, "The New Institutional Economics, Business Associations and Development," Discussion Paper 110, ILO, International Institute for Labour Studies, Geneva, 2000.

dominant party system (led by the People's Action Party). As a result, officials are able to formulate policies with a view toward longer-term objectives nested within a vision based on dynamic clusters of related activities. These processes are themselves predicated on the assumption that the government's role is to catalyze, not replace, the private sector.

This requires monitoring of and engagement with the private sector. Government officials are sufficiently informed and organized to monitor and to hold firms accountable for their use of incentives and subsidies. The criterion of accountability is a firm's or industry's capacity to succeed in the market. In the case of state support for local companies in the Local Industry Upgrading Program, market performance is interpreted through a local firm's success in linking up with and supplying export-oriented, foreign firms.

Such monitoring overlaps with engagement. At the sectoral level, there is evidence of extensive collective engagement with business on issues of human resources, supplier development, and technology diffusion. As noted, for example, the Economic Development Board actively sought out multinational corporations to establish industrial training centers, institutes, and programs in its promotion of electronics-related skills development. Similarly, the Data Storage Institute (whose chair is the head of Hewlett-Packard in Singapore) is also highly attentive to demands emanating from the industry, which has been drawn into the Institute through its governance structure. In effect, the Data Storage Institute serves as a mechanism for organizing the disk drive industry in Singapore. Finally, the success of the Skills Development Fund is predicated on close ties with organized labor (National Trade Union Congress) as well as with business.[79] Extensive input from business has ensured that participation in the Skills Development Fund is high; amazingly, as of 1999, 100 percent of firms with more than ten employees participated. Cooperation between labor and the Skills Development Fund has made it possible for the National Trade Union Congress to implement a new Skills Redevelopment Program using existing funds from the Skills Development Fund and infrastructure to train both union and nonunion workers, avoiding costly duplication.[80]

Thailand's institutional capacities are distinctly weaker. First, Thailand lacks any kind of politically powerful and cohesive agency focused on technological upgrading. The country's macroeconomic agencies, historically the most powerful and cohesive government bodies, assumed that macro-

---

[79] Bryan Ritchie, "Innovation Systems, Collective Dilemmas, and the Formation of Technical Intellectual Capital in Malaysia, Singapore, and Thailand," *International Journal of Business and Society* 2, no. 2 (2001): 21–48.

[80] In addition, the SDF does not directly administer any funds. All fund disbursement is handled through a financial department in the Productivity and Standards Board (PSB), which coordinates with the Ministry of Finance. Thus, those that distribute the funds do not determine where they go, and those that determine where they go do not distribute them (interview by author, Singapore, July 2000).

economic stability was sufficient for growth (as indeed it was for many years). Second, policy implementation is weakened by splits between the macroeconomic agencies and sectoral ministries as well as fragmentation among the latter. Finally, since the 1990s the country's competitive party system, driven by rural-based politicians with little support for industrial promotion, have politicized the sectoral ministries and further undermined support for industrial upgrading.

These conditions have severely hindered the development of effective R&D and training institutions and policies. As part of the Sixth Plan (1986–91), the government created the partially autonomous Science and Technology Development Board (STDB) to strengthen applied research in the public sector, diffuse public-sector R&D expertise to local firms, and offer direct support to private-sector research initiatives. Nevertheless, these objectives were undermined when the Ministry of Science, Technology and the Environment (MOSTE) created three technology institutes to pursue the same objectives as the STDB. Fragmentation is even more severe in technical training. At least seven ministries have a major role in education and training leading to duplication, waste, and intense bureaucratic infighting.[81]

Bureaucratic rivalries have also hampered initiatives to develop public institutions devoted to technology acquisition and diffusion. For example, the Fifth Development Plan (1982–86) called for the creation of a Public Technology Transfer Corporation. Nevertheless, the effort was blocked by interministerial rivalry. Likewise, the Thailand Institute of Scientific and Technological Research (TISTR), patterned after Korea's Advanced Institute for Science and Technology (see Chapter 6), foundered under a combination of bureaucratic controls and political interference.[82] Finally, all of these initiatives have suffered from a lack of systematic private-sector input.

At first glance, institutions in Malaysia appear significantly more centralized and cohesive than those in Thailand. In fact, however, once outside the inner sanctum of the prime minister's executive offices and agencies, the bureaucracy is highly fragmented, disconnected, and duplicative with few linkages to the private sector.[83] Rather than the line ministries, it is executive-level bodies, such as the Economic Planning Unit, Office of Technology Policy, and Malaysian Business Council that coordinate economic, investment, and

---

[81] Bryan Ritchie, "The Recourse Curse, Ethnicity, and the Origins of Technical Education and Training," paper prepared for the annual Meeting of the American Political Science Association, Atlanta, September 1999. For example, both the Ministries of Education and Interior provide primary education; the Ministries of Education, Labor, Industry, Interior, and Agriculture all provide vocational education; and the Ministries of Education and University Affairs both provide tertiary education.

[82] Peter Brimble and Chatri Sripaipan, "Science and Technology Issues in Thailand's Industrial Sector: The Key to the Future," paper prepared for the Asian Development Bank, Bangkok, June 1994.

[83] Ritchie, "Innovation Systems, Collective Dilemmas."

technology policy. Line ministry implementation at the sectoral level has been hampered by a lack of qualified personnel and by institutional fragmentation. The Malaysian Industrial Development Agency (MIDA), for example, lacks responsibility for fostering subcontracting linkages, while the Prime Minister's Office exercises significant discretion over some of the country's most important industrial initiatives. This discretion is in turn justified by the need for distributive policies to favor ethnic Malays (Bumiputera) over ethnic Chinese.[84]

Ethnic politics have had two deleterious effects. One is to direct most upgrading efforts, such as SME promotion, toward promoting the entry of new Bumiputera firms, rather than toward broad technological support for existing manufacturers.[85] The second is to generate mistrust on the part of ethnic Chinese manufacturers who fear that participation in government assistance programs will lead only to more exposure to tax and regulatory authorities.[86] The overall result is to weaken public-private linkages.

The exception to this fragmentation is Penang, where the Penang Development Corporation (PDC) has been relatively unified, consulting effectively with and linking both multinationals and local firms. The fact that local firms in Penang are just as ethnic Chinese as elsewhere in Malaysia suggests the impact of broader political factors on institutional capacities.

Explaining Institutional Capacity: External Threats, Domestic Coalitions

Explaining these policy and institutional differences, at least prior to the 1997 crisis, requires understanding the incentives of politicians in building institutions and devising industry-specific policies. Our explanation emphasizes two related factors: external pressures and coalitional bases.[87]

External pressures, including security challenges from other countries and economic shocks of various sorts, typically have an important influence on the course of national development. Most generally, they expand the ability of political leaders to build new institutions and launch policy initiatives. More specifically, external shocks can influence the attention national leaders give to manufacturing, and to export-oriented manufacturing as a way of garnering foreign exchange in particular.

Singapore's national institutions emerged in the 1960s as the country faced a diverse set of external challenges: security threats from Indonesia,

---

[84] It is interesting that the prime minister feels it necessary to retain control over these initiatives to "ensure that the interests of the Bumi's are safeguarded" when that was the main rationale and mandate behind the creation of the Majlis Amanah Rakyat Agency, which is part of the Ministry of Entrepreneurial Development. Ritchie, "Innovation Systems, Collective Dilemas."

[85] Felker, "Malaysia's Innovation System," p. 20.

[86] Ibid., p. 22.

[87] This is drawn from McKendrick et al., *From Silicon Valley to Singapore,* chap. 9, pp. 246–51.

the loss of a domestic market and access to natural resources after its 1965 expulsion from Malaysia, and the departure of British military protection in the late 1960s. In response, the People's Action Party (PAP) developed a national security strategy that had a strong economic component. The weakness of the country's manufacturing base (most indigenous firms were in trade and finance) led the government toward an emphasis on foreign-investment-led growth.

Penang is, of course, part of Malaysia and therefore was not faced with Singapore's security challenges. But in other respects, Penang resembled Singapore. It not only lacked natural resources but also lost a key revenue-generating resource when its port facilities were made redundant as the bulk of Malaysia's entrepôt trade activities were transferred to a newly built, modern port in Klang, just outside of Kuala Lumpur. Penang's political leaders reacted to these challenges by consciously emulating Singapore's development strategy and institutions, albeit under constraints associated with Malaysia's federal structure.

Thailand illustrates another institutional variant based on a slightly different combination of threats. Like Singapore but unlike Penang, Thailand has faced significant external security threats – first from colonialism in the late nineteenth and early twentieth centuries and subsequently from the wars in Indochina. Unlike both Singapore and Penang, however, Thailand was able to gain ample foreign exchange through large exports of natural resources, especially rice. National independence and political legitimacy therefore required a central bank and Finance Ministry sufficiently cohesive and expert to provide the macroeconomic bases for sustained natural resource exports. A bureaucracy focused on manufactured export promotion, however, was not critical.

But the simple existence of threats does not necessarily mean that institutions will emerge to address them. Political elites' ability to create institutions is also a function of their coalitional bases. Singapore's ruling People's Action Party came to power at least in part in opposition to indigenous business interests. Challenged on the left, the PAP needed to expand its support from within the working class. The result has been a regime that, despite its reliance on multinationals, is best described as an authoritarian social democracy. On the one hand, the PAP-led government has historically had significant leeway to develop institutions that make use of foreign capital, even to the detriment of local firms. On the other hand, the PAP's emphasis on increasing value added and on local skills development reflects the importance of satisfying an important working-class constituency.

Decline in electoral support for the PAP in the early- to mid-1980s reflected working-class frustration over increasing income inequalities and the resentment of a middle class deprived of political rights and corporate participation in the country's economy. The government responded with programs such as the Local Industry Upgrading Program designed to strengthen indigenous firms, albeit through linkages to foreign producers. This subtle turn to domestic business contributed to policies that in turn had the effect of promoting a local supplier base, one of Singapore's key location-specific assets.

Coalitional factors were equally important for Penang's ability to respond to its external challenges by promoting both the expansion of foreign-based multinationals and the growth of an associated group of local suppliers. Penang is the only Malaysian state with an ethnic Chinese majority. As a result, the state's political leadership is more inclined to pursue a development strategy that promotes the interests of local Chinese firms than are governments in the rest of Malay-dominated Malaysia. Second, because of its utility as an alliance partner to the ruling coalition, Penang's political elite has been given the policy autonomy to pursue its own development strategy, including promoting industry-specific institutions and policies for advancing the electronics sector. The result is an effort to integrate MNC upgrading with indigenization.

Thailand again differs, both with regard to coalitional bases and the cohesion of the state elite more generally. Historically, the key supporters of Thailand's political leadership were found in the urban-based banking and industrial sectors. Both of these sectors developed in large part through revenues generated from agricultural exports. Until quite recently, none of these three sectors pressed for the kind of industry-specific institutions and collective goods evident in Singapore or Penang. This is obvious for agriculture and banking, less so for industrialists. Many local manufacturers expanded simply through cheap labor; indeed, labor-intensive manufactured goods such as textiles constituted the key to Thailand's boom in the 1980s and early 1990s. Another group of more skill- and capital-intensive local firms – presumably those with the potential to supply the disk drive firms – expanded through access to a protected domestic market in areas such as automobiles and consumer electronics. Thai governments have provided tariffs in part for revenue purposes but also due to the political strength of these producers.

Meanwhile the government provides incentives for foreign-based multinationals to operate freely in Thailand but not to increase value added. All of this has resulted in powerful constituencies that do not need and/or are suspicious of industry-specific support. They have therefore accommodated themselves to the bureaucracy's fragmentation. And they have reinforced the bureaucracy's lack of interest in and capacity for institutions, goods, and services necessary for competitive upgrading. The result is a highly fragmented industrial structure in which multinationals operate in isolation not only from one another but also local suppliers. Unlike Penang, and more recently Singapore, indigenization has occurred at the expense of upgrading.[88]

---

[88] An illustrative case: A Singaporean baseplate producer, MMI, grew in part through development of extrusion techniques. Support from Conner, subsequently part of Seagate, was key to MMI's growth. Presumably this relationship was "fostered" either directly or indirectly by Singapore state officials and incentives. Wong et al., "Singapore." There are similar cases in Penang. We can find no such cases in Thailand.

The Crisis and National Responses

The disk drive industry experienced a severe cyclical downturn in 1997–98. This fall occurred prior to and independently of the region's broader economic crisis. But, given the region's heavy reliance on electronics exports, the fall in exports of "computers and parts" (led by hard drives) exacerbated the crisis.[89] The national impact varied. For Singapore, this combination of disk drive problems and regional crisis exposed the country's high reliance on key electronics sectors.[90] For Thailand, the persistent current account deficit contributing to the crisis was a further wake-up call regarding the country's lack of supporting industry and resulting high import content in exports.[91] For Malaysia, however, the crisis does not seem to have been a wake-up call. Rather, Malaysia saw the crisis as something completely exogenous: as an externally induced calamity that had little to do with any structural weakness of its own (with the possible exception of the banking sector).

How then did each of the three countries respond to these threats? Perhaps not surprisingly, given its continued concern with reducing its external vulnerability, the crisis seems to have had the most obvious and far-reaching impact on Singapore. But while the primary influence has been to accelerate existing direction and strategy, elements of a more nationalist approach to technological development have also emerged, albeit not in the traditional, mercantile sense.

In the mid-1990s the Singapore government began to talk of transitioning from an intensive industrial economy to a knowledge-based economy. To do so, Singapore would have to create a world-class science and technology base.[92] The original National Science and Technology Plan (NSTP) envisioned that it would take between ten and fifteen years to reach these objectives. An official at the Ministry of Trade and Industry indicated that the crisis had compacted the original ten- to fifteen-year estimates into five to seven years.[93] As an indicator of this acceleration, since 1997 there has been an explosion of government initiatives designed to foster the development of science and technology, with regard to both training and R&D (see Table 8.1).

---

[89] The impact of the crisis on disk drive firms depended on whether they had denominated their transactions in local currencies versus the U.S. dollar. Those that denominated transactions in the Thai baht suffered significant financial losses as a result of the baht's devaluation (interview by author, Read-Rite engineer, Thailand, March 2001).

[90] Wong, "The Role of the State in Singapore's Industrial Development," p. 11.

[91] Lauridsen, "Financial Crisis, Structural Problems and Linkage Policy in Thailand in the 1990s," p. 18, who also notes that concerns about supporting industries expressed in the mid-1980s faded away in the wake of the 1987–94 boom.

[92] Singapore National Science Technology Board Report, *National Science Technology Plan (NSTP)* (1996), 6.

[93] Interview by author, Singapore, July–September 2000.

TABLE 8.1. *New Government Initiatives since 1997*

Initiative/Program	Objective	Lead Agency[a]	Details
Education and Training			
People Developer Standard	Corporate training systems	PSB	S$50,000 per firm to set up holistic training programs
Skills Redevelopment Fund	Training of retrenched and older workers	NTUC	Pays for both training and compensates employers for training time away from work
Manpower Development Assistance Scheme	Develop training facilities inside firms	MOM	Reimburses costs up to a specified amount to create in-house training
Initiatives in New Technology	Train high-level technical talent	EDB	Reimbursed up to 70 percent for training outside of Singapore or to bring in outside expertise to train Singaporeans
Manpower 21	Engage government, labor, and the private sector to meet human resource needs in the next century	MOM	Government is evaluating several new peak cooperative organizations to facility training and education
No official name	Recruit highly trained foreign labor	NSTB	Subsidized housing, salary reimbursement, extended visas, etc. for foreign workers
Technopreneurship 21	Develop tertiary institutions into generators of both manpower and business opportunities	NSTB	Undisclosed amount of funds

Program	Objective	Agency	Details
Manpower Upgrading for Science and Technology	Develop R&D and technopreneurship capacity in local firms through training and postgraduate studies	NSTB	1. Training attachment/internship to local and overseas companies and local and overseas trainers to the companies. Help with financial, legal, and information services. 2. Grants for advanced degrees at local and overseas universities
Critical Infocomm Technology Resource Program	Create specialized IT talent	IDA	S$2 million to train 1,000 IT professionals. Reimburse up to 50 percent of costs
Research and Development			
NSTB Venture Funding	Provide seed funds for new technologies	NSTB	Funds for university incubators, public research institutes, and private firms
University Technology Incubators	Provide opportunities for students to develop new technologies while learning "culture" of high-tech productization	MOE	Provide space and infrastructure to encourage technology development
Pioneer Tax Incentives (or extensions)	Encourage private firms to invest in formal R&D centers	EDB	Renew or provide tax incentives to firms doing product and design R&D
Technopreneurship Fund	Attract venture capital activities	NSTB	US$ 1 billion fund to invest in new technologies
INTECH	Upgrade the technology in local firms	EDB	Reimburse costs for transferring technology (both process and product) to Singapore

[a] PSB = Productivity and Standards Board; NTUC = National Trade Union Congress; MOM = Ministry of Manpower; EDB = Economic Development Board; NSTB = National Science and Technology Board; IDA = Info-Comm Development Authority; MOE = Ministry of Education.

Much of this effort continues to be focused on acquiring technology and expertise directly from multinationals. Nevertheless, although MNCs continue to play the primary role in Singapore's ongoing technological development strategy, new elements of technology development with a distinctly nationalist orientation are emerging, albeit not in a traditional technonationalist sense. By the mid-1990s it was clear that two problems existed with the MNC-led technology strategy. First, most of the smaller firms that foreign-based multinationals had helped to create were rooted in low- to mid-level technologies.[94] Firms with higher-level technologies, such as those supplying precision-engineered parts to the disk drive industry, were involved much more in process as opposed to design development. But, second and perhaps more troubling, the number of spin-offs was low, although it was clear that the multinationals were upgrading the level of technology within their organizations, even to the point of high-level product R&D. Thus, the economy was technologically top-heavy, with many large MNCs and few small, "technopreneurial" firms. To respond to this gap, the government has expanded its strategy to include the creation of new, and in many cases publicly funded, technology ventures.

There are at least two reasons for this additional policy direction, one more closely approximating the technonationalist model and the other not. First, this thrust is not technonationalist in that rather than seeking to replace foreign-based multinationals, it simply seeks to fill an economic gap not met by existing strategies. As a director at the NSTB put it, "We need to support the MNCs with a vibrant source of new, niche technologies that can enhance the capacities and technologies of foreign MNCs. In this way, new MNCs will be attracted to Singapore and existing MNCs will be encouraged to upgrade their facilities." If spin-offs from the MNCs had been filling this gap, there would have been no reason for government to get involved. But, second, the crisis placed in stark relief the vulnerability of Singapore's having all its proverbial eggs in one basket. In a very real sense, the government saw this effort as an opportunity not only to support and enhance the multinational sector but also to create indigenous firms with the capacity to develop at the technological frontier. Thus, the ideal technological relationship between MNC and indigenous smaller firms would be bidirectional with the public research institutes playing a critical linking role between the two.

Malaysia's response, on the other hand, focused less on industrial efficiency and more on ethnic redistribution and what might be termed financial nationalism. The government responded to the crisis by committing itself to a more selective industrial policy driven primarily by private-sector patterns of specialization rather than state plans. In addition, it has also

---

[94] Clearly this was not the case for all firms. Firms such as Creative Technologies led their respective industries in technological development.

formally announced a revamping of the educational and training system to meet the requirements of a rapidly evolving industrial structure.[95] Nevertheless, more than a year after this announcement was made, there had been little agreement on the substance of the reforms, let alone any concrete action. Part of the difficulty in carrying out educational reform may be due to the government's continued commitment to intervene in the economy to promote Bumiputera interests. But equally problematic, the bureaucracy responsible for education and training is highly fragmented and politicized, making agreement and cooperation on education and training policy difficult.

Unlike Thailand or Singapore, Malaysia responded to the crisis by implementing capital controls, which suppressed foreign direct investment in the near term. The response marks an obvious departure from the country's precrisis technoglobalist approach to economic growth. Perhaps, however, the response is best understood not in terms of ideology but in terms of the creativity and talents of Malaysia's Mahathir Mohamad himself. While undoubtedly ideologically driven and institutionally constrained, Mahathir was able to implement a nationalist response to the crisis that would have been unthinkable in either Thailand or Singapore.

Both to manage and to evaluate the new policy strategy, the prime minister's office convened a National Economic Action Council, which met every morning to assess the effects of the crisis. Capital being siphoned to Singapore, primarily by ethnic Chinese business owners, was given one month to return or it would not be allowed to return at all. Although initially viewed with skepticism, many in the international community are grudgingly admitting that these controversial initiatives have been effective: the Malaysian economy grew 5.6 percent in 1999 and 8.3 percent in 2000.

Many in government, including Mahathir, see this evidence as vindicating Malaysia's strategy of fostering foreign investment while actively working to ensure distributional equity. From the government's perspective, Malaysia is on track to reach vision 2020.[96] But while financial nationalism may have worked to restore FDI-led growth, the underlying institutional focus has not changed. Thus, as has been the case historically, the government continues to call on businesses to "forgo some short-term profits in exchange for longer-term ethical [read ethnic] goals."[97] Indeed, the government's primary focus is not on increasing technological capacity through training, education, and R&D, but rather on "trying to balance

---

[95] Felker, "Malaysia's Innovation System," p. 24.

[96] Mahathir Mohamad, "Malaysia on Track for 2020 Vision," January 10, 1999, Prime Minister's Office.

[97] Speech given by Mahathir on August 29, 2000, at the 21st Century Conference to Commemorate the Establishment of the Un Ismail Ali Chair in Monetary and Financial Economics, Kuala Lumpur.

TABLE 8.2 *HRDF and SDF Comparison*

	HRDF		SDF	
	1997	1998	1997	1998
Training places committed	533,227	409,242	502,686	530,755
Grants committed	RM159.49 million	RM138.79 million	S$86.52 million	S$88.41 million
Applications received	Not reported	Not reported	52,990	53,368

Sources: SDF, *Annual Report,* 1998–99; HRDF, *Annual Report,* 1998.

the development of the indigenous people with the non-indigenous Chinese and Indians."[98]

This attempt is reflected in a comparison between the Skills Development Fund (SDF) in Singapore and the Human Resource Development Fund (HRDF) in Malaysia (see Table 8.2) and their respective responses to the crisis. First, Singapore increased its training and education efforts in the face of the crisis, whereas in Malaysia the tendency was to decrease the amount of training. At the same time both countries tried to lessen the burden of the levy on business. Singapore dropped the wage-level requirement from S$1,500 to S$1,000 during the crisis (although it has since raised it again). This ensured that all firms with low-cost labor would continue to bear the costs of the program evenly; it simply reduced the amount each would pay. Malaysia, on the other hand, exempted twenty-eight industries from paying their levy for eleven months while another ten were given six additional months' reprieve. The remaining industries continued to pay the levy through the downturn (the Malaysian report does not detail which industries were exempted, although it is widely believed that politics played a significant role).[99]

The Thai response to the crisis was perhaps the most impressive with regard to policy and institutional initiatives, if not in terms of achievements. The outbreak of the crisis spawned extensive discussion and research on Thailand's declining competitiveness. These concerns were especially serious in light of increasing pressures for liberalization under new WTO agreements and imminent regional trade agreements (AFTA). The World Bank sponsored major research on weaknesses in the manufacturing sector[100] as foreign experts lambasted Thai producers for their high costs and low quality, and

[98] Mahathir Mohamad, "Many Challenges Lie Ahead," June 5, 2000, Collection of speeches by Mahathir, Prime Minister's Office.

[99] SDF annual report 1998/1999; HRDF annual report 1998.

[100] See the papers prepared for the conference on Thailand's Dynamic Economic Recovery and Competitiveness. Lall, "Thailand's Manufacturing Sector."

local industry association officials claimed that Thai firms could cut costs as much as 50 percent by identifying inefficiencies in manufacturing.[101]

Simultaneously, officials in the Ministry of Industry initiated an extensive set of public-private discussions with representatives of almost all sectors of the economy. In terms of process, this was a real effort to promote bottom-up exchanges and reach consensus on both problems and solutions. These discussions highlighted Thai producers' general lack of attention to productivity issues and resulted in a comprehensive Industrial Restructuring Plan. The plan explicitly recognized the need to move out of low-wage, mass-production activities through measures such as skills upgrading and SME support. To these ends, it proposed specific productivity-enhancing measures for thirteen of Thailand's most important industries (including electrical appliances and electronics). Some of these efforts, especially in the area of training, drew on Singapore's programs. More broadly, the plan explicitly proposed "inducing FDI in strategic industries with technologies for the future."[102] And in terms of process, the plan called for more systematic public-private consultation.

The crisis also prompted significant efforts at institution building. This included measures to strengthen the BOI's capacity for technology promotion and the creation of eight public-private institutes designed to address productivity issues in key sectors such as textiles, autos, food, and electronics. It also led to calls for greater bureaucratic centralization, cohesion, and insulation from political influences. In fact, in May 2000 the Civil Service Commission proposed the creation of a Ministry of International Trade and Industry.[103] Although immediately opposed by the Foreign Affairs Ministry as an out-of-date, Japanese-style institution,[104] the MITI proposal is significant because it highlights government awareness of the need to combine responsibilities for manufacturing (presently under the Ministry of Industry) and export promotion (under the Ministry of Commerce).

The results of these efforts thus far are uncertain at best. Although Thai manufactured exports grew in a number of sectors, the core problems of low productivity and a weak supplier base persist. Indeed, a senior Ministry of Industry official stated outright that, owing to "red tape and lack of cooperation from the private sector," the industrial restructuring program "was a failure in terms of boosting efficiency and cooperation."[105] Whether or not

---

[101] Yuthana Priwan, "Production Defects Pushing Up Costs," *Bangkok Post,* June 23, 1998.
[102] National Industrial Development Committee, "Thailand's Industrial Restructuring Plan," Industrial Executive Plan, Executive Summary, June 15, 1998.
[103] "Revamp Spawns New Ministries," *Nation,* May 26, 2000.
[104] Maneerungsee Woranuj, "New Ministry a Blunder, Say Kobsak – Japanese Model Soon Will Be Out of Date," *Bangkok Post,* August 9, 2000.
[105] "New Lease on Life for Manufacturing," *Bangkok Post / Mid-Year Economic Review,* July 2000.

this is the case in all sectors, it seems clear enough in electronics and disk drives: government agencies have not given much support to initiatives for a disk drive training program along the lines of Singapore's course.[106]

Conclusions and Implications

Sources of Policy and Institutional Change

An analysis of national responses to a crisis requires greater attention to the factors influencing policy and institutional change. In our effort to explain cross-national differences in preferences and institutional capacities, we emphasized structural factors: external vulnerability and coalitional bases. But these may not be all that powerful for explaining the shorter-term impact of external shocks even if, as we have argued, there are strong pressures for convergence. After all, there is a long tradition of scholarship demonstrating divergent national responses to similar external pressures. To draw a parallel with the endogenous growth literature, economic institutions have a lot of tacitness; many "need to be developed locally, relying on hands-on experience, local knowledge, and local experimentation."[107]

Several approaches might be useful in this regard. One, a "national systems" literature, asks whether new institutions are complementary with existing arrangements; perhaps even more important, it notes that institutional systems, as well as capacities for adaptation and quick evolution within these systems, vary across countries. A second assesses the impact of ideas and norms on policy and institutional reforms. This approach is particularly relevant in an era of increasing globalization. How much of a country's technological strategy is influenced by the dissemination of norms and ideas through increasing economic liberalization? A third evaluates the influence of individual leadership, which has certainly been important, particularly in the case of Singapore's Lee Kuan Yew and Malaysia's Mahathir Mohamad. Even so, we conclude that the explanatory power of individual creativity, like ideology, must take a back seat to institutional capacity. A fourth emphasizes the impact of "veto players" – the number and cohesion of actors with decision-making authority. The veto player literature brings us to the broader political topic – namely, the impact of various types of electoral rules and various types of democratization. This seems especially important in light of the contrast between Singapore's cohesive response to the crisis and Thailand's game but comparatively ineffectual efforts.

---

[106] Interviews by author, Bangkok, 1999–2000.
[107] Dani Rodrik, "Institutions for High-Quality Growth: What They Are and How to Acquire Them," paper presented at the IMF Conference on Second-Generation Reforms, Washington, D.C., November 8–9, 1999, p. 16.

Regional Options?

We argued at the outset of this chapter that successful engagement with globalized production networks requires convergence toward technology upgrading through strong local institutions. However, where value chains contain labor-intense activities, and where such components are best located proximate to higher value-added activities, opportunities remain for low-wage countries without the capacity for upgrading. This does, however, assume a regional convergence to the Southeast Asian standard of free-trade and investment regimes.

Technomodels

Our review of Southeast Asian policies and institutions provides evidence that globalist-nationalist categories for technological trajectories are of limited use when viewed in isolation. The strategy of "MNC-induced technological learning" implies a technohybrid strategy that combines more nationalist objectives (greater autonomy seeking) with relatively globalist means (reliance on foreign firms for technological spillovers). Globalist means may in turn be mixed up with strong nationalist means in the form of strong support for indigenous producers. And if Singapore's recent moves into the promotion of "technopreneurship" are an indication, more successful developing countries may move toward increasing nationalist means. Indeed, Singapore's recent initiatives are beginning to resemble Taiwan's strategy of promoting local firms through its own public research institutes rather than through multinational auspices. But such a strategy may be more useful in a more stable industry such as autos or even CD-ROMS than in an industry with highly rapid technological change such as disk drives.[108]

---

[108] This is the conclusion from an examination of Taiwan's ambitious but ultimately unsuccessful effort at local disk drive production. McKendrick et al., *From Silicon Valley to Singapore*, chap. 10.

9

Continuity and Change in Asian Innovation

William W. Keller and Richard J. Samuels

The Asian "Financial Crisis" Revisited

The Asian "financial crisis" of 1997–98 was in fact a number of crises, both economic and political. They did not begin in all affected states in Asia in 1997, nor did all end in 1998. It may be comforting to view the "financial crisis" as a limited and discrete phenomenon, during which investors temporarily abandoned a number of "bubble" economies until adjustments could be made and confidence restored, all in just eighteen months. But the evidence presented by the contributors to this volume clearly paints a different picture.

For some countries, the crisis began before 1997 and continued on past the turn of the millennium. In Japan, for example, the "crisis" only served to deepen a period of slow to no growth that prevailed throughout most of the 1990s, and worsened thereafter. For others, like Indonesia, the crisis was catastrophic. Financial disruptions of 1997 set events in motion that led to the collapse of a regime that had been in power for decades. With rampant political instability, direct investment flows to Indonesia turned negative in 1998 and continued to erode for the next several years.[1] Taiwan, which at first appeared not to register the 1997–98 financial crisis, slipped in 2001 into its first recession in thirty years. In Singapore, the year 2001 marked an abrupt reversal, with the economy entering a technical recession with two consecutive year-on-year quarterly declines in GDP.

For much of the rest of Asia the downward slide, following a brief "recovery" from the financial crisis, may well be attributed to decreased demand caused by the end of a decade of sustained growth of the U.S. economy. The end of the 1990s bull market in 2001 began well before the September 11 terrorist attacks on the World Trade Center in New York City and the

---

[1] Inward direct investment flows fell from $4.7 billion in 1997 to $–0.4 billion, $–2.7 billion, and $–4.6 in 1998, 1999, and 2000 respectively. UNCTAD, *World Investment Report 2001* (New York, 2001), annex tables B, 1-6.

Pentagon in Washington. But the economic effects of the attacks were palpable, even if difficult to distinguish from the steadily slowing growth of the U.S. and global economies. These events doubtless contributed to the financial distress and general economic weakness spreading across much of Asia.

But even though they can now be recognized as a prolonged and interrelated set of political and economic events, the Asian crises – whatever their duration and form – did not necessarily change the ways firms interact or the ways in which technological innovation occurs in the region. The institutions of research and dominant ideas about technology in several of the countries, notably Japan and Taiwan, proved remarkably durable. Despite financial pressure, established technological trajectories were maintained. In other cases, change was more apparent, particularly in South Korea and Singapore.

Most important, we have observed that production and innovation in the states under consideration in this book did not converge on a common set of standards nor did they seem to change in any wholesale way in direct response to economic crisis. The changes documented by our authors point toward continued variation in the ways in which production and innovation are organized in Asia. Each of the Asian countries studied in this volume responded differently to the Asian financial crisis of 1997–98, and to subsequent political and economic perturbations.

Our central finding is that despite considerable pressure to converge on more open, liberal norms, the Asian economies retained distinct approaches to innovation and technological interaction. Even in the face of crisis and escalating global competition, they superimposed change at the margins, often seeking unique technohybrid solutions to build or maintain internal technical and industrial capabilities to compete in local, regional, and even global markets.

Crisis and Choice in Asian Innovation

In the introduction to this volume, we identified four classes of factors that affect the organization of science, technology, and innovation, and the ability of states to respond in the face of the financial contagion that swept the region: institutions of innovation, techno-ideologies, capabilities, and leadership. In the sections that follow we take each category in turn and apply what we have learned in this collective research endeavor.

Institutions of Innovation
Some states seemed to respond differently because the choices available to them were conditioned on the different ways in which innovation and production had been organized in the past. Clearly, the institutional arrangements through which innovation is carried out have varied widely among the different polities in Asia. Japanese companies, for example, tend not to rely

on research universities to train their scientists and engineers. Compared with other Asian countries, moreover, Japan sends very few independent graduate students abroad for training in science and engineering, even after a decade in which it has become painfully obvious that something is amiss in Japanese postgraduate education. Most advanced technical training in Japan still takes place inside major companies and the research consortia that they and the government sponsor. Japanese graduate students abroad are predominantly "lifetime" employees of particular firms. Although there have been rumblings of change, there is very little hard evidence to indicate that university research conducted in Japan will figure prominently in Japanese innovation in the foreseeable future.[2] If the state of the economy is any indication, it would appear that some of the institutions of Japanese innovation may have persisted beyond the expiration date of their economic utility.

The response to crisis in Korea in this regard was very different. It was based, at least in part, on different choices made in the past. Korea, like Taiwan, has traditionally sent large numbers of graduate students to the great U.S. research universities for training in the scientific and engineering disciplines. The vast majority of professors of science and engineering, for example, at the Korea Advanced Institute for Science and Technology (KAIST) and at Seoul National University received their doctorates in the United States. Again, like Taiwan but unlike Japan, Korea has in recent years made major strides in developing indigenous technical institutes and universities in order to upgrade the quality of its work force. But in contrast both to Japan and Taiwan, the crisis provoked the Korean government to set a goal of having 10 Korean universities ranked among the top 100 research institutions worldwide, and that goal is backed with substantial funding.

More broadly speaking, South Korea would seem to have adopted significant changes in its technology development system, and this would appear to have occurred in relation to democratic transformation of the polity. In contrast to Japan, the financial contagion that struck East Asia in the spring of 1997 provided an opening for newly elected democratic leaders in South Korea to attack the *chaebol* – family-owned business conglomerates – which were already weakened by significant withdrawal of foreign capital, with many on the brink of insolvency. But here our authors draw a more complex picture, rooted in the sectors they have studied and their views of the Korean policy apparatus for science and technology.

One insider observer, Linsu Kim, contends in Chapter 4 that the Asian financial crises of 1997–98 proved to be a critical juncture for Korea. In the short term, he argues, the crisis caused widespread disruption and hardship for the Korean people, many of whom lost their livelihoods and their dreams of a stable, middle-class existence. On the other hand, in the context of rapidly

---

[2] See, for example, "Academia Builds High-Tech Ties with Private Sector Companies," *Nikkei*, October 22, 2001.

changing economic and political institutions, the crisis provided an opportunity to rid the country of outmoded industrial structures and policies. In particular, the freely elected government of Kim Dae Jung sought to reform the *chaebol*, severing their collusive and corrupt relationships with government cronies. It was an opportunity to revamp many aspects of South Korea's innovation system with the aim of enhancing industrial competitiveness and a higher standard of living for Koreans in the long term.

It seems that some states will develop the requisite local institutions of innovation and skilled labor force, but many will not. Some will continue to participate in high-technology areas – like the hard disk drive industry examined in Chapter 8 by Richard Doner and Bryan Ritchie – but others will not, depending on their ability to capture an adequate portion of the value added in what is essentially a regional production system dominated by foreign producers. Our contributors indicate the need in developing countries for a blend of generic and sector-specific policies to promote domestic suppliers and develop a highly skilled technical labor pool. In terms of its ability to produce the necessary technical and industrial ingredients, for example, Singapore would appear to have more in common with Hong Kong or Taiwan than with Malaysia and Thailand, the other two major participants in East Asian disk drive production.

This raises the question of whether the national innovation system is the proper unit of analysis. On one view, national institutions may be less relevant than before because multinational corporations can decide at any time to reallocate the production system, and they may do so for any number of reasons. Control and composition of the innovation system may have become exogenous to the nation-state. But this is not what our contributors have learned. The political, economic, and social institutions that make up the innovation systems of the ASEAN states, for example, are not static. Nor have they been subjugated to the preferences of foreign corporations. There is considerable persistent variation, even in the hard disk drive industry that spans Singapore, Malaysia, and Thailand. Singapore and Malaysia's Penang have created economies that are as much the result of public policy and indigenous innovation systems as they are of foreign corporate decision making and other externalities.

This circumstance leaves open the possibility that other Southeast Asian states will develop institutions for innovation comparable with those found in Penang or Singapore. We have seen hints, moreover, that the institutions of production and innovation in Singapore may be changing, and that the process may have accelerated in response to the Asian financial crisis of 1997–98. Since 1997 there has been a proliferation of education and training programs together with science and technology initiatives sponsored by the government of Singapore (see Table 8.1). The purpose of these efforts is to transform Singapore from an economy structured to serve as the regional headquarters of foreign-based corporations to a more entrepreneurial knowledge-based economy, structured to build up local technological infrastructure and competencies.

Singapore's National Science and Technology Plan of 1996 sought to create a work force and indigenous small and medium-sized firms that could prosper at the cutting edge of niche technologies. This was a dual strategy to build up local technological and industrial infrastructure and, at the same time, support and even attract foreign multinationals. In response to the Asian financial crises, our authors indicate, the time horizon for implementation of this state-led strategy was shortened by half, from ten to fifteen years to five to seven years. With heavy government involvement in creating an MNC-supporting, yet indigenous high-technology sector, the Singaporean innovation system began to resemble more closely its better-insulated Taiwanese cousin.

Techno-Ideologies

At the outset of this study, we entertained the possibility that Japan's and South Korea's technonational orientations might have eroded or at least softened considerably. After all, Japan had endured many years of economic malaise. And with the advent of financial contagion throughout much of East Asia in 1997 and 1998, it was not inconceivable that government officials and corporate managers might begin to think differently about innovation and industrial policy. Moreover, it seemed unlikely that Japan could indefinitely continue to adhere to its traditional pattern of nurturing a more insular technology development system, especially when the more open approach in the United States garnered technological and economic success in the 1990s almost in inverse proportion to the failures in Japan.

The research of our contributors confirms these expectations to some extent with respect to South Korea but not in the case of Japan. As D.H. Whittaker asserts in Chapter 3, "it is inconceivable that policy makers and business leaders in Japan will stop believing that technology is a fundamental element in national security, that it must be indigenized, diffused, and nurtured in order to make a nation rich and strong." But he adds the caveat that Japan in recent years has reached out technologically and economically to rediscover Asia. And this, he believes, will add an increasingly regional perspective to future Japanese patterns of innovation, informing and perhaps even changing some aspects of traditional Japanese technonationalism.

It is certainly the case that Japan reached out to its Asian neighbors, especially during and after the onset of the Asian financial crisis in 1997. Japanese companies and banks took the opportunity to increase direct investment flows to South Korea, Thailand, and Malaysia, among others. But according to Walter Hatch, the author of Chapter 2, Japanese investment in – and many other forms of assistance to – its Asian neighbors was a way to strengthen and extend Japanese technonationalism and industrial policy throughout the region. Japanese companies remained more insular than others. They contained technology in intrafirm networks, supporting Japanese subsidiaries or "transplants" in a number of Asian states. They also acquired or increased equity positions in many Asian firms at crisis basement prices.

In this way, Japan was able to extend its web of *keiretsu*-like relationships farther into Asia and, in the process, prolong the life of the embattled system of "relationalism" at home, very possibly to its own detriment. In this view, developing and newly developed countries in East Asia provided – even in their distress – a kind of lifeline to Japanese technonationalism. Instead of responding according to more liberal norms welcoming of Schumpeterian creative destruction, Japan opted to resist. It tried to maintain the status quo, making only incremental changes in response to a regional economy under great pressure to change. This strategy did not pay immediate dividends: according to a survey of Japanese firms, from June to September 2001, Japanese companies reported that business conditions steadily worsened in Southeast Asia, especially in the information technology industries that depend so heavily on exports to American companies and consumers.[3]

In retrospect, it seems clear that the transformation of the South Korean technonational ideology was ripe for a crisis. The Korean *chaebol* had diversified far afield from their core competencies. Most were highly leveraged, relying on debt instead of equity financing, and many of the most "successful" had not turned a significant profit in years, preferring to gain market share and service debts in lieu of making a profit. The Asian financial crisis, which hit Korea with full force in November 1997, may merely have been the straw that broke the camel's back. As John Ravenhill, the author of Chapters 5, observes, the three top electronics companies – Samsung, Hyundai, and LG Semicon – accounted for 70 percent of the net profits of the thirty top *chaebol* in Korea. When the "silicon cycle" took a downturn in 1996, underlying weaknesses in the economy came to the fore. We note that when the silicon cycle staged a comeback in 1999, it brought the Korean economy with it. And, when U.S. consumers turned their backs on information technology products in 2001, the fortunes of the Korean semiconductor makers sank again.

But shifts in the technonational orientation of the Korean economy varied by sector. In the information technology sector, Korean corporate and government leaders opted to retain key elements of technonationalism and yielded only grudgingly to technoglobal solutions as a last resort and in the national interest. In the automobile sector, by contrast, the technonational posture eroded. As Ravenhill points out, several automakers in South Korea were already in deep trouble by the middle 1990s. Although the Asian financial crisis may have been the proximate cause of the collapse, global overcapacity was a key

---

[3] Hiromichi Ozeki, Deputy Director, Research and Analysis Division, Trade Policy Bureau, METI, "Asia Business Sentiment Survey (Asia Quick DI Survey) – Business Conditions Worsen for Japanese Companies in Southeast Asia," *IIST Mail Magazine*, no. 0006, October 1, 2001, pp. 7–9 <http://www.iist-info.jp/magazine/#ozeki>.

accomplice. Taken together, by the mid-1980s, South Korea had come under intense pressure to open its markets to imports, but by employing a variety of nontariff barriers, foreign penetration of the Korean automobile market was kept to less than 1 percent throughout the 1990s, in effect creating a sanctuary market for the domestic industry. In the end, however, if Hyundai is unable to retain its dominant position, those markets will be forced open not by the U.S. trade representative or the World Trade Organization, but by foreign automakers who acquire the assets of the Korean companies.

Even with substantial foreign direct investment, political transformation to democracy, reform of the financial, educational, and R&D sectors, and greater transparency and accountability in the *chaebol*, South Korea – our research indicates – continues to embrace technonational norms. South Korea, a large country with a population comparable with that of France or the United Kingdom, will strive to advance its own product brands and to compete at the leading edge in a number of global high-technology industries. Indeed, many of the reforms undertaken by South Korea immediately following the onset of the 1997 financial crisis were aimed at increasing the competitiveness of Korean industry, even if that meant undertaking large-scale transformation of indigenous political, economic, and production systems.

On the evidence in this volume, Korea – like Japan – remains determined to retain its nationally centered system of technological innovation, moving only reluctantly toward technohybrid solutions in the face of new global financial and investment incentives. As William Keller and Louis Pauly suggest in Chapter 6, this view was reflected in the electronics field, where the "crisis" was the apparent cause of the takeover of LG Semicon by Hyundai Electronics. More precisely, it was a forced union to maintain two national champions – the Hyundai and Samsung *chaebol* – a marriage that was arranged using the full panoply of state powers at the highest level in government.

One of the characteristics of the technohybrid category, introduced in the first chapter of this volume, is the orientation of technology acquisition strategies and industrial policies toward strategic alliances and partnerships in multinational production networks. With or without state support, firms do so with an eye to building up the capabilities of conationals to compete in global markets and, indeed, to further the objective of making the nation strong and secure by capturing a significant portion of the value-added in large-scale enterprises.

As the authors of Chapter 6 argue, Taiwan is the quintessential technohybrid state. From the outset of its industrialization, Taiwanese business and government leaders sought to entice multinational corporations to undertake production in Taiwan. They saw foreign direct investment as a means to build up the island's technological infrastructure. As Taiwanese firms acquired technology, however, they continued to cultivate interdependence with U.S., European, and Japanese multinational corporations.

But even as the state pursued the globalist posture of supporting foreign corporations through tax incentives, the development of technology parks, and many other inducements, there was always a second, more nationalist agenda in the background.

Government laboratories engaged in the acquisition, for example, of semiconductor technology, and in hiring and training local engineers and other technologists to support indigenous companies. When government research institutes mastered a particular set of industrial technologies, they "spun off" research teams to form new private-sector companies, including such powerhouses as the Taiwan Semiconductor Manufacturing Company and the United Microelectronics Company. Concurrently the government fostered the development of science-based industrial parks, technically oriented universities, and public- and private-sector research laboratories. Government, and then industry, sent the best and brightest Taiwanese nationals abroad to study at the major research universities, typically in the United States.

But unlike the Japanese model in which the majority of advanced "students" were actually employees on temporary assignment, upon graduation, and often with advanced degrees, many Taiwanese engineers went to work for high-technology companies in the United States. As Taiwan built up its technological and industrial infrastructure throughout the 1990s, these students – now expatriates in the United States – returned in large numbers to work for Taiwanese companies, universities, and research institutes. In the 1990s, for example, approximately 3,000 U.S.-trained technologists returned to take jobs in the Hsinchu Science-Based Industrial Park near Taipei. This dual strategy of embracing foreign direct investment as a means of technological learning, and simultaneously building up world-class national industrial competencies, positions Taiwan midpoint between the technonationalist orientation of Japan and the technoglobalist ambitions of Hong Kong or Singapore.

In the longer term we think that the technohybrid model will become predominant, particularly in smaller newly industrialized and industrializing Asian states. This may occur on a sector-by-sector basis. Although we have emphasized the technonationalist character of Korean innovation and industrialization, there is no doubt that the automobile sector in Korea was penetrated by foreign companies during and after the Asian financial crisis of 1997–98. If the export-led strategy of Hyundai and its subsidiary Kia should fail, Korea would lose its national champion in this economically critical sector. In that case, there would be very little likelihood that South Korea could continue to make automobiles competitively for global markets. A technonationalist posture would no longer be an option for South Korea in this sector.

Capabilities: The Dynamics of Innovation

As we review the findings of our authors, it is apparent that there are different small-state and large-state dynamics in the development of an innovation system, and the ways in which it interacts with economic volatility and multinational production networks. In the 1990s, the consolidation of corporate power in almost every sector made it difficult for smaller states in Asia to establish or maintain their positions in increasingly competitive global markets. Consider first the ability of Japan to preserve its system of relationalism, even in the face of severe regional economic crises and sustained political pressure from the advanced industrial states of North America and Europe. Likewise, the size of Korea's population, and its rapidly expanding GDP over the past two decades, gave Korean government and corporate leaders the sense that they could follow Japan's developmental trajectory. They sought to create and maintain the large-scale economic center of gravity necessary to support technonationalist policies.

But like many smaller and middle-sized states in Europe in the 1980s, South Korea has come face-to-face with its vulnerability to the bracing winds of global competition. This became evident as the Asian financial crisis of 1997–98 unmasked structural and financial weaknesses in the automobile sector of the Korean economy. The Korean *chaebol* were emulating the Japanese *keiretsu* of a decade earlier. Like the Japanese technocrats, the Koreans sought to insulate their auto sector from imports and majority foreign direct investments. The difference was one of scale, however, with Japan convinced it would be able to absorb a decade-long economic slump and to ride out financial storms and market penetration by foreign competitors.

The large state – small state dynamic is also apparent in the inability of some of the Southeast Asian nations to become more than cogs in the regional machinery of multinational production networks. The range of innovation strategies available to Southeast Asian states has narrowed. Thailand, Malaysia, and the other ASEAN countries face relegation to the status of "technonothings" in most industries, at least until they can develop strategies to build enabling national innovation systems. This will require constructing policy and technological infrastructures that place them beyond the role of suppliers of unskilled or semiskilled labor to shifting alliances of multinationals that are based predominately in the United States, Japan, and Western Europe. As the contributors to this volume suggest, that bar has been raised. The level of technological sophistication necessary to sustain growth and participate in regional and global production networks is steadily increasing in Asia. This reinforces our view that the technohybrid trajectory will come to dominate the innovation systems and overall economies of the newly industrialized and industrializing states of Asia after the millennium.

If this dynamic works to the disadvantage of small states, or at a minimum, forces them to emulate a particular technological trajectory, it also has major implications for China and possibly for other large states in Asia as well. As Barry Naughton and Adam Segal remind us in Chapter 7, China contains 65 percent of the population of East Asia, but accounts for only about 10 percent of East Asian GDP. But with such an enormous population, potential productivity, and great-power ambitions, the leaders of China can pursue two or more paths of technology acquisition and industrial policy that are not necessarily related. On one hand, China today embodies a kind of technonationalism – defined as a large-scale effort to obtain high-technology competencies in a variety of industrial sectors, and to do so in a self-sustaining way, with minimal reliance on outside powers, particularly the United States. This posture is reinforced by the dictates of Chinese national security, and the acquisition of military technology in particular, which will continue to figure prominently in Chinese innovation and industrial strategies.

At the same time, however, it is possible for provincial governments to experiment with other technology strategies, for example, in the southern province of Guangdong, where technology policy is based more on developing human resources and cooperation among corporations, both foreign-based and domestic. Here the reach of the central state is far more circumscribed, government research institutes play a less prominent role, state-owned enterprises have been pushed to the side, and technological autonomy is less highly prized. It is quite possible that these varying approaches to technology acquisition will coexist as experiments in China for the foreseeable future, and that they may continue to embody inconsistent and even contradictory elements. As our authors indicate, for example, it is unlikely that China will seek to develop national champions modeled either on the Korean *chaebol* or the Japanese *keiretsu*, because Chinese leaders view this element of traditional Asian technonationalism as outmoded and unlikely to succeed.

Leadership

Leadership – especially the creative and nimble kind that one most hopes for during times of crisis – was in short supply in Asia in 1997. In the introduction to this volume we discussed briefly the extraordinary cases of Chinese and Malaysian leadership. We noted how the Malaysian leader, Mahathir Mohamad, who, by refusing to cooperate with the International Monetary Fund, and by freezing currency transactions, succeeded in alleviating many of the worst effects of the crisis. He maintained – indeed, he consolidated – power while he watched the regime in neighboring Indonesia collapse.

Chinese leaders were similarly audacious. As Naughton and Segal demonstrate clearly in Chapter 7, the Chinese leadership took a series of major, unprecedented decisions in the aftermath of the financial crisis. The events of 1997 strengthened the hand of central leaders like Zhu Rongji, ensuring their ability to consolidate promarket policies and to act upon their skepticism toward large state-owned enterprises and national champions. This greatly enhanced the political and economic space in which private sector entrepreneurs and companies could maneuver. China's sharp turn in economic policy was not directly linked to the financial crisis but to its leaders' ability to use that crisis to drive China in new directions.

Our contributors documented only one additional case in which political or business leaders took demonstrable steps to "stretch" the considerable constraints within which they were forced to operate after the 1997–98 financial crisis: South Korea. As Kim reported in Chapter 4, the democratic administration of Korean president Kim Dae Jung targeted government reform as one of its highest goals. Productivity in the public sector was a high priority. So too was the stimulation of science and technology. But the Asian financial crisis also triggered the government to restructure its administrative apparatus for coordinating public-sector science and technology. President Kim was determined to integrate science and technology policy across different industries and agencies, and he used the occasion of the crisis as a window of opportunity. His government established a National Science and Technology Council, which he chaired. He thus attempted to place more than a dozen separate ministries and agencies under his personal control. He used this newly consolidated power to bring private firms up on the carpet and was personally instrumental in forcing the consolidation of LG Semicon and Hyundai Electronics.[4] Whether these reforms will prove effective in the long run is open to debate, but there can be little doubt of the agency that President Kim sought to impose.

Meanwhile, Japanese leadership failed miserably in its repeated efforts to jump-start the Japanese economy. Each time there were signs of recovery, Japan's political and bureaucratic leadership intervened with tax increases that drove the economy back into recession. Their uneven fiscal policies of stimulus and restraint, and their experiments with eased monetary policy, "whipsawed" the economy.[5] By 2000 Japanese public debt was at least 130 percent of GDP, the highest ever recorded by a developed economy, larger even than Italy's public debt at its worst point in the early 1990s.[6] Still, "extraordinarily inept" political managers of the Japanese economy pursued failed stimulation after failed stimulation.[7] They injected more than 1 trillion yen into the reeling economy – ten times more than the entire Marshall Plan, even adjusting for

[4] Interview with meeting participant, Seoul, November 1999.
[5] Edward J. Lincoln, *Arthritic Japan: The Slow Pace of Economic Reform* (Washington, D.C.: Brookings Institution Press, 2001), p. 65.
[6] John Makin, "Japan: It's the Economy, Stupid!" *AEI Economic Outlook*, April 2000, estimates that the Japanese debt in 2000 was more than three times the Italian debt of the early 1990s. David L. Asher and Robert H. Dugger, *Could Japan's Financial Mount Fuji Blow Its Top?* MIT International Science and Technology Initiative, Center for International Studies, MIT Japan Program, Cambridge, Mass., 2000, provide even higher estimates, and projected Japanese public debt would grow to 220 percent of GDP within a few years. See also David L. Asher, "The Bush Administration's Japan Problem," *AEI Economic Outlook*, March 2001, p. 2, who argues that in 2000 nearly 65 percent of Japan's tax revenues were needed to service its debt – a figure three times higher than in Italy at the same time.
[7] Makin, "Japan: It's the Economy, Stupid!" p. 1.

inflation – mostly on construction projects of marginal economic benefit.[8] After each new package, a temporary economic boost was followed hard upon by slowed or negative growth. Repeated claims of incipient recovery were belied by lackluster economic performance, and even recession.

Nor was it only the government that was mired deeply in debt. The private sector was inundated by unrecoverable loans; a mountain of bad debt forced unprecedented downgrading in the credit ratings of many of Japan's leading firms. Now each of the characteristics of the Japanese economy that had been invoked as sources of Japan's extraordinary strength and resiliency during the high growth era – *keiretsu*, cartels, developmental bureaucrats, high levels of investment and savings, lifetime employment, industrial policy – were reinterpreted (if not revealed) as liabilities. What had been the sources of Japan's "economic miracle" now were sources of excessive rigidity and "inner rot."[9]

Questions That Remain

Related questions remain unanswered. We think that further research might yield a better sense of how the Asian economic downturn and financial crises affected the foreign technology acquisition strategies of firms based in different parts of Asia. Did some Asian states and firms aggressively develop technology assets located abroad, taking advantage of competitive opportunities, even when the net result would be the development of technical infrastructure in competing economies? There is some evidence to support this view; specifically, a number of Japanese companies made the decision to outsource their more risky R&D activities to U.S. universities.[10] Or did Asian firms redouble their efforts to develop technology indigenously?

Second, to what extent have Asian firms changed their patterns of technology licensing? Have they begun to view technology trade as a profit center? If technoglobalism increased, we would expect that firms in need of foreign capital would have adjusted their strategies to market technology assets abroad. In an ideal technonational world, technology transfer would remain embedded in equipment sales, very often a generation behind the state of the art. According to a survey by Japan's leading business association, domestic technology transfer within Japan increased sharply (from 67 percent to 79 percent of total interfirm technology transfer) after 1992,

---

[8] Note, however, that as much as 40 percent of each "new" package comprises commitments carried over from previous ones. The amount of "real water" (*mamizu*) is usually less than half the official figures.

[9] Lincoln, *Arthritic Japan*, p. 66.

[10] There is a trend for more cooperation in research between Japanese corporations and U.S. universities. As part of a broader pattern, Cannon planned in 1998 to give $7–10 million to research universities in the United States to "outsource some of the more risky research." Interviews with Cannon executives, San Jose, Calif., October 21, 1998.

while the share of technology transferred to Asia, Europe, and the United States dropped commensurately. Other data are more ambiguous.[11]

Third, we need a more systematic account of the extent to which foreign-based multinationals were and are able to acquire significant R&D assets in East Asian countries. Surely the answer to this question varies widely from one country in Asia to another, and over time. Receptivity to foreign buyers may have changed in some countries and in some sectors in response to extraordinary financial and political pressures. If global market forces were generating convergence, we would expect firms to seek opportunities to sell R&D assets to foreign multinationals, especially if the technology in question is not essential to their core business operations. If, however, the more mercantile logic prevailed, firms, aided by their governments, would continue to invest in innovation at home to preserve and build capability to compete in global markets.

Fourth, we still lack a full understanding of the extent to which Asian systems and policies for producing technologists (scientists and engineers) are changing, and why. Under both technoglobal and technonational assumptions, increased pressure for rapid technological advances leads states to train and otherwise acquire scientists and engineers from any source, foreign or domestic. Under the former logic, however, the nationality of the technologist matters little as he or she rises in the firm. Under the latter logic, foreign training is pursued to create domestic specialists, and foreign specialists are used and then discarded. Many of the Asian states have long sent their best and brightest graduate students abroad for technical training. As we have seen, some of these countries, especially Taiwan, have been extremely successful in repatriating their students and avoiding a "brain drain" of domestic talent. Others, like China and Korea, recently began to staunch the flow of their most talented scientists and engineers.[12]

Fifth, are some Asian states and firms less willing to participate in international strategic alliances that involve significant two-way technology transfer? We would anticipate wide variation with Japan or Korea at one end of the spectrum and Taiwan or Hong Kong at the other. Technonationalists would be expected to share technology through joint ventures and other international collaborations in contexts where both companies believe they

---

[11] The Asian share dropped from 15 to 11 percent, the European share dropped from 8 to 5 percent, and the U.S. share dropped from 6 to 4 percent between 1992 and 1996. See *Sangyô Gijutsuryoku Kyôka no tame no Jissei Chôsa: Hôkokusho* (Survey research on the strengthening of industrial technology: A report) (Tokyo: Keizai Dantai Rengôkai Shuppan Guruupu, September 1998), pp. 82–83.

[12] Figures based on National Science Foundation data. "Global Access to Applied Research: A Report to the Semiconductor Research Corporation," Monterey Institute of International Studies, Monterey, Calif., February 12, 1997, executive summary. Also see "University-Industry Cooperation for Technology Innovation in Japan," Special Scientific Report #98-09 (April 21, 1998), prepared by Dr. Win Aung, Senior Staff Associate, Division of Engineering Education and Centers, National Science Foundation, Arlington, Va.

can achieve a clear benefit that would otherwise elude them. On the other hand, from a more mercantile perspective, one-way technology transfer could be a bargaining chip for foreign access to domestic markets. This was the key that unlocked the Japanese market for IBM in the 1960s, and that is playing the same role for Japanese firms in much of Asia today. As one Japanese research executive explained, R&D conducted by Japanese companies in the rest of Asia, mainly in China, India, and the Philippines, is typically the price for admission to conduct large-scale business in the country in question. In his words, "You have to have a research lab in China to make volume sales."[13]

Finally, we think further research is needed to understand the impact that regional economic and political crises in Asia at the end of the past century had on the technology-intensive regional production networks in Asia. Under liberal assumptions, the economies of the industrial states in Asia should have become progressively less dependent on manufacturing and more service-oriented. As a result, the crisis ought to have struck with a differential force on the economies to which they had moved manufacturing capacity, jobs, and technology. The technonational perspective, on the other hand, posits an ideological brake on this movement. It would predict that the more advanced economies would have resisted "hollowing out." On this account, as national firms develop new products, they should shift domestic production capacity to higher value-added innovation to maintain a leading market position. Parent companies would continue to turn over production of more standardized but still viable product lines to their domestic subcontractors.

Conclusion

As an empirical matter, the government of every industrializing and industrialized state puts substantial funding into building up the local innovation infrastructure. Whether government support is applied to military technology or to complex civil engineering projects, it is always an inherently political process, involving patronage of a large number of stakeholders and other interested groups. Even those who appreciate the role of government in promoting technological innovation are concerned that technonationalist responses could slow down the global innovation

---

[13] Interviews with Cannon executives, San Jose, Calif., October 21, 1998. There are also recent indications that once a technology is introduced to China, the government may take steps to transfer foreign technology to local firms, with the result that the foreign presence in the market is reduced. With respect to mobile telephones, see James Kynge, "Beijing to Break Foreign Grasp on Cell Phone Market," *Financial Times*, December 16, 1998, p. 10. For the IBM Japan entry story, see Mark Mason, *American Multinationals and Japan: The Political Economy of Japanese Capital Controls, 1899–1980* (Cambridge, Mass.: Harvard University Press, 1992).

process if misapplied.[14] But this, of course, assumes that there is a global process of technological development that is moving inexorably toward a generally higher level or common end. Each of the chapters in this book adds considerable weight to the idea that distinct innovation systems are associated with particular sectors and with particular developing and industrialized nations in Asia.

We asked the contributors to this volume – virtually all political scientists – to develop a fuller, empirically grounded institutional and ideational understanding of innovation that incorporates politics in Asia. Despite the advent of the World Trade Organization – and the *tsunami* of trade, cross-border investment, and international finance that has swept the globe in recent decades – they found that some states nurture more insular systems of innovation and apply science and technology to statist developmental goals. They found further that much of this persistent insularity can be quite independent of state policy.[15] It is a norm that has been deeply assimilated in the institutions of the private sector. As anticipated, we learned that ideas about the purposes and modalities of science and technology may be realized as often by states with resources led by bureaucrats and politicians as by firms that operate within their borders led by managers whose political interests ought to be made explicit.

The editors of this volume proceeded from the assumption that the Asian response to economic crisis might frame fundamentally different approaches to the development and character of vibrant domestic innovation systems. Each approach has costs and benefits, and each would suggest a different future. A more open, technoglobal approach would have led national systems of innovation to converge upon a common set of institutional norms.[16] Although it may be premature to draw final conclusions, we observe no universal logic of research

---

[14] Sylvia Ostry and Richard R. Nelson, *Techno-Nationalism and Techno-Globalism: Conflict and Cooperation* (Washington, D.C.: Brookings Institution Press, 1995).

[15] Japan may be the most insular system among the industrial democracies. According to a study by Japan's leading business federation, Japanese firms employed on average fewer than one foreign technologist as a regular employee in 1996. They employed only slightly more than one foreign technologist per firm on a contract basis. Keizai Dantai Rengôkai, ed., *Sangyô Gijutsuryoku Kyôka no tame no Jittai Chôsa* (Survey to strengthen industrial technological competitiveness) (Tokyo: Keizai Dantai Rengôkai, September 1998).

[16] For supporting literature, see Lowell L. Bryan and Diana Farrell, *Market Unbound* (New York: John Wiley, 1996); John H. Dunning, *Alliance Capitalism and Global Business* (London: Routledge, 1997), and *Multinationals, Technology and Competitiveness* (London: Unwin Hyman, 1988); Francis Fukuyama, *The End of History and the Last Man* (New York: Free Press, 1992); Robert Z. Lawrence et al., *A Vision for the World Economy* (Washington, D.C.: Brookings Institution, 1996); Thomas H. Lee and Proctor P. Reid, eds., *National Interests in an Age of Global Technology* (Washington, D.C.: National Academy Press, 1991); Kenichi Ohmae, *The End of the Nation State* (New York: Free Press, 1995); John M. Stopford et al., *Rival States, Rival Firms* (Cambridge: Cambridge University Press, 1991); Susan Strange, *The Retreat of the State* (Cambridge: Cambridge University Press, 1996).

and education rising to overwhelm national differences and produce similar solutions to common problems of design and development.

A more closed, technonational approach would lead firms to maintain their nationality – that is, to restrict reciprocal technology flows and to prefer design and subcontract interactions with conationals – even when operating abroad.[17] This, too, is not uniformly observed. Instead, our authors have documented a range of intermediary approaches in which there is regional or even globally oriented technological integration among local and foreign firms, but in which the goal of such interactions clearly revolves around the national interest. In the last years of the twentieth century, a large-scale crisis – or series of crises – punctuated "expected" economic development, shifting the trajectories of economic growth and innovation for several countries in Asia. This volume has attempted to capture the nature, direction, and scope of that change. Further research, as outlined here, will be required to monitor these transformations and refine our understanding of the relationship between crisis and innovation.

[17] For supporting literature, see Alice H. Amsden, *Asia's Next Giant: South Korea and Late Industrialization* (New York: Oxford University Press, 1989); Paul N. Doremus, William W. Keller, Louis W. Pauly, and Simon Reich, *The Myth of the Global Corporation* (Princeton: Princeton University Press, 1998); Chi-Ming Hou and San Gee, "National Systems Supporting Technical Advance in Industry: The Case of Taiwan," in Richard R. Nelson, ed., *National Innovation Systems* (New York: Oxford University Press, 1993); Chalmers A. Johnson, *Japan, Who Governs? The Rise of the Developmental State* (New York: Norton, 1995); Linsu Kim, *Imitation to Innovation: The Dynamics of Korea's Technological Learning* (Boston: Harvard Business School Press, 1997); and Richard J. Samuels, *"Rich Nation, Strong Army": National Security and the Technological Transformation of Japan* (Ithaca: Cornell University Press, 1994).

Index

Administration Reform Council, Japan, 80–1
aerospace industry, 8
AFL-CIO, 42
alliances, 63, 127, 140, 146, 150, 152, 153, 159; manufacturing, 10
Amsden, Alice, 133
Anglo-Saxon ideas, 68, 84
Anwar Ibrahim, 15
Asia, *see individual countries*
Asian Development Bank, *see* banks
Asian financial crisis of 1997–98, 2–3, 42, 226, *see also individual countries*; and foreign reserves, 13; responses to, general, 16–19, 83, 226
Asian Monetary Fund, 84; *see also* Chiang Mai Initiative
asset inflation, 27
asset swaps, 124
asset values, 16, 57, 59, 124
Association of South East Asian Nations (ASEAN), 6, 13, 32, 33, 39; ASEAN Industrial Cooperation, 3; ASEAN plus three, 85; ASEAN plus four, 37
atomic bomb, 182
autarky, 84
automobile industry, 19, 24, 43–4, 48, 63, 143, 153, 169, 176, 192, 231, *see also* automobile manufacturers; automobile components industry, 132–3; automobile parts industry, 37, 132; Automotive Industry Promotion Law of 1962, South Korea, 116; bankruptcy, 122–3, 129, 132–3; effects of financial crisis on, 114; R&D, 95–6, 120, 127, 130; exports, 95, 109–10, 114, 118, 128–9, 132; weakness of, 110, 234
automobile manufacturers, 31, 39–40; Alfa Romeo, 127; Asia Motors, 117, 119, 121, 123; Chrysler, 230; Daewoo, 94–6, 108,
112–15, 119, 123–6, 128–9, 131; Daimler Chrysler, 24, 113–14, 129, 132; Ford, 113, 123–4, 126, 129; General Motors, General Motors Korea, 95, 113, 115, 117–19, 126, 128, 131–2; Honda, 24, 40, 44, 111; Hyundai, 94–6, 110, 113–14, 117–19, 122–5, 127–31, 136, 232; Kia, 96, 112–14, 117, 119–20, 122–4, 129; Mazda, 119; Mitsubishi, 24, 43–4, 117, 127; Nissan, 24, 40–1, 44, 112–13, 117, 120–1, 129; Renault, 24, 125, 127, 131–2; Saenara Motors, 117; Samsung Motors, 112, 114, 120–1, 123–5, 129, 131, 136; Shinjin Motors, 117; Ssangyong Motors, 111–12, 114; Toyota, 24, 31, 43–4, 130; Volkswagen, 113, 127
autonomy, 6, 47, 90, 115, 127–30, 135, 141, 144, 159, 161, 182, 187–9, 201, 235, *see also* technonationalism; technological autonomy, 163–4

badge engineering, 131
bailout, 59, 88, 112, 114
banking, 92–3, 141; collapse, 59; lending, 73, 109, 120, 172, 176
banks: Asian Development Bank, 17; Bank for International Settlements (BIS), 59; Bank of Korea, 92; bankruptcy of, 73, 89, 106; development banks, 143; Korean Development Bank, 124–6; Japan Export-Import Bank, 35
Bayh-Dole Act, United States, 75, 77–8
Big Deal program, South Korea, 124–5
Blair, Tony, 14
bond markets, 145
bottom-up communications, 105
bottom-up investment, 64
brain drain, 51, 178, 233, 238
Brain Korea, 21, 102
Brazil, 209

bubble economy, 11, 16, 20, 27–8, 51, 57, 59, 61, 82, 226
Bush, George W., 14
business process reengineering (BPR), 64, 67

California Fuel Cell Partnership, 96
capabilities, 13–15, 23, 161
capacity utilization rate, 111, 147
capital adequacy ratios, 60–1
capital controls, 3, 15, 221
capital goods sector, 62–3, 95, 199
capital investment, 27, 51
capital outflows, 2–3
capitalism, 3, 6, 60, 83
captive firms, 10
cartels, 144
central planning, 161, 163
chaebol, 18, 88–90, 92, 98, 104, 112, 143–4, 231, 234; bankruptcy of, 106, 109; definition of, 87; reform of, 89, 93–4, 105, 124, 153, 228–9; weakness of, 176
Chang, Morris, 138, 147, 151
Chiang Mai Initiative, 84–5
China, 6, 32, 130, 138; and capabilities, 13, 163; central government, 163–6; and Communist Party, 16; Economics and Trade Commission, 177; effects of crisis on, 3, 13, 15–16, 18, 162, 164; effects of size, 182, 185; and entrepreneurship, 79; 15th Party Congress, 177–8; global standards, impact on, 184–6; Guangdong province, 169–70, 235; investment in, 84; Ministry of Information Industry, 185; Ministry of Post and Telecommunications, 166; Ministry of Science and Technology (State Science and Technology Commission) (SSTC), 167; People's Liberation Army (PLA), 182; planned economy, 175; and reunification, 182; State Council, 172; State Council Decisions (1993, 1995, 1999), 179; State Economic Commission (SEC), 165, 168
Chinese Communist Party (CCP), 161, 172; *see also* communism
Chinese Company Law, 179
Chun Doo Hwan, 144
coalitional factors, *see* institutions
Cold War, 143
Commercial Code and Antimonopoly Law, 65
communism, 1; *see also* Chinese Communist Party
comparative advantage, 30, 31, 134, 141, 183, 197, 210
competition, 12
competitive advantage, 147, 159, 181
competitiveness, 100–2, 105, 144, 159, 177
computer industry, 8, 137; Legend Computer, 172–3

computer-assisted design (CAD), 154
Confucius, 105
conservation-of-power rationality, 104
consolidation, *see* merger
contagion effect, 112
convergence, 20, 225, 238; policy convergence, 190; pressures for, 25, 189, 224
core businesses, 97, 120, 122
core competency, 19, 20, 88, 109, 129, 231
core technology, 181
corruption, 88, 90–1, 116, 144
cross-credit guarantees, 94
cross-lending, 145
cross-shareholding, 20, 26, 60–1, 145
culture, 106, 138, 160; sociocultural environment, 105
currency appreciation, 142
currency crisis, 123
currency depreciation, 2, 17
currency devaluation, 101

Daewoo, *see* automobile manufacturers
debt, 61, 112, 122–3, 136, 145, 153; China, 15; debt burden, 88, 109, 111, 143; debt obligations, 150; debt-financing, 138, 231; debtservicing, 114; public debt, 17, 236
debt-to-equity ratio, 93–4, 104, 111, 124
decentralization, 164–6
deepening, 196, 198
deflation, 60
denationalization, 133
Deng Xiaoping, 165, 170
Denki Rengô, 42
dependence, *see* technology dependence
deregulation, 90, 144
developing countries, 102, 192; and capacity, 193
developmental states, 89–90, 137
diehard statists, 134
differentiated economies, 13–14
direct foreign investment, *see* foreign direct investment (FDI)
diversification, 88, 109, 115, 128, 138, 144; market diversification, 113; product diversification, 113, 155; of technology, 163
Dore, Ronald, 83
downsizing, 64–5, 131, 177
dumping, 147, 157
Dunning, John, 189
duties, 174

earthquake of September 1999 (Taiwan), 21, 148
economic development, 3
economic growth, types of: static efficiency, 195–7; structural change, 195–7; *see also* upgrading
economic miracle, 3, 23, 58

economic nationalists, 114, 116, 124, 131
economic rationalists, 114, 116, 118, 120, 123
economies of scale, 40, 109, 116–17, 120–1, 132, 135, 146
economies of scope, 132, 135
education, 12, 91, 102–3, 133
education, higher, 204, *see also* universities; Engineering Research Centers (ERCs), South Korea, 102; and entrepreneurship, 78–9; and military exemption, 154; and research, 77–8, 102; Science Research Centers (SRCs), South Korea, 102
education reform, *see* reform
863 Project, China, 166–8
electronics companies: LG, 94; Samsung Electronics, 87, 94, 97
electronics industry, 30, 33–5, 108, 124, 130, 139, 145, 147, 157, 181, 203, 223–4, 232, *see also* electronics companies, semiconductor industry; in Japan, 36–8, 48, 52, 63, 157
End of Market-ism, The, 83
endogenous growth theory, 209–10, 224
enterprise groups, 176
enterprise resource planning systems (ERP), 64
entrepreneurship, 2, 142, 209, 230, *see also* technoentrepreneurship; Bit Valley, 74; in China, 160–1, 178–9, 186; and communism, 16; initial public offerings (IPOs), 74, 80; in Japan, 54, 64, 74, 79, 82; and SMEs, 70, 80; start-up firms, 54–6, 62, 70, 80, 142, 172–3, 177–8
equity, 92, 142; equity resources, 150; equity-based deferred compensation arrangements, 142
ethnic politics, 214, 216, 220
Europe: and direct investment, 19; economic slowdown, 3; European firms, 12; expertise, 129
European Union, 136
excess capacity, 117
exchange controls, 3
exchange rate, 3, 42, 143
export credits, 35
export-led growth, 133, 233
exports, *see individual industries*

fabrication facilities (fabs), 147–51, 159
Fair Trade Commission, South Korea, 121, 125
Federation of Korean Industries, 125
financial contagion, 22, 228, 230
financial deregulation, 83
financial sector, 92–3
First Five Year Development Plan, South Korea, 116
Fiscal Investment and Loan Program (FILP), 35

flying geese pattern of regional economic development, 32
Ford, *see* automobile manufacturers
foreign direct investment (FDI), 6, 19, 20, 200, 205, 223, 230, 232; in China, 160, 165–6, 170–6, 180; convoy-style, 38; and Japan, 24, 35, 37, 57, 82; in Singapore, 95; in South Korea, 87, 95, 125, 129; in Taiwan, 95; and technoglobalism, 11; and techno-hybrids, 12; and technonationalism, 9
foreign exchange reserves, 18
foreign invested enterprises (FIEs), 170, 174, 181
foreign reserves, 2, 13
foundry model of chip production, 12, 138, 140, 159, *see also* semiconductor industry; capabilities, 150–2; and economies of scale, 146; and interdependence, 147; origins of, 140–3
fragmentation, 117, 122
France, 49, 82
free trade, 5, 136, 225; and technoglobalism, 11
free-market economy, 90

Gang of Four, *see* newly industrialized economies (NIEs)
GE, 65
General Agreement on Tariffs and Trade (GATT), 16
Germany, 104, 154
Gandhi, 14
global economic downturn, 68
global supply chains, 113
globalism, 86, 88, 114
globalization, 5, 19, 25, 63, 87, 113, 115, 120, 157, 224–5; effects on technoindustrial regimes, 23; globalized economy, 133, 135
growth enterprise market, 179
guarantees, financial, 139

hard disk drive industry (HDD), 21, 174, 190, 229, *see also* hard disk drive industry manufacturers; and Asian financial crisis, effects of, 190, 217; and Asian financial crisis, responses to, 191, 217–24; in China, 194; downturn, 217; Local Industry Upgrading Program (LIUP), Singapore, 207, 212, 215–16; national capacities, of Malaysia, 194–5, 198–200, 203–6; national capacities, of Singapore, 199–200, 206–9; national capacities, of Thailand, 195, 200–3
hard disk drive industry manufacturers (*see also* hard disk drive industry): IBM, 193, 202, 239; Seagate, 190–1, 193, 195, 202, 207–8; Sharp, 202
Hashimoto, 81

Heavy and Chemical Industries Project, South Korea, 92, 116–17, 134
heavy industry, 141
Hitachi, *see* manufacturing sector
hollowing out, 36, 49, 57, 62, 239
Honda, *see* automobile manufacturers
Hong Kong, 11
host economy, 7, 30, 32–5, 37, 49
human resource development, 162, 201, 210; Human Resources Development Fund (HRDF), Malaysia, 204, 222
human resources, 102, 235
hyperinflation, 17
Hyundai, *see* automobile manufacturers; semiconductor manufacturers

"I told you so" approach, 133
Icarus, 88
ideology, 7, 9, 15, 139, 157, 160–1, 200, 231
import substitution, 143
incentives, 138, 150, 205, 212, 216; economic, 103; financial, 35, 148; tax, 116, 200, 204, 233
indigenization, 216
India, 79
Indonesia, 226, 235
industrial economies, 109, 136
Industrial Master Plan, Malaysia, 203
industrial planning, 143–4
industrial policy, 33, 35, 116, 127, 133, 137, 139, 175–6, 235; and institutional challenges, 209–11
industrial property applications, 101
Industrial Regeneration Law, Japan, 80
industrial relations, 63–4
industrial restructuring program, 223
industrial sector, 87
industrial sequencing, 31
industrialization, 47, 86, 93, 102, 134, 141, 143, 232; late industrializers, 121, 210
inflationary pressures, 144
inflationary shortage economy, 176
information colonialism, 184; *see also* technology dependence
information revolution, 183
information technology, 3, 13, 81, 84, 137, 151, 205, 231; e-Japan campaign, 81; in Japan 26, 55, 67–8, 75, 77, 81; Information Technology Agreement, South Korea, 136; IT Strategy Council, Japan, 81; in the semiconductor industry, 137–8; in South Korea, 94
innovation, 2, 9, 21, 47, 53, 63, 139, 156, 162, 227; character of, 8; in China, 160, 177–9; corporate model, 75; diffusion of, 11; in Indonesia, 17; institutions of, 6, 227–30; Japanese model, 75; in South Korea, 94–5, 143; theory, 3, 5

innovation system (*see also* national innovation system), 6, 7, 107, 140, 172, 240; new innovation system, 173; response to crisis, 19; sectoral innovation system, 8
institutional capacity, 190, 209–16; coalitional factors, 215–16; external pressures, 214–15
institutions, 2, 7, 9, 15, 20, 23, 199–200, 227; for innovation, 88; institutional change, 21, 224; in Japan, 40, 53, 227; in Malaysia, 213–14; in Singapore, 189; social contract institutions, 83; in Taiwan, 189, 211–13
integrated circuit production, 148, 150
integrated device manufacturing (IDM) model, 138, 140, 146, 153, *see also* semiconductor industry; Japanese, 150, 159; origins of, 143–6
intellectual property, 151, 156, 174; intellectual property rights, 77–8, 100, 140
intercontinental ballistic missiles, 182
interest payment, 122
interest rates, 2, 18
International Monetary Fund (IMF), 15, 17, 18, 84, 88, 235
internationalization, 73, 124, 131, 136
internet, 2, 66, 177
isolationism, 84

Japan, 6, 138; and Asian financial crisis, 16, 57–62; Asian financial crisis, effects of, 3, 20, 45, 82, 226; Asian financial crisis, effects on SMEs, 73–4; Asian financial crisis, responses to, 83; companies, 129, 132, 140; and differentiated economies, 14; Economic Planning Agency of Japan, 25, *see also* Ministry of International Trade and Industry (MITI/METI); and education, 80, *see also* education; elites, 23, 25, 28, 42–3, 47; exports, 29; FDI in, 13, 74; investment in Asia, 28–9, 36–40, 43, 230; Japan International Cooperation Agency (JICA), 28–9, 33, 45; Japanese system, 57, 61; Ministry of Education, 76, 80; Ministry of Finance (MOF), 27, 80; Ministry of Foreign Affairs, 32; Official Development Assistance (ODA), 28, 45–6; and technology dependence, 10; and trade associations, 33–4; training programs, 44–5
Japan Finance Corporation for Small Business (JFS), 36
Jiang Zemin, 161, 182
joint ventures, 95–6, 113, 119, 121, 128, 132, 141–2, 166, 169, 172, 238
joint-stock company, 173, 180

Keidanren, 28
keiretsu, 33, 60, 231, 234, 237; horizontal, 24; vertical, 24, 38–40

Key Technology Promotion Center, 77
Keynesianism, 1
Kia, *see* automobile manufacturers
Kim Dae Jung, 90, 92, 93, 123–4, 145, 153, 229, 236
Kim Young Sam, 120, 144
King, Martin Luther, 14
knowledge-based economy, 230
Korea, *see* South Korea
Korea Asset Management Corporation (KAMCO), 92
Korea Development Institute, 124–5
Korea Institute for International Economic Policy, 125
Korean Auto Industries Cooperation Association, 125
Korean Federation of Small Business, 125
Korean Research Councils for science & technology, 154
Kosovo crisis, 182
Kôzuki Yatsugo, 47
Krasner, Stephen, 2

labor market, 105, 141
labor unions, *see* unions, labor
laissez-faire, 163
Lall, Sanjaya, 197–8
layoffs, 65, 154, 177
leadership, 7, 15–16, 224, 235–7
leaking out, 49
Lee Kuan Yew, 224
Legend Computer, *see* computer industry
liberal economics, 5–6, 114
liberalization, 6, 122, 130, 135, 144, 175–6; economic liberalization, 120, 134, 160; financial liberalization, 59, 111, 120, 134; market liberalization, 144; policy liberalization, 141; pressures for, 222; trade liberalization, 121, 191
licensing, *see* technology licensing
Lin Biao, 165
List, Friedrich, 5
loans, 35, 46, 134
localization, 121
lock-in effects, 183

macroeconomic policies, 133
Mahathir, Mohamad, 15, 221, 224, 235
Malaysia, 35; effects of Asian financial crisis, 2–3, 13; Penang, 194–5, 199, 214, 229; Penang Development Corporation (PDC), 214; People's Action Party, 212, 215; responses to Asian financial crisis, 15, 220–2
manufacturing sector: in China, 167; Hitachi, 41, 64–9, 73, 75; "i.e.Hitachi Plan", 66, 68–9; in Japan, 43, 62, 64, 73, 76, 82; in South Korea, 97, 115

Mao, 14
market-based economy, 160
market-based solutions, 83
market-value-based asset accounting, 61
mass-production, 12, 95
mergers, 113, 116, 126, 132, 144, 153; and acquisition, 97, 133; in Japan, 24, 60
Ministry of International Trade and Industry (MITI/METI), Japan, 10, 28, 37, 45–6, 75–77, 168; AEM-MITI Economic and Industrial Cooperation Committee (AMEICC), 33, 45; Asian Industrial Network Program, 34; Association for Overseas Technical Scholarships, 45; Cambodia-Laos-Myanmar Working Group (CLM-WG), 33; and complex international work sharing, 32; Japan External Trade Organization (JETRO), 34; and national strategy, 25–6; New Asian Industries Development (New AID) plan, 32
Miyazawa Kiichi, 46
mobile phone industry, 180–1, 184
monopoly, 93, 114, 117, 125, 169; in China, 16, 166
Moore's Law, 156
moral hazard, 92, 104, 134, 139
Morris-Suzuki, 58
multilateral economic organizations, 135
multinational corporations, 11, 22, 31, 35, 38, 87, 108–9, 141, 202, 207, 215, 230, 238; and China, 160–1, 165–6, 168–9, 175, 179, 181; incentives for, 216, 232; investment of, 7, 30, 205, 212; Japanese, 43, 45, 47–9; MNC-induced technological learning, 189, 208, 225; in regional production networks, 13; and South Korea, 96–8, 106; in technohybrids, 12; and technology, 220
multinational design and production networks, 139
multinationalization, 86

NASDAQ, *see* stock markets
nation building, 21
national champions, 143, 163, 176–7, 178, 186, 232–3, 235; promotion of, 129, 136; and state intervention, 116; strengthening of, 123
National Economic Action Council, 221
national economists, 5
national industrial base, 144
national innovation system (*see also* innovation system), 7, 53, 86–9, 92, 138, 149, 157, 229, 234; definition, 25; in South Korea, 133, 136
National Investment Fund, South Korea, 145
national laboratories, 142
National Science and Technology Board (NSTB) (Singapore), 207

National Science and Technology Council
(South Korea), 91, 236
National Science and Technology Plan
(NSTP) (Singapore), 217, 230
national security, 230, *see also* security
threats; China, 163, 235; Japan, 10, 25
nationalism, 83–5, 88, 114, 160, 164, 189,
221, 225, 233; financial nationalism, 220–1
nationalization, 112
natural resources, 102, 215
neoclassical economists, 134
neoclassical paradigm, 9
New Zealand, 87
newly industrialized countries (NICs), 100,
188, 198
newly industrialized economies (NIEs), 30,
32, 88; Gang of Four, 108, 165
Nikkei, 16
Nikkeiren (Japanese Federation of
Employers Associations), 45
1988 Torch Plan (China), 167–8; Torch
Development Center, 167
nonstate enterprises, China, 161, 172–3,
178, 181, 185
norms, 8–11, 19, 20, 23, 40, 224, 230, 240
North American Free Trade Agreement
(NAFTA), 42

oil crisis of the 1970s, 141, 147
Okinawa Summit (2000), 79
oligopoly, 120, 132
open capital markets, 139
Organization for Economic Cooperation
and Development (OECD), 106, 108, 135
Organization of the Petroleum Exporting
Countries (OPEC), 118
organizational continuity, 53
original equipment manufacturing (OEM), 95
outsourcing, 91
overcapacity, 113, 120–1, 231
overinvestment, 140
overproduction, 114

paradigm shift, 1
parent companies: in Japan, 38, 43–4, 46,
47, 73; in South Korea, 96
patents, 77–8, 87, 100–2, 108
Philippines, 2–3
policy loans, 145
political patronage, 104
price-driven dependencies, 158
pricing cycles, 157
privatization, 91, 186
product cycles, 191
production capacity, 111, 122, 130, 177
production networks, 115, 190
production structures, 187–9
productionist model, 68

productivity, 106, 130, 223, 236; of capital,
109; labor productivity, 96, 199; productivity gap, 64; white-collar productivity,
64–5
profit dilution, 152
profitability, 109, 143
protectionism, 9, 18, 70, 88, 111, 142–3,
188, 191, 199–201, 209–10
public enterprise sector, 177
public funds, 59
public goods, provision of, 10
punctuated equilibrium, 1
punctuation, 1–2, 241

quality control, 130

rationalization, 73, 118–19, 121–3, 127, 131
recapitalization, 114
recession, 21, 28, 35, 62, 65, 95, 118, 226,
236; effect of foreign reserves on, 13; of
1985, 207
reciprocal consent model, 58
reform, 84, 86–7, 200; agricultural reform, 164;
economic reform, 160; education reform, 80,
102, 106, 204, 218–19, 221, 229; enterprise
renovation, 165; export-oriented reform, 201;
financial reform, 18, 60, 89, 92, 176; government reform, 82; human resources management, 67; labor reform, 89, 176; national
strategy reforms, 77; organization reforms,
see layoffs; public-sector reform, 89, 103;
R&D, 103, 217; reform period, China, 162,
164–70; regulatory reform, 23–4; stimulus
for, 57, 82, 90–1; tax reform, 176; technology
reform, 191
regional currency stabilization system, 84;
see also Chiang Mai Initiative
regional integration, 29, 85
regional production networks (systems), 13,
22, 30–1, 37
regionalization, 25, 32, 35, 37, 40, 42–4, 47,
50, 56, 162
relational contracting, 83
relationalism, 20, 23, 31, 42–5, 47, 50, 53,
231, 234; business-business ties, 26,
36–40; costs and benefits, 27, 56; definition, 25–7; extension into Asia, 25;
government-business ties, 26, 31–6; labor-
management ties, 27, 40–2
rent seeking, 116, 209
Republic of Korea, *see* South Korea
research and development (R&D), 11, 50–1,
238; in China, 162–3, 172; government
research institutes, 103–4, 167, 168;
corporate, 64, 69, 101, 103, 207; and
education, 52, 167; funding of, 7, 87; in
Japan, 100; in Malaysia, 205–6; regional
R&D production systems model, 8;

in Singapore, 100; in South Korea,
97–104, 106, 159; in Spain, 100; in
Taiwan, 100; and technoglobalism 9–11;
and technonationalism, 9–11
research consortia, 75–7; and development
cycle, 10–11
reverse engineering, 100, 105
Ricardo, David, 5
ROE, 65–7
Roh Tae Woo, 144

Samuels, Richard, 47, 58–9, 129
science and technology (S&T), 75–6, 91, 160,
167, 172, 179, 201, 213, 217, 229, 236
Science and Technology Advisory Group,
Taiwan, 142
Science and Technology Basic Law (1995), 76
Science and Technology Basic Plan (1996),
Japan, 50–1, 76–7
Science and Technology Policy Council, 77
science parks, 143, 167; Route 128, 167;
see also Silicon Valley; technology parks
security dilemma, 163
security threats, 182, 214–16; *see also*
national security
semiconductor industry, 3, 136, 137, 199,
205, 233, *see also* foundry model of chip
production, integrated device manufacturing (IDM) model, semiconductor manufacturers; and Asian financial crisis, 140,
153; downturn in, 140; exports, 146; and
Japan, 63, 68, 75; R&D, 139, 145, 149,
154–5; and Singapore, 12; in South
Korea, 96, 109, 111, 127, 138, 140;
standard memory chip (DRAM), 140,
145, 147, 153, 156–7; in Taiwan, very
large scale integrated (VLSI) chip
design, 97
semiconductor manufacturers (*see also* semiconductor industry): Hynix Semiconductor
Inc., 153, 155–7; Hyundai Electronics, 97,
100, 109, 153, 232; investment in China,
148; LG Semiconductors, 97, 100, 109,
153, 232; Lucky Goldstar *chaebol*, 145,
153; Motorola, 98; Samsung Electronics,
97, 100–1, 109, 153, 155–7, 232; Taiwan
Semiconductor Manufacturing Company
(TSMC), 142, 151, 233; Toshiba, 96;
United Microelectronics Company (UMC),
142, 233
September 11, 2001, 14, 226
service sector, 84
Shenzhen Special Economic Zone, 180
silicon cycle, 13, 65, 146–8, 153, 155,
158, 231
Silicon Valley, 65, 79, 155, 159, 167, 177
Singapore: Economic Development Board
(EDB), 206–8, 211–12; effects of Asian

financial crisis on, 13, 22, 226; responses
to Asian financial crisis, 217–20
Skills Development Fund, 204, 212, 222
small and medium-sized enterprises (SMEs),
199, 202, 204–6, 214, 223, 230; in Japan,
34–7, 46, 53–4, 57, 70–5, 80; and joint
ventures, 34; Small and Medium Enterprise
Agency, Japan, 54; in South Korea, 93–4,
101, 104, 132; in Taiwan, 151
Smith, Adam, 5
social networks, 58
socialism, 160
South Korea, 6, 137; and Asian financial
crisis, 86, 109; The Blue House, 121;
causes of Asian financial crisis, 122, 134;
competition with Japan, 143; democratization, 105; Economic Planning Board
(EPB), 118–21, 168; effects of Asian
financial crisis on, 2–3, 13, 18, 19, 21,
87, 92, 101, 104, 106, 123, 133, 158;
Financial Supervisory Commission, 92,
112; foreign investment in, 87; government intervention, 90–1, 93; Government
Reform Office (GRO), 90; Grand
National Party, 125; and industrialization, 86; military coup, 90, 144; Minister
of Finance and Economy, 123, 125;
Ministry of Commerce and Industry
(MCI), 121; Ministry of Science and
Technology, 91; Ministry of Trade and
Industry, 116, 119; National Assembly,
92; Office of the Prime Minister, 154;
responses to Asian financial crisis, 228–9;
state control, 144
Southeast Asia, 97, 172, 193; *see also individual countries*
Southern Tour, 171
Soviet Union, 182
specialization, 109, 113, 119, 193
spillover, 174–5, 190–1, 194, 202, 225
spin-offs, 56, 103, 142, 178, 207,
220, 233
standards, Western, 83, 113, 184
start-up firms, *see* entrepreneurship
state enterprise, 123
state intervention, 133–4, 163; and
technoglobalism, 11; and technonationalism, 10
state-owned enterprises (SOEs), 160–1,
167–8, 172, 176–9, 235; elimination of,
16; joint-venture partners, 174
state-owned sector, 141
stock markets, 2–3, 61, 74, 133, 173;
NASDAQ, 74, 179; share prices, 59–60
Strategic Industries Program, Taiwan, 142
structural features, *see* capabilities
subcontracting, 36, 47–8, 72–3, 122, 201–2,
204–5

subsidies, 36, 93, 139, 142, 145, 204, 206, 209, 212; cross-subsidization, 112; elimination of, 177; export subsidies, 116, 168; financial subsidies, 129; interest subsidies, 179; public subsidies, 144; and technonationalism, 11
Suharto, 17
summit, November 2001, 85
supply networks, 39–40, 47
surplus capacity, 109, 111, 130, 144
Sweden, 87

Tainan, 151
Taiwan, 100, 121, 137; and Asian financial crisis, 138; Central Finance Committee, 142; companies, 73; effects of Asian financial crisis, 3, 13, 21, 146, 226; Kuomintang Party, 141
Taiwan Straits crisis, 182
tariffs, 11, 31
taxes, 179, *see also* incentives, reform; taxation rates, 116; value-added taxes (VAT), 174, 179
technoentrepreneurship (*see also* entrepreneurship), 57–8, 77, 80–1; technopreneurial firms, 220, 225
technoglobalism, 18–19, 22, 188–9, 221, 237–40; definition of, 11; in China, 163, 182; in Hong Kong, 233; in Japan, 58–9, 75, 84; in Singapore, 233; in South Korea, 87, 107, 114–15; in Taiwan, 141, 233
technohybrid, 21–2, 189, 225, 232; and China, 175; definition of, 12; future predominance of, 233–4; and South Korea, 87, 107, 138; and Taiwan, 138–9, 152, 159, 232
technoindustrial regime, 23, 26, 31; definition of, 25
technological development, 196, 200
technological sourcing, 128
technological upgrading, *see* upgrading
technology acquisition, 19, 127–8, 162–3, 166, 171, 173, 205, 220, 232, 235, 237
technology and industrial policies (TIPS), 11, 203
technology champion sector, 58, 61–4
technology dependence, 6, 20, 152, 161, 182–5, 235, *see also* information colonialism; and information security, 184; and Linux, 183–5; and technonationalism, 10
technology development, 162, 164–6, 168, 201, 220, 230
technology diffusion, 202, 205
technology gap, 169
technology highways, 10
technology import, 164–6, 168, 170–1
technology licensing, 20, 49, 67, 95, 97, 112, 127, 129, 150, 152, 171, 175; technology-licensing offices (TLOs), 79

technology parks, 103, 151, 173, 205, 230, *see also* science parks; Hsinchu Science-Based Industrial Park (Taiwan), 149, 151, 233; Research Triangle Park (South Korea), 159; Technology Park Malaysia, 205; Xi'an International Business Incubator, 173
technology transfer, 32, 78, 96, 168, 178, 205, 237
technonationalism, 18–22, 139, 188–9, 220, 230, 237–41; and autonomy, 10, 25; and China, 160–1, 163–4, 167, 172, 175, 182, 185–6, 235; definition and characteristics of, 9–10, 47; and Japan, 10–11, 25, 47–9, 58–9, 84, 108, 161, 175, 186, 230–1; and South Korea, 86, 106–7, 108–9, 114–15, 121, 123, 127, 129, 133–6, 143, 145, 161, 175, 230–2; and Taiwan, 233
telecommunications industry, 3, 98, 100, 137, 176; *see also* mobile phone industry; telecommunications industry companies
telecommunications industry companies: Alcatel, 166, 169; AT&T, 166; Huawei, 180; ITT Belgium, 166; Nortel, 166; Shanghai Bell, 16
Thailand, 42; effects of Asian financial crisis, 2–3, 13, 18; investment in, 43; Ministry of Industry, 33, 223; MITI Plan, 223; responses to Asian financial crisis, 222–4; and static efficiency, 197; Thailand Board of Investment (BOI), 202
Thatcher, Margaret, 77
Tiananmen Incident of 1989–90, 170
Tokyo Stock Exchange, *see* stock markets
top-down investment, 64
top-down management, 104
Toshiba, 65
total factor productivity, 196
trade associations, 33–4
trade liberalization, *see* liberalization
trade surplus, 59, 76
21st Century Frontier Technology R&D Program, South Korea, 87
tying, 45

unemployment, 89, 106, 136; in Japan, 17, 62
unified market, 84
unions, labor, 103, 105–6
unions, trade, 136
United Kingdom, 25, 47, 49, 87; influence in Asia, 83, 104; research model, 154; and technology development, 69
United States, 25, 47, 49, 50, 53, 143; companies, 12, 97, 102, 132, 185, 191, 233; and direct investment, 19; dominance, 163–4; economy, 3, 82, 86, 226; and education sector, 79, 149, 155; influence

in Asia, 68, 83, 84, 102; and the IT
revolution, 81; as a model, 102, 163,
230; reaction to economic crisis, 75; and
technology development, 69
universities, 149, *see also* education, higher;
Beijing University, 172, 186; Chinese
Academy of Sciences, 172, 186; Institute
of Management Development (IMD),
South Korea, 91; Korean Advanced
Institute of Science and Technology
(KAIST), 154, 228; Malaysian Science and
Technology University, 204;
Massachusetts Institute of Technology
(MIT), 204; National Chiao Tung
University, Taiwan, 149; National Tsing
Hua University, Taiwan, 149; Seoul
National University (SNU), 154, 228
upgrading, 188, 190, 197, 199–201, 209,
214, 216; definition of, 196; industrial
upgrading, 187, 213; technological
upgrading, 188, 198, 225

value-added taxes (VAT), *see* taxes
vendor development programs, 202, 205
venture businesses, 101
venture capital, 173, 176, 179
venture "incubating" centers, 103
veto players, 224

wage restraint, 63
Welch, "Neutron Jack," 65; *see also* GE
welfare corporatism, 65
Western Europe, *see individual countries*
World Bank, 17, 118–19, 134, 222
World Trade Organization (WTO), 16, 130,
135, 160, 180, 186, 222, 232
Wu Jichuan, 176

Yamaichi, 62, 82

Zhu Rongji, 176–7, 235